Kennedy, Johnson, and the Quest for Justice

KENNEDY, JOHNSON, AND THE QUEST FOR JUSTICE:

THE CIVIL RIGHTS TAPES

Jonathan Rosenberg
and
Zachary Karabell

W. W. NORTON & COMPANY
NEW YORK • LONDON

Manufacturing by the Maple-Vail Book Manufacturing Group
Production manager: Amanda Morrison

Library of Congress Cataloging-in-Publication Data

Rosenberg, Jonathan, date.
Kennedy, Johnson, and the quest for justice: the civil rights tapes /
Jonathan Rosenberg and Zachary Karabell.—1st ed.
p. cm.
ISBN 0-393-05122-6 (hardcover)
1. Civil rights movements—United States—History—20th century. 2. Civil rights
movements—United States—History—20th century—Sources. 3. African Americans—Civil rights—History—20th century. 4. African Americans—Civil rights—History—20th century—Sources. 5. Kennedy, John F. (John Fitzgerald), 1917–1963. 6.
Johnson, Lyndon B. (Lyndon Baines), 1908–1973. 7. United States—Politics and government—1961–1963. 8. United States—Politics and government—1961–1963—
Sources. 9. United States—Politics and government—1963–1969. 10. United
States—Politics and government—1963–1969—Sources. I. Karabell, Zachary. II. Title.
E185.61 .R816 2003
323'.0973—dc21
2002009782

W. W. Norton & Company, Inc., 500 Fifth Avenue, New York, N.Y. 10110
www.wwnorton.com

W. W. Norton & Company Ltd., Castle House, 75/76 Wells Street, London W1T 3QT

1 2 3 4 5 6 7 8 9 0

MILLER CENTER OF PUBLIC AFFAIRS
UNIVERSITY OF VIRGINIA

Presidential Recordings Project

Philip Zelikow
Director of the Center

Timothy Naftali
Director of the Project

Michael Beschloss
Taylor Branch
Robert Dallek
Allen Matusow
Richard Neustadt
Arthur Schlesinger, Jr.
Robert Schulzinger
Editorial Advisory Board

Kennedy, Johnson, and the Quest for Justice

Jonathan Rosenberg & Zachary Karabell
Editors

Kent Germany
Max Holland
Robert D. Johnson
David Shreve
Associate Editors

Sarah Stewart
Assistant Editor

Philip Zelikow & Ernest May
General Editors

Contents

The Presidential Recordings Project

BY

PHILIP ZELIKOW AND ERNEST MAY

The civil rights struggle of the 1960s seemed a second Reconstruction, perhaps the prelude to a second Civil War. This book begins in 1962 with an explosive clash in Oxford, Mississippi, where President John F. Kennedy sought to enforce the right of a black student, James Meredith, to enroll in the state university. It ends in 1964, with President Lyndon B. Johnson signing a Civil Rights Act outlawing discrimination in all schools and places of public accommodation.

The story is familiar. At least, part of it is. Many scholars have traced the struggle for civil rights from the ground up, as has Diane McWhorter in her moving chronicle of contests in Birmingham, or through the lives of movement leaders, as in the probing studies of Martin Luther King by Taylor Branch and David Garrow. The story from the top down has not been equally well told. In writings on Kennedy and Johnson, the civil rights struggle is only one theme among many.

In this book, Jonathan Rosenberg and Zachary Karabell blend a thorough knowledge of the story we know with what is new: the missing top-down story. They start at the very top, using unique and previously inaccessible records of meetings and conversations in the White House secretly taped by the two Presidents. They allow the reader to listen at a keyhole as Kennedy and Johnson learn about the bottom-up struggle and decide on the strategies and actions of the U.S. government.

Between 1940 and 1973, the presidents of the United States secretly recorded hundreds of their meetings and conversations in the White House. Though some recorded a lot and others just a little, they all created a unique and irreplaceable source for understanding not only their presidencies and times but also the office of the presidency itself and, indeed, the essential process of high-level decision making.

These recordings, of course, do not displace the more traditional sources of historical knowledge such as official documents, private diaries and letters, memoirs, and contemporaneous journalism. Rather, they augment these sources much as photographs, films, and recordings augment printed records of presidents' public appearances. But they also do much more than that.

Because the recordings capture an entire meeting or conversation, not just highlights caught by a minute taker or recalled afterward in a memorandum or memoir, they can have two distinctive qualities. In the first place, they can catch the whole complex of considerations that weigh on a president's mind on a particular day. Most of those present at an individual meeting with the president know chiefly the subject of that meeting; even key staff advisers have compartmentalized responsibilities. However, the tapes and transcripts of successive meetings or conversations reveal the interlocked concerns of which only the president is aware. They provide hard evidence, not just bases for inference, about presidential motivations.

Desk diaries, public and private papers, and memoirs and oral histories all show how varied and difficult a president's responsibilities are and how little time there is for meeting those responsibilities. But only the tapes provide a clear picture of how these responsibilities constantly converge— how a president can be simultaneously, not consecutively, a commander in chief worrying about war, a policymaker conscious that his missteps in economic policy could bring on a market collapse, a chief mediator among interest groups, a chief administrator for a myriad of public programs, a spokesperson for the interests and aspirations of the nation, a head of a sprawling political party, and more.

Another distinctive feature of the tapes is that they reveal not only what the president says but what he hears as well. While people vary in their ability to learn visually versus verbally, action-focused individuals tend to take in more of what they hear than what they read, especially when they can directly question a speaker. A document read aloud or summarized to a president thus has a much better chance of registering than that same document simply being placed in his in box. Though listening and reading can both be selective, the tapes probably show—better than any other records—the information and advice guiding presidential choices.

Perhaps most usefully, the secret tapes record, as do no other sources, the *processes* that produce decisions. Presidential advisers can be heard debating with one another, adapting to the perspectives of others, and changing their minds. The president's own views are often reshaped as well, sometimes by a subtle but profound shift in the definition of an issue or the stakes involved. While participants rarely have a clear memory of such changes, the tapes record them word for word.

Casting about for analogies, we have thought often of Pompeii. As the ruins uncovered there have given students of Greco-Roman civilization knowledge not to be found elsewhere, in any form, so the presidential recordings give students of the presidency, American and world history, and decision making knowledge that is simply without parallel or counterpart. They are a kind of time machine, allowing us to go back and listen as history was being made. And, unlike even the finest archaeological site, what we uncover are the words and deliberations of the people themselves in not one but multiple moments of action.

.   .   .

Though Franklin Roosevelt, Harry Truman, and Dwight Eisenhower had all made a few secret recordings, Kennedy was the first president to install an elaborate taping system and to make extensive use of it. His family and aides removed the system almost immediately after his murder in 1963. Johnson then installed a different system, of which he, too, made frequent use. The details of how those quite different recording systems were installed and operated, as well as the provenance of how the tapes ultimately became available to scholars, is fascinating but intricate. Those interested should consult the specific prefaces that introduce the reference volumes in the Presidential Recordings series (also published by W. W. Norton & Company). The first three volumes in the Kennedy series have already been published. The first volumes in the Johnson series will be in print soon.

The existence of Kennedy's taping system was known at the time only to the President himself, his private secretary (Evelyn Lincoln), and the two Secret Service agents who installed and maintained it. President Kennedy's brother Robert learned of the system at some point, and the circle probably eventually extended to include also the President's close aide Kenneth O'Donnell. Other senior White House officials, like special counsel Theodore Sorensen or national security adviser McGeorge Bundy, knew nothing about it. President Kennedy had to activate the system with a buzzer press, and he tended to use it as a kind of electronic diary to record meetings he considered important, probably with a view to the later preparation of the memoirs he never had the chance to write. He paid little attention to the tapes while he was president, leaving them to Mrs. Lincoln to store away for later. There is no evidence that President Kennedy ever intended to make the tapes public.

During the period covered by this book, President Johnson only recorded telephone conversations, using a popular dictation device of the time known as a Dictaphone. Fortunately for historians, Johnson did much of his work over the phone—much more than Kennedy had. Johnson was more attentive than Kennedy to transcribing tapes and reflecting on them while he was still president. Yet, as any reader can see, this self-consciousness had little apparent effect on Johnson's candor. He planned for the tapes to remain secret for decades after his death, but for various reasons, the executors of his estate, including his widow, were able and willing to expedite their release.

On the premise that these and the other secretly made presidential recordings will remain important historical sources for centuries to come, the University of Virginia's Miller Center of Public Affairs is producing transcripts and aids for all accessible recordings of all six presidencies. The work must be done principally by trained historians. For those unfamiliar with the history and personalities of the period, transcribing presidential tapes can be a bit like trying to assemble a jigsaw puzzle without being able to see the picture on the puzzle box. The task of transcription is especially hard when the audio quality is bad. Tapes of telephone conversations tend to be easier to transcribe, both because the speakers are using a machine directly linked to the original recording system (a Dictaphone) and because there are usually only two participants in the telephone conversation. Recordings of meetings are much harder to transcribe.

The Miller Center is preparing this material in reference volumes, organized chronologically for each presidency. Some scholars working with the center also pull out portions of the tape transcripts to tell a particular story. This book is an example of one such policy volume.

In consultation with our editorial advisory board and our scholars, we developed a number of guidelines for the Miller Center's work, focused mainly on the preparation of the reference volumes. This work is organized in the Center's Presidential Recordings Project, directed by Tim Naftali. Among the most important methodological principles are:

First, the work is done by trained professional historians who have done deep research on the period covered by the tapes and on some of the central themes of the meetings and conversations. They are listed on the title page of every reference volume and at the front of this book. The historians not only delve into documentary sources but sometimes interview living participants who can help us comprehend the taped discussions. Our voice identifications are based on samples we have compiled and on our research. We list only the names of the participants we can identify.

Second, each reference volume uses the team method. Usually one or two scholars painstakingly produce a primary draft. Two or more scholars then carefully go over that transcript, individually or sometimes two listening at the same time, with their suggestions usually going back to the primary transcriber. In the case of meeting tapes, like the Kennedy recordings, every transcript has benefited from at least four listeners. The reference volume editors remain accountable for checking the quality and accuracy of all the work in their set of transcripts, knitting together the whole. We, as the general editors, then review this work, advised regularly by members of the project's editorial advisory board.

Third, we use the best technology that the project can afford. As of 2001, we work from Digital Audio Tape (DAT) copies of the recordings (not the less expensive analog cassettes ordinarily sold to the public by presidential libraries). Our transcribers increasingly transfer this digital data onto CD-ROMs and use software as a further aid to deciphering what was said.

Fourth, we strive to make the transcripts accessible to and readable by anyone interested in history, including students. This requires a considerable amount of subjective editorial work. Since people often do not speak in complete and grammatically correct sentences, the transcriber has to infer and create sentence structure, paragraphs, commas, semicolons, and the like. We omit verbal debris such as the *uh*s that dot almost anyone's speech. Listeners unconsciously filter out such debris as they understand what someone is saying. Judgments must be made. Someone says, for example, "sixteen . . . uh, sixty. . . ." The transcriber has to decide whether the slip was significant or not. But the judgment calls are usually no more difficult than those involved in deciding where to insert punctuation or paragraphing. In the effort to be exhaustive, sometimes there is a temptation to overtranscribe, catching every fragmentary utterance, however unclear or peripheral. But the result on the page can add too much intrusive static, making the substance less understandable to readers now than it was to the hearers then. Obviously, what to include and omit, balancing coherence and comprehension against the completeness of the record, also requires subjective judgment. The object is to give the reader or user the truest possible sense of the actual dialogue as the participants themselves understood it.

Fifth, we go one step further by including in each reference volume explanations and annotations intended to enable readers or users to understand the background and circumstances of a particular conversation or meeting. With rare exceptions, we do not add information that participants would not have known. Nor do we comment often on the significance of items of information, except as it might have been recognized by the participants. As with all historical sources, interpretations will have to accumulate over future decades and centuries.

· · ·

Jonathan Rosenberg and Zachary Karabell have drawn on the tapes being transcribed in the wider Miller Center project (in which they have both taken part) in order to create this volume. They alone are responsible for the analysis, narrative, and interpretation. As for the tape transcripts, the Kennedy material for 1962 is excerpted from Volume 2 of the comprehensive Presidential Recordings reference series for the administration of John F. Kennedy, published in 2001. The Johnson material for 1963 and early 1964 is derived from volumes Miller Center scholars are preparing for the Johnson reference series. The Kennedy material for 1963 and the Johnson material for the spring and summer of 1964 have not yet received the full reference-level review described above but have nevertheless benefited from multiple listenings and listeners.

The Civil Rights Act of 1964 and the follow-up Voting Rights Act of 1965 were landmark achievements in the long struggle to make all Americans both free and equal. This book enables readers to understand for the first time the full roles of Presidents Kennedy and Johnson in these achievements and the events leading up to them.

Kennedy, Johnson, and the Quest for Justice

Introduction

On July 16, 1973, Alexander P. Butterfield, an unprepossessing man who had served as deputy assistant to President Richard Nixon, testified before the Senate Watergate Committee. In a nationally televised hearing, Butterfield informed the committee that all conversations in the Oval Office had been routinely tape-recorded. The news created a firestorm and the Senate subpoenaed the White House tapes, demanding that the President release this potentially crucial evidence. Nixon refused to surrender the tapes, but after a year of legal wrangling, the Supreme Court ordered him to do so. The Court's order provided the Senate with the smoking gun that would finally implicate the President in the Watergate cover-up.

Most political observers assumed Nixon's penchant for taping his activities in the White House was unique. But if Nixon did tape more energetically than had previous chief executives, we have since learned he was not alone. As rumors of other presidential taping programs made their way through the Washington establishment, the Kennedy family decided to reveal the recording practices of President John Kennedy, who had installed his own taping system in the White House. Those in charge of Lyndon Johnson's papers confirmed that Johnson, too, had taped thousands of telephone conversations and meetings. Richard Nixon, therefore, was carrying on a tradition begun by his predecessors, a tradition practiced not just by John Kennedy and Johnson, but also by Dwight Eisenhower, Harry Truman, and Franklin Roosevelt, each of whom employed a rudimentary taping system.

Clearly, in conducting the nation's business, presidents have had a powerful desire to preserve a detailed record of their actions. For Kennedy and Johnson, it seems likely that they taped their White House meetings and telephone calls not to help future generations write the history of their presidencies but to create a detailed and secret account of the historical record for themselves. They would then be able to use the tapes in writing their memoirs, which would shape how their presidencies were assessed. But in the wake of Watergate, public pressure for full disclosure of the presidential recordings intensified, and the civil rights conversations on which this volume is based became available to the general public. Now anyone who wishes to do so can eavesdrop on these leaders as they conducted the nation's business.

The Miller Center of Public Affairs at the University of Virginia has recently begun a multiyear project of transcribing, editing, and publishing the presidential recordings from the Roosevelt through the Nixon administrations. These volumes will contain verbatim transcripts of the tapes—complete and without deletions.

This book is different. Blending edited transcripts and historical narrative, it tells the story of the preeminent social and political issue in the United States in the 1960s: the struggle for racial justice. More precisely, it examines one part of that story over the course of two years, from the crisis in the fall of 1962 caused by the effort to integrate the University of Mississippi to the passage of the Civil Rights Act in July 1964. And it does so from the vantage point of the White House and the two presidents who worked there during this period.

Transcripts of tape recordings made by Kennedy and Johnson make up the bulk of the book. By and large, these transcripts are excerpts from longer conversations and meetings. We have then added historical narrative and commentary to provide the reader with background and context, as well as our thoughts on how Kennedy and Johnson responded to the challenges presented by the civil rights struggle. In short, by interweaving passages of narrative with the tape transcripts, we have tried to create a coherent story about the presidency and civil rights during these two years.

The two Presidents were as different in their taping styles as they were in their leadership styles. Kennedy mainly recorded meetings, which often involved numerous participants in times of crisis, while Johnson (at least through 1964) recorded almost only telephone conversations, which typically involved himself and one other person. The distinctions between a meeting and a telephone conversation are important: meetings tend to be multilayered and, during a crisis, chaotic. Some continue for hours, unfolding in rambling, disjointed fashion. While telephone conversations are simpler to transcribe, they can be difficult to place in context since they often take up where an earlier (perhaps unrecorded) conversation left off. No matter how significant, such calls can appear trivial. In order to enable the reader to appreciate fully what is happening, both types of tapes—meetings and telephone calls—require an understanding of the historical context and an explanation of unfolding developments. Throughout the volume, we have sought to provide contextual and explanatory material.

Another challenge concerns the wide variance in the quality of the White House recordings. For the Kennedy material, some meetings are extremely difficult to decipher, even after the tapes have been technically enhanced. The hidden microphones in the White House picked up all manner of ambient noise, and with telephones ringing, people speaking simultaneously, papers shuffling, and drinks being poured, the effect can be confusing, challenging even the most diligent transcriber. The Johnson telephone conversations, on the other hand, are generally clearly recorded and easy to understand.

Beyond the matter of sound quality, LBJ recorded his telephone conversations almost daily, whereas Kennedy recorded civil rights meetings only intermittently. In fact, Kennedy's recorded meetings were sometimes separated by months, and at times, he did not record important meetings at all. Thus, much of the history of Kennedy's civil rights policies is not part of the taped record. We have done our best to fill these gaps by composing brief segments of narrative in order to connect and clarify the recorded material.

The differences in what Kennedy and Johnson taped (meetings versus telephone calls) have significant implications for understanding the way each leader worked. In general, the Kennedy tapes provide little insight into how JFK handled people individually, whereas the Johnson recordings contain ample evidence of what has been called the "Johnson treatment." The Johnson material shows the President practicing the art of one-on-one politics—cajoling, convincing, and wooing—for which he was justly acclaimed. The Kennedy material, by contrast, provides a remarkable view of President Kennedy's performance as a political leader, illuminating his *modus operandi* in White House meetings—listening, probing, and deciding.

A Word about the Words

In order to enhance the flow of the narrative and the readability of the meetings and telephone conversations, we have edited the transcripts. The meetings, especially those with numerous participants, were frequently chaotic and sometimes confusing. In presenting the transcripts, we have attempted at all times to remain faithful to the historical record, and, at the same time, to help the reader comprehend the significance of what was happening.

For the Kennedy material, almost all the meetings he recorded are presented in excerpted form; some have not been included at all. In the interest of readability, we have omitted some passages we found unintelligible, as well as some exchanges in which the participants were speaking over one another. These deletions and elisions are clearly indicated. At times, in place of the transcripts themselves, we have included narrative passages that explain what was discussed. We have tried to make these distinctions apparent and easy for the reader to understand.

Most of the Johnson telephone conversations were sufficiently brief so as to make substantial editing unnecessary. We were, however, selective about which conversations we included in the volume, and we excluded some of Johnson's civil rights telephone calls. When a telephone conversation covered more than one topic, we have typically presented only that portion that pertained to civil rights.

Thus, in exploring how and why the White House came to propose and then push for civil rights legislation, we have not presented a verbatim text of every conversation on civil rights recorded during the Kennedy and Johnson years. That does not, however, mean the transcripts are inaccurate. The Kennedy transcripts are the product of hours of careful work conducted by several people and the Johnson transcripts are the product of more than one set of ears. While each transcript presented was listened to by at least two people, and is the result of many hours of arduous work, it is inevitable that it may contain some errors. We believe that those which may occur do not substantially alter the overall thrust of a meeting, a telephone call, or the larger story. But perfection surely eludes us. We would encourage those readers who desire verbatim transcripts to turn to the reference volumes that have been and continue to be prepared by the Miller Center and its team of scholars.

Overview

In the broadest sense, the tapes cover two distinct but related aspects of the civil rights struggle in the Kennedy and Johnson years: the crises at Ole Miss and Birmingham in 1962 and 1963, and the struggle in Washington over civil rights legislation in 1963 and 1964. In the Kennedy period, we encounter a president confronting grave crises, one in Mississippi over the battle to integrate the University of Mississippi in 1962, the other in Birmingham, where civil rights leaders organized a campaign in 1963 to break the back of segregation in one of the South's most oppressive cities. We see President Kennedy responding to the violence that exploded at Ole Miss in 1962 after the court ordered the segregated institution to enroll James Meredith, a black man, who wished to attend the university. The following year, in the spring of 1963, Martin Luther King and other leaders targeted Birmingham in their ongoing crusade—a decision that resulted in the brutal and infamous response orchestrated by the city's police chief, Eugene "Bull" Connor.

These two crises, and Birmingham especially, contributed to Kennedy's June 1963 decision to present his proposal for civil rights legislation to the Congress. How the proposal was forged, made its way to Congress, and became law in 1964 constitutes the other major story of the book. Kennedy taped many hours of meetings on civil rights legislation, including gatherings with his own advisers and with civil rights leaders such as Martin Luther King, Roy Wilkins, and A. Philip Randolph. Although we have included less than half the total amount of recorded material on civil rights legislation under Kennedy, we do not support the notion that the making of laws, like the making of sausage, is better left unseen. Rather, we have included those meetings and discussions that seem most interesting and illuminating.

After President Kennedy was assassinated in November 1963, Lyndon Johnson made civil rights the centerpiece of his new administration. The transcripts indicate that Johnson devoted a great deal of time and energy to the cause between November 1963 and July 1964, although once the bill entered the Senate in February, its day-to-day management was left to the Senate's majority whip, Hubert Humphrey, and the number of relevant telephone conversations dwindled considerably in April and May. Though Johnson worked behind the scenes more than the tapes suggest, he chose to adopt a low profile during the many weeks of the southern filibuster and did not try to force the issue in a Senate that might have resented the interference of a president, even one as skillful as LBJ. We have included most of the relevant telephone conversations that Johnson recorded and have tried to provide sufficient narrative description to give readers a sense of the bill's changing status during these seven and a half months.

While much is known about the black freedom struggle in these years, the civil rights tapes made by Kennedy and Johnson are a revealing and often dramatic addition to the history of the quest for racial justice. By adding a missing piece to that history, the tapes help enrich our understanding of the way U.S. leaders reacted to events in the Jim Crow South, and deepen our appreciation of the way their response to the crises of 1962 and 1963 helped catalyze the more prosaic but critically important legislative process that unfolded in the nation's capital. And lest one forget, it was legislation that ultimately helped abolish institutionalized racial oppression—long the goal of civil rights leaders. We hope that once readers have encountered the words recorded in these years, they will gain a new perspective on the civil rights movement. By presenting an aural picture of government officials grappling with one of the great social and political challenges the United States faced in the twentieth century, the civil rights tapes afford us a rare opportunity to listen as history unfolds.

Chapter 1
The Twentieth-Century Struggle

"Let us close the springs of racial poison. Let us pray for wise and understanding hearts. Let us put aside irrelevant differences and make our nation whole." So declared President Lyndon Johnson, in a speech to the nation on a July evening in 1964, the day he signed the Civil Rights Act into law.

The Civil Rights Act was a milestone in the history of the U.S. civil rights movement. In the eyes of many, the complex legislation, which outlawed discrimination in public accommodation, employment, and federally funded programs, was the most important civil rights law in nearly a century, and leaders in the struggle for racial justice hailed its passage enthusiastically. The Reverend Fred Shuttlesworth described it as "the second emancipation of the America Negro," while the NAACP's Roy Wilkins likened it to the Magna Carta. And Dr. Martin Luther King, Jr., the country's foremost African American leader, declared that this "monumental" legislation had emerged from the cauldron of mass meetings and marches, and was then "polished and refined in the marble halls of Congress." The result, he said, was an "historic affirmation of Jefferson's ringing truth that 'all men are created equal.'"

In asking Americans to "help eliminate the last vestiges of injustice" from their country, Lyndon Johnson, the first southerner to occupy the White House since Woodrow Wilson, noted that the bill was the product of months of "careful debate and discussion," which had been initiated by John Kennedy, "our late and beloved president." While true in the narrowest sense, Johnson's observation did not convey a larger and more significant truth, namely, that the 1964 legislation was the product of decades of toil by countless men and women who had devoted their lives to working for racial justice in twentieth-century America.

If the movement to abolish American slavery was the noblest cause of the nineteenth century, then the civil rights struggle was the most heroic crusade of the twentieth. Indeed, the quest for racial justice in modern America was a continuation of the historic effort of a century before, when a group of determined individuals sought to compel the nation to end slavery and realize America's age-old promise. While it had taken a bloody war to sweep slavery from the national landscape, the twentieth-century civil rights movement was wrenching in its own right and, if not as cataclysmic, nearly as dramatic.

The story of the civil rights crusade has become part of the mythos of America, as towering heroes, possessed of great dignity and greater courage, labored energetically in the quest for justice. Arrayed against them were less noble figures, who, with equal zeal, worked to thwart the aspirations of the reformers. Whether a particular figure was a hero or a villain was of course a matter of one's perspective.

Thurgood Marshall, Martin Luther King, and Rosa Parks; Bull Connor and George Wallace—the names have become part of the nation's collective memory, as have the events that brought them to prominence. The 1954 Supreme Court decision, which famously declared segregation in education to be "inherently unequal"; the determination of the residents of Montgomery, who chose to walk rather than ride on Jim Crow buses in December 1955; the gathering on a peaceful August afternoon in 1963 when thousands came together in the nation's capital; and the shocking murder of four little girls in Birmingham that same year—the story of the struggle is etched in the minds of Americans, whether they lived through the events themselves or viewed them on the film clips that have become a staple part of the diet of American schoolchildren.

While many recognize the significance of the civil rights movement of the 1950s and 1960s, few recall that the struggle began not in those years but decades earlier. Emerging late in the nineteenth century, the modern quest for racial justice was peopled by extraordinary figures, many of whom are now remembered only dimly or not at all. Black and white freedom fighters worked tirelessly and often at great personal risk to extract justice from the heart of a nation that had long proclaimed itself the source of freedom and democracy in the world. That the United States was unwilling to provide either to all its citizens was one of the supreme ironies of the struggle, a campaign that unfolded slowly but inexorably over the first half of the twentieth century.

To have believed early in the last century that schools would one day be integrated and legal racial discrimination ended would have seemed a case of hope vanquishing reality. Yet in the 1950s and 1960s, it would begin to happen, and the Civil Rights Act of 1964 represented the culmination of years of work. With its passage, and the enactment the following year of the Voting Rights Act, the legal wall that had stood for so long between African Americans and full citizenship came tumbling down.

The history of the struggle has been told many times before, often as the story of courageous African Americans whose collective actions forced a reluctant federal government to defend and protect the rights of all Americans against a system that had long denied justice to blacks. And that is as it should be told, for what finally compelled the federal government to act were the assiduous efforts of black Americans who were determined to end legal discrimination.

Unlike earlier civil rights legislation in 1957 and 1960, the legislation of 1964 mandated an aggressive expansion of federal power and represented a convergence between grassroots activism and decisions made on the national political level. For a variety of reasons both noble and pragmatic, the Civil Rights Act was supported by northern and western legislators, Justice Department officials, and the White House, all of whom responded to the words and deeds of civil rights leaders and activists who had worked for racial justice in the 1950s and 1960s. The law's passage in 1964 was the product of local efforts and federal activism. Neither by itself would have been sufficient, a fact amply demonstrated by decades of unsuccessful efforts to enact civil rights law. But together, grassroots reformers and national political leaders overcame formidable obstacles that had long made the passage of effective legislation unlikely if not impossible.

In many accounts of the civil rights movement, the federal government has been portrayed as either passive or, worse yet, hostile to the aims of the reformers. It has been said that Truman, Eisenhower, and Kennedy were unwilling to kneel before the altar of civil rights and that it was not until Lyndon Johnson entered the White House that the executive branch demonstrated a genuine commitment to work for change. And there is much to commend this view, although Truman and Kennedy were considerably more supportive of the movement's aims than Eisenhower was. If Truman and Kennedy feared that endorsing civil rights would spell the end of their political careers or the fragmentation of their party, Eisenhower seemed at best ambivalent about the moral necessity of the domestic struggle. The former general evinced little willingness to lead the country toward confronting institutionalized racial discrimination in the 1950s, and just as white Americans preferred to maintain the status quo, Eisenhower was content to do the same.

The tape recordings made by John Kennedy and Lyndon Johnson open a new window onto the civil rights struggle. Although they do not invalidate earlier pictures of presidential uneasiness with civil rights reform, they do demand that we consider the obstacles two presidents faced in working for change. By allowing us to examine more clearly than before each man's commitment to the domestic crusade, these transcribed conversations reveal a dimension of the civil rights story that has never been fully considered, and they show that the White House played an active and constructive part in the quest for racial justice.

In highlighting the role played by the executive branch, the tapes in no way minimize the determination, skill, and heroism manifested by countless black Americans—leaders and followers—who helped transform the landscape of American race relations. The story of the struggle over civil rights should not be written according to the rules of a zero-sum game: there is not a fixed amount of credit to go around. Adding to the list of those who contributed to the passage of the 1964 bill does not mean that others need to be removed.

Until midway through the Kennedy administration, the White House was a reluctant partner in the civil rights struggle, as the President and some of his advisers viewed the demands of the movement's leaders as politically naive and even unreasonable. But that changed in 1963, largely because of the brutal events in Birmingham that May, which made an often apathetic country sit up and take notice. In response to the violence in Alabama, the Kennedy administration proposed legislation more sweeping than any federal civil rights reform since the 1870s, and while Kennedy never fully overcame his ambivalence about the bill, his reservations were political not moral.

But Lyndon Johnson would be different, for unlike his predecessor, he was wholly determined to do whatever was necessary to pass effective civil rights legislation. About this, Johnson was passionate and adamant, and he staked his political future on passing the 1964 bill. Had Johnson not made civil rights the number one priority of his first months in office, it might have been some time before Congress passed meaningful legislation. While Johnson has rightly been blamed for his failings in Southeast Asia, it is appropriate to credit him for his achievements on civil rights at home.

To be fair, the two Presidents faced different challenges, and the transcripts highlight different aspects of their presidencies. A substantial portion of the Kennedy tapes shows the President responding to crises, whether at Ole Miss or Birmingham. Confronted with dangerous and unpredictable situations, Kennedy did not have the luxury of careful deliberations, and his primary concern was to contain the chaos that threatened to engulf the South. Johnson, on the other hand, faced only a legislative crisis. The moral stakes may have been high, but violence and social disorder were not immediate concerns. Only in the weeks before the passage of the Civil Rights Act, confronted with the murder of three volunteers in Mississippi and the specter of a white backlash against the act, did Johnson have to contend with the same level of immediate danger on a civil rights issue as Kennedy had to in 1962 and 1963. Kennedy's ambivalence toward reform, therefore, may have been aggravated by his understandable sense that the South was a tinderbox waiting to ignite, while Johnson had the more straightforward task of dealing with a complicated congressional morass.

Both Kennedy and Johnson were political animals, who rarely made a decision without closely considering its political consequences. But civil rights had long been framed as a moral question, and those who led the campaign for race reform based their demands not on the ephemera of domestic politics but on timeless questions of right and justice. In the discussions and debates on the 1964 bill, the moral and the political were often merged. In the halls of Congress as well as in the Oval Office, advocates and opponents of the bill made it clear that what was just would have to be reconciled with what was possible in Washington and throughout the country.

This tension between morality and pragmatism has led some to question the motives of those political leaders who championed civil rights in the 1960s. Johnson has been susceptible to the charge that he endorsed civil rights reform largely to enhance his political standing, while Kennedy has been criticized for not moving more aggressively on the matter because he feared the political consequences for himself and his party. But if politics was never far from the mind of either man, the morality of civil rights weighed on both. Indeed, Johnson, the quintessential Texan, was more committed to civil rights than was Kennedy, a son of Massachusetts, home of the abolitionists. Just as many said that only a hard-line anti-Communist like Nixon could go to China, it is perhaps equally true that only Johnson—the southern politician par excellence—could engineer meaningful civil rights reform.

But the question remains: Why did Kennedy and Johnson come to believe that civil rights reform was the single most important domestic issue facing the nation and decide it was worth fighting for? What the tapes depict is an unfolding process between 1962 and 1964. At first, a reluctant Kennedy resented civil rights leaders for their failure to understand the obstacles to change. But as events proceeded, his position shifted, and he became determined to craft meaningful reform, even as he remained unsure about how far to go. Then, in the Johnson period, we see an administration willing to move without hesitation to ensure the passage of the 1964 act. Perhaps most interestingly, the tapes suggest that for both administrations, any attempt to separate moral from political concerns is a futile enterprise.

It is impossible to determine whether Kennedy cared more about the justness of civil rights than about the domestic political implications of the issue. Nor can one separate morality from politics when talking about Johnson. Each man was fully capable of fusing the two, of compromising moral imperatives because of political concerns, or of ignoring political concerns because of moral imperatives. Had Kennedy not believed that the political climate had changed such that ignoring civil rights was no longer politically feasible, it is difficult to imagine he would have acted as he did. And few would argue that Johnson would have invested his political capital in civil rights had he not been convinced that it was, quite simply, the right thing to do.

Civil Rights before 1960

The transcripts begin in 1962, but there is, of course, a rich history that preceded the events covered in the following pages, a history that informed and shaped how the various participants approached the issue of civil rights. The leading figures in the brief but intense drama of the early 1960s stood on the shoulders of thousands of committed people who preceded them, some well known, but most obscure.

To be black in early-twentieth-century America was by any measure to live a life of deprivation and oppression. Black Americans were poorer, hungrier, and less educated than their white countrymen were, and the black population in the South was victimized by Jim Crow, a wide-ranging system of legalized oppression that denied blacks the right to vote and enforced discrimination in housing, education, transportation, and employment. In addition, the oppressive system, which white southerners had constructed late in the nineteenth century, was made up of countless smaller indignities, which were no less humiliating. If it was demoralizing to be denied the vote in a country that prided itself on its love of democracy, then it was no doubt equally painful to be forced to take the oath on a special "colored" Bible in a southern courtroom. Separation and oppression sometimes took imaginative forms, as in New Orleans, which adopted a law segregating black from white prostitutes. Moreover, an unwritten code of racial deference made additional demands on black citizens, like the custom that forbade a black man in a car from passing a white driver, even if the latter was riding in a wagon.

Emerging from the miasma of prejudice and oppression, African American thought at the dawn of the century consisted of two distinct streams. The views of two men, Booker T. Washington and W. E. B. Du Bois, both of whom would someday occupy prominent places in the black pantheon, pointed the struggle in different directions. For Washington, born and bred in the rural South, the guiding idea was vocational education, which emphasized practical training, especially cultivation of the soil. In Washington's mind, this constituted the most effective path to advancement. Moreover, in a period when the accumulation of wealth had achieved an almost sanctified character in the United States, Washington emphasized hard work and thrift.

Had he stopped there, he might have been remembered as a modest advocate of black self-help. But for all his apparent mild-manneredness, he was destined to become a controversial figure in the African American community. Along with his call for education and hard work, in the short term, he explicitly ruled out for blacks what white America feared most of all: social equality between the races.

For white Americans in 1900, the term *social equality* was in truth a euphemism for interracial social contact, which might lead to interracial sex and miscegenation. Those possibilities terrified mainstream America, and Washington's clear rejection of such aims was reassuring. In his most-celebrated speech, he asserted in 1895, "In all things that are purely social we can be as separate as the five fingers, yet one as the hand in all things essential to mutual progress." Thus, Washington's means and ends were congenial to influential segments of white America, which believed that black uplift was not necessarily a bad thing—so long as it was narrowly circumscribed.

W. E. B. Du Bois thought differently. Cerebral, assertive, and utterly determined, Du Bois was born and reared in Massachusetts, graduated from Fisk University, studied in Berlin, earned a doctorate from Harvard, and was an altogether different type of leader than Washington was. Du Bois's views on the clearest path to racial progress differed markedly from Washington's, and the two became ideological rivals. In time, Du Bois's influence would surpass that of the elder man. He would become the leader of the black freedom struggle, and the most important black figure in the United States in the first half of the twentieth century.

Du Bois believed an elite group of black Americans, which he called the Talented Tenth, should be responsible for helping to elevate the rest of the race, economically, politically, socially, and culturally. In order to prepare for its leadership role, this black elite (representing approximately 10 percent of the black population) would need solid training in the liberal arts. According to Du Bois, "Progress in human affairs is more often a pull than a push, a surging forward of the exceptional man, and the lifting of his duller brethren." With his elite credentials and his Ph.D., Du Bois was convinced that reform, to be effective, had to come from above. In a celebrated critique of Washington, Du Bois wondered in 1903 whether it was possible to achieve racial progress with a philosophy that allowed only a "meager chance" for the development of "exceptional men." The answer, he asserted, was an "emphatic No."

While there were points of overlap between the visions of Washington and Du Bois, their differences marked the civil rights movement early in the century. But this was an age in which highly educated, reform-minded experts were gaining increasing prestige, power, and authority throughout American society, and Du Bois's elite-centered approach to race reform came to dominate the campaign for racial justice.

Reflecting the ascendence of Du Bois, the National Association for the Advancement of Colored People (NAACP) was founded in 1909. Composed of blacks and whites in the early days, the NAACP was destined to become the organizational engine for race reform for the next fifty years. Well-educated, articulate spokespersons, committed to helping the downtrodden, would spearhead the movement for racial justice by working to challenge segregation, end occupational discrimination, and gain the right to vote. A new spirit of abolitionism had been born.

In addition to the emergence of an organized movement for race reform early in the century, a key development in the black experience at this time was the northward migration of large numbers of African Americans. This was the beginning of the so-called Great Migration, which saw hundreds of thousands of blacks leave the South for the North between 1910 and 1920. (Equally significant was the simultaneous black migration within the South, which saw rural blacks move into southern cities in record numbers, a development that in later years would have enormous implications for the civil rights movement.) While World War I accelerated the exodus, blacks started to move even before the guns sounded. Nature, too, played a role, as the boll weevil and flooding wreaked havoc on southern agriculture (especially cotton), which upset the always precarious economic balance of the black farmer.

The movement of peoples was significant, as nearly all blacks heading north settled in urban areas. The black population grew spectacularly in places like Detroit, New York, and Chicago; the latter two gained more than 60,000 black residents and Detroit acquired 36,000. The percentage increases of the black population in northern cities ranged from 150 to 600 percent.

The quest for a better life—an idea that combined economic, political, and social aspirations—was the prime motivation. According to Adam Clayton Powell, a prominent black leader of the time, "we were tired of being kept out of public parks and libraries, of being deprived of equal educational opportunities." They were tired also of being denied the vote and of being the object of unchecked violence perpetrated by white southerners who knew they would never be brought to justice. Blacks thus left the South in record numbers, a trend that continued for several decades, transforming the political, social, and cultural landscape of twentieth-century America.

World War I provided black Americans with the opportunity to serve their country in a war that was fought, as President Woodrow Wilson famously observed, to "make the world safe for democracy." Whether or not this was actually the case, leading race reformers sought to use Wilson's noble rhetoric to energize their followers and to legitimize their aims to the nation and the international community. If the United States had embarked on a crusade to bring democracy to the world, surely it was right and proper to bring democracy to Mississippi and Alabama. Civil rights leaders made this claim repeatedly at home and abroad during the Great War.

But for all his noble rhetoric, Woodrow Wilson was no progressive on the subject of race relations, and while fulminating for justice abroad, he issued an executive order that reimposed segregation in government offices in Washington, D.C. Black federal employees were once more forced to use separate eating facilities and rest rooms, despite the fact that nearly 400,000 African Americans were serving their country overseas in the war for democracy.

With the end of World War I, much of the fervor for domestic reform evaporated, and the postwar decade saw little tangible progress in race relations. The NAACP, in particular, had few notable successes in these years, and the northward black migration continued, as an estimated 750,000 to 1 million blacks left the South for the urban North. By 1930, of the five cities with the largest black populations, not one was located in the South.

Among the most significant developments in African American life in the 1920s was the cultural flowering known as the Harlem Renaissance. Literature, painting, and music blossomed in Harlem, a place one observer described as the "great Mecca for the pleasure-seeker, the curious, the adventurous, the enterprising, the ambitious, and the talented." Contributing to a developing sense of black identity, the cultural movement was part of the larger social and political struggle for racial justice, and its implications would be felt for years to come.

The twenties also saw the emergence of the black nationalist leader Marcus Garvey, a Jamaican possessed of a powerful, controversial message. Beyond urging black Americans to take pride in their African heritage, he also encouraged them to return to their ancestral African homeland. As head of the Universal Negro Improvement Association, Garvey attracted hundreds of thousands of supporters. In huge numbers they attended rallies, drawn to Garvey's assertive message, which rejected the notion that the black population would ever achieve equality in the United States. Garvey stands somewhat apart from the traditional race reform struggle for he advocated leaving the United States, rather than working to change it. If his program did not directly influence the trajectory of civil rights reform in the decades to come, his was the first genuine mass movement among the African American population.

Although the 1920s was not a decade notable for great achievements in race reform, the NAACP did work for change through legislative and judicial channels. Federal anti-lynching legislation was one of the association's key objectives, and civil rights reformers worked tirelessly to gain passage of a law to outlaw that gruesome crime. While such legislation never became law (it passed the House but not the Senate), many believed agitation for the bill contributed to a drop in the number of lynchings in this period. At the same time, the NAACP's energetic effort, which was led by a black man, James Weldon Johnson, represented the first time an African American leader had spearheaded the drive to pass civil rights legislation. It would not be the last.

But the dynamics of Congress prevented civil rights legislation from passing in these years. The key obstacle was the Senate. Under arcane and complicated senatorial rules, a small group of senators could block any legislation by filibustering. Essentially, that meant talking continuously, which in turn would prevent the Senate from voting before adjournment. A filibuster, or even the threat of a filibuster, could halt nascent legislation before it ever reached the full Senate. That, in effect, gave a minority of senators veto power over what the majority might want. In short, senatorial procedure was one factor that blocked civil rights reform during these decades.

Stymied on the legislative front, the NAACP did achieve some significant victories in court, the first of which was a 1923 ruling, *Moore v. Dempsey*, in which the Supreme Court ruled against mob influence in an Arkansas courtroom, by reversing a verdict that had wrongly sentenced a group of black man to death. In 1927, in *Nixon v. Herndon*, the Court struck down a Texas statute that excluded blacks from voting. While the NAACP realized there was still a long way to go on the franchise question, the decision represented a significant step along the road to full citizenship rights for black Americans.

If progress for African Americans was difficult to measure during the twenties, the Depression decade posed still greater challenges and obstacles to black advancement. The economic problems that befell the country in the age of Franklin Roosevelt hit African Americans particularly hard. In the words of the noted scholar Harvard Sitkoff, the Depression dealt the black population a "staggering blow," making an already difficult existence harsher than ever. Black unemployment rates were often twice that experienced by white Americans, reaching 50 percent in some northern cities. And lest one forget, there was precious little governmental assistance to be had. Relief in Philadelphia was inadequate to sustain a sufficient diet, and Detroit paid out 15 cents per day per individual before running out of funds altogether.

In response to the nation's dire economic problems, Franklin Roosevelt moved to establish a variety of programs, known as the New Deal, which sought to alleviate the hardships caused by the worst economic depression the country had experienced in some forty years. The Roosevelt administration established myriad agencies and programs, laying the groundwork for the modern welfare state. Social Security, the Public Works Administration, the Works Progress Administration, the Farm Security Administration—these were but a few of the ways the federal government responded to the crisis of the 1930s.

One of the most striking political developments of these years was the movement of African Americans into the Democratic Party. Until the 1930s, when blacks did vote—if they were allowed to do so at all—they supported Republicans, the party of Lincoln, the man who freed the slaves. But with the Republican Party's apparent indifference to the plight of the poor, and with the active efforts of the Roosevelt administration to ease the pain of the Depression, many blacks, having recently arrived in northern cities, began to vote Democratic. In response, northern Democrats attended to the issues black Americans cared about. In time, this would create an uneasy and untenable situation in which northern Democrats would work to curry favor with blacks while southern Democrats would work energetically to maintain Jim Crow.

With the onset of World War II, economic opportunities increased for black Americans as the country's booming factories worked overtime to produce war materials. Even before the United States entered the war in December 1941, A. Philip Randolph, the founder of the Brotherhood of Sleeping Car Porters, and one of black America's most-revered figures, sought to organize a march on Washington to highlight the persistent inequities in American race relations. A White House meeting with FDR, in which Randolph promised the President thousands of blacks would march, led Roosevelt to sign Executive Order 8802, which barred racial discrimination in the government and in defense contract employment, and established the Fair Employment Practices Committee (FEPC). Although its effect was limited, the order marked the first time in the twentieth century that the executive branch of the federal government had responded directly to the demands advanced by black leaders.

Despite the apparent responsiveness of the executive branch, racial tensions did not abate during the war. Race riots erupted in northern cities like Detroit and New York, exposing tensions that continued to plague the entire country. As the riots made clear, injustice was not confined to the American South; blacks in every region were more determined than ever to gain their rights as citizens in a democracy. The wartime cry among blacks was encapsulated in the notion of the Double-V, which asserted that it was essential to achieve victory not only against dictators abroad but also against the tyranny of racism at home.

Indeed, the war strengthened the determination of the African American population to claim their rights as American citizens. The United States and its allies had assumed the burden of sweeping the racist ideologies of Nazi Germany and Imperial Japan from the world scene. With the successful conclusion of the global conflagration, the notion of state-sanctioned racial, ethnic, or religious persecution lost legitimacy throughout the world. And that in turn undermined such thinking in the United States. If it had been worth fighting to stamp out racial persecution in Europe and Asia, then it was surely reasonable to stamp out racial persecution in Alabama. This argument, which had been made throughout the war, came to have considerable power once peace was achieved.

Another significant implication of the war was the movement of blacks from the rural South to the urban North. Due to increasing economic opportunities in the North and the mechanization of southern agriculture (especially in the harvesting of cotton, which decreased the demand for black labor), some 700,000 blacks headed north during the war years. Nor did this northward migration end once the war was over. In fact, during the 1940s as a whole, over a million blacks left the region, while in the 1950s, more than 1.5 million blacks moved north, abandoning their rural roots for cities from New York to California. As the historian Harvard Sitkoff has noted, this mass migration "fundamentally altered the configuration of the race problem." And over time, it would transform social, cultural, and political life in postwar America, affecting everything from presidential politics to popular music.

In the postwar political realm, Harry Truman built on the actions of his predecessor, issuing an executive order in 1948 that ended segregation in the military. This was a significant milestone, though it would be some time before the armed forces fully implemented the President's directive. During the first months of 1948, Truman also spoke out forcefully on behalf of civil rights reform. When the Democrats assembled for their convention in the summer of 1948, northern Democrats such as Minneapolis mayor Hubert Humphrey pushed for a strong civil rights plank in the party platform. This led to a rupture in the Democratic Party during the presidential campaign. Led by Strom Thurmond of South Carolina, some southern Democrats refused to endorse Truman and formed a States' Rights party that was dedicated to preventing any supporter of federal civil rights reform from reaching the White House. That fall, Thurmond captured four southern states. Though Truman won the White House, the lesson was clear: the civil rights struggle had the potential to break up the Democratic Party.

After the war, the NAACP turned its attention more energetically than before to the federal courts, where the country's leading race reform organization continued to batter the walls of institutionalized racial discrimination. In the late 1940s and 1950s, a series of successful cases brought against the persistent indignities of Jim Crow culminated in the momentous Supreme Court decision of 1954, which declared famously that separate educational facilities were "inherently unequal." With the successful verdict in *Brown v. Board of Education*, a once-impregnable barrier had fallen, and while obstacles to black liberation remained, it is easy to understand why the NAACP's Roy Wilkins described May 17, when the court's verdict came down, as "one of life's sweetest days."

The High Court's epic decision ordering the desegregation of public schools was the result of years of labor by the NAACP's legal division, headed by a talented lawyer named Thurgood Marshall, who would later become the first African American to sit on the Supreme Court. Marshall built patiently on prior cases in which the NAACP had challenged the constitutionality of the "separate but equal" doctrine, a misguided notion that had been enshrined by the Supreme Court in its 1896 decision in *Plessy v. Ferguson*. The NAACP legal team argued that separate facilities could never be equal and presented a considerable body of evidence to support this claim.

Chief Justice Earl Warren worked hard to ensure the court would speak with one voice, and in a 9–0 ruling, the court held that segregation in public education denied African Americans their rights under the equal protection clause of the Fourteenth Amendment to the Constitution.

While the ruling represented a stunning victory for the civil rights movement, the court allowed the states and school districts to devise specific remedies to the problem. Not surprisingly, this plan generated years of heated, bitter, and sometimes violent confrontations between civil rights leaders and local and state officials who were utterly determined to prevent the full realization of the Supreme Court's decision.

In state after state, the NAACP brought suits demanding an end to segregation, and even when the courts ordered a school district to do so, local officials rarely enforced such rulings, remaining unwilling to comply with judicial decisions. In Little Rock, Arkansas, in the fall of 1957, Governor Orval Faubus refused to enforce a federal court order to admit African American students to the city's public schools. After weeks of failed negotiations, President Eisenhower reluctantly federalized the Guard, ordering guardsmen to escort and protect black children who walked through the hate-filled mobs that had surrounded one of Little Rock's schools. No firebrand on civil rights, Dwight Eisenhower was compelled by events to act. (As the tapes in this book document, a similar crisis would confront John Kennedy five years later, when James Meredith tried to enroll at the University of Mississippi, a bastion of southern segregation.)

In the mid-1950s, the momentum for progress on civil rights accelerated. In December 1955, Rosa Parks, a 42-year-old seamstress in Montgomery, Alabama, refused to surrender her seat to a white person on a city bus and move toward the back as the rules of Jim Crow demanded. The bus driver called the police and Mrs. Parks was arrested. The events that flowed from this solitary act would capture the attention of the nation and the world, as a large-scale, grassroots movement, the Montgomery bus boycott, began. Thousands of African Americans refused to ride Montgomery's buses, and because they made up a substantial portion of the daily ridership, the boycott struck a severe financial blow to the bus company and to the city's merchants.

The Montgomery bus boycott brought Martin Luther King to the forefront of the civil rights movement. The 26-year-old Baptist preacher, charismatic, courageous, and possessed of mesmerizing oratorical skills, proved to be a superb strategist. As the boycott continued throughout 1955 and 1956, its leaders faced threats and harassment that came in a variety of forms: they were fired from their jobs; they were jailed; and in an act of terror that only stiffened the resolve of the boycotters, King's house was bombed.

In the Montgomery campaign, King honed his skill as a practitioner of nonviolent resistance, a philosophy that owed a great deal to the Indian leader Mohandas Gandhi. King was jailed for his role in the Montgomery campaign—the first of many times he would be imprisoned over the next decade, each sentence serving to enhance his stature as the leading figure in the civil rights struggle. Because of the determined actions of thousands of black citizens in Montgomery, in December 1956, the city was ordered to desegregate its buses. A great victory had been won and countless ordinary people had helped to achieve it.

The bus boycott marked a new stage in the civil rights struggle. While after Montgomery, the NAACP continued to pursue its legal strategy, the movement's energy would begin to flow from broad-based efforts led by King, the Southern Christian Leadership Conference, the Congress of Racial Equality, and other organizations. Seeking to mobilize thousands of young black men and women, such groups were often closely linked to southern black churches. Instead of the methodical, if at times momentous, legal challenges waged by black elites in American courtrooms, after 1955, the civil rights struggle came to be defined by peaceful marches, freedom rides, lunch counter sit-ins, inspirational sermons, demonstrations, and arrests.

The Brown decision and events in Montgomery generated pressure in Washington. In response, Eisenhower's attorney general, Herbert Brownell, presented Congress with a draft for a civil rights bill. The proposed legislation, introduced in 1956, included the establishment of a civil rights division in the Justice Department and provided for the prosecution of federal voting rights abuses, both of which were central concerns of American civil rights leaders.

The Democratic Party, which controlled the House and the Senate in this period, was unwilling to move on civil rights, mainly because it was paralyzed by the opposition of southern senators. Led by northerners and midwesterners, the Republicans perceived a golden opportunity to take advantage of the Democrats' reluctance to act. While Eisenhower was largely indifferent to federal civil rights reform, the potential political gains that could be derived from proposing a bill were too great to forgo, and if nothing was achieved on the legislative front in 1956, the fact that the administration had decided to act pulled some northern black voters back into the Republican Party.

The following year, the Democrats took up the bill. Senate majority leader Lyndon Johnson, aware of the damage that intransigence on civil rights was doing to his party and to his own political aspirations, intended to shepherd some sort of legislation through the upper chamber. At the same time, Johnson also realized that the southern bloc would never permit passage of a genuinely effective bill and that he would harm his own political future in Texas if he was thought to be too far out front on civil rights. In what would serve as a preview of his adept handling of the far broader 1964 bill, Johnson steered the legislation through the Senate. First, he mollified northern liberals like Hubert Humphrey by convincing them half a loaf was better than none. And then he satisfied the southern bloc, led by Georgia's Richard Russell, by allowing them to gut those portions of the bill that permitted federal troops to be used to enforce desegregation and that gave federal courts the power to impose criminal penalties on those who infringed on black voting rights.

The bill passed by a wide margin, and civil rights leaders took solace from this fact, even though the bill itself was weak. In the words of the NAACP's Clarence Mitchell, "not only did it have some substantive value, but it also represented a breakthrough. Up until that time, it had been assumed that Congress would not and could not pass any civil rights legislation." Roy Wilkins, the head of the NAACP who had tirelessly lobbied members of Congress, dismissed the bill's critics as unrealistic. While he recognized the bill's limitations, Wilkins kept his eyes on the big picture. As he and other civil rights leaders knew, Congress had last passed civil rights legislation in 1875, a law the Supreme Court had declared unconstitutional. Eighty-two years later, the High Court was no longer an obstacle, and Congress had taken a small step down a road it had rarely traveled before.

Notwithstanding the 1957 legislation, Congress and the White House were reacting to events, not leading them, and the 1957 bill was a response to the ferment caused by King, the NAACP, and the courts. The same could be said of the 1960 civil rights bill. In February of that year, in Greensboro, North Carolina, four students from a local college sat down at a lunch counter marked "for whites only" and refused to move. Within days, their ranks had swelled, and suddenly there were sit-ins everywhere. Countless young men and women throughout the South planted themselves at whites-only lunch counters, where they would remain until the stores closed for the day or the police arrested them for disturbing the peace. The sit-in movement attracted widespread publicity during the presidential campaign, as yet again, grassroots organizers forced civil rights onto the national stage.

Events in Greensboro marked a sea change within the civil rights movement. Since Montgomery, the more traditional tactics of the NAACP were being eclipsed by the activities of mass-based organizations such as King's SCLC. Moreover, there was an immediacy to the actions of these nascent organizations. The students who began the Greensboro sit-in seemed to have acted spontaneously, and, while such an approach was not completely novel, in the climate of the early 1960s, their protest was like touching a match to dry tinder. Eventually, the effects of the conflagration would spread to policymakers in the nation's capital.

No longer would the civil rights protest be an elite-driven phenomenon, as had been the case for decades. The new leaders were mostly young men, who, at times, could scarcely conceal their scorn for the staid ways of the NAACP. However unfair their attacks on the NAACP—it was too conservative, too patient, and ineffective, they asserted—the proverbial torch had been passed to a new generation of leaders who were swept up in the passions of the moment. And indeed, such grassroots activism would lead Washington to act.

In the Senate, Lyndon Johnson used the sit-ins as a pretext for pushing through a new civil rights bill. But this time, unlike in 1957, the southern bloc was more adamant in its opposition. Richard Russell, the courtly Georgian who was devoted to the traditions of the Senate and the South, was the most moderate leader within the southern bloc. According to Russell, it was imperative to hold the line: the South had to prevent passage of federally mandated desegregation of public facilities and the provision of voting rights for black Americans. But Lyndon Johnson knew a civil rights bill, even an anemic one, would help the Democrats in the upcoming contest for the White House. While the final bill was largely symbolic, it contributed to the sense that progress on race reform was inevitable, and, more importantly, it suggested that the southern bloc could no longer stand in the way.

The Civil Rights Acts of 1957 and 1960 have been viewed as hollow pieces of legislation that achieved little in the struggle for justice. And while neither bill did much to improve the lives of African Americans, they did set a precedent and served as a crucible for policymakers like Humphrey, Kennedy, and Johnson. Johnson, especially, came to realize that a strong presidential push was necessary to achieve passage of meaningful civil rights legislation. Having managed both bills as majority leader in the Senate, Johnson would be prepared to take decisive action on civil rights when he became president in late 1963.

In the first months of 1960, as the sit-ins became increasingly widespread, John Kennedy and Lyndon Johnson fought a close contest to be their party's nominee for the White House. It was an odd primary campaign, with Johnson's remaining in Washington and Kennedy's entering only a handful of primaries. This was still an era when party leaders selected the nominee, and Johnson believed he had a good chance of securing enough party backing to win the nomination at the convention. But with more backing and more money, Kennedy would ultimately emerge on top, beating out Johnson, Humphrey, and Missouri's Stuart Symington.

In the debates over who would receive the nomination, the platform committee conducted its business out of the public spotlight, and the language it adopted on civil rights was surprisingly powerful. The Democrats' platform committed the party to removing all barriers to the right to vote, especially the poll tax and the literacy test. It called for aggressive action on school desegregation and promised that a Democratic president would end discrimination in the federal government and in federal housing. Coming to the convention, Kennedy had made a brief statement endorsing the sit-ins: "It is in the American tradition to stand up for one's rights," he told a group of African diplomats, "even if the new way to stand up for one's rights is to sit down." It was, like so many of Kennedy's public utterances, a pithy line, but civil rights was not a key aspect of his campaign.

Chapter 2
Ole Miss

A child of privilege, John Fitzgerald Kennedy had long seemed destined to achieve great things. The son of the ambitious and intensely political multimillionaire Joseph Kennedy, John graduated from Harvard, and, while still in his early twenties, authored a 1940 bestseller on contemporary affairs, *Why England Slept*. Although young Jack Kennedy's authorship of the work has long been questioned, the book created a public profile for Joe Kennedy's son, as did his service as a naval officer in the Pacific during World War II, when he conducted himself heroically after his PT boat was sunk by the Japanese.

In 1948, the young war hero glided into politics, becoming a congressman at 29 and the junior senator from Massachusetts just four years later. If Kennedy did not stand out as a legislator, his marriage to Jacqueline Bouvier attracted the attention of the nation's society pages. The publication of his second book, *Profiles in Courage* (whose authorship has also been questioned), won him the Pulitzer Prize and greater name recognition than anything he had achieved in the Senate.

His emergence as a factor in the 1956 presidential election was a surprise, and while many thought him to be smart, charismatic, and self-possessed, some believed he was merely the political creation of his father. Narrowly defeated for the vice presidential nomination on Adlai Stevenson's ticket, Kennedy emerged from the 1956 Democratic convention as a new force in the party. If anything, Kennedy was fortunate to escape political association with Stevenson, who would lose the 1956 presidential contest to Dwight Eisenhower, after having lost in 1952. By the start of the new decade, Kennedy could claim that it was time for new blood in the party and that he represented the Democrats' best chance to unseat the Republicans.

During the 1960 campaign, Kennedy made few overtures to the country's leading civil rights figure, Martin Luther King, who was on trial for his actions in Montgomery. With civil rights still a divisive issue in the Democratic Party, Kennedy kept these contacts quiet. Perhaps the most public action candidate Kennedy took was a telephone call to a distraught Coretta Scott King, the wife of the young activist, who was upset about her husband's arrest and imprisonment in Georgia. In a brief call, Kennedy comforted Mrs. King. While some in the campaign worried that the telephone call might harm Kennedy's candidacy, the incident did little political damage and may have done some good. Though the call was not widely reported in the mainstream media, African Americans took note of the gesture, and the action won Kennedy praise from Dr. King himself.

Neither John Kennedy nor his brother Robert, his campaign manager, had closely examined the civil rights plank of the 1960 Democratic platform, and both would probably have been surprised by its forceful language. But as the campaign headed into the fall, Kennedy did not retreat from the platform, although it was hardly necessary for him to do so since civil rights was not a significant campaign issue. Moreover, the Republican platform strongly favored civil rights legislation, and, as was true on foreign policy, Kennedy and Nixon shared many views on the struggle for racial justice. The 1960 election was decided less on policy differences than on matters of personal style, and in one of the closest elections in American history, Kennedy's appeal won the day.

As president-elect, John Kennedy worked with his brother Bobby, who would become the Attorney General, to come up with a capable civil rights team in the Justice Department. Like his older brother, Robert Kennedy had no obvious commitment to civil rights. He had spent the 1950s focusing more on the domestic threat of Communism and on Jack's political fortunes than on the plight of black Americans. Though one day he would become the exemplar of a distinctive brand of American liberalism, in the 1950s, Robert Kennedy was more a street fighter than a social reformer, serving as a lawyer on Senator Joseph McCarthy's committee and later as a political operative. He cared about race only to the extent that it helped the electoral fortunes of the Democrats. For that reason, he had been unequivocal in arguing that the Kennedy team should not appear to side with Martin Luther King during the campaign.

Along with Bobby Kennedy at Justice, Nicholas deB. Katzenbach was named assistant attorney general, Harris Wofford became special assistant to the President on civil rights, and Burke Marshall was chosen to head the Civil Rights Division at the Justice Department. A Yale Law School graduate, Marshall was a highly capable corporate lawyer with little prior civil rights experience. The selection of the understated Marshall struck many as an uninspired choice, which suggested the new administration was planning to play it safe on civil rights. But those who thought Marshall's lack of charisma reflected a lack of commitment to civil rights soon learned otherwise. As it turned out, this unassuming attorney proved to be one of the new administration's most ardent and effective supporters of the freedom struggle.

Kennedy entered the White House with a shaky congressional base, and while the Democrats had a majority in the Senate, the party was so fractured between North and South, conservative and liberal, that a bloc of moderate Republicans and conservative southern Democrats had an effective majority. On domestic matters, the young President had little room to maneuver, no great problem at first since his administration was more concerned with foreign than domestic affairs. Crises in Laos, Cuba, Berlin, and Vietnam occupied most of Kennedy's attention; the African American crusade had not yet reached the top of his agenda.

By early 1961, the civil rights campaign had become a mass movement led by a variety of people with divergent approaches. At times, black leaders worked together, but tensions frequently impeded their efforts. Nevertheless, if the movement had lost some of its earlier cohesiveness, it had gained a following of hundreds of thousands of young men and women who were willing—quite literally—to lay their lives on the line for the cause. In addition, the struggle had the support of a growing number of Americans outside the South who viewed the persistence of Jim Crow as an affront to American values. The movement could also rely on the backing of the federal courts, which, in case after case, had ruled that discrimination violated the Fourteenth Amendment. But still, civil rights activists could not count on the full support of the executive branch, and until the President decided to place the weight of his office behind the movement, the struggle would remain arduous, its outcome in doubt.

Given their background, one might have imagined that the Kennedys would have been more sensitive to the grievances of black Americans. As Catholics, the Kennedys had learned to tread delicately around the subject of prejudice, which had stung the family for many years. Indeed, John Kennedy's religion had been a significant issue during the presidential campaign, but with deft handling, the candidate had neutralized the problem to become the nation's first Catholic president. Although John and Robert Kennedy had developed no obvious compassion for the struggles of African Americans, the persistence of institutionalized racism disturbed the Kennedy brothers. Having grown up in a world of boarding schools, large estates, and Ivy League manners, they had rarely encountered southern-style racism, and its virulence did not sit well with them.

In responding to the civil rights movement, the administration seemed at first to oscillate between respect and annoyance. Kennedy and his inner circle believed the country was moving about as quickly as it could on civil rights, and they were convinced it was not feasible for the Democratic Party to take energetic action in Congress. The votes simply were not there, and, having won a close election, Kennedy was not prepared to spend his limited political capital on trying to gain additional support in Congress for civil rights.

To consolidate his southern flank, Kennedy's choice for vice president was the Senate majority leader from Texas, Lyndon Johnson. Though Johnson had successfully steered two civil rights bills through the Senate, in the eyes of most black activists, he was little more than a good old boy from the South. But Johnson was unlike most of his southern colleagues, for he actually cared about civil rights reform—far more deeply than the Kennedys. While this commitment would become clear when he succeeded Kennedy in November 1963, in the administration's early days, Johnson's tone was muted on the race question.

In those first days, Kennedy's focus on foreign policy would become an unexpected boon to the civil rights movement. After the Bay of Pigs debacle in 1961, which saw the collapse of a U.S.-sponsored invasion of Cuba by anti-Castro Cuban exiles, Kennedy was pilloried abroad. Communist countries ridiculed the United States, and Castro and Nikita Khrushchev, especially, pointed to the hypocrisy of the United States, the self-proclaimed bastion of freedom, which continued to oppress its black population.

In the spring of 1961, events provided added grist for the Communist propaganda mill, as civil rights activists settled on a novel strategy for desegregating buses. Organized by the Congress of Racial Equality (CORE), the Freedom Rides would force the Kennedy administration to attend to civil rights. The head of CORE was James Farmer, who had been one of the organization's founders in the early 1940s. A student of Gandhi and an advocate of nonviolence, Farmer had come to see the value of highly publicized protests that might provoke a violent reaction in the South. Tough-minded and highly educated, Farmer seized on the Freedom Rides as a way of showing the country that racial inequality persisted. Carrying out a well-coordinated plan, a small interracial group of young men and women would ride Greyhound and Trailways intercity buses across the Deep South, challenging segregated seating, terminals, and restaurants along the route. As expected, the Freedom Rides generated a wave of unrest, as southern mobs assaulted the riders for having the temerity to demand their rights.

The mounting tension and violent outbursts demanded a response from the White House, and the Justice Department was soon drawn into the fray. As bus companies like Greyhound violated court rulings, which had made clear that businesses involved in interstate commerce could not segregate their facilities, CORE sought the protection of Robert Kennedy and the Department of Justice. The images of angry mobs assaulting riders like John Lewis, who was beaten and bloodied, spurred the administration to act. As historian Carl M. Brauer has written, the Attorney General "worked behind the scenes to ensure order," and this made it possible for the Freedom Rides to go on. Robert Kennedy ordered the FBI to investigate the violence and within a short time arrests were made by the federal government. He then instructed his staff to draw up plans to prevent more violence from exploding as the Freedom Rides continued.

The administration was particularly concerned about the potential international repercussions of such damning domestic images. As people around the world witnessed the violent behavior of white southerners, President Kennedy was forced to confront the possibility that southern brutality could impair the ability of the United States to wage an effective propaganda war against the Soviet Union. How could the administration continue to claim that the United States was a beacon of freedom and democracy in the world while vivid pictures of southern violence visited on the freedom riders were flashed across the globe? This was especially disturbing to the President and his foreign policy team as he prepared to go to Vienna in early June to meet with Soviet leader Nikita Khrushchev.

Cornered by events, President Kennedy and Robert Kennedy privately lashed out at civil rights leaders. As Evan Thomas has noted in his biography of Robert Kennedy, when the Attorney General met with NAACP lawyer Thurgood Marshall in the midst of the Freedom Ride crisis, he displayed an astonishing insensitivity. "The problem with you people," Robert Kennedy snapped, "[is that] you want too much too fast." And that was the Kennedy administration's attitude throughout the year. But whatever the administration's attitude, the Freedom Rides achieved a measure of success, as the Justice Department decided to push for the desegregation of businesses involved in interstate travel.

With these successes providing momentum for the movement, civil rights activists continued to agitate for change as groups like CORE and a new force, the Student Nonviolent Coordinating Committee (SNCC), worked to register voters throughout the Deep South. But the Justice Department remained aloof from such efforts, which it considered the actions of private citizens seeking to redress issues of state law. Focusing on foreign and defense policy, the President gave little indication that he intended to fulfill either the spirit or the letter of the Democratic Party platform on civil rights, and not for a year and a half would the subject return to the top of the presidential agenda.

Although some of RFK's deputies in the Justice Department were sympathetic to the movement, on the whole, relations between civil rights leaders and the Kennedy administration became increasingly strained in 1961 and 1962. John Kennedy simply was not that interested in civil rights. From his vantage point, the denial of black rights was an old wrong that would take many years to fix, and compared to the challenges of the international situation, the African American struggle was of secondary importance. In these less than propitious conditions, James Meredith tried to enroll at the University of Mississippi in the fall of 1962, and shortly thereafter, all hell broke loose.

The Background to the Crisis

Inspired in part by the strong civil rights plank in the Democratic platform, James H. Meredith, a 28-year-old Air Force veteran, decided to apply to the leading institution of higher learning in Mississippi. Requesting an application to the University of Mississippi, widely known as Ole Miss, Meredith described himself as an "American-Mississippi-Negro citizen" who had been moved by all the changes "in our educational system taking place in the country in this new age." He noted that the application would probably not come as a surprise to the university and hoped the matter would be "handled in a manner that [would] be complimentary to the University and to the State of Mississippi. Of course, I am the one that will, no doubt, suffer the greatest consequences of this event." Convinced that his goal of ending segregation at the university was but one part of the great struggle for racial justice, Meredith would later write of his "Divine Responsibility" for ending "White Supremacy" in Mississippi, observing that desegregating Ole Miss was "only the start."

Over the next 18 months, as Meredith's case moved through the courts and finally exploded on the grounds of the Mississippi campus, it would receive national and even international attention, and Kennedy administration officials, including the President and the Attorney General, devoted a great deal of time to managing the crisis. Before the episode ended with the registration and matriculation of Meredith at Ole Miss in the fall of 1962, tense standoffs, rioting, and death would come to the university, and President Kennedy would order thousands of U.S. Army troops to the campus in order to protect Meredith and enforce the rule of law. Meredith's determination to attend Ole Miss, Mississippi's steadfast efforts to prevent him from doing so, and the conviction of the President and his aides that it was essential to allow Meredith to enter the university combined to make the episode one of the most celebrated in the history of the civil rights movement.

Having decided to transfer from all-black Jackson State to segregated Ole Miss, Meredith recognized that he would need legal assistance; this led him to contact Medgar Evers, Mississippi field secretary of the NAACP.[1] Evers put him in touch with the NAACP Legal Defense Fund, where his case would be handled by Constance Baker Motley, one of the Defense Fund's talented young attorneys. With the nation's leading civil rights organization behind him, Meredith embarked on what would become a tortuous legal battle to enter the segregated institution. After Ole Miss had denied him admission on clearly specious grounds, the struggle moved to the courts, and over the next several months, Meredith continued to seek admission to the university. In September 1962, the federal courts established Meredith's legal right to attend the institution. But the struggle was far from over, as white Mississippians, a collection of politicians, Ole Miss students, local journalists, and ordinary citizens united to block the young black man from entering their beloved university.

Spearheading the movement against the integration of the university was Governor Ross Barnett, who combined the soft-spoken demeanor of the southern planter with the overheated rhetoric of the southern populist. Barnett's performance during the crisis is not easy to characterize: in speaking to the Kennedys, he was generally conciliatory, searching, or so it seemed, for a way out of the legal and political morass. But the governor was equally capable of appealing to the basest instincts of those who would stand in Meredith's path. In one of the most highly charged moments of the crisis, Barnett declared to a crowd of more than 40,000 football fans attending an Ole Miss game: "I love Mississippi. I love our people. I love our customs." The throng laughed, cried, and roared its approval, the moment, a spectator recalled, resembling "a big Nazi rally." In showdowns that saw Barnett and his colleagues confront U.S. marshals and Justice Department officials, many Mississippians came to see the crisis as pitting the federal Goliath against the southern David, or perhaps more aptly, as providing a second chance to fight for the honor of the South against the northern invader.

The U.S. Department of Justice developed an early interest in the case; Burke Marshall, Assistant Attorney General for Civil Rights, told Mere-

---

[1] As William Doyle, the author of *An American Insurrection*, points out, Ole Miss was not an all-white institution. It was a multiracial, multiethnic university open to peoples of color from the United States and overseas. It was not, however, open to African Americans.

dith the Civil Rights Division was following his efforts and was prepared to do everything it could to assist him. In August 1962, one month before the federal courts established Meredith's right to enter the university, the Justice Department had become officially involved in the case, filing an *amicus curiae* brief, which argued that several delays issued by Justice Ben F. Cameron of the Fifth Circuit were improper. On September 10, Justice Hugo Black of the U.S. Supreme Court concurred, paving the way for the federal order that Meredith be admitted to Ole Miss.

Although by August 1962 the Justice Department had become an active participant in the case, the Attorney General himself only became personally involved when the impasse in Mississippi exploded into public disorder. Bobby Kennedy was not just the head of the Justice Department; he was one of the administration's more important political advisers and was closer to the President than anyone in the White House. With midterm congressional elections looming in November, the dispute over Meredith threatened to become a political issue that could adversely effect the fortunes of the Kennedy administration. During the latter part of September, Robert Kennedy had more than twenty conversations with a recalcitrant Governor Barnett in an effort to work out a plan to register Meredith. Over the next week, Barnett and the Kennedys engaged in a complicated dance, with each party trying to lead. Barnett knew his position was tenuous, but it was his turf and that gave him an advantage.

Meredith was scheduled to start classes at the university, after registering on September 25. But Barnett prevented him from enrolling. The governor, in one of his many acts of grandstanding, blocked Meredith's entry into the room in a state office building in Jackson, where the registration was scheduled to take place. Accompanied by John Doar of the U.S. Justice Department and James McShane, chief U.S. marshal, Meredith was forced to leave after Barnett willfully refused a court order to admit him, saying "I hereby finally deny you admission to the University of Mississippi." The large crowd roared its approval, an onlooker cried "Three cheers for the governor," and Meredith departed, along with his federal escorts.

Robert Kennedy thought Barnett was a typical southern demagogue, agreeable, even charming at times, but capable of lying when it suited him. The next day, September 26, Meredith, again accompanied by Doar and McShane, headed to the Ole Miss campus in Oxford to register for classes. The car carrying the three men, escorted by the highway patrol, was forced to stop a few blocks from the entrance to the campus. Backed up by state troopers, county sheriffs, and a line of patrol cars, Lieutenant Governor Paul Johnson approached Meredith, Doar, and McShane. Filling in for Governor Barnett (low clouds had prevented him from flying up from Jackson to Oxford), Johnson said, "I would like to read this proclamation," which stated that Mississippi was "interposing" its powers and would deny Meredith admission to the university. After some gentle pushing between McShane and Johnson, it was apparent the Mississippian would not yield. After they exchanged some words, McShane turned in retreat, and Meredith, Doar, and a retinue of federal marshals departed the scene, prevented once more from fulfilling their court-ordered task.

On September 27, the group again tried to register Meredith. This time an elaborate plan had been worked out in discussions between Bobby Kennedy, Barnett, and the governor's friend, Tom Watkins. According to the plan, U.S. marshals would draw their guns on Barnett and Paul Johnson in a "show of force." Once this symbolic act had been completed, the Mississippi politicians would stand aside and allow Meredith and his escorts to pass and register for classes.

But the plan was thwarted. Some 2,000 people, including students, farmers, and self-styled vigilantes, converged that day on Oxford from all over Mississippi, determined to stop Meredith from registering at the university. A worried Barnett telephoned the Attorney General late in the day to report that he was uncertain if he could maintain order, claiming he had been unable to disperse the crowd. The Attorney General, never comfortable with the planned "show of force," ordered Meredith's convoy, which was heading from Memphis to Oxford, to turn back. Less than 50 miles from Oxford, the group halted, recrossed the Tennessee border, and returned to Memphis.

On Friday, September 28, the Fifth Circuit Court of Appeals found Governor Barnett guilty of contempt. Barnett, who did not appear in court, was found guilty in absentia and given until the following Tuesday to clear himself by retracting his proclamation and allowing Meredith to register. In the event he failed to do so, the Court declared, Barnett would face arrest and a fine of $10,000 a day for each day he remained in Meredith's path.

On Saturday, September 29, President Kennedy became personally involved in the crisis. Until then, he had let Bobby assume primary responsibility in the affair, but with the election looming and events in Oxford attracting national attention, he thought it prudent to become directly involved. That morning Robert Kennedy had been on the telephone with Ross Barnett and Barnett's chosen intermediary, Thomas Watkins, an attorney from Jackson, Mississippi. The deal reached the day before had fallen through. Now the Mississippians wanted an even larger show of federal forces before giving in and letting Meredith register at Ole Miss.

The President had to decide whether the U.S. Army or a federalized Mississippi National Guard would be needed to cope with the increasingly tense situation. For the next five days, the White House was consumed by the crisis, and Kennedy activated the newly installed taping system to record the many hours of meetings. Kennedy was cautious and hoped he could avoid using federal troops. Barnett, perhaps sensing the reluctance of the administration to get involved, played an elaborate game of chicken, hinting that federal action would make an already volatile situation more dangerous. The lines had been drawn. The next few days would determine the fate not just of Meredith, Barnett, and Mississippi, but of the next phase of the civil rights movement.

September 29, 1962, 2:00 P.M.

Conversation with Ross Barnett

President Kennedy: Hello? Hello, Governor?

Ross Barnett: All right. Yes.

President Kennedy: How are you?

Barnett: Is this . . .

President Kennedy: This is the President, uh . . .

Barnett: Oh. Well, Mr. President [*unclear*].

President Kennedy: Well, I'm glad to talk to you, Governor. I am concerned about this situation down there, as I know . . .

Barnett: Oh, I should say I am concerned about it, Mr. President. It's a horrible situation.

President Kennedy: Well, now, here's my problem, Governor.

Barnett: [*Unclear.*] Yes.

President Kennedy: Listen, I didn't put him in the university, but on the other hand, under the Constitution . . . I have to carry out the orders, carry that order out, and I don't, I don't want to do it in any way that causes difficulty to you or to anyone else. But I've got to do it. Now, I'd like to get your help in doing that.

Barnett: Yes. Well, uh, have you talked with Attorney General this morning?

President Kennedy: Yeah. I talked to him and in fact, I just met with him for about an hour, and we went over the situation.

Barnett: Did he and Mr. Watkins have a talk this morning, Tom Watkins, the lawyer from Jackson, or not?[2]

---

[2]Thomas H. Watkins was the Mississippi lawyer and Barnett adviser who served as an intermediary in the crisis.

President Kennedy: Yes, he talked to Tom Watkins, he told me.

Barnett: Yes, sir. Well, I don't know what . . . I haven't had a chance to talk with him . . .

President Kennedy: Now just wait . . . just one minute because I got the Attorney General in the outer office, and I'll just speak to him.

Barnett: All right. [*Long pause.*]

President Kennedy: Hello, Governor?

Barnett: Yes. Hold on.

President Kennedy: I just talked to the Attorney General. Now, he said that he talked to Mr. Watkins . . .

Barnett: Yes.

President Kennedy: . . . and the problem is as to whether we can get some help in getting this fellow in this week.

Barnett: Yes.

President Kennedy: Now, evidently we couldn't, the Attorney General didn't feel that he and Mr. Watkins had reached any final agreement on that.

Barnett: Well, Mr. President, Mr. Watkins is going to fly up there early tomorrow morning.

President Kennedy: Right.

Barnett: And could you gentlemen talk with him tomorrow? You . . .

President Kennedy: Yes, I will have the Attorney General talk to him and then . . .

Barnett: Yes.

President Kennedy: . . . after they've finished talking I'll talk to the Attorney General . . .

Barnett: All right.

President Kennedy: . . . on the phone and then if he feels it's useful for me to meet with him . . .

Barnett: I thought . . .

President Kennedy: . . . I'll do that.

Barnett: I thought they were making some progress. I didn't know.

President Kennedy: Well, now . . .

Barnett: I couldn't say, you know.

President Kennedy: . . . he and Mr. Watkins, they can meet tomorrow. Now, the difficulty is, we got two or three problems. In the first place, what can we do to . . . First place is the court's order to you, which I guess is, you're given until Tuesday. What is your feeling on that?

Barnett: Well, I want . . .

President Kennedy: What's your position on that?

Barnett: . . . to think it over, Mr. President.

President Kennedy: Right.

Barnett: It's a serious matter, now that I want to think it over a few days. Until Tuesday, anyway.

President Kennedy: All right. Well, now let me, let me say this . . .

Barnett: You know what I am up against, Mr. President. I took an oath, you know, to abide by the laws of this state—

President Kennedy: That's right.

Barnett:—and *our* constitution here and the Constitution of the United States. I'm, I'm on the spot here, you know.

President Kennedy: Well, now you've got . . .

Barnett: I, I've taken an oath to do that, and you *know* what our laws are with reference to . . .

President Kennedy: Yes, I understand that. Well, now we've got the . . .

Barnett: . . . and we have a statute that was enacted a couple of weeks ago stating positively that no one who had been convicted of a crime or, uh, whether the criminal action pending against them would not be eligible for any of the institutions of higher learning. And that's our law, and it seemed like the Court of Appeal didn't pay any attention to that.[3]

President Kennedy: Right. Well, of course . . .

Barnett: And . . .

President Kennedy: . . . the problem is, Governor, that I got my responsibility, just like you have yours . . .

Barnett: Well, that's true. I . . .

President Kennedy: . . . and my responsibility, of course, is to the . . .

Barnett: . . . I realize that, and I appreciate that *so much*.

President Kennedy: Well, now here's the thing, Governor. I will, the Attorney General can talk to Mr. Watkins tomorrow. What I want, would like to do is to try to work this out in an amicable way. We don't want a lot of people down there getting hurt . . .

Barnett: Oh, that's right . . .

President Kennedy: . . . and we don't want to have a . . . You know it's very easy to . . .

Barnett: Mr. President, let me say this. They're calling, calling me and others from all over the state, wanting to bring a thousand, wanting to bring 500, and 200, and all such as that, you know. We don't want such as that.

---

[3]On September 20, Meredith was found guilty in abstentia of false voter registration and was fined $100 and costs and sentenced to one year in the Hinds County jail. The conviction on this clearly specious charge occurred the same day that Mississippi Senate Bill 1501 passed the legislature. The bill barred persons guilty of a criminal offense from attending state institutions of higher learning. In addition, on September 20, Governor Barnett was appointed registrar of the university. Five days later, the Board of Trustees rescinded the appointment.

President Kennedy: I know. Well, we don't want to have a, we don't want to have a lot of people getting hurt or killed down there.

Barnett: Why, that's, that's correct. Mr. President, let me say this. Mr. Watkins is really an A-1 lawyer, an honorable man, has the respect and the confidence of *every* lawyer in America who knows him. He's of the law firm of Watkins and Eager. They've had an "A" rating for many, many years, and I believe this, that he can help solve this problem.

President Kennedy: Well, I will, the Attorney General will see Mr. Watkins tomorrow, and then I, after the Attorney General and Mr. Watkins are finished then, I will be back in touch with you.

Barnett: All right. All right. I'll appreciate it so much, now, and there . . . Watkins'll leave here in the morning, and I'll have him to get into touch with the Attorney General as to when he can see him tomorrow.

President Kennedy: Yeah, he'll see him and . . .

Barnett: Yes, sir.

President Kennedy: . . . we will, then you and I'll be back and talk again.

Barnett: All right.

President Kennedy: Thank you.

Barnett: All right.

President Kennedy: Okay.

Barnett: I appreciate your interest in our poultry program and all those things.

President Kennedy: Well, we're . . . [*laughs softly*].

Barnett: Thank you so much.

President Kennedy: Okay, Governor. Thank you.

Barnett: Yes, sir. All right now.

President Kennedy: Bye now.

Barnett: Thank you. Bye.

.   .   .

Less than an hour passed, and the President and the Governor spoke again, this time with the Attorney General present. The Kennedy brothers made it clear that their primary objective was to maintain order, and that they fully expected the Governor to cooperate. Barnett had been using his friend, Tom Watkins, as a liaison with the Attorney General, but Robert Kennedy had not been satisfied with what Watkins had suggested. Barnett, through Watkins, had wanted to craft a compromise that would allow Meredith to register, but in secret in Jackson, rather than in the glare of publicity in Oxford. That would allow Barnett to claim that he had opposed desegregation, but that the feds had tricked him and the state of Mississippi by whisking Meredith away to Jackson. The Kennedys, however, did not intend to let Barnett transform the crisis into a victory for the Jim Crow South.

September 29, 1962, 2:50 P.M.

Conversation with Ross Barnett

President Kennedy: Hello.

Ross Barnett: All right.

President Kennedy: Governor.

Barnett: Mr. President. Yes, sir.

President Kennedy: Oh, will you talk to Mr. Watkins? The Attorney General did.

Barnett: No, I haven't talked with him now in a couple of hours . . .

President Kennedy: Oh. Well, now . . .

Barnett: . . . I talked with him though about two hours ago, Mr. President, and he said he was going to *talk* with the Attorney General and go *see* him tomorrow morning.

President Kennedy: Oh. Well, in the meanwhile, then, the Attorney General talked to Mr. Watkins to see whether there was some . . . Wait just a second. The Attorney General's right here. He'll tell you what he talked to Watkins and Watkins was going to talk to you. Wait a minute.

Barnett: All right. All right.

President Kennedy: He'll come right on the other phone.

Barnett: Yeah, sure.

President Kennedy: Wait just a [*unclear*].

Barnett: All right. All right.

Robert Kennedy: Hello?

Barnett: Yes, sir, General. How are you?

Robert Kennedy: Fine, Governor. How are you?

Barnett: Fine, fine.

Robert Kennedy: I talked to Mr. Watkins, you know, earlier this morning.

Barnett: Oh, yes?

Robert Kennedy: And he really did not have much of a suggestion. He had mentioned yesterday the possibility of our coming in tomorrow Monday with marshals, and . . .

Barnett: Yes.

Robert Kennedy: . . . that under our understanding for Thursday that the marshals would show up and that you and the others would step aside and Mr. Meredith would come into the university. Well, he felt that when he mentioned he talked to me today, he said that he thought that would create some problems, which they could not overcome. And he suggested at that time, some alternatives which were not very satisfactory.

Barnett: Well . . .

Robert Kennedy: And then he mentioned the fact that he might come up early tomorrow morning.

Barnett: Well . . .

Robert Kennedy: I called him back after I heard the President's conversation with you . . .

Barnett: Yes.

Robert Kennedy: . . . and said that I thought I'd be glad to see him, but I thought that unless we had some real basis for some understanding and working out this very, very difficult problem that really he was wasting his time; and that one of the basic requirements, in my judgment, was the maintenance of law and order, and that would require some very *strong* and vocal action by you, yourself . . .

Barnett: Well, I'm certainly going to try to maintain law and order, Mr . . .

Robert Kennedy: Yeah.

Barnett: . . . General, just the very best way that I can.

Robert Kennedy: But in the . . .

Barnett: I, I talked with the student body the other day and told them to really, to have control of the physical and mental faculties. But it didn't do much good it seemed like.

Robert Kennedy: Well . . .

Barnett: They cheered and carried on, but then they just started raving and carrying on, you know.

Robert Kennedy: Yeah. I think, Governor, that if we as a very minimum and as a start, an order by you and the state that people could not congregate in Oxford now in groups of three or five, larger than groups of three or five; the second, to get the school authorities to issue instructions to the students that if they congregate in groups that they are liable for expulsion. If that was done this afternoon, I think that would be a big step forward. And that anybody carrying an arm or a, arms or a club, or anything like that would be liable to punishment.

Barnett: Well . . .

Robert Kennedy: Those kind of steps by you . . .

Barnett: Yes.

Robert Kennedy: . . . would indicate a interest in maintaining law and order.

Barnett: Well, General, I certainly, I'll tell the chancellor to announce to all the students to keep law and order and to keep cool heads. But the trouble is not only the students, but it's so many thousands of outsiders will be there.

Robert Kennedy: Yes, but I think, if you said, Governor, not just to . . .

Barnett: Yeah.

Robert Kennedy: . . . keep cool heads, but that they couldn't congregate.

Barnett: How many do you figure on sending down?

Robert Kennedy: Well, that's a . . . I think that the President had some questions for you that he thought that maybe if we could get some answers to them that . . .

Barnett: Yeah.

Robert Kennedy: . . . that would be what depend. [*speaks to President Kennedy in the room*] Mr. President . . .

Barnett: Mr. General, why don't you . . . I believe that if you and Tom Watkins could get together it would help a lot. He's a very reasonable man, and, and he's, he knows, he knows the situation down here as well as anybody living. If you all could get together tomorrow morning, *I* really think that it would pay. I think it would help.

Robert Kennedy: Well, he doesn't have any suggestions, he just told me, Mr. Governor.

Barnett: Yes. Well, I . . .

Robert Kennedy: So I don't know what . . .

Barnett: . . . I thought he did have.

Robert Kennedy: Well, he didn't. I mean he said something about sending Meredith, sneaking him into Jackson and getting him registered while all of you were up at . . .

Barnett: Yeah.

Robert Kennedy: . . . at Oxford. But that doesn't make much sense, does it?

Barnett: Well, I don't know. Why? Why doesn't it? That's where they'd ordered him to go at first, you know.

Robert Kennedy: Yeah.

Barnett: You see, there's an order on the minutes, Mr. General, for him to register . . .

Robert Kennedy: Well, would you . . .

Barnett: . . . [*unclear*].

Robert Kennedy: . . . you'd get . . . As I understand it, you'd get everybody up at Oxford, and then we'd, and then . . .

Barnett: Oh, well, that's exactly what Tom Watkins must have had in mind, you know.

Robert Kennedy: Yeah.

Barnett: Let me talk with Tom and call you back in a little while. He's not but a block from me. That's what he had in mind, I think. And, of course, you know how it is in Jackson. Monday they, no school's going on here, you know, and . . . Uh, of course nobody would be anticipating *anyone* coming here, you know.

Robert Kennedy: Are you going up to Oxford on Monday? Is that your plan?

Barnett: Well, that's what I planned to do, yes, sir. The lieutenant governor and I, both, *I* guess, we'll have to be up there to try to keep order, you know. And, we're to be up there pretty early Monday morning.

Robert Kennedy: Will you?

Barnett: We'll be up there, unless you ask us not to.

Robert Kennedy: Yeah.

Barnett: Well, like, you see, we'll be up there and that's where all the people will be. Yeah. I thought you and Watkins were going to talk about that kind of a situation, then what'd be the best thing to do under those conditions, you know.

Robert Kennedy: Yeah, I think, Governor, that the President has some, uh, questions that he wanted some answers to . . .

Barnett: Well . . .

Robert Kennedy: . . . make his own determination.

Barnett: . . . that's right. He wanted to know if I would obey the orders of the court, and I told him I, I'd have to do some . . . study that over. That's a serious thing. I've taken an oath to abide by the laws of this state and our state constitution and the Constitution of the United States. And, General, how can I violate my oath of office? How can I do that and live with the people of Mississippi? You know, they're expecting me to keep my word. That's what I'm up against, and I don't understand why the court, why the court wouldn't understand that.

President Kennedy: Oh Governor, this is the President speaking.

Barnett: Yes, sir, Mr. President.

President Kennedy: Now it's, I know that your feeling about the law of Mississippi and the fact that you don't want to carry out that court order. What we really want to have from you, though, is some understanding about whether the state police will maintain law and order. We understand your feeling about the court order . . .

Barnett: Yes.

President Kennedy: . . .and your disagreement with it. But what we're concerned about is how much violence is going to be and what kind of action we'll have to take to prevent it. And I'd like to get assurances from you that the state police down there will take positive action to maintain law and order.

Barnett: Oh, they'll do that.

President Kennedy: Then we'll know what we have to do.

Barnett: They'll, they'll take positive action, Mr. President, to maintain law and order as best we can.

President Kennedy: And now, how good is . . .

Barnett: We'll have 220 highway patrolmen . . .

President Kennedy: Right.

Barnett: . . . and they'll absolutely be unarmed.

President Kennedy: I understa—

Barnett: Not a one of them'll be armed.

President Kennedy: Well, no, but the problem is, well, what can they do to maintain law and order and prevent the gathering of a mob and action taken by the mob? What can they do? Can they stop that?

Barnett: Well, they'll do their best to. They'll do everything in their power to stop it.

President Kennedy: Now, what about the suggestions made by the Attorney General in regard to not permitting people to congregate and start a mob?

Barnett: Well, we'll do our best to, to keep them from congregating, but that's hard to do, you know.

President Kennedy: Well, they just tell them to move along.

Barnett: When they start moving up on the sidewalks and different sides of the streets, what are you going to do about it?

President Kennedy: Well, now, as I understand it, Governor, you would do everything you can to *maintain* law and order.

Barnett: I, I, I'll do everything in my power to maintain order . . .

President Kennedy: Right. Now . . .

Barnett: . . . and peace. We don't want any shooting down here.

President Kennedy: I understand. Now, Governor, what about, can you maintain this order?

Barnett: Well, I don't know.

President Kennedy: Yes.

Barnett: That's what I'm worried about you see. I don't know whether I can or not.

President Kennedy: Right.

Barnett: I couldn't have the other afternoon.[4]

President Kennedy: You couldn't have?

---

[4]Barnett is undoubtedly referring to Thursday, September 27, when some 2,000 people, including students, farmers, and self-styled vigilantes, converged on Oxford from all over Mississippi, intent on stopping Meredith from registering.

Barnett: There was such a mob there, it would have been impossible.

President Kennedy: I see.

Barnett: There were men in there with trucks and shotguns, and all such as that. Not a lot of them, but some, we saw, and certain people were just, they were just enraged.

President Kennedy: Well, now, will you talk . . .

Barnett: You just don't understand the situation down here.

President Kennedy: Well, the only thing is I got my responsibility.

Barnett: I know you do.

President Kennedy: This is not my order, I just have to carry it out. So I want to get together and try to do it with you in a way which is the most satisfactory and causes the least chance of damage to people in Mississippi. That's my interest.

Barnett: That's right. Would you be willing to wait awhile and let the people cool off on the whole thing?

President Kennedy: 'Til how long?

Barnett: Couldn't you make a statement to the effect, Mr. President, Mr. General, that under the circumstances existing in Mississippi, that, uh, there'll be bloodshed; you want to protect the life of, of, of James Meredith and all other people? And under the circumstances at this time, it just wouldn't be fair to him or others to try to register him at this time.

President Kennedy: Well, then at what time would it be fair?

Barnett: Well, we, we could wait a, I don't know.

President Kennedy: Yeah.

Barnett: It might be in, uh, two or three weeks, it might cool off a little.

President Kennedy: Well, would you undertake to register him in two weeks?

Barnett: Well, I, you know I can't undertake to register him myself . . .

President Kennedy: I see.

Barnett: . . . but you all might make some progress that way, you know.

President Kennedy: [*Laughs.*] Yeah. Well, we'd be faced with, unless we had your support . . .

Barnett: You see . . .

President Kennedy: . . . and assurance, we'd be . . .

Barnett: . . . I say I'm going to, I'm going to cooperate. I might not know when you're going to register him, you know.

President Kennedy: I see. Well, now, Governor, why don't, do you want to talk to Mr. Watkins?

Barnett: I might not know that, what your plans were, you see.

President Kennedy: Do you want to, do you want to talk to Mr. Watkins then . . .

Barnett: I'll be delighted to talk to him, we'll call you back.
President Kennedy: Okay, good.
Barnett: Call the general back.
President Kennedy: Yeah, call the general, and then I'll be around.
Barnett: All right. I appreciate it so much ...
President Kennedy: Thanks, Governor.
Barnett: ... and I thank you for this call.
President Kennedy: Thank you, Governor.
Barnett: All right.
President Kennedy: Right.
Barnett: Bye.

.   .   .

After the conversation ended, President Kennedy went to the swimming pool, while Burke Marshall and the Attorney General returned to the Justice Department. Significantly, as the conversation indicates, the administration and Barnett had apparently agreed on a plan the Kennedys hoped would end the dilemma. In the words of the popular historian Walter Lord, it was "sort of a hidden ball play," whereby Meredith would be registered in secret on Monday at the University's Jackson campus, while Barnett made a public show for the benefit of the segregationists on the main campus in Oxford, thus allowing him to declare that he had been "tricked" by the Kennedy administration. By having tried to bar Meredith from the campus, even as the young African American was being registered "secretly" behind the Governor's back, Barnett would be able to maintain his allegience to southern "traditions." Barnett could then pretend he had not willingly yielded to the federal government's demands.

Shortly after 7:00 P.M. on Saturday, September 29, Barnett and the President spoke again, their third conversation of the day. (Due to an apparent error with the recording system, the call was not taped.) Beyond discussing the Monday plan for Meredith's sneak registration, Barnett assured Kennedy that the highway patrol would maintain law and order and guarantee Meredith's safety. But later that night, the deal to register Meredith in secret came apart, news Barnett conveyed to the Attorney General, who then passed it on to the President. That same evening, Barnett attended an Ole Miss football game, where he was cheered wildly by more than 40,000 fans for his ongoing defiance of the federal government. And back at the White House, in the wake of the failed plan to register Meredith in secret, President Kennedy signed an order that would federalize units of the Mississippi National Guard and order all those obstructing justice in Mississippi to "cease and desist" and to "disperse and retire peaceably."

The next morning, Sunday, September 30, with the previous day's deal off, Robert Kennedy threatened Barnett, telling him he would make public that the Governor had been negotiating with the Kennedy brothers behind the backs of the segregationists. The Attorney General's threat resulted in a new Barnett scheme, by which the federal government would sneak Meredith onto the campus that afternoon, a day earlier than had originally been planned. Barnett would then announce in a speech that he had been tricked and that Meredith was already on the campus.

At 6:00 P.M. September 30, James Meredith flew into Oxford, accompanied by Justice Department officials. Before his arrival, a force of approximately 200 U.S. marshals had assembled around the Lyceum, the main administration building at Ole Miss. The deputy attorney general, Nicholas Katzenbach, who was in charge of operations on the campus, had expected that Meredith would be able to register that day. But this was impossible. As Governor Barnett issued a press release stating that Meredith was on campus, U.S. marshals remained posted around the Lyceum, while some distance away, in Baxter Hall, a dormitory, Meredith was under federal protective guard for the night. The goal was to keep him safe so that he could register in the morning.

At 10:00 P.M., the President spoke to the nation about the crisis in Mississippi, having delayed his speech two hours to await word that Meredith was safely on campus.[5] The text was vintage Kennedy, and it concluded with soaring oratory. "Let us preserve both the law and the peace, and then, healing those wounds that are within we can turn to the greater crises that are without and stand united as one people in our pledge to man's freedom."

As the President began to address the nation, the situation was unraveling in Oxford. According to the arrangement made earlier that day, Kennedy called the Mississippi governor, who was expected to announce ruefully that the state of Mississippi had been "physically overpowered" and that Meredith was on campus. Kennedy was then supposed to give a conciliatory speech stressing the triumph of the rule of law. But the rule of law was not winning where it counted this night—on the streets of Oxford.

In the hours before Kennedy's address, violence exploded at the university. A crowd of 2,500 surged toward the Lyceum. With a few hundred federalized U.S. marshals and handpicked border patrolmen now on campus and ringing the Lyceum, the governor's representatives on campus decided to withdraw the Mississippi highway patrolmen who had pro-

---

[5]Due to the two-hour time difference between Washington and Oxford, it was 8:00 P.M. in Oxford.

vided the campus with a semblance of calm in the tense days since the appeals court had ordered Barnett to admit Meredith. Sensing a shift in the balance of power, the crowd surged forward, and the federal marshals, in self-defense, launched a volley of tear gas canisters.

All this was unfolding unbeknownst to Kennedy, who was addressing the nation. "I would like to take this occasion to express the thanks of this nation to those southerners who have contributed to the progress of our democratic development. . . ." Aides tried to catch the President before he went on the air to stop him from giving the speech, but they were too late. As Kennedy was laying the crisis to rest, the crowds in Oxford were injecting it with new and dangerous life. A cloud of tear gas was rising from the campus while Kennedy spoke.

In the half hour following the speech, the news from Mississippi got progressively worse, and the President, Attorney General, and a handful of advisers retired to the Cabinet Office, which became a crisis war room. President Kennedy activated the taping system, and the meeting lasted until the early morning hours of Monday, October 1. Because of daylight saving time, events in Mississippi were occurring two hours behind Washington time.

A jerry-built communications setup relayed information from the campus to the White House. A series of walkie-talkies carried by the marshals and Justice Department aides in and around the Lyceum kept Nicholas Katzenbach, Attorney General Robert Kennedy's field commander, informed. Using a pay telephone in the basement of the building, Katzenbach or Ed Guthman conveyed information to Robert Kennedy or his assistant Burke Marshall in the White House. Meanwhile, at the Justice Department in Washington, another Kennedy aide, Ramsey Clark, monitored what was happening at Justice's makeshift communications center in Oxford, which was located in a post office building a few minutes from campus. Periodically, Clark called the Attorney General with updates.

With telephones ringing continually, and various people having conversations (some with persons in the room, others on the telephone with aides in Mississippi), the meeting has a chaotic quality. Much of the information coming from Mississippi is conflicting or inaccurate, which only heightens the confusion in the White House. There are also frequent lulls as the President waits to be updated on the rapidly changing situation in Oxford. With the sole source of external information coming via the telephone, at times the meeting has a deceptive calm, but this peacefulness is belied by the chaos in Oxford.

President Kennedy started taping as the impromptu domestic crisis team was absorbing news that the mob had turned violent. Burke Marshall was handling the telephone in the Cabinet Room for the Attorney General, with the President a worried observer.

September 30, 1962, 10:40 P.M.–1:00 A.M.

Meeting on Civil Rights

Including President Kennedy, Robert Kennedy, Burke Marshall, Lawrence O'Brien (special assistant to the President), Kenneth O'Donnell (special assistant to the President), and Theodore Sorensen (special counsel to the President).

Robert Kennedy: [*on the phone*] Now don't you have to . . . Do you have some other men? Yeah. Did you get all the marshals there now?

President Kennedy: State police or . . .

Robert Kennedy: [*on the phone*] How many you've got? And they're all there? Yeah. How are the state police? Is the crowd getting bigger?

Unidentified: [*talking to Robert Kennedy in the room*] [*Unclear*] wants you?

Robert Kennedy: That's fine.

[*on the phone*] Okay, well I'll get back. I'll let you know.

[*off the phone*] Well, I think that—

President Kennedy: What?

Robert Kennedy: They think they have it in pretty good shape. [*Puts down the receiver.*]

President Kennedy: [*Unclear.*]

Robert Kennedy: Did one marshal get his arm broken?

President Kennedy: His arm broken?

Robert Kennedy: The lousy, I mean, there you are appointed, some politician gets you appointed deputy marshal and you're sitting in the courtroom . . . [*telephone rings*] moving . . . close to the judge . . . and suddenly . . .

Burke Marshall: [*on the phone*] Hello. Yes, he is.

President Kennedy: His arm broken, what, by a bottle?

Unidentified: No, but he said they're throwing [*unclear*]. It's Ed.

President Kennedy: Who?

Unidentified: Ed.

Robert Kennedy: [*on the phone*] Oh, Ed.[6] Well, how's it look to you?

---

[6]Probably Edwin Guthman, Director of Public Information, Department of Justice.

Kenneth O'Donnell: Yeah, there might not be quite as much rush for those bumps they're handing out right after . . .

Robert Kennedy: [*on the phone*] Is it under control? Would you bring the guard in?[7]

Theodore Sorensen: Yeah, but tomorrow's going to be worse than today.

Several people then talk at once, in fragments, until we hear RFK on the phone.

Robert Kennedy: [*on the phone*] Are they mad at the marshals?

As the Attorney General talks on the phone, several conversations are taking place simultaneously, little of which is intelligible on the tapes.

Robert Kennedy: [*on the phone*] Okay, well, I'm going to see if I can get these troops started anyway.[8] We can see. Well, I think if they, I think it's better that we can control the situation. I don't think it's worth screwing around. The weekend.[9]

President Kennedy: It's going to be a long fall in Oxford, I think.

Robert Kennedy: [*on the phone*] I'll see if I can't get them going anyway. Okay.

While Robert Kennedy is speaking, in the background an unidentified man says, "Kermit's having trouble with his homework."

Unidentified: What's the story now?

Robert Kennedy: Well, he thinks the situation's under control now, but you know—

President Kennedy:—I think we ought to get the guard within, you know, shouting distance outside of town. I think it's probably [*unclear*].

Unidentified: Blocked off those roads?

Robert Kennedy: Yeah. There's enough people coming in from . . . They got the . . .

Unidentified: That's [*unclear*].

Robert Kennedy: Well, [*unclear*] they got the people on the roads, just to keep them informed about it.

Marshall: [*on the phone*] Hello?

Robert Kennedy: Then we get all around the city so as to [*unclear*].

Marshall: [*on the phone*] This is Burke Marshall.

---

[7]Earlier in the day President Kennedy federalized the Mississippi National Guard. There are units in Oxford, Jackson, and throughout the state of Mississippi that could be deployed if necessary.
[8]The crisis has entered a new phase. It is about 10:45 P.M. in Washington and two hours earlier in Mississippi and the Kennedy administration is preparing to deploy the U.S. Army in Oxford.
[9]Task Force Alpha is waiting for orders in Memphis. Organized in the last 24 hours, it includes the 503rd Military Police Battalion, the 31st Light Helicopter Company, the 138th Truck Company, a medical detachment, and two tear gas experts. The Attorney General is pressing the introduction of these troops on his men in Oxford.

Robert Kennedy: . . . came in and get control of . . . and then we have control over the air. But if you have gas, you've got a pretty good operation going. They got 500 marshals . . . [*Laughter in background.*]

Marshall: [*on the phone*] [*Unclear.*]

Unidentified: [*Unclear.*]

Robert Kennedy: You see, they're sitting there and they're throwing iron . . .

President Kennedy: Spikes?

Robert Kennedy: . . . spikes, and they're throwing Coke bottles, and they're throwing rocks.

Unidentified: I gather they're [*unclear*]—

Robert Kennedy: Well, you tell that guy that just came out of Cleveland from . . . just appointed by . . .

Marshall: [*on the phone*] Dean?[10]

President Kennedy: [*Unclear.*]

Robert Kennedy: Miller.

Marshall: [*on the phone*] I know that [*unclear*].

President Kennedy: But Bobby [*unclear*]'s a bookie from [*unclear*]—

Sorensen: [*Unclear.*]

O'Brien: That isn't the way the American people envision marshals [*unclear*].

Marshall: [*talking to people in the room*] Is it Johnny Vaught?[11]

Unidentified: [*Unclear.*]

Robert Kennedy: Yeah, the coach. What's the good coach's name?

Unidentified: Johnny Vaught.

Robert Kennedy: Let's see if we can get him.

Unidentified: He won't believe it.

Robert Kennedy: He might . . .

President Kennedy: What's Barnett doing?

Marshall: [*on the phone*] . . . TCU or . . .

Robert Kennedy: [*Unclear.*]

Marshall: Did he come from Tennessee? TCU, wasn't it?

President Kennedy: Texas Christian University then.

Robert Kennedy: Where he came from originally?

Unidentified: Yeah.

President Kennedy: I think he was out of Texas. Yeah.

Unidentified: He was.

Marshall: [*on the phone*] Dean [Markham]?

---

[10]Dean P. Markham.

[11]John H. Vaught, University of Mississippi football coach.

President Kennedy: What are we waiting for . . . Cy Vance to tell us how long it will take?

The U.S. Army had forces on stand-by in Memphis, Tennessee, to calm the situation in Oxford, Mississippi, and there was a local Mississippi National Guard unit available for reinforcing the federal marshals on campus.

Marshall: [*on the phone*] Do you think you could find him and talk to him?

President Kennedy: Why don't we just tell him to get on and tell him to take them out [*unclear*].

Marshall: [*on the phone*] Yeah. Vaught saw the [*unclear*].

Unidentified: [*Unclear.*]

Marshall: [*on the phone*] Yeah.

President Kennedy: Let's see this article.

Marshall: [*on the phone*] See if he talks to the kids, yeah.

President Kennedy: [*reading*] "Ross Barnett, Jr., son of the Mississippi governor [*unclear*]."[12]

Marshall: [*on the phone*] Well, did Vaught talk to them tonight?

President Kennedy: [*reading*] "[*Unclear*] National Guard Patrol [*unclear*]." [*Laughter.*]

Marshall: [*on the phone*] Why don't you do it, and then if you think it would do any good to have some.

Unidentified: Did he get called up?

Robert Kennedy: Do we have any other phone system other than that, this we're using here?

Marshall: No.

Unidentified: We don't have anything else?

President Kennedy: You want to get [*unclear*] and Secretary on it.

Marshall: All right.

Unidentified: Do you want in or out?

Marshall: [*on the phone*] All right.

[*Pause.*]

Marshall: [*to people in the room*] He said he wants to keep all the football squad out of it if there were any demonstrations.

O'Brien: That would have been a hell of a squad. [*Unclear*] a couple of hundred [*unclear*].

Unidentified: They want [*unclear*].

Unidentified: Yeah.

---

[12]Ironically, the Governor's son was called up with his Mississippi National Guard unit to fight against his father's segregationism.

Unidentified: This reminds me a little bit of the Bay of Pigs.[13]
Unidentified: Yech!
[*Laughter.*]
O'Brien: [*Unclear*], I will say that . . .
Sorensen: Well, especially when Bobby said we'd provide air cover.[14]
[*Laughter.*]
O'Brien: Yeah [*unclear*] they know [*unclear*].
Sorensen: We could control the air . . .
Unidentified: Except on one of the [*unclear*].
[*Laughter.*]
O'Brien: Ed described [*unclear*].
Unidentified: [*Unclear.*]
O'Donnell: What do you think the response to Jim McShane's men without the President protecting them.[15] As you say, they [*unclear*].
Unidentified: [*Unclear.*]
O'Donnell: What about Jim?
[*Laughter.*]
Unidentified: One of the two places.
Sorensen: My guess is, Bobby, that we'll have the control of outsiders down pretty good.[16] You may be able to introduce—
Marshall:—Well, we don't have . . .
Robert Kennedy: Well, the only thing is to keep . . .
Marshall: . . . control of outsiders, I don't think [*unclear*].
Robert Kennedy: Yeah, we haven't had any trouble from outsiders yet. I suppose you'll always have the difficulty of people storming onto the campus. They have a lot of gates. It's a hell of a big campus, you know. So you have a few marshals and a few people at each gate, and I suppose you can stick a car in [*unclear*] . . .
Marshall: [*on the phone to Justice Department officials in Mississippi*] Hello [*unclear*]. Yeah. All right.
Robert Kennedy: . . .we can always storm in there at 8:00 tomorrow morning or 10:00 tomorrow morning. The problem is, you see, when you

---

[13]In April 1961, the United States backed an invasion force composed of Cuban nationals that sought to overthrow the Castro regime in Cuba. The invasion, marred by a series of errors in planning and execution, failed miserably, much to the chagrin of the new administration.
[14]The reference here is to the U.S. decision not to provide air cover to support the invasion force during the Bay of Pigs landing. Some claimed the administration's failure to do so doomed the operation.
[15]James McShane, chief of the federal marshals.
[16]"Outsiders" was the codeword for Ku Klux Klansmen, John Birchers, and other extremists who had been threatening to descend on Oxford from across the Deep South to keep Ole Miss white.

don't have anybody there that's really interested in maintaining law and order, and where their primary interest is to get us to bring troops in.[17] You can imagine what would have happened if we'd gone through with what he wanted to do tomorrow morning.

Marshall: [*on the phone*] It's now against them.

Sorensen: Yeah.

Robert Kennedy: Walk in there and try to get through and he's there with all his . . . That's what his plan was. That he'd be there with his state police and sheriffs, and then assistant sheriffs and then volunteers behind him, four lanes. And then we were to push our way through.

Unidentified: His agreement was they wouldn't fire.

Marshall: [*on the phone*] [*Unclear*] the state troopers.

Unidentified: . . . tend to resist them anyhow.

Robert Kennedy: Yeah. With nobody else knowing the plot but him and me.

Evelyn Lincoln: Peter Lawford is on the phone.[18]

Marshall: [*on the phone*] Well, he called on the students to act as responsible citizens.

President Kennedy: That's slightly ironic. I wish we'd taken that part out.

Marshall: [*on the phone with Joseph Dolan*] Yeah. All right, Joe . . . [*to the people in the room*] He says that the state police are against us.

President Kennedy: Who does?

Marshall: [*on the phone*] Hello. Yeah.

Robert Kennedy: Of course, filled with all this poison.

Several moments of fragmentary exchanges follow.

Marshall: [*to the people in the room*] Dean [Markham] tried to call the coach and his wife says he's out.

Robert Kennedy: [*Unclear.*] Why don't I try [*unclear*]?

Marshall: [*on the phone*] Well, Bob will try to call him. Dean?

Robert Kennedy: Get the number.

Marshall: [*on the phone*] Dean? Oh, Dean. Dean? Listen, why don't we get Bob to try to call him from here? Well, he may . . . His wife may be lying to you.

---

[17]Robert Kennedy is referring to his failed negotiations with Ross Barnett, whose primary concern seemed to be to maneuver the Kennedy White House so that it would overplay its hand in Oxford and make political martyrs out of Barnett and his supporters.

[18]According to the White House telephone memorandum, Peter Lawford, the well-known screen actor and brother-in-law of the President, called Kennedy at 10:50 P.M. Evelyn Lincoln Collection, Box 5, John F. Kennedy Library.

Sorensen: What do you think the chances are that Barnett is being honest with you and he's not . . .

Marshall: [*on the phone*] All right. Well, we'll see what happens.

Sorensen: [*unclear*] . . . the state police? He's just . . .

Robert Kennedy: I don't think he would.

Marshall: [*on the phone*] All right.

Robert Kennedy: I don't think he's telling them to lay off, but I don't think they're enjoying this. You know, it's one thing to get in for the wrong reason and not have a problem, and they see we're having problems and then, might have a sense of greater problems.

Sorensen: He said he didn't want to get anyone killed, though, or does he mind that?[19]

Marshall: [*on the phone*] Sounds like it's out of the country.

Robert Kennedy: The only thing, like he said the other day to me, if 50 people get killed down here, it might be embarrassing for the two of us.

[*Laughter.*]

Robert Kennedy: It might hurt us, and then he went on to say that [*unclear*].

Marshall: [*Unclear*] two, three, four.

Lincoln: Secretary Vance.

Marshall: [*on the phone*] See, now, we'll give that a try.

Robert Kennedy: [*Unclear.*]

It appears that Robert Kennedy had gone to speak with the secretary of the army, Cyrus Vance, who briefed him on the readiness of the forces in Memphis to intervene.

Marshall is heard on the phone as several unidentified voices talk in the background.

Marshall: [*on the phone*] Gee whiz. Well, can't we get them some food?

Unidentified: Hear that?

Robert Kennedy: So they go to the armory in Oxford. And they'll be someone there within an hour.[20]

Marshall: [*on the phone*] I know, but I mean, can't we get . . .

Robert Kennedy: . . . company.

President Kennedy: They'll be at . . .

Robert Kennedy: And they'll be . . .

President Kennedy: . . . they'll be at the armory in Oxford?

---

[19]Ross Barnett.

[20]The Attorney General had been given inaccurate information. The first contingent of U.S. troops would not reach the Oxford airport until 12:30 A.M. Oxford time, when 117 men from A company of the 503rd Military Police Battalion arrived.

Robert Kennedy: Yeah. Well, in four hours they'll have about 800, 900.

President Kennedy: In Oxford? But that's not *in* the, that's not at . . .

Robert Kennedy: Well, that's the armory there, so they're not at the university.

President Kennedy: Yeah.

Robert Kennedy: I think that's the . . .

President Kennedy: That's the best. I think that's fine. The problem is really the time lapse, isn't it?

Robert Kennedy: Well, I think that it's in the . . . They're going to be . . . I mean, if you can tell, from what they say, they're going to be all right for an hour.

Marshall: [*on the phone*] Well, I know, but I . . .

President Kennedy: Then what happens after that?

Robert Kennedy: Well, then you could . . . We have company of . . .

President Kennedy: Oh, you're, so they're flying them in?

Robert Kennedy: . . . couple of hundred. No, we'll have a couple of . . .They'll be a couple of hundred there within an hour.

The President was relying on the Attorney General for information about the troop movements. The order went out to Memphis at 11 P.M. to load the first contingent of 200 men aboard helicopters for the one hour flight to Oxford. The White House assumed that the military operation was already in progress. In fact, it had not even started.

President Kennedy: Oh, I see. The others . . .

Robert Kennedy: And there'll be eight within four hours if he needs them.

President Kennedy: Oh, I see.

Unidentified: [*Unclear*] said there'd be 200 within . . .

Marshall: [*on the phone*] Yeah.

President Kennedy: Where will they go?

Robert Kennedy: They'd all go into the armory.

President Kennedy: I see.

Robert Kennedy: And they're all Mississippians.

Unidentified: They're dying in there.

Robert Kennedy: And they got gas masks.

Marshall: [*may be on the phone*] How long are they going out to . . .

Unidentified: Yes.

Robert Kennedy: And the general's getting in touch with Nick, and he can use them any time he wants.[21] I'll tell Nick or you can.

---

[21]Nicholas Katzenbach, deputy attorney general.

President Kennedy: So they'll be 200 there within an hour?

[*Unclear exchange.*]

Marshall: [*on the phone*] Oh, Dean? Can we get Nick?

Robert Kennedy: He did a hell of a job on the narcotics thing.

President Kennedy: Who?

Robert Kennedy: Yeah.

President Kennedy: Was it a success? The conference?[22]

Robert Kennedy: Certainly. It really was.

President Kennedy: Background.

Marshall: How long will it take?

Robert Kennedy: They'll have a company there within an hour.

Marshall: Yeah.

Robert Kennedy: And 800 within four hours.

Marshall: Oh, I see, a company. [*Unclear*] uniforms [*unclear*] Mississippians.

President Kennedy: [*Unclear.*]

Robert Kennedy: Well, I think that what we at least show that the marshals couldn't do it by themselves, so.

President Kennedy: Are we showing him or are they showing us?

[*Laughter, followed by several unclear exchanges.*]

Robert Kennedy: [*on the phone*] Hello, Nick? Well, there'll be a company there at the armory within an hour. And there'll be 800 there, as I understand it, within four hours.[23] Now, General Billingslea is going to get in touch with you.[24] Blakerslee or whatever the hell he's named.

Marshall: Billingslea.

Robert Kennedy: So, how does that sound?

President Kennedy: Need any more marshals or some equipment? Are the marshals holding up for some tear gas?

Robert Kennedy: [*on the phone*] Is the gas coming in there?

Unidentified: Now, what is next?

Marshall: They gassed some of our own marshals.

President Kennedy: Did they?

Marshall: Dean says it's bad for their morale.

---

[22]The White House Conference on Narcotics and Drug Abuse, organized by Dean Markham, was held September 27–28, 1962.

[23]This is Task Force Alpha, a 687-man team stationed at Millington Naval Air Station in Memphis. The advance group of 170 were supposed to have left by helicopter already. The rest were to travel by Interstate 55 to reach Oxford in the early morning. At this point, no troops from the Task Force had yet left Millington.

[24]Brigadier General Charles Billingslea, commander of the Second Infantry Division, Fort Benning, Georgia.

Robert Kennedy: [*on the phone*] [*Unclear.*]
Unidentified: What?
Unidentified: Which isn't too high, anyway.
Marshall: Well, they're doing a good job.
O'Brien: You're not kidding.
Marshall: They haven't had anything to eat.
Unidentified: They'll manage it.
Robert Kennedy: [*on the phone*] I don't mind that.
Unidentified: It's [*unclear*].
Robert Kennedy: [*on the phone*] And they should be home watching the President on television.
Unidentified: [*Unclear.*]
Robert Kennedy: [*on the phone*] Listen, Nick. You got enough gas there now? Okay, you're in pretty good shape now, though?
Marshall: [*whispering*] We'll make these decisions tomorrow.
Robert Kennedy: [*on the phone*] Well, is anybody trying to get . . .

. . .

With Robert Kennedy on the telephone and another conversation going on simultaneously in the Cabinet Room, the recording becomes very difficult to understand. The President was distracted by news that James Reston had just filed a story for the *New York Times* alleging that Nikita Khrushchev was inviting Kennedy to a summit meeting, and for the next few minutes, the conversation turned to Reston and the Soviet Union. Then the conversation turned back to Oxford, and Bobby Kennedy assured the President that reinforcements were on their way. Bobby and John had a brief discussion with Burke Marshall about whether to allow a group of female secretaries to assist Nicholas Katzenbach in Oxford.

. . .

Marshall: I think that General Abrams and General Billingslea are working on it.[25] Do you want to send those women down there?
Robert Kennedy: I guess I better not.
Marshall: What about the others? The lawyers?
President Kennedy: What women are these?
Marshall: Secretaries.
Robert Kennedy: Secretaries.
President Kennedy: Down to where, Oxford?
Marshall: Yeah.

---

[25]Major General Creighton Abrams, Director of Operations, Deputy Chief of Staff for Military Operations, U.S. Army.

President Kennedy: Oh, you mean Nick's secretaries?

Marshall: Yeah.

Robert Kennedy: Yeah. Well, why don't I put a hold on it and I'll talk to him later on tonight.

Marshall: Hold on [*unclear*].

President Kennedy: You don't have any men secretaries?

Marshall: [*Unclear*] could probably find them. I would think [*unclear*].

President Kennedy: The FBI must have them.

Sorensen: At least one or two here in the correspondence section.

Marshall: They must have one.

. . .

The conversation becomes unclear and appears to wind down. Only a few fragments are understandable before there is a break in the tape. When taping resumed, the President had a brief conversation with Ted Sorensen about the upcoming election, while Robert Kennedy was on the telephone trying to ensure that the new shipment of tear gas was on its way to the marshals on the campus of Ole Miss. Evelyn Lincoln seemed to bring some of the participants drinks.

. . .

Robert Kennedy: [*on the phone*] Do you? [*Pause.*] Well, would you favor that I had troops coming in there? Yeah. Well, they're on their way. [*Pause.*] Okay. No. [*Pause.*] Well, you can just stay there. What about . . . Is Nick there? Well, I'd just like to find out what he's heard on getting that gas in there.

Marshall: Do you want to talk to Cy [Vance]? Cy would know.

Robert Kennedy: [*on the phone*] Yeah. Well.

President Kennedy: Can we get, what's his name? The governor's man?[26]

Marshall: [*starts speaking on the phone*] Hello?

Robert Kennedy: He's getting him.

Marshall: [*on the phone*] Hello? Oh, listen, he went off and I'm on.

Unidentified: [*in the background*] What about gas?

Marshall: [*on the phone*] Well, are they on their way, do you know? [*A telephone rings.*]

President Kennedy: [*faintly in the background*] Should I talk with the general directly?

Lincoln: Jim, did you want your girl to stay?

Unidentified: If she could do me one last favor, which is to bring me a glass of milk.

---

[26]Apparently a reference to Tom Watkins, the intermediary in the Barnett-Kennedy negotiations.

Marshall: [*on the phone*] All right. Where were they, at the airport?

Lincoln: A glass of milk?

[*Unintelligible exchange.*]

Robert Kennedy: [*Unclear*] from now?

Marshall: [*on the phone*] [*Unclear*] well that's something to . . .

Unidentified: Evelyn's got some beers in the refrigerator.

Marshall: [*on the phone*] Well, they're coming in. Well, have they walked out on you? They don't have any gas masks.

It appears that Sorensen and the President have reentered the room.

Sorensen: [*Unclear*] matter, did we like [*unclear*] the troops on the ground?

President Kennedy: It seems to me [*unclear*].

Sorensen: Yeah.

President Kennedy: The governor has said the troops withdrew. The marshals were . . . with nothing to do.

Sorensen: We'll announce that. Yeah, but . . .

Marshall: [*on the phone*] The gas should be in there in a few minutes.[27]

Robert Kennedy: Is that Nick?

Marshall: [*to Robert Kennedy*] This is Ed [Guthman].

President Kennedy: How do we get the gas in and out of there?

Robert Kennedy: [*apparently speaking to someone else*] I guess you can come in.

Unidentified: I know, but one of us.

[*Chuckles.*]

Marshall: [*on the phone*] They have?

Unidentified: Students [*unclear*] when they have a riot like this one, do they?

President Kennedy: Well, that's what I said. [*Unclear.*]

Unidentified: [*Unclear.*]

Robert Kennedy: You what?

President Kennedy: There weren't any riots like this at Harvard just because some guy yells . . .

[*Chuckling.*]

Unidentified: What's that?

Unidentified: That's the only thing that [*unclear*].

Unidentified: Um huh.

---

[27]The federal force protecting the Lyceum ran out of tear gas. Because the Mississippi National Guard lacked their own supply, canisters of tear gas had to be flown in from Memphis. Soon the White House would face the problem of arranging a convoy to bring the gas from the airport in Oxford to the campus.

Unidentified: Move [*unclear*].

President Kennedy: What?

Robert Kennedy: [*could be on phone*] Well, you ought to leave it to the [*unclear*].

Sorensen: [*Unclear*] have student riots like this and it is [*unclear*] you ought to be prepared for the worst, but . . .

President Kennedy: That's it. That's what we're preparing for.

[*Laughter.*]

Unidentified: Yeah, and evidently we got it.

President Kennedy: Where is Nick? Is he up in the attic or just . . .

[*Laughter.*]

Sorensen: He's in the pillbox.

President Kennedy: He's a candidate [*unclear*]. Get him out of there.

O'Donnell: Nick might see that this is a job that he was [*unclear*] every year.

Unidentified: And almost died [*unclear*].

Unclear exchange.

O'Brien: You know, with the marshals, Bobby, at least they were out booking numbers or something . . . [*unclear*] in Chicago.

Marshall: [*possibly on the phone*] No one saw it [down there].

[*Laughter.*]

Marshall: [*on the phone*] No, no. [*Unclear.*]

President Kennedy: [*Unclear.*]

Marshall: [*possibly on the phone*] No. [*Unclear.*]

President Kennedy: There are no Boston marshals, are there?

Marshall: [*to the President*] The coach is going to go out and talk to them.

President Kennedy: Perhaps, perhaps . . .

Marshall: [*to the people in the room*] Perhaps?

Unidentified: Yeah [*unclear*].

President Kennedy: That's why the . . . police . . . I remember in a riot at Harvard, these guys go around and start asking for your identity card.

Unidentified: University police.

President Kennedy: Yeah. That's the only one that scared the shit out of me.

Unidentified: We just got three points in the [*unclear*] match.

President Kennedy: This [*unclear*] department.

Marshall: [*on the phone*] He wants . . . Well, here's Bob. He'll talk to you himself.

Robert Kennedy: [*on the phone*] Hello? Yeah. Right. Okay. Now, the question I think we have to decide, and Nick's going to have to talk to that general, if 200 fellows walking up there in uniforms, whether that's going to help or, whether it's going to really make it a . . . They're all Mississippians. No, I don't know. They all have tear gas. But I think he should talk to the military fellow there and see whether that would be of . . . Well, they said he'd been in touch with them. [*Pause.*] All right. Have we got the gas in there yet? [*Pause.*] Yeah. Could you if you had your uniform on?

President Kennedy: Are we going to get this every night?

Robert Kennedy: [*on the phone*] Hello?

Unidentified: [*responding to the President*] Huh?

President Kennedy: Are we going to get this every night?

Robert Kennedy: [*on the phone*] Are you in touch with the military?

Sorensen: [*to the President*] I think that may well be Barnett's strategy.

President Kennedy: [*Unclear.*]

Sorensen: You know it's what happened to Autherine Lucy.[28] She had some trouble—

Robert Kennedy: [*on the phone*] Well now, is the gas on the way?

Unidentified: What did she do, withdraw?

Unidentified: Yeah, personally [*unclear*]. Isn't that right?

Robert Kennedy: [*on the phone*] Will you? Do you want these troops in there?[29] Yeah. Okay. [*Pause.*] He got hit by what? Yeah.

Unidentified: Who?

Robert Kennedy: Is he going to live? The state police have left? [*Unclear*] put them in?

Marshall: I [*unclear*] talk with the governor.

President Kennedy: What'd he say?

Marshall: He said they can't have pulled them out.

Sorensen: What?

Marshall: Watkins.

Robert Kennedy: [*having heard Marshall's exchange with the President*] And he said, Watkins says, "They can't have pulled out of there." Yeah. They have, though?

President Kennedy: What's Watkins say otherwise?

Robert Kennedy: [*on the phone*] Six what?

Marshall: [*to the President*] He said it's dead.

---

[28]In February 1956, a black woman, Autherine Lucy, entered the University of Alabama under a court order. Rioting ensued, and university officials suspended Lucy for her own protection. When she criticized the decision, she was expelled from the university, a ruling upheld by a federal judge.

[29]At this point Katzenbach tells the Attorney General that he does not need any troops.

Robert Kennedy: [*on the phone*] [*Unclear.*]

Marshall: He just talked to the governor and the governor had just talked to the highway patrol [and] that everything was under control.

· · ·

At this juncture, concerns rose in the Cabinet Room as news arrived that General Edwin Walker was in Oxford to rally extremists in defense of a segregated University of Mississippi. The President and the Attorney General urgently wanted to deploy the U.S. Army on campus, and they started to become frustrated that it was taking so long to get the troops from Memphis, where the Army forces were stationed, to Oxford, less than an hour away by helicopter. We pick up the meeting with the Attorney General informing the participants of what he has just learned.

· · ·

Robert Kennedy: [*to the people in the room*] General Walker's been out downtown getting people stirred up.[30]

[*on the phone*] Can we get it arranged to get him arrested?

President Kennedy: By the FBI.

Robert Kennedy: [*on the phone*] [*Unclear.*] Well, let's see if we can arrest him. Will you tell the FBI that we need an arrest warrant.

President Kennedy: What's his crime?

Robert Kennedy: [*to the people in the room*] He's been stirring people up.

Sorensen: Incitement.

President Kennedy: Inciting.

Sorensen: Inciting insurrection.

Robert Kennedy: Obstruction of justice.

President Kennedy: [*Grunts.*] Would the FBI have trouble arresting him on . . .

Robert Kennedy: [*on the phone*] Yeah.

President Kennedy: How many agents do you have down there? I think you ought to get those MP's into there and over near the airport. I don't see what you've got to lose, if they're at the airport. You can always send them back.

Robert Kennedy: [*on the phone*] Yeah. Okay. All right. I'll do that. Now, will you clear it with Nick? He said we didn't need them a minute ago.

O'Brien: As far as [*unclear*].

Unidentified: [*Unclear*] is no longer . . .

O'Brien: . . . it depends on which is, you know, but I think that the thing is, you have less risk [*unclear*] they do and bring 'em in.

---

[30]Major General Edwin A. Walker, ret.

Robert Kennedy: [*on the phone*] Yeah. All right. Oh, can somebody sit on this? That's it. [*Hangs up the phone.*]

[*to the people in the room*] He [Katzenbach] said that if they get the gas, they don't have a problem.

President Kennedy: When do they think they are going to get it?

Robert Kennedy: Well, they think a couple of minutes, at least.

Unidentified: Somebody's injured? [*Unclear.*]

President Kennedy: Who got hurt?

Robert Kennedy: They're going to have . . .

Unidentified: No way, I tell you.

Marshall: [*on the phone*] [*Unclear*] terrible [*unclear*].

President Kennedy: Imagine them coming in there with gas masks and beginning again.

Unidentified: Yeah.

President Kennedy: That's what happens to all of these wonderful operations. War.

O'Brien: They haven't [*unclear*] some of the gas in those gas masks so they all be [*sound of sniffling*].

Unidentified: And the next group.

[*Laughter.*]

Unidentified: Well do you have . . .

President Kennedy: General Walker. Imagine that son of a bitch having been commander of a division up till last year. And the army promoting him.

Unidentified: You're right.

Unidentified: Yes.

Sorensen: Have you read *Seven Days in May*?[31]

President Kennedy: Yeah.

Unidentified: Damned good book.

President Kennedy: I thought that . . .

Sorensen: It's pretty interesting.

Unidentified: Yeah.

Sorensen: I read it straight through. It's interesting.

Unidentified: I didn't really like it.

O'Brien: Unrealistic?

[*Laughter.*]

Sorensen: And you thought it was too far-fetched, then?

---

[31]Popular novel of 1962, written by Fletcher Knebel, about a military plot to overthrow the U.S. government.

President Kennedy: No, I thought this sort of awful amateur's dialogue.

Unidentified: Yeah, it was a [*unclear*].

Unidentified: No, it's not great writing, but I mean—

President Kennedy: It's not even good . . . The only character that came out at all was the general. The President was awfully vague. But I thought the general was a pretty good character.

[*Extended pause.*]

Robert Kennedy: . . . well, then General Walker starts bringing those fellows, you know . . .

President Kennedy: What?

Robert Kennedy: If General Walker starts bringing in fellows from [*unclear*] and that—

Marshall: There are rumors all over the place.

President Kennedy: He's bringing in what?

Robert Kennedy: He's getting them all stirred up. If he has them march down there with guns, we could have a hell of a battle.

Unidentified: Thugs.

Sorensen: Did the FBI say Walker's there [*unclear*]?

Robert Kennedy: No. No. Walker's baiting them.

Marshall: [*on the phone*] John?[32]

Robert Kennedy: They need to keep an eye on him.

Marshall: [*on the phone*] Is that football coach doing any good?

Lincoln: Tom Watkins is calling you.

Robert Kennedy: Why don't you get it?

Two simultaneous telephone conversations proceed: the Attorney General tried to get some information about whether or not the marshals have enough tear gas, while Marshall continued working the phones. After listening for about a minute, the President wanted to know what was happening.

President Kennedy: What are they saying? He's there now?

Robert Kennedy: They're saying . . .

President Kennedy: Where are they? Up around the third floor? Where are they? Are they in the administration building with Meredith?

Robert Kennedy: No. Meredith is in another building.[33]

President Kennedy: Nobody knows where he is?

Sorensen: How many are guarding the administration building?

---

[32]Probably John Doar, on the staff of the Civil Rights Division, Department of Justice.

[33]Meredith was in a dorm room in Baxter Hall. Evidently the President was unfamiliar with the geography of the campus or the plan to protect Meredith.

Robert Kennedy: He's got 40 or 50 marshals. The gas is a quarter of a mile.

President Kennedy: But they can't get it through the . . .

Robert Kennedy: Well they just . . . Yeah. You know.

Marshall: They're not guarding anything there.

Sorensen: Then why don't . . .

Marshall: . . . the students.

Sorensen: . . . why don't they just let . . . The marshals just left?

Marshall: What do you mean?

Sorensen: [*Unclear*] spend the night . . .

Unidentified: Where are the marshals?

President Kennedy: Why don't they go inside the building? I think they would. I haven't had such an interesting time since the Bay of Pigs. [*Chuckling.*]

Unidentified: Cuba [*unclear*]?

Robert Kennedy: Since the day what?

President Kennedy: Bay of Pigs.

Unidentified: Does Tom Watkins sound like he's—

Robert Kennedy: The Attorney General announced today, he's joining Allen Dulles at Princeton University.[34]

[*Laughter.*]

Marshall: He sounds . . .

Unidentified: You might take up this [*unclear*].

Marshall: So he is. He's a very reliable fellow.[35]

President Kennedy: What?

Marshall: He's been a very reliable fellow. But he sounds—every time . . . every time there's a suggestion that that conversation would get out, he sounds concerned.

Robert Kennedy: [*on the phone*] Hello? No, I'm just wondering if you heard. No.

Unidentified: Do you want to hold that?

Marshall: Yeah.

Robert Kennedy: [*on the phone*] When they say he's sending more gas, we'll know we're in.

Marshall: Sending what?

Robert Kennedy: More gas.

Marshall: [*on the phone*] Oh, I'm just holding it. Who?

---

[34]Dulles was the retired director of Central Intelligence.
[35]The "reliable fellow" is most likely Tom Watkins.

Unidentified: [*Unclear*] is loose as a goose.

[*Laughter.*]

Marshall: [*on the phone*] That's all right. This is Burke Marshall. A what? A priest. Oh.

O'Brien: That's the best shot they could take. That'll [*unclear*] in Mississippi.

Unidentified: Tell him to get that collar on quick.

Marshall: [*on the phone*] Do you know if the football coach has talked to the students?

O'Brien: More appropriately [*unclear*] if his sweatshirt's on.

President Kennedy: Yeah. [*Unclear.*] He may be down there [*unclear, followed by several brief exchanges*].

Marshall: Where was that company?

Robert Kennedy: Right there. It's just forming up.

Marshall: Oh, it's just forming?

Robert Kennedy: The only question is you want them there now? That's up to Nick.

Marshall: Yeah.

Robert Kennedy: All you're going to have up to assist is 150–200 fellows.

Marshall: Yes, it's all there.[36]

Robert Kennedy: I think it's all there. It's within the hour, and that was 50 minutes ago. I am [*unclear*].

President Kennedy: Yeah, I think we ought to, I wouldn't hesitate to put them there. I don't think that's where we're going to have the difficulty. Not way beyond it. The problem is looking as if we're not doing enough rather than too much right now.

Marshall: Yeah.

President Kennedy: Good.

O'Brien: Oh, I agree.

President Kennedy: Better get them over there.

Marshall: I wonder if we shouldn't just put them over there.

Robert Kennedy: Yeah, but if it's forming up and we can't put—

Marshall: Because it might discourage some of these people from . . .

Robert Kennedy: Throwing?

Marshall: Yeah.

Robert Kennedy: That's why, he's in a . . . They're just guessing.

[*Pause.*]

---

[36]The advance contingent of MPs in Task Force Alpha was landing at the Oxford airport at 12:30 A.M. Oxford time.

Robert Kennedy: If they get the gas, it's not really a—

President Kennedy: Problem?

Robert Kennedy: . . . problem because they're going to get the . . .

Marshall: Unless the Bureau . . .See the Bureau says that their people are moving in.

Unidentified: From outside?

Marshall: Yeah. And they might be armed.

President Kennedy: You see, once some one fellow starts firing, everybody starts firing. That's what concerns me.

Marshall: Yeah.

President Kennedy: If one person fires . . .

.   .   .

The meeting continued in this vein, as information slowly trickled in. The President was concerned that events were spiraling out of control, and, as he would demonstrate during the Cuban Missile Crisis (which was only weeks away), he was determined not to authorize federal actions that would exacerbate the situation. The fundamental goal was to preserve Meredith's safety, and both JFK and RFK were prepared to authorize the federal marshals to open fire on the mob only if Meredith's room came under attack. In the meantime, the force was kept to strict rules of engagement. While the marshals were ordered to hold their fire, on at least three occasions, they felt sufficiently threatened to disregard the no-fire order. Not surprisingly, well over 100 marshals were wounded. Shortly after midnight in Washington, amidst unconfirmed (and inaccurate) reports that Meredith's room had been stormed, President Kennedy again talked to Governor Barnett by phone.

October 1, 1962, 12:14 A.M.

Conversation with Ross Barnett

Ross Barnett: . . . the commissioner of the highway patrol to order every man he's got.

President Kennedy: Yeah. Well, now, how long's that going to take? We don't want somebody . . .

Barnett: Well, I haven't been able to locate him.

President Kennedy: You can't locate . . .

Barnett: He went to the . . . Here's what happened. He went to the doctor's office with this man that was hurt.

President Kennedy: Yeah.

Barnett: And I finally located him there after you'd told me to get, have him to get more people, don't you see, if . . .

President Kennedy: Yeah.

Barnett: You needed 'em.

President Kennedy: Yeah.

Barnett: And he thought then that 50 he had would be sufficient.

President Kennedy: Yeah.

Barnett: But I told him by all means to order out every one he had if he needed it.

President Kennedy: Yeah.

Barnett: And I'm certainly trying in every way . . .

President Kennedy: Well, we can't consider moving Meredith as long as, you know, there's a riot outside because he wouldn't be safe.

Barnett: Sir?

President Kennedy: We couldn't consider moving Meredith if we haven't been able to restore order outside. That's the problem, Governor.

Barnett: Well, I'll tell you what I'll do, Mr. President.

President Kennedy: Yeah.

Barnett: I'll go up there myself . . .

President Kennedy: Well, now, how long will it take you to get there?

Barnett: . . . and I'll get a microphone and tell them that you have agreed to re-, to, for 'em to be removed . . .

President Kennedy: No. No. Now, wait a minute. How long . . .

Barnett: [*Unclear.*]

President Kennedy: Wait a minute, Governor.

Barnett: Yes?

President Kennedy: Now, how long is it going to take you to get up there?

Barnett: About an hour.

President Kennedy: Now, I'll tell you what, if you want to go up there and then you call me from up there. Then we'll decide what we're going to do before you make any speeches about it.

Barnett: Well, all right. Well . . .

President Kennedy: No sense in . . .

Barnett: . . . I mean, whatever you, if you'd authorize . . .

President Kennedy: You see, if we don't, we got an hour to go, and we may not have an hour.

Barnett: This, this man . . .

President Kennedy: It won't take you an hour to get up there.

Barnett: . . . this man has just died.

President Kennedy: Did he die?

Barnett: Yes.

President Kennedy: Which one? State police?

Barnett: A state policeman.[37]

President Kennedy: Yeah, well, you see, we got to get order up there, and that's what we thought we're going to have.

Barnett: Mr. President, please. Why don't you, can't you give an order up there to remove Meredith?

President Kennedy: How can I remove him, Governor, when there's a riot in the street, and he may step out of that building and something happen to him? I can't remove him under those conditions. You . . .

Barnett: Uh, but, but . . .

President Kennedy: Let's get order up there, then we can do something about Meredith.

Barnett: . . . we can surround him with plenty of officials.

President Kennedy: Well, we've got to get somebody up there now to get order and stop the firing and the shooting. Then when you and I will talk on the phone about Meredith . . .

Barnett: All right.

President Kennedy: . . . but first we got to get order.

Barnett: I'll, I'll call and tell them to get every official they can.

President Kennedy: That's right and then you and I will talk when they get order there, then you and I will talk about what's the best thing to do with Meredith.

Barnett: All right then.

President Kennedy: Well thank you.

Barnett: All right.

Kennedy hangs up.

· · ·

The President then returned to the Cabinet Room to brief the others about Barnett's position. Information continued to trickle in, and the situation in Oxford seemed to be deteriorating. It was dark; students and white civilians were rioting; and the Justice Department officials on the ground had limited resources and strict orders not to authorize retaliation against the students unless Meredith's life was in immediate danger. The last thing Kennedy wanted was for federal marshals or Army troops to fire on students. In the meantime, injuries mounted, and the White House learned that death had come to the Ole Miss campus.

· · ·

---

[37]Barnett is wrong about this. Two people were killed that night: the reporter Paul Guihard, who was with Agence France Press, and Ray Gunter, a local man who repaired jukeboxes for a living.

President Kennedy: He wants us to move him again. And I say, "Well, we can't move him if the situation's like this." And he says, "Well, we'll take care of the situation if you move him."

Robert Kennedy: I can't get him out. How am I going to get him out?

President Kennedy: That's what I said to him. Now, the problem is, if he can get law and order restored. . . . Okay, we'll move him out of there if he can get order restored.

Unidentified: I don't see how we can . . .

Long pause. Sounds of doors opening and closing. Evelyn Lincoln can be heard murmuring in the background.

Robert Kennedy: [*on the phone*] Now we'd better get this . . . Now, they might not recognize the kids today. Get him . . . get him up there and get him out or something. I don't know what the exit is. Yeah, yeah, they're shooting at other . . .

Unidentified:. [*Unclear.*] He said [*unclear*] to you immediately.

Robert Kennedy: I'm glad to see that . . . They always make sure of everything, even if they don't know what time it is.

[*on the phone*] Can we be all right? Will they be all right? Have they gotten into the room? I think we just have to protect him no matter what it is.

O'Donnell: [*Unclear.*]

Robert Kennedy: [*on the phone*] All right. Would you get that, Ed? See if we can get Barnett to get [the] highway patrol to bring doctors in.

[*Door opens.*]

Robert Kennedy: [*on the phone*] Nick? I'll hold.

O'Brien: Doctor.

Sorensen: From the inside of the arm[ory] or wherever [*unclear*].

O'Brien: [*on the phone*] Hello.

President Kennedy: What about removing him if Barnett says that he can restore law and order?

Robert Kennedy: Well, that's not what they, they're firing at the marshals.

Unidentified: I'd sure as hell put all those bastards in the can.

Unidentified: Yeah. That's for sure.

O'Brien: [*on the phone*] Hello. What's it look like?

O'Donnell: Guthman's so scared he can't talk. Helpless feelings on the other end of that phone. You have to [*unclear*].

O'Brien: [*on the phone*] This is Larry O'Brien. [*Pause.*]

O'Donnell: [*in the background*] I hate to say it, but I [*unclear*].

Unidentified: Well, we ought to do that [*unclear*] to Barnett. [*Indistinct exchange.*]

O'Brien: [*on the phone*] Yes. Yes. Hello? Yes. Hello? [*to the people in the* *room*] Two marshals have been shot. [*on the phone*] Yes, we're on this line down there. We're on this line. Well, we're talking down there. This is Larry O'Brien in the Cabinet Room. Hello? Yeah. So I understand. Yeah. Yeah. Are you able to move them out of the administration building to where the boy is?

Marshall: Have they got authority to return, Bobby?

O'Brien: They know it.

Unidentified: [*Unclear.*]

O'Brien: First. I thought they said haven't eaten since haven't eaten since this morning. [*Unclear.*] [*Unclear*] in the field, probably didn't spend a lot of time on the campus.

Evelyn Lincoln: [*Heard faintly in the background.*]

Unidentified: [*Unclear*] people [*unclear*].

Unidentified: [*Unclear*] one reason was that the people [*unclear*].

O'Brien: They say they can't determine just what his next move is. Let's see what's going to happen. He says these students are getting ready with a flying wedge to hit the dormitory and [face] these guys. He says, "No, they just have to face us, and somebody's going to get it."

Unidentified: Have they not shot back yet? The marshals?

O'Brien: Apparently not. Said some of them were hit with buckshot. But there are two of them seriously hurt. They really don't know how badly yet. The problem . . . One's bleeding in the throat.

[*Possible door sound.*]

President Kennedy: Well, can I talk to them directly and on . . .

Robert Kennedy: Do you want to get Nick for me?

O'Brien: [*on the phone*] Hello? Is Nick there? All right.

Robert Kennedy: The problem is, if we move him they're liable to [*unclear*].

Sorensen: About two hours.

President Kennedy: What about the Guard?

Robert Kennedy: Well, can't the 82nd [*unclear*].

Unidentified: How long before they get any more guards?

Robert Kennedy: He told me he'd have several bunches in an hour.

President Kennedy: An hour from now?

Robert Kennedy: And in a pinch they'd have about [*unclear interjection*]. They took two hours.

Marshall: And they [*unclear*].

Continues speaking faintly in the background.

Unidentified: [*Unclear.*]

O'Brien: [*on the phone*] Yeah? Nick? Hold on, here's Bobby.

Robert Kennedy: [*on the phone*] Hey, Nick? Oh, I just got, Ramsey just asked me for . . . if they had permission to fire back. Do you have to do that? Well, can't they just retreat into that building? [*Pause.*] Is he safe over the other place? Oh, I think that they can fire to save *him*. But now, can you hold out for an hour there? [*Pause.*] Can you hold out if you have gas? Is there much firing? Is there any way you could figure a way to scare them off? [*Pause.*] I'm sorry for that. I think that if we start a battle with . . . Up in the air? Except then it might really start them . . . Once *you* start firing they can forget this . . . Will that help? Okay. Okay. [*Puts down the receiver.*]

President Kennedy: [*on the phone*] Will you hold? [*to the people in the room*] Do you think they can hold for an hour?

Robert Kennedy: If they have gas.

President Kennedy: And do they?

Robert Kennedy: I think it really depends on how much firing.

[*Phone rings in the background.*]

Unidentified: Pardon.

Lincoln: [*answering phone*] Hello? Hello?

Unidentified: How much firing?

Robert Kennedy: The guards have arrived since you . . .

Lincoln: [*on the phone*] This is Evelyn Lincoln. [*calls out*] Cy—

Robert Kennedy: Cy Vance . . . The President can take it.

O'Brien: [*on the phone*] Hello. [*Long pause.*] Hello. [*to the people in the room*] Pretty damn hard once firing takes place, to shut it off.

Unidentified: Yeah, I know.

Operator: Hello?

O'Brien: [*on the phone*] Hello.

Operator: Yes, do you want a line?

O'Brien: [*on the phone*] Just leave it open. Hello. Yeah. Yeah. Yeah. Well, we'll leave this line open. All right. Right. [*Puts the receiver down.*] [*to the people in the room*] Well, they can't even get the injured guy to the college dispensary. They're trying to get a wedge to get him through.

O'Donnell: Trying to get him through the crowd? [*Long pause.*]

Sounds of a door opening and closing can be heard as Robert Kennedy returns to the room, probably after a conversation with Cyrus Vance, the Secretary of the Army.

Robert Kennedy: Damn army! They can't even tell if [*unclear*] the MPs have left [yet].[38]

O'Brien: [*on the phone*] Hello?

O'Donnell: Whether they've left yet?

---

[38]It is about 12:17 A.M., over 90 minutes since the Attorney General ordered the movement of the troops from Memphis.

Robert Kennedy: Won't even attempt to tell us.

O'Brien: [*on the phone*] Hello? Yeah. All right.

Sorensen: You mean they're not in contact with anyone . . .

Robert Kennedy: Well, who knows what the reason is? Cy Vance doesn't know yet.

[*Pause.*]

Robert Kennedy leaves the room again.

Lincoln: [*Unclear.*]

Pause. Sound of door opening. It appears that a midnight snack is being served.

Unidentified: Cheese on this?

Unidentified: Yes.

O'Brien: [*on the phone*] Hello?

Unidentified: [*referring to the snack*] And a roll.

O'Brien: [*on the phone*] Nothing, huh? Right.

[*Unclear voice in the background.*]

O'Brien: [*on the phone*] Huh? Yes.

O'Donnell: [*Unclear.*]

O'Brien: Well, where were they?

O'Donnell: [*Unclear.*] Out of the way. [*Unclear.*] I'll be a son of a bitch if the President of the United States calls up and says, "Get your ass down there." Yeah, I would think they'd be on that fucking plane in about five minutes.

Unidentified: They sort of roped them in.

O'Brien: So, where they are afraid the problem is the . . . now this flying wedge of students that's going to tackle the dormitory.[39] Half these guys, you know, they've about had it.

O'Donnell: But what's the point of it . . . these guys . . . burning and looting. I suppose they are going to kill us when they get here.

O'Brien: Yeah.

O'Donnell: You start firing at a bunch of students?

O'Brien: They're afraid it's going to happen.

O'Donnell: Uh?

O'Brien: That's what they're afraid is going to happen.[40] . . . marshal seriously hurt, the others, some others got buckshot. Well, this must have been done under the premise that something's going to happen [*unclear*]. [*on the phone*] Hello?

---

[39]Baxter Hall, where Meredith is located.

[40]Tape 26 ends. There appears to have been some conversation lost before the Secret Service replaced the tape reel.

Pause. An indistinct conversation can be heard in the background.

O'Brien: [*puts down the receiver*] If necessary, is there any way that we could get an ambulance?

Sorensen: The police ought to be able to get an ambulance to the [*unclear*].

Unidentified: The governor said, "Make sure and take that boy out of there, and everything will be all right."

O'Brien: That's the main thing.

Unidentified: I'd take him out. By tomorrow, with those 5,000 bayonets.

Unidentified: Certain that there be no repercussions whether you choose to bring troops in or not.

Unidentified: No. No. I agree.

Unidentified: [*Unclear.*]

O'Brien: . . . write this thing off now. Obviously, the townies [*unclear*].

Robert Kennedy: They had in mind.

[*Doors open.*]

Sorensen: One that was hit by the gas?

Unidentified: Yeah. [*Unclear.*]

[*Unclear exchange.*]

Robert Kennedy: Well, we can't last that long.

[*Doors close.*]

O'Brien: [*talking on the phone*] Hello. Yeah. Hmm. Don't worry. Oh yeah.

Robert Kennedy: The son of a bitch. He knows [*unclear*].

Door opens and closes.

President Kennedy: What? Yeah.

Robert Kennedy: [*Unclear.*] It's not about the policemen. It's about other people being shot. If you get Barnett to get Meredith off the campus . . .

President Kennedy: What?

Robert Kennedy: Just to get Meredith off the campus. That's what he wants.

Unidentified: Well he can [*unclear*].

[*Sound of water being poured.*]

Robert Kennedy: That's what he said.

President Kennedy: Well, he wants to be able to say that he asked me to get him off. And that I refused.

Robert Kennedy: Now, he's too . . .

President Kennedy: You've got to get law and order and then you can discuss what to do about Meredith. But he can't do anything. He doesn't even get a hold of the head of the state police.

Robert Kennedy: What do they say?

O'Brien: They don't know. Nothing at the moment.

Robert Kennedy: We'll have to stick it to that [General] Walker. [*Door opens and closes.*]

Sorensen: Can't you get him arrested?

Robert Kennedy: Well, I can't do it now.

Sorensen: Why not?

Robert Kennedy: Well, he's out there in the field.

Unidentified: You mean there's nobody that can go out and arrest him?

Robert Kennedy: Yeah.

O'Brien: [*talking on the phone*] Hello?

Robert Kennedy: Is he still being shot at, Larry?

O'Brien: [*talking on the phone*] No. Any shooting? Things quiet now? Quiet. Yeah. Yeah. [*talking to people in the room*] Everything's quiet around there, but he doesn't know . . . they're trying to check the dormitory.

Robert Kennedy: The what?

O'Brien: Trying to check around as to what's going on in the dormitories. He says it's quiet around the area. One fellow's seriously hurt and they're trying to get an ambulance.

Marshall: There's supposed to be an ambulance going in, too. [*Door sounds.*]

Unidentified: Jesus!

Sorensen: Sad day in our country.

No conversation as they wait for information to come in.

[*Doors open and close.*]

Sorensen: Any word yet on the military?

Marshall: Well, they're just leaving Memphis.[41]

Sorensen: Can they handle that [*unclear*]?

[*Unclear exchange.*]

Bobby Kennedy and Marshall have a brief exchange before the President enters the room.

President Kennedy: [*Unclear*] casualties [*unclear*] unless we're lucky.

O'Brien: The state policeman died. It's too bad.

President Kennedy: Shotgun wound in his back.

O'Brien: [*talking on the phone*] Hello? [*Pause.*] Right. No. All right. [*talking to people in the room*] He told me they ought to get [*unclear*] the fighting was [*unclear*] the campus [*unclear*] the assistant dean [*unclear*].

---

[41]Task Force Alpha's choppers began leaving Memphis at 11:50 P.M. The lead chopper would reach the Oxford airport at 12:30 A.M.

Unidentified: I understand it was [*unclear*]. [*Voices can be heard murmuring in the background.*]

O'Brien: Yeah.

The Attorney General enters the room.

Robert Kennedy: What's he say, Larry?

O'Brien: Nothing at the moment. He just said that we've got a stretcher. [*on the phone*] Hello? Maybe he . . .

Robert Kennedy: [*on the phone*] Hello? Well, how does it look now?

O'Brien: So they sent 18 men out to the dormitory.[42] They weren't sure if they were receiving fire or not.

Robert Kennedy: [*on the phone*] And what about there, they firing at all now? [*Pause.*] Is Nick there? [*Pause.*] Well, I'd like to talk to him to see what the . . . Oh, they're there? Yeah. Who's this?

Marshall: Let the people pick [*unclear*].

Robert Kennedy: [*in an aside*] Now, they told them they had to land.

Unclear exchange.

Robert Kennedy: They think we shouldn't do that.

Unidentified: Not today.

Robert Kennedy: You shouldn't just, you shouldn't say things.

Unidentified: Why don't you pick up the phone? That will get them flying.

Robert Kennedy: [*Unclear*] probably shouldn't say anything [*unclear*]. These guys have capable fellows there.

O'Brien: Yeah.

Robert Kennedy: The national guard. They can [*unclear*].

O'Brien: Yeah.

Robert Kennedy: [*talking on the phone*] Yeah. Oh Nick? How's it look? The fellow from the London paper was there, was he?[43] London paper. [*talking to the people in the room*] He says the fellow from the London paper died. . . . Yeah.

President Kennedy: We ought to get some more troops. I wonder if it takes this long to get people ready around here.

Robert Kennedy: [*on the phone*] Have the troops, have the national guard showed up? Did they fire? Are they firing at all down there?

Unidentified: [*Unclear.*]

---

[42]Originally, Katzenbach posted six men to guard Meredith; as the situation deteriorated on campus, eighteen additional men were dispatched from the Lyceum front to reinforce Baxter Hall.

[43]At approximately 12:30 A.M., Jack Rosenthal of the Justice Department called the White House to report that reporter Paul Guihard had been killed in the riot. His body was found next to a women's dormitory on campus.

Robert Kennedy: [*on the phone*] Is it quieter?

Marshall: [*Unclear.*]

Robert Kennedy: [*on the phone*] Who've you got up there at the other place? Yeah, but I mean I think you want to get somebody that's up there that knows how important it is to keep Meredith alive. Yeah, but I mean it should be somebody that you know. And that should stay right by Meredith and shoot anybody that puts a hand on him. And it has got to be the absolute . . . Okay? [*The telephone rings in the background.*]

[*Speaking to the people in the room*] It's a little quieter. [*Unclear.*]

. . .

For the next hour, Bobby tried to find out exactly when Army Task Force Alpha would arrive in Oxford, but Secretary of the Army Cyrus Vance could not give him precise details. In the Cabinet Room, there was a rising sense of urgency, and though the participants finally received confirmation that the helicopters carrying the troops were on their way, President Kennedy and his advisers were concerned it would be too little too late. In disgust, Kenneth O'Donnell remarked sarcastically that "Khrushchev would get those troops in faster," and several others seemed to feel the same way. Ted Sorensen quipped that "a few hundred students and rednecks have got the U.S. Army" pinned down.

Although the White House was unhappy with its inability to keep the peace in Mississippi, there was anger with Barnett for not having done his job as governor. At one point in the meeting, Bobby tried to come up with a response strategy to Barnett, who he believed would claim the next morning that the state of Mississippi had been tricked by the federal government and that the whole situation could have been avoided if the White House had not tried to "sneak" Meredith onto the campus. The younger Kennedy wanted to make sure word got out that it was Barnett who tricked the President and not the other way around. The Attorney General was also worried about the international ramifications of a foreign journalist's getting killed in the melee, and he knew that in the days ahead the administration would be in for some hard knocks in the foreign press.

At about 1:00 A.M., the meeting broke up, but the President and his brother stayed up for three and a half more hours, during which the President again talked to Barnett and to General Creighton Abrams about the troop deployment. Kennedy was fed up with Barnett, and on learning that there were 150 state troopers near the campus, sitting in their cars and not lifting a finger to halt the violence, he called the Governor personally. The tape begins in the middle of the conversation.

October 1, 1962, 1:45 A.M.

Conversation with Ross Barnett

President Kennedy: Yeah. Well, our people say that it's still a very strange situation. They wouldn't feel that they could take a chance on taking him outside that building. Now if we, can we get these fellows? I hear they got some high-powered rifles up there that have been shooting sporadically. Can we get that stopped? How many people have you got there? We hear you only got 50.

Barnett: Well, I have approximately 200 there now, Mr. President. That's not that . . .

President Kennedy: You got 200?

Barnett: Sir, about 200.

President Kennedy: Well, now let me get in touch with my people.

Barnett: . . . and we don't have but 210 of 12, patrolmen, you see.

President Kennedy: I see. Well, now, let me get my people back again.

Barnett: I'm doing everything in the world I can.

President Kennedy: That's right. Well, we've got to get this situation under control. That's much more important than anything else.

Barnett: Yes. Well, that's right.

President Kennedy: Now, let me talk to my people, and let me find out what the situation is there.

Barnett: Yes.

President Kennedy: They called me a few minutes ago and said they had some high-powered rifles there. So we don't want to start moving . . .

Barnett: Mr. President . . .

President Kennedy: . . . anybody around.

Barnett: . . . people are wiring me and calling me saying, "Well, you've given up." I said, I had to say, "No, I'm not giving up, not giving up any fight."[44]

President Kennedy: Yeah, but we don't want to . . .

Barnett: "I never give up. I, I have courage and faith, and, we'll win this fight." You understand. That's just to Mississippi people.

President Kennedy: I understand. But I don't think anybody, either in Mississippi or anyplace else wants a lot of people killed.

---

[44]Throughout the evening, the Governor was deluged with calls and telegrams urging him not to "sell out" to the Kennedys. In response to such talk, Barnett went on the air shortly before midnight (local time), and declared, "I call on Mississippians to keep the faith and courage. We will never surrender."

Barnett: Oh, no. No. I . . .

President Kennedy: And that's what, Governor, that's the most important thing. We want . . .

Barnett: . . . I'll issue any statement, any time about peace and violence.

President Kennedy: Well, now here's what we could do. Let's get the maximum number of your state police to get that situation so we don't have sporadic firing. I will then be in touch with my people and then you and I'll be talking again in a few minutes, see what we got there then.

Barnett: All right.

President Kennedy: Thank you, Governor.

Barnett: All right now.

President Kennedy: I'll be back. [*Phone hangs up.*]

The conversation resumes a few minutes later, at 1:50 A.M.

President Kennedy: Hello.

Unidentified: Just one moment, sir.

Unidentified: There you are, sir. There's the President.

President Kennedy: Hello. Hello.

Ross Barnett: Mr. President?

President Kennedy: Yes, Governor.

Barnett: I just talked with Colonel Birdsong . . . [45]

President Kennedy: Right.

Barnett: . . . who is our director of the highway patrol . . .

President Kennedy: That's right.

Barnett: . . . and he assures *me* that he has *approximately* 150 men there now.[46]

President Kennedy: Now, we got a report that they're all in their cars two or three blocks away.

Barnett: I told 'em, just like you asked me, to get *moving*.

President Kennedy: I see. Now, can you get them so that we stop this rifle shooting? That's what we got to stop.

Barnett: Well, he says he's doing all that he can. He says they're strangers in there.

President Kennedy: I know it, well that's what we hear.

Barnett: And he's calling for 50 more, and that'll put it up around 200.

President Kennedy: Can they get those students to go to bed?

Barnett: Well, he says he's trying to, and I don't think it'll be long before he can get them all to bed.

---

[45]T. B. Birdsong, head of the Mississippi Highway Patrol.

[46]This is presumably the 150 men seen sitting in their cars near campus.

President Kennedy: Okay. Will you stay at . . .

Barnett: Maybe not, I can't tell.

President Kennedy: Well, let's stay right at it. We ought to be, that's what we got to do before we can do anything.

Barnett: . . . he's reporting constantly to a gentleman who has control of the activities of the troops there.

President Kennedy: Yeah.

Barnett: And he understands that he's doing all he can.

President Kennedy: Well, I think that it's very important, Governor, aside from this issue, we don't want a lot of people killed just because they, particularly, evidently two or three guardsmen have been shot. And, of course, our marshals and then that state trooper, so we don't want . . .

. . .

Over the next two hours, the President and his brother each talked with General Abrams about the progress of Task Force Alpha. The troops finally arrived on the campus in the early morning hours of Monday, October 1, and they immediately calmed the situation. Confronted with Regular Army forces, the student mob scattered, and when the sun rose, the campus was in a state of imposed calm. Hearing the news, the President went to bed for a few hours of sleep, but first thing in the morning, he called Barnett.

Monday, October 1, 1962, 8:46 A.M.

Conversation with Ross Barnett

Begins in midconversation.

President Kennedy: Well, now, the thing is, Governor, I want your help in getting these state police to continue to help during the day because they're their own people. And we are going to have a lot of strange troops in there, and we are going to have paratroopers in and all the rest. And I think the state police should be the key, and that depends on you.

Barnett: Oh, I . . . You'll have, you'll have the whole force that we have.

President Kennedy: Well, now, you tell them . . .

Barnett: The [*unclear*] men are not equipped like yours.

President Kennedy: I understand that. But during the daytime they can help keep order on these roads and keep a lot of people from coming in. And I think that doesn't change your position on the issue, but at least it helps maintain order, which is what we've got to do today.

Barnett: All right, Mr. President.

President Kennedy: Thank you, Governor.

Barnett: I'll stay here now.

President Kennedy: Thank you very much.

Barnett: Thank you so much.

President Kennedy: And keep after your state police now.

Barnett: I will.

President Kennedy: Thanks.

Barnett: I'll call him as soon as we hang up . . .

President Kennedy: Thanks.

Barnett: . . . 'n tell him to do all he can to keep peace.

President Kennedy: Okay, thanks, Governor.

Barnett: And when'll I hear from you again?

President Kennedy: I'll be talking to you about noon, my time.

Barnett: Okay. Thank you so much. Good-bye.

President Kennedy: Okay, Governor.

[*Phone hangs up.*]

．　　．　　．

Still upstairs at the White House, the President called the solicitor general, Archibald Cox, to discuss some legal issues raised by the Oxford riot. In particular, the President was considering seeking the arrest of Governor Barnett and Major General Edwin Walker. Walker was eventually arrested, though he was never tried. Barnett, however, escaped arrest because the Kennedy administration believed the potential costs were too high. The last thing the administration wanted was to make a martyr of the Governor, and in the days ahead, Kennedy would decide not to pursue an arrest.

Monday, October 1, 1962, 9:31 A.M.

Conversation with Archibald Cox

[*Phone rings.*]

Evelyn Lincoln: Hello.

Unidentified: I have Mr. Archibald Cox, the solicitor general, returning the President's call.

Lincoln: Okay.

President Kennedy: Hello.

Archibald Cox: Good morning, Mr. President.

President Kennedy: Good morning. . . . Now, the only question I had was whether there are any additional proclamations or powers, etc., that we might need in the Mississippi matter if it gets worse, for arresting people, and under what charge and what legal penalties they face and so on. For example, we want to arrest General Walker, and I don't know whether we just arrest him under disturbing the peace or whether we arrest him for more than that. I wonder if . . . How long are you going to be at the court this morning?

Cox: Not beyond half past ten.

President Kennedy: Yeah, well then I wonder if we can get more precise information on where we are legally on arresting people, including the governor if necessary and others?

Cox: Right.

President Kennedy: And what the penalties are because we might want to announce that on the radio and television that anyone involved in any demonstration or anything would be subject to this penalty, and maybe the General could announce it.[47]

Cox: Right. Good-bye.

.   .   .

Later that day, Kennedy talked with Cyrus Vance and Secretary of Defense Robert McNamara. By the end of the day, about 10,000 Regular Army soldiers and federalized National Guard troops had arrived in Oxford and its environs. Thousands more would follow, and according to some reports, at peak, there were around 23,000 troops of various sorts stationed in and around Oxford, which had a population of only 10,000. Between October 1 and October 8, the Army set up checkpoints, and every car trying to get on the campus was searched. Not until October 9 did the Army begin to withdraw significant numbers of troops.

Though Barnett had been forced to back down and Meredith was successfully registered, the Kennedy administration had won few friends. Public opinion in the North heavily endorsed what the President had done, but the White House had alienated the Deep South, and Meredith himself charged the Army with institutional racism. In a handwritten statement released on October 8, he asserted that the U.S. Army had resegregated the troops stationed on the campus. "The first two days of my stay at the University," Meredith wrote, "the military units looked like American units. All soldiers held their positions and performed the task for which they had been trained." But since then, Meredith continued, "Negroes have been purged from their positions in the ranks."

On learning of Meredith's protest, President Kennedy called Cyrus Vance for confirmation and was told the Army was indeed no longer using black troops on patrol because the commanders were worried that

---

[47]Attorney General Robert Kennedy.

the use of such troops would be interpreted by white Mississippians as a provocation.[48]

Trying to keep the situation in Oxford from spinning out of control, the administration had satisfied neither the demands of civil rights leaders to move more quickly on desegregation nor the desires of white southerners who wanted to leave civil rights to state and local authorities. Though Kennedy had sent federal troops to protect Meredith, black leaders were aware that on many other occasions court orders had been thwarted by men like Ross Barnett and that Washington had done nothing. Far from seeing the Kennedy brothers as friends, civil rights leaders concluded from the events in Oxford that only a violent crisis—in the public eye—would compel the White House to become involved.

For his part, the President was glad the troops had restored order, and he quickly began to focus on the upcoming congressional elections. Even if Kennedy had intended to follow up events in Oxford with greater attention to civil rights, the Cuban Missile Crisis, which began on October 16, 1962, would push all else to the back burner. By the time the missile crisis ended and the election was over, Oxford, Mississippi, was something of a distant memory. The decisive resolution of the missile crisis had boosted the President's popularity, and the midterm elections saw the Democrats lose only four seats in the House, which was considerably less than the party of a sitting president typically lost, while gaining four seats in the Senate.[49]

But if civil rights leaders hoped Kennedy would use his increased popularity and his party's edge in Congress to introduce civil rights legislation, they would be disappointed. The President did use the electoral success as a cover to fulfill his delayed promise to issue an executive order to end segregation in federal housing projects, but on the whole, Kennedy showed no more enthusiasm for federal action on civil rights after November 1962 than he had during the previous year and a half. Civil rights leaders concluded the only way to break the logjam on civil rights was to capture the country's attention in a bold way in order to show the White House and the nation that racial oppression persisted.

---

[48]As William Doyle notes, it was Robert Kennedy who had approved the segregation order in a September 27 meeting with military leaders.

[49]The margin was 259–175 in the House and 62–38 in the Senate.

Chapter 3
Protest in Birmingham

For the next few months, civil rights leaders debated the course of the movement. Nearly a decade had passed since the victory in *Brown v. Board of Education*, and as the struggle engaged increasing numbers of African Americans, voices were raised about the best way to achieve justice, with some questioning the NAACP's approach and even that of the Southern Christian Leadership Conference (SCLC). Although the Kennedy brothers maintained considerable popularity among the black population, the administration's reluctance to move boldly on civil rights left the movement's leaders altogether discouraged.[1]

Perhaps Kennedy sensed that some black leaders were prepared to turn away from the Democratic Party, but whatever the explanation (and the historical record remains unclear about this), on February 28, the President sent a civil rights message to Congress. Recommending legislation that would quicken progress on black voting and educational rights, Kennedy used bold rhetoric to assert that all was not well in America. "Our Constitution is color blind," he declared, but "the practices of the country do not always conform to the principles of the Constitution. . . . Equality before the law has not always meant equal treatment and opportunity." In unambiguous language, the President spoke of the disparities between the races—in education, in employment, and even in life expectancy.

But if the words were powerful, as historian Hugh Davis Graham has written, the specific legislative proposals were "frail."[2] There was no cause

---

[1]It is striking that in this period average African Americans throughout the country seemed to support the President and the Attorney General, a point noted by historian Carl Brauer in *John F. Kennedy and the Second Reconstruction*.

[2]Hugh Davis Graham, *The Civil Rights Era: Origins and Development of National Policy*, 70.

for optimism in the proposed changes, which would have achieved little, and the fact that Kennedy failed to include discrimination in public acco-modations or in employment was a great disappointment to those com-mitted to the cause. And so, despite Kennedy's powerful rhetorical thrust, it was clear the White House remained reluctant to consider effective pro-posals that would advance the freedom campaign, and the more the administration stalled, the more difficult it became for the movement's leaders to maintain control. King and other key figures were caught between the administration's caution and the rumble of criticism coming from those who wanted to move more aggressively.

The SCLC concluded that the President and his staff would only take action on civil rights if forced to do so, while at the same time, the move-ment's leadership was convinced that without federal intervention, grass-roots activism would face an insurmountable task. After lengthy debate and discussion, the SCLC decided to create a crisis that would attract national media attention and force the Kennedy administration and white America to take notice of the injustices black Americans yet endured. The place they chose to do battle was Birmingham, Alabama, an industrial steel city—a symbol of the new South. But in many ways, Birmingham was mired in the past.

In the late 1950s and early 1960s, Birmingham was the scene of dozens of bombings directed at civil rights activists and frequent cross burnings organized by the Ku Klux Klan. According to the SCLC's Rev-erend Ralph Abernathy, black Americans thought Birmingham was the "worst city this side of Johannesburg, South Africa." They would drive 30 miles out of their way to avoid this "bastion of southern racism." These sentiments were shared by Martin Luther King, who said Birmingham was "a city which had been trapped for decades in a Rip Van Winkle slum-ber," a city whose fathers had "apparently never heard of Abraham Lin-coln, Thomas Jefferson, the Bill of Rights . . . or the 1954 decision . . . outlawing segregation in the public schools."

The city's hostility to civil rights was epitomized by one man, police chief Eugene "Bull" Connor. Connor bore the official title of Public Safety Commissioner, but Birmingham's byzantine municipal bylaws made him perhaps the most powerful individual in the city. From the perspective of the civil rights movement, Connor was a figure straight out of central casting, a round, scowling good old boy, with a well-deserved reputation for brutality and violence. But for the movement's purposes, Connor was ideal, for civil rights leaders knew he could be counted on to do something outrageous, which would so offend common notions of decency that it would cause otherwise ambivalent white Americans to sympathize with the freedom struggle. The leadership also knew that one of those ambivalent white Americans was the President himself. But if John Kennedy had not acted boldly during the riots at Ole Miss, he had not stood by idly, either. The movement's leaders hoped Kennedy's sense of justice would transcend his political calculations.

Taking the pulse of Birmingham, King and his colleagues decided to implement what they called Project C (for confrontation), and they fixed early April 1963 as their starting point. As organized by Fred Shuttlesworth's Alabama Christian Movement for Human Rights and the SCLC, the protests that began in Birmingham in April 1963 were designed to force existing tensions to the surface. King and others hoped that by creating a "crisis situation," the protests would "open the door to negotiation." Shuttlesworth was equally blunt, claiming "Birmingham's where it's at." If the protests yielded the desired results, Shuttlesworth predicted, the movement would "gain prestige" and "really shake the country." It was a strategy born of desperation, a plan that aimed to provoke a confrontation with an ornery police chief and a racist city establishment. But the potential payoff was undeniable, for a victory in Birmingham would have enormous value, both symbolic and real. If "we could crack that city," one activist remarked, "then we could crack any city."

In deciding to target Birmingham, King and other black leaders recognized that its black residents lacked the votes to influence the city's political system. But they were convinced blacks possessed, in King's words, "enough buying power to make the difference between profit and loss in almost any business." The movement thus directed its energy at the city's "economic power structure." As King told a church audience, "We must no longer spend our money with businesses that discriminate against Negroes." To this end, black leaders decided to focus on one of the most disturbing aspects of the city's race relations: segregated lunch counters at stores in the city's business district. The objective was nothing less than the abolition of decades of institutionalized racial oppression.

On the morning of April 3, 1963, the protests began at five lunch counters in downtown Birmingham. At Britling Cafeteria, seven blacks seated themselves at the "whites only" counter and asked to be served; eight more did the same at Woolworth's. Similar scenes were played out in three other locations. One of the participants described how a white man came up to him and spat in his face. "I looked at him and smiled," he recalled. Birmingham police arrested more than twenty protesters. The second day more activists were arrested, and on the third day, still more were jailed.

On April 4, the leaders of the Birmingham campaign announced their objectives. They called for the desegregation of lunch counters and all public facilities in downtown stores; the immediate establishment of fair hiring practices in those stores; the dropping of all charges against those arrested in the sit-ins; the establishment of fair hiring practices in all city departments; the reopening of city parks and playgrounds, which had been closed to avoid desegregation; and the establishment of a biracial group to work out a timetable for the desegregation of Birmingham's public schools. Speaking to a church group, Ralph Abernathy articulated the ultimate goal of these multifaceted demands. He compared life in Birmingham with African American life in another southern city, Atlanta, where blacks could "go to the finest, most exclusive restaurant, sit down, and order . . . a steak." In Atlanta, Abernathy said, "business and civic leaders will call you down to their office [and] shake your hand. . . ." As his black listeners well knew, in Birmingham, such experiences were impossible.

Over the next several days, the Birmingham effort expanded to include the boycott of downtown department stores, which was a bitter pill for white merchants during the Easter season. Speaking about the arrests of the protesters, King told a church crowd, "We can't all go to jail, but we can all keep our money in our pockets and out of the hands of the downtown merchants. . . . If we can do that, then the downtown businessmen will sit down and talk this thing out with us." As the economic boycott gathered momentum, sales dropped significantly in the city's department stores. At the same time, the arrests of protesters continued. But already, there were signs of trouble. The protests depended on a massive mobilization of Birmingham's black population, akin to the Montgomery boycott of the previous decade. But with the protests barely a week old, black leaders were having trouble finding volunteers willing to go to jail.

On April 6, the Reverend Fred Shuttlesworth and about thirty others walked through the black ghetto toward the city hall where they were planning to hold a prayer meeting to protest the denial of a permit for picketing. Bull Connor's forces met the crowd and promptly arrested them, despite Shuttlesworth's declaration: "We are taking an orderly walk. We are not parading." The arrests were orderly and peaceful. The following day, however, the confrontation between blacks and police became considerably more antagonistic, and Bull Connor's forces resorted to precisely the sort of tactics the movement's leaders had anticipated.

After church on April 7—Palm Sunday—a group of protesters marched toward the center of town, singing "Hold My Hand While I Run This Race." Connor's men again lined the route, stopping the protesters and arresting them as they knelt on the street in prayer. Twenty were taken to jail, charged with parading without a permit. The protesters themselves submitted without resisting, but black spectators who witnessed the arrests were not so forbearing. Connor had deployed not just officers, but police dogs. A young black man named Leroy Allen got into a tussle with one of the dogs and suddenly, officers and dogs violently forced young Allen to the ground. Pandemonium followed.

For some 15 minutes, the police used nightsticks and German shepherds to clear spectators from the scene. Seven were arrested for disorderly conduct and carted off to jail. With this confrontation, which the media reported the next day, the civil rights leadership had achieved part of its aim: an outbreak of police brutality witnessed by the press and, ultimately, the nation. Some of those spearheading the Birmingham movement were relieved. Bull Connor had not let them down. "We've got a movement. We had some police brutality. They brought out the dogs. We've got a movement!"

On April 10, Birmingham authorities obtained a temporary restraining order from a state circuit court judge, which ordered Martin Luther King, Shuttlesworth, Abernathy, and others to cease further demonstrations and public protests in the city. Good Friday was two days later, and, seizing on the symbolism, King, Abernathy, Shuttlesworth, and several others decided they would defy the order and make Connor arrest them. When they began a peaceful Good Friday procession, Connor obliged by tossing them into the back of paddy wagons and hauling them to jail.

The leaders were separated, placed in solitary confinement (for their own safety, they were told), and locked in cells, each with a small window and a metal slat bed. Recalling his feelings of isolation and distress, King said that without any contact, "I was besieged with worry. How was the movement faring?" That first night in Birmingham jail, he said, represented the "longest, most frustrating and bewildering hours I have lived."

King's arrest made instant news. During the preceding week, the Kennedy administration had paid no more attention to the events in Birmingham than it had to similar protests in cities throughout the South during previous months. But the events of Easter weekend forced the White House to focus on civil rights. At about midnight on Good Friday, Wyatt Walker of the SCLC, a leader of the Birmingham movement, contacted Burke Marshall at his Washington home to ask for help, and the next day Walker sent a telegram to the President: "We ask that you use the influence of your high office to persuade the city officials of Birmingham to afford at least a modicum of human treatment" to King and Abernathy.

On Easter Sunday, Coretta Scott King tried to reach Kennedy, and after some difficulty, she contacted his press secretary, Pierre Salinger, who was relaxing in Florida with the President. Salinger promised he would pass along her message, and less than an hour later, the Attorney General telephoned Mrs. King, expressing the administration's concern for her husband. The next day, April 15, the President called Mrs. King to convey similar sentiments. A short time later, Coretta King talked with her husband by phone and shared the news of Kennedy's overture. Hoping to derive maximum public relations benefit, King encouraged her to make the President's call publicly known. While he had also telegramed Kennedy to thank him for his "encouraging words" and "moral support," King was intent on bringing the Birmingham movement to fruition, and using Kennedy's private call as a public endorsement could only help.

But the most enduring aspect of King's jailing in Birmingham concerned neither telegrams nor telephone calls. While imprisoned in Birmingham, King penned one of the great documents in the long history of the civil rights struggle, a declaration that would serve as a powerful statement in the quest for human liberation. King's "Letter from Birmingham City Jail" was written in response to eight white Birmingham clergymen who had criticized the movement's tactics if not its aims. In a prepared statement, the clergymen had pointedly suggested that the protests, far from helping the cause of justice, only incited "hatred and violence" and failed to contribute to "the resolution of our local problems."

King's jailhouse response was written in the margins of the newspaper, on scraps of toilet paper, and on whatever shreds of paper he could find. Though he addressed the clergymen directly, the letter was clearly aimed at a wider audience. Writing that "injustice anywhere is a threat to justice everywhere," he claimed that, "we are caught in an inescapable network of mutuality, tied in a single garment of destiny." He spoke of just and unjust laws and racial oppression in American history and explained the reasons for the movement's "direct action" campaign. If the history of race relations was grim, he looked toward a time when "the dark clouds of racial prejudice will soon pass away" to reveal "the radiant stars of love and brotherhood [that] will shine over our great nation. . . ."

The Birmingham letter was a testament to King's passion, a call to people everywhere to fight moral injustice. High school and college students throughout the country are now expected to read King's statement, but its impact at the time was slight. The eight clergymen to whom King had responded seemed unmoved by his words, and felt, as one of them remarked, that they had been "put in a position of looking like bigots."

King and Abernathy were released from jail on April 20, and two days later, along with several others, they went on trial for violating the city's injunction banning demonstrations, sit-ins, and other activities. On April

26, the judge found the defendants guilty of criminal contempt and sentenced them to five days in jail and a $50 fine. Imposition of the jail sentences would be delayed, pending appeal.

Though King, Abernathy, Shuttlesworth, and other activists were now out of jail, the campaign was beginning to flag. It was once again becoming difficult to recruit volunteers willing to go to jail. As Wyatt Walker recalled, "We needed more troops. . . . We had scraped the bottom of the barrel of adults who could go." Facing the challenge of injecting vitality into the struggle, the leadership was unsure of its next move. Like the others, King was increasingly concerned about the declining interest of the press. "You know, we've got to get something going," he said. Everyone in the inner circle acknowledged that unless they hit on a new tactic, the Birmingham movement would fizzle.

The SCLC had staked much of its political capital on the outcome in Birmingham, and if the movement failed, it would do substantial harm to King and his circle. While other groups stood poised to assume a more prominent role, the movement could not easily sustain a defeat at the hands of Bull Connor. By the end of April, the situation in Birmingham threatened to squeeze the life out of the crusade. Nor did anyone think a telephone call from President Kennedy was going to transform southern race relations or make it easier for blacks to vote in the South.

To continue the demonstrations, it would be necessary to enlist additional support. More people were needed—and that was precisely what the movement lacked. So King and the leaders of the movement turned to a more enthusiastic (and pliable) group: children. To some, the decision to recruit children to participate in the Birmingham campaign was an immoral act. Not only were the city's children asked to miss school, but they were also recruited to engage in protests, to risk arrest and even physical harm.

Martin Luther King was persuaded that the righteousness of the ultimate goal justified such problematic means. One reformer, offering a pragmatic observation, noted the "parents were working . . . [and] couldn't go and march" because they might have lost their jobs, while the kids had "nothing to lose." What's more, the community supported the plan. If parents had not endorsed the idea, there would not have been enough children to make a difference, and as the world would shortly see, the decision to put children in the line of fire paid enormous dividends. When Bull Connor unleashed his dogs and his firehoses on Birmingham's children, the outrage could be heard throughout the nation.

On May 2, the children's crusade began. That morning, thousands of children gathered in the Sixteenth Street Baptist Church. From there, they departed in groups of ten to fifty and set off toward designated locations in the city, including city hall and the downtown shopping district. Marching in orderly fashion, the youngsters sang, clapped, and laughed as they went, some carrying picket signs, all aware of the movement's aims. Some were as young as six years of age. Bull Connor, uncertain about what to do, had never confronted such a mass of orderly, determined—and youthful—protesters. By the end of the afternoon, hundreds of children had been arrested, taken off first in police cars, then in paddy wagons, and finally in school buses. Presaging the difficulties to come, Connor had posted fire trucks with high-pressure hoses at a number of intersections, although this day they went unused. The canine corps was also kept at bay.

That night, Martin Luther King expressed a sense of wonderment over the day's events, telling 2,000 people gathered at the Sixth Avenue Baptist Church, "I have been inspired and moved today. I have never seen anything like it." In Washington, Attorney General Robert Kennedy was less sanguine, asserting, "School children participating in street demonstrations is a dangerous business. An injured, maimed, or dead child is a price none of us can afford to pay." Black leader Malcolm X was still more direct, declaring that "real men don't put their children on the firing line." If the first day of the children's crusade had been memorable, the next would be impossible to forget.

On May 3, more young protesters headed to the Sixteenth Street Baptist Church, where King told them, "If you take part in the marches today, you are going to jail but for a good cause." Early that afternoon, they began to emerge from the building in a repeat of the previous day's activities. Connor's men arrested seventy children, some of whom were chanting, "Freedom . . . freedom. . . ." Concerned about the growing numbers of marchers, the police did not know what they would do with them all; the municipal jails were running out of room. In an effort to end the demonstrations, Connor ordered his firemen to turn their hoses on the children, hoping this might keep them inside the churches. Thus began one of the most infamous episodes in the movement's history, an event, which, according to historian and White House aide Arthur Schlesinger helped convince President Kennedy that action had to be taken to meet the challenge of southern intransigence on civil rights.[3]

The force of the water from the fire hoses lifted children off the

---

[3]Schlesinger made this point in a conversation with the editors, Charlottesville, Virginia, April 10, 1999.

ground, bloodying some and peeling the clothes off others. As the pressure was increased to 100 pounds, students were hurled down the streets like pieces of paper in the wind. Watching in horror, bystanders became enraged and began hurling bricks, rocks, and bottles at Connor's troops. In response, the canine corps went to work; the snarling dogs charged at blacks in the crowd. The German shepherds tore at clothes and flesh, until finally the police managed to subdue the crowd and regain control of the situation. Several hundred protesters were arrested, and by the time the riot ended at 3:00 in the afternoon, Connor had provided civil rights leaders with precisely the sort of spectacle they had sought.

Newspapers around the country and the world recorded images never to be forgotten: a German shepherd lunging at the stomach of a black man and firemen pinning black youngsters against a wall with a powerful jet of water. One of the civil rights movement's leaders recalled the impact Connor's violent tactics had on the struggle in Birmingham: "Bull Connor had something in his mind about not letting these niggers get [through]. I prayed that he'd keep trying to stop us." If he had let the protesters go through, there would have been "no movement, no publicity. . . . We had calculated for the stupidity of Bull."

Like many Americans, the President was sickened by the events in Birmingham and decided to send Burke Marshall there, an indication of the administration's concern about the situation in the southern city. On May 4, Marshall boarded a plane and headed south in an effort to mediate the dispute. In the days ahead, he would meet with the city's African American and white leaders and play a key role in helping to ameliorate the situation. According to historian Adam Fairclough, Marshall was the "crucial intermediary" in Birmingham, and many have credited him for the landmark agreement that was reached several days later.

On the day Marshall arrived, the situation remained volatile, and violence erupted once more as blacks marched, bricks and rocks were hurled at the police, and Connor turned his hoses on the demonstrators. Against the backdrop of this mayhem, Marshall would negotiate with both sides in the Birmingham dispute. He described his approach later, noting, "First I had a meeting with the merchants and then I'd have a meeting with some Negro leaders and then it was arranged so that . . . local Negroes would meet with a very small group of whites, and then I'd go and meet with King in the middle of the night." Then the process would begin again, and Marshall or his deputies would "see if any agreement or consensus could be reached on the issues."

This juxtaposition of events continued over the next few days; Marshall attempted behind the scenes to reach an agreement that would satisfy the demands of civil rights leaders, while demonstrations and arrests continued on the streets of the city. On the afternoon of May 7, as a meeting with white leaders was concluding, violence again rocked the streets as Connor's fire hoses blasted away at black protesters, including the Reverend Fred Shuttlesworth, who was pinned against the wall of a church even though the demonstration had largely ended. As an injured Shuttlesworth was taken by ambulance to a nearby black hospital, an unrepentant Bull Connor was heard to declare, "I waited a week to see Shuttlesworth get hit with a hose. I'm sorry I missed it. I wish they'd carried him away in a hearse."

Connor's lack of empathy notwithstanding, Marshall seemed to be making progress in his negotiations with African American and white leaders. But King and Shuttlesworth were growing impatient. As the discussions continued, they warned that unless an agreement was reached soon, they would step up the pressure and increase the size of the demonstrations. The city's jails were filled beyond capacity, and some of the city fathers were becoming nervous about the mounting business losses on the one hand and the tarnishing of the city's reputation on the other. They were willing to meet most of the demands, including gradual desegregation of public facilities and lunch counters. The sticking point was the release of the jailed demonstrators.

King demanded the protestors' release without bail, contending their arrest had been unlawful and unjust. City authorities refused. Recognizing an impasse, Burke Marshall worked out a solution with Robert Kennedy. While in public the administration maintained that the dispute in Birmingham involved state law and was thus beyond the scope of federal authority, in private, the Kennedy brothers understood that a solution was both politically prudent and absolutely essential. In order to raise the money for bail, Robert Kennedy and his aides contacted figures like singer Harry Belafonte and labor leader Walter Reuther. And finally, the qualms of the city's white business leaders were met, and on May 10, King announced a settlement had been reached.

Without disclosing the role of the Kennedy administration, King could present the May 10 agreement as a great victory for the movement. In addition to progress on desegregation, he had won concessions on the hiring of more African Americans in the city government. It was a triumphant moment for King, who was crowned with laurels by Ralph Abernathy. "All these preachers are great men," Abernathy shouted from the podium of St. John's Church that night, "but there isn't but one Martin Luther King! God has sent him to lead us to freedom. Are you going to follow him? Is he our leader?" The crowd roared its approval. Birmingham had catapulted King to the forefront of the movement, and it meant he would serve as a broker in all subsequent challenges.

But there would be no peace in Birmingham. Although the city's business leaders had been willing to compromise, Bull Connor and his crowd were not yet prepared to back down. The Ku Klux Klan rallied around the police chief, and in the days after the accord was reached, bombs rocked the city, including one that exploded near King's motel and another that blew a hole through the living room in the home of King's brother.

In response, young blacks began rioting. They hurled bricks and bottles at police and burned and looted stores, even though their violence was confined to the city's black neighborhoods. Adding to the fury was the sense that Alabama authorities had intentionally set up the movement's leaders. Just hours before the bombs exploded, 700 state troopers, ordered to Birmingham on May 8 by Governor George Wallace, had been patrolling the areas where the blasts would occurr. But suddenly they had been withdrawn on orders of their commander, whose friendship with Bull Connor and Governor Wallace was well known. Such developments did little to quell the emotions of the crowd.

Despite the success of May 10, it now appeared as if the crisis was about to enter a new and deadlier phase. In Washington, the Kennedy administration was torn between anger at King's tactics and outrage at Bull Connor's brutality. With the agreement about to collapse, the President confronted the prospect of the breakdown of civil order in Birmingham, and after the Oxford fiasco of the previous fall, Kennedy was determined to contain the situation.

Whatever the White House may have thought of him, King desperately wanted to end the violence. Indeed, the race leader even tried to contact the White House but only managed to reach the FBI. Shouting into the telephone, he said that federal troops were needed. "You've got to do something, the whole town has gone beserk. . . . [T]he Negroes are up in arms." By Sunday morning May 12, Mother's Day, it was clear the damage was severe: several businesses, houses, and an apartment building had burned to the ground, dozens of cars had been destroyed, and almost seventy people had required hospitalization.

This burst of rioting precipitated a series of high-level meetings in the White House, which President Kennedy recorded. That Sunday, Kennedy met with top aides to discuss how best to respond to events in Birmingham. The most pressing question was whether to order federal troops to Alabama. With the lesson of Oxford in mind, President Kennedy wanted to make sure that if he decided to send troops to Alabama, it would be done without delay. The May 12 meeting begins with a briefing from

Robert Kennedy, who first presents an overview of the Birmingham riot and then turns to the question of whether it would be prudent to order federal troops to the area.

Sunday, May 12, 1963, 5:35 P.M.

Meeting on Birmingham

Including President Kennedy, Robert Kennedy, Burke Marshall, Robert McNamara, and others.

Robert Kennedy: Now, have you got what happened last night? You want to hear a few things?

President Kennedy: Okay.

Robert Kennedy: I guess, shortly before 12:00, maybe 11:30, they had this explosion that took place, I guess first at Martin Luther King's brother's house, Reverend King, and virtually demolished his house, so that he was very fortunate to escape. About 30 minutes later, an explosion took place 4 miles away at a motel where Martin Luther King stays, and badly damaged it. Immediately, at both places, crowds gathered. And, then the crowds got angry, but the police said the sheriff's office were able to have the situation reasonably under control. There was some brick throwing, and the crowd was unfriendly, but by 2:00 or so in the morning they had the situation reasonably under control.

At that time, the Governor moved in 2[00] or 300 of these special deputies. And the newsmen, Claude Sitton and others, heard the police tell them to put their guns back in the cars, that they didn't need them, but they got out anyway and they started shoving people around, sticking their guns into people, and hitting them with billies . . . and then the crowd became more [*unclear*] riots and brickthrowing. All of this lasted for the next three or four hours and almost got out of hand. A number of the policemen were badly hurt, and I guess a number of the Negroes were badly hurt. And it was very close to becoming complete chaos.

During the course of it a couple of buildings were set on fire and it appears that a Negro was responsible for that. When the fire department came to put the fire out, a number of Negroes gathered and started throwing rocks and stones and all kinds of things and wouldn't let them put the fire out. And then another building caught on fire and the fire department then refused to come back because they said it was so difficult. The result is, I guess, both buildings burned down.

The crowds dispersed as of about daylight this morning, 5[:00] or 6:00. And all of the police, all of the sheriff's office were up, around and active. The leaders of the Negroes feel that the sheriff's office and the police handled themselves reasonably well. And the leaders at least don't have any complaints about them. They do have very bitter complaints about the people who were sent in by the Governor.

The sheriff said that he didn't think that those who were responsible for the violence as far as the Negroes were concerned were those who were associated with Martin Luther King, but they were the criminal element of Birmingham, and the individuals who never liked the police. Today everybody on both sides, the police department side and to a considerable extent the Negroes, were all worked up about it.

The Negro Reverend Walker, whose wife got hit by a butt of a rifle (she had headaches all day), he said that the Negroes, when dark comes tonight, that they're going to start going after the policemen—headhunting—and try to shoot to kill the policemen. He said it's completely out of hand.

Martin Luther King is coming back; I guess he is probably in Birmingham at the present time. He is going to have a rally or meeting at 5:00 in which he is going to ask all the Negroes to go back home and stay home tonight and stay off the streets, and that violence has no role to play in this. And that they should pray for what they did last night, causing disorder. He'll have some effect on those that attend; the rest, it's questionable. On the other side, they've got, I suppose, 6[00] or 700 policemen now, with the ones that they've deputized, the ones the Governor sent in, the police that are there anyway in the sheriff's office. . . .

So they're going to have the city pretty well patrolled. They're going to be careful, be on top of the situation. On the other side, the Negroes who are tough and mean and have guns, who have been bitter for a long period of time, who are worked up about this, and figure one of the best services they can perform is to shoot some of them.

So if you have an incident, and the incident, another bombing for instance, or something like that, or a fire, and it attracted large numbers of Negroes, the situation might very well get out of hand. The sheriff's office said that he thought that if they had the same kind of situation as last night, that they probably wouldn't be able to control them because of the feeling of the policemen, et cetera.

Now we have, as far as sending the troops in, we discussed it for a long period of time and of course there are the obvious drawbacks. We don't have the clear-cut situation that we've had in the other situations where we sent either marshals or troops in. We don't have the situation getting completely out of hand as it did in Montgomery a year ago with the Freedom Riders. In addition to protecting the riders traveling through the state, and then you sent your personal emissary down, John Siegenthaler, and then he was beaten, after the Governor had given you assurances he would maintain law and order.[4] We had an excuse, really, sending marshals in at that time. We had certainly as far as Oxford.

We don't have the same type of situation at the present time. The Governor has indicated publicly that he is going to maintain law and order. The group that has gotten out of hand has not been the white people, it's been the Negroes, by and large. So to work up a proclamation, which you'd give us, the basis of which to send troops in, at this time, is far more difficult.

The argument for sending troops in and taking some forceful action, is what's going to happen in the future. You're going to have these kind of incidents: the Governor has virtually taken over the city. You're going to have his people around sticking bayonets in people, and hitting people with clubs and guns, et cetera, you're going to have rallies all over the country calling upon the President to take some forceful action, and why aren't you protecting the rights of the people in Birmingham? And we feel that based on the success that they had in Birmingham, and the feeling of the Negroes generally, and the reports that we get from other cities (not just in the South), but that this could trigger off a good deal of violence around the country now. The Negroes' saying that they have been abused for all these years, and they are going to have to start following the ideas of the Black Muslims, not go along with the white people.

If they feel, on the other hand, that the federal government is their friend, and is intervening for them, is going to work for them, this could head some of that off. I think that's the strongest argument for doing something: the fact that we're going to have more difficulties down in Birmingham. It won't perhaps be as clear cut, as it is at the present time about sending somebody in because there're going to be smaller incidents, and perhaps be more difficult to hang our hat on as to why we should send it in.

Now I want to suggest an alternative or a possibility. What we could perhaps do in this case. It's got some disadvantages and some advantages. It's sort of a halfway step, of landing these 3[00] or 400 troops in Birmingham and just saying that they are going to stand by. Put a statement out

---

[4]John Seigenthaler was Robert Kennedy's administrative assistant. On May 20, 1961, during the Freedom Rides through the South, he was brutally attacked by a mob in Montgomery, Alabama, when he came to the aid of one of the Freedom Riders.

by you that you're greatly concerned: maintenance of law and order, the rights of people, et cetera. That these troops will stay in Birmingham and we'll make a determination as time goes by as to whether they should be used, and whether you're going to issue a proclamation to move them into the city. The second alternative to that would be to move them to Fort McClellan.

Unidentified: About 30 miles away.

Robert Kennedy: Thirty miles away. And have it get out that you sent 4[00] or 500 troops in there and that perhaps that more will go in tomorrow morning.

President Kennedy: The problem really isn't the maintenance of law and order, as you said, is it, because it might be that if we send the troops into Birmingham or McClellan, there would be no disturbances, because there was sort of a repression of the city?

Robert Kennedy: That's right.

President Kennedy: Then they might tear up that paper agreement they made. Therefore, you'd have the Negroes knocked out again without getting the agreement and then we wouldn't have any reason to go in there.

Robert Kennedy: The committee that made the agreement, that backed up the agreement, is meeting right now. And it's going to be suggested to them by one of their leaders that they make their names public. To say that they made this agreement and that they come out publicly for it. Maintenance of law and order and say that we are going to live up to it. So let it be spread throughout the city. Now these are the people that really control Birmingham: the wealthy, the important.

President Kennedy: They've been able to keep that agreement quiet; I don't know how.

Robert Kennedy: The names, you mean? Yeah.

President Kennedy: Yeah. What is King? I mean King has said that we should issue a statement. . . .

Robert Kennedy: Now as part of sending the troops to some other place. The preference would be, the first thing we'd do, we'd announce that Burke Marshall is going back. The second thing is probably you would get out that you already have a general in Birmingham. And that's already landed there, and that's making this available. And that Burke Marshall is going back and that you are watching the situation. And the third step is the fact that you are sending these troops in and they'll be landing in another hour and some more will come tonight. And, then—

President Kennedy: Let's see, under that strategy, I would issue some sort of a statement from here which would be asking the Negroes to stay off the streets, and so on, and then asking that the agreement which was made be implemented and so . . . Then, uh, Burke Marshall will be going back, then we put the troops in at the airport. How far is the airport?

Unidentified: It's 5 miles from the center of the town, Mr. President.

President Kennedy: The General, let's say you began to have trouble during the evening. Once we announce that the troops had arrived, the Governor would probably issue a statement saying that he had complete . . .

Robert Kennedy: Well then I think you'd probably have to nationalize the Guard, too. So he doesn't take over the Guard.[5]

President Kennedy: . . . He would announce that he has control of the city. . . . So it really is just a question, we have to have two things: First, we have to have law and order, and therefore the Negroes not to be running around the city. And then secondly, we have to get this arrangement working. . . . We can't just have the Negroes not running around the city and then have that agreement blow up because . . . If the agreement blows up, the other remedy we have under that condition then is to send legislation up to the Congress this week as our response to that action happening. Say there's this case; unless there's a means of getting relief, we have to provide legislation. We may have to do that anyway, but at least that would be our public response if that agreement blows up.

Kennedy pauses briefly while several people make interjections.

The only thing is, supposing we put our troops in there and then these whites then say, "Well now we are going to withdraw from the agreement." Or do you think they would?

Burke Marshall: I can't tell what they'd do. I think, Mr. President, the Governor and the outgoing city government are doing everything they can to make that agreement blow up—the basic reason the situation is so difficult. I shouldn't wonder but what these highway patrol are deliberately being awfully tough to provoke incidents on the theory that the more incidents they can provoke, the more [*unclear*] in the city and the more scared everyone gets, including the white businessmen.

President Kennedy: Do we have any idea what the white businessmen would think if we put troops in there?

Unidentified: They would not like it.

President Kennedy: They wouldn't like it?

Marshall: No. I'm quite sure. . . .

President Kennedy: You haven't talked to any of them today, have you?

---

[5]By nationalizing the Guard, the President, rather than the Governor, would have authority over the National Guard.

Marshall: No. . . . You see, their whole desire is to prevent that. They want Birmingham to look like Atlanta, and they want it to solve its own problems.[6] So their desire is to prevent that. So they wouldn't like it. And they might rather have that than have a racial war down there, but those are the alternatives, and they understand them clearly as they did last week. They made concessions to the Negroes because they'd rather make concessions then have a great deal of racial disturbances. So again if the alternatives were clear to them, maybe they wouldn't mind. But the immediate reaction of sending troops in there would be very bad, I'm sure. As the Attorney General says, I think in the case of Montgomery, in the case of Oxford, a great many people in the South who are white really thought we had to do what we did. And I don't think a great many white people in the South would think we'd have to send troops into Birmingham.

President Kennedy: This has a lot of Oxford in it, doesn't it?

Marshall: Yes it does, but it's different, because there we had a white mob against a Negro, a single Negro. Here we have a Negro mob. . . .

President Kennedy: Well, except, that's why one of [the] things would be to control the Negro mob. That's one of our purposes. That's the only purpose; what we've got is twofold: to provide an atmosphere in which this agreement can be carried out, and in the meanwhile to prevent the Negroes from rioting, and therefore prevent the whites from reacting against it. That's our purpose. The question really would be, what would be the thing about landing the troops at the airport—outside, without going in.

Responding to Kennedy, various participants, including McNamara, discussed the nuts and bolts of deploying troops. Seemingly uninterested in that level of detail at this stage in the meeting, Kennedy cuts them off and asks Burke Marshall how freely he talks to Martin Luther King.

Marshall: I talk to him freely. I'll tell you what he intends to do, Mr. President. He intends to go to this church and call upon his people to [*unclear*] the Attorney General said. And then tomorrow, he intends to go around the city and visit pool halls and saloons and talk to the Negroes and preach against violence. Those are his intentions.

President Kennedy: Now what has he, he's issued a statement calling upon me to make a statement. But what our problem is here, we can make the statement, but if there is going to be violence there tonight, that is obviously what Governor Wallace wants. We don't want to, we don't like

---

[6]With respect to race relations, Atlanta was considered a far more enlightened city than Birmingham.

to put troops in there because then we think it is going to be more difficult for a success to be made of this agreement. But we will if there's going to be violence there tonight. Now, what is his judgment about that?

Marshall answers that he hasn't discussed this with King.

President Kennedy: Well, I think you ought to look like you're talking just on your own, without saying we're considering it then. What our problem is, is to try to make a judgment on whether the Negro community is going to be out in the street tonight. If it is, then we are going to have to put troops in there because they're either going to get beaten up or they're going to beat somebody up. Maybe he can't tell us that. The other thing is, he [King] wants me to make a statement. I don't know what a statement . . . He said today that he hopes would not jeopardize. [*reading from the Martin Luther King statement*] "these bombings, et cetera." Now there's one other thing where he's asked me to make a statement. [*shuffling of papers, again reading from King statement*] ". . . said today the new outbursts would make it mandatory to take a forthright stand against the indignities as to . . ."

Robert Kennedy: I think you can make a statement because I mean you can say about the fact that these two places have been bombed. His brother's house was bombed . . .

President Kennedy: Yeah.

Robert Kennedy: . . . and the motel was bombed.

President Kennedy: We'd also urge the Negroes to . . .

Robert Kennedy: I mean you can make a pretty strong statement, I think, this time.

President Kennedy: In fact, also though, in this one that came in. The Negroes ought to keep off the street. Otherwise, we're just saying that the Negroes are being mistreated. I mean I've got to put some word about the Negroes staying home because otherwise it's just inflammatory about their abuses again without urging them to keep quiet to permit an atmosphere to develop where the agreement of this week can be carried out. Anyway, Burke, why don't you see what he has to say? What I'd like to find out from him is, if it's possible for us to tell him, is whether the atmosphere is going to be such that we're liable to have violence in the streets tonight and therefore . . .

Robert Kennedy: I think it will be tough for him to tell us.

·   ·   ·

The meeting then turned to the situation on the ground in Birmingham. Robert Kennedy argued that while troops might have to be sent, it was not necessary to do so that night. The problem, he noted, was a long-term one. Order could be restored, but if the indignities against Birmingham's blacks continued, the result would be many weeks of unrest and potential violence. No one in the room joined Bobby in ruminating about the big picture, and the discussion once again turned to the logistics of a possible deployment. Would the troops be sent to the airport or to Fort McClellan? Where would they stay once they arrived? Perhaps remembering how difficult it was to deploy troops in Oxford, the President was particularly concerned about how long it would take to get troops into Birmingham, and he spent several minutes trying to pin down the exact number of hours it would take from the time he gave the order. He then turned again to Burke Marshall, who had just gotten off the phone with King.

.   .   .

President Kennedy: What does he say?

Marshall: [*very softly, parts inaudible*] Well, he says that he thinks if there are no other incidents, no other bombings, that he can control his people. Of course he just got there and he says that. I asked him, I said I saw that he had called upon the President to give a statement. I asked him what kind of a statement. He didn't really know—a statement calling on everyone to be decent and respect law and order, not condoning violence at all, but pointing out [*unclear*] Attorney General said, that this kind of thing stands [*unclear*] right. So that was all. He's leaving for the church in about 25 minutes. And he's going to call upon, he's going to try to get on radio and call for law and order. He's going to try to organize the Negroes to go around to the communities. He said a lot of those people were drunk last night.

President Kennedy: Yeah.

Marshall: And Sunday's a better night than Saturday.

President Kennedy: He didn't say anything about troops, did he?

Marshall: No he didn't. Well, I didn't bring it up.

President Kennedy: Well now, it seems to me, let's just say we initiated the troops now. We've got one group who wouldn't get there, anyway, for an hour and a half anyway if we put everybody in the air. The only question really would be whether you just stick them out at that airport.

Robert Kennedy: I don't know that you can rescue the thing tonight in any case because of the fact that you wouldn't have enough and you're going into a strange city and all and trying to put the thing together. And if a real riot broke out and the only way a riot's going to break out, it's going to get out of hand from the local people, that means you have 2[,000] or 3,000 Negroes. And then suddenly march 300 fellows in, who've never seen anything [*unclear*] in that city. Twenty-five percent of it would be Negroes themselves; I think it would be damned tough. I think if you just got the Army into it, you'd want to be able do it in such a way that you'd want to so overwhelm them.

I think that the alternative to that is that this is more a psychological move, that you say that you hope law and order be maintained so that you're moving these people to Fort McClellan. You put out your statement. Burke goes down there and says that they're available, but with no hint to anybody or feeling that we can ever move tonight. You might issue a proclamation tomorrow morning or issue a proclamation tonight, which would bring more troops in. I mean for instance if you had a riot tonight at midnight, then you'd issue a proclamation and say I'm going to bring in large troops. We're going to start to take over, but you would not have the feeling that you're going to start to take over until 6:00 tomorrow morning or 8:00 tomorrow morning. I think it would be pretty tough, don't you?

Unidentified: It would be very difficult, Mr. Attorney [General].

Several people speak at once.

President Kennedy: The law and order isn't any good unless we can get the agreement implemented; otherwise—

Marshall: He made that point, Mr. President; just as I said to you, he said that if this causes the businessmen to go back on their agreement, he says I can't control the people.[7] I think that's absolutely—

President Kennedy: That's right. Well, in other words, if they went back on their agreement, it would seem to me that would be sufficient then for us to decide that we ought to get in there. Now the thing is, if we are going in there, let's just say we don't go in there now, how can we get a buildup so we can really; I think one of the important things about Oxford was we got so goddamn many in there.

.   .   .

For the rest of the meeting, the participants turned again to the logistics of the deployment. A consensus emerged that it would be best to deploy some federal troops and to restore law and order, and that it was important to signal to all parties that the federal government would not allow the situation to be resolved by violence. Kennedy wanted to make sure that all contingencies were considered, and he repeatedly mentioned the Oxford episode. As a result of that experience, Kennedy factored in potential delays of several hours. It was not merely a question of how long the transport flight might take, but also a matter of assembling the troops and establishing communications and liaison with local officials.

Kennedy and his advisers were also concerned that Governor Wallace might use the deployment to announce large-scale resistance to the civil rights movement's aims and claim that federal troops were proof that "the

---

[7]"He" refers to Martin Luther King, who made the point in a telephone conversation with Marshall.

President had invaded the state of Alabama." That could mean a mini–civil war between Klu Klux Klan members and young black rioters. While no one thought this was a likely course of events, such concerns suggested just how tense the situation was.

In the end, the President decided to place all Army forces near Birmingham on alert and prepared to federalize Alabama's National Guard in case Wallace tried to resist the President's actions. Kennedy then gave a televised address to the nation that evening (May 12), the outlines of which had been hashed out at the end of the meeting. "The Government will do whatever must be done to preserve order, to protect the lives of its citizens, and to uphold the law of the land," he declared. "The Birmingham agreement [of May 10] was and is a fair and just accord. It recognized the fundamental rights of all citizens to be accorded equal treatment. . . . The Federal government will not permit it to be sabotaged by a few extremists on either side who think they can defy both the law and the wishes of responsible citizens by inciting or inviting violence."

It was an unusually strong statement from Kennedy, marking an unambiguous stance in support of the civil rights movement. Kennedy had several more meetings on the Birmingham situation, including one he taped on May 21. More important, Birmingham was a turning point for the administration, and the events of that May became a catalyst that caused Kennedy to introduce a civil rights bill in Congress just a few weeks later. The May 21 meeting came a day after a meeting that focused on the outlines of the administration's bill. For King, the SCLC, and the civil rights movement, the Birmingham gamble had paid off.

President Kennedy convened the meeting on May 21 in order to conduct a postmortem on Birmingham. Calm had returned to the city, but the President and his brother wanted to review what had happened. Having dealt with Oxford and now Birmingham, they realized they could well face similar situations in the months to come. It was imperative, therefore, to understand what had occurred, and it was essential to look for ways to respond more effectively in the future. Like generals going over a recently concluded battle, the Kennedy brothers considered how to improve the administration's performance should the need arise again.

Robert Kennedy began the meeting by providing a compelling summary of the way the crisis had evolved. After completing this taut overview, he turned to the matter of black grievances, noting that southern blacks felt they lacked effective means to register their frustrations. Though Birmingham officials had promised to hire more blacks in the municipal government, Robert Kennedy acknowledged that the hiring record of the federal government in the South was abysmal and asked

John Macy, the chairman of the Civil Service Commission, to brief the President on proposed steps to remedy the problem. Following the lead of the Attorney General, Macy recognized that it was necessary for the administration to act quickly to address the matter, lest it be revealed as lagging behind Birmingham in rectifying discriminatory hiring practices.

Tuesday, May 21, 1963, 10:15 A.M.

Meeting on Birmingham

Including President Kennedy, Robert Kennedy, John Macy, Lawrence O'Brien, and others.

The tape begins midsentence.

Robert Kennedy: . . . to come out for some accommodation with the Negroes were as against him coming back and we were against him coming back.[8] And we tried to prevail upon him to wait until Boutwell had been able to take over the administration of the city and put in the reforms that he indicated that he would do.[9] So we were not successful.

He came back and, as I say, did not have the support of the Negro community and he sought a license to parade and to put on a demonstration and Bull Connor refused. So he went out and got eight or ten people and they were all arrested. So the next day he decided to have another demonstration and this time because ten people had been arrested, twenty people came out, and then they were arrested. And then when they were arrested, that got a little bit more publicity, although the papers had arranged between them that they would never put this on the front page and that they would play it down. Television played it up and it got around the Negro community. So then he started to get more and more support as more and more of his people were arrested.

Then he got himself arrested on Good Friday so that he stays in jail over Easter Sunday and then of course he got everybody around the Negro community and then he came out. And he started having larger and larger demonstrations and as more and more people were arrested, the Negro community, the local Negro community, felt that they couldn't let him do all these things by himself cause they didn't have the support. So they started to support him.

---

[8]Robert Kennedy is referring to Martin Luther King.
[9]Albert Boutwell was the mayor of Birmingham.

And then the NAACP, which had been strongly against him going in there and having these demonstrations, they started to feel that they had to support him because they were losing everything to him. And so finally you start getting more and more people who come his way. And then he hit upon the idea of having children come out and that's when the thousands of people started to gather.

He got these large groups of people out, Friday or Saturday about two and a half weeks ago. And there was then of course with all those children and all those people, there was great danger. The problem at that time was that the white people and the Negro people weren't talking to one another. Many in the Negro leadership didn't know what they were demonstrating about. They didn't know whether they were demonstrating to get rid of Bull Connor or whether they were demonstrating about the stores or whether they were demonstrating against the city government. Ninety percent of the people who were demonstrating certainly didn't know what they were demonstrating about and none of the white community knew what they were demonstrating about. None of the white community would get near the Negro community at that juncture because they felt that they were being disorderly and so nobody was talking to anybody. And you had all these demonstrations, which were getting larger and larger.

So then the President sent Burke Marshall down . . . [to] Birmingham to see if something could be done about getting people together. First, he went to the Negro community to find out what they wanted. And that was difficult because a lot of them didn't know what they wanted. And finally, through efforts with Martin Luther King, found out what they wanted, which [*unclear*] to desegregate the lunch counters, which was to take the signs off the toilets and the drinking fountains, to have a better hiring system in Birmingham in the department stores, and to hire at least one clerk in one of the stores.

So he went back to the white community to the department store heads, the majority of whom were branch stores and had their main offices outside the city, and told them this. So they started having meetings: Douglas Dillon and some others called the heads of the big chains.[10] I spoke to some of them and expressed our concern. Burke met with the local people in Birmingham, and finally they said that they'd be willing to do some of these things, but that they would want to wait until something else happened in Birmingham. They wanted to have some other desegregation take place before they took the first step. And what they hit upon was the schools. When the schools were desegregated, they said that they would

---

[10]C. Douglas Dillon was President Kennedy's Treasury Secretary.

then do these other things. Well, the earliest the schools would be desegregated was September, so the Negroes were unwilling to wait until that happened. And the department stores said they were unwilling to take the first step so the result was, this was into Monday, Tuesday. And then the demonstrations got larger and larger, and then as demonstrations got into thousands, of course, they got out of hand. Then Martin Luther King preaches nonviolence and "if you're hit, you kneel down and say your prayers, and don't hit back," which is all very good. And those who hear him, they follow him exceptionally well. I mean there is no violence as far as the Negroes are concerned.

But the Negro community of Birmingham has probably the toughest group of Negroes in the country. And so when some of them started to turn out, they [*unclear*] with the police for a long period of time. And they came out with their bricks and their knives and they stood on the fringe and they started throwing bricks and started running through the park and going into the department stores. And so the situation had gotten completely out of hand.

The white community, then, became, itself, became exercised, concerned as to what they should do. And we felt that if we could get the substantial white citizens who owned the, ran the financial life of Birmingham behind the department store heads, that perhaps we could get the department store heads to move. So they had a meeting down there, and Burke attended it, and said that what you were going to have in Birmingham was complete chaos. You would have bloodshed unless something was done—that the Negro demands were quite reasonable, and that they should support the department store heads and urge them to make this agreement. Finally, some of these meetings went to 4:00 or 5:00 in the morning and Burke was the only contact between the whites and the Negroes, and finally brought them together and the white financial, economic leaders agreed to support the department store heads and then they would go down the line and they also would take steps to improve the lot of the Negroes. When that happened, the department store heads said that they would make this agreement.

Then we got in touch with Martin Luther King and said that they had agreed to make the agreement and he said, "Well, I've had businessmen tell me in Albany that they'd made an agreement and then they didn't keep their word, so we are going to go on with the demonstrations." We said to him that you had the demonstrations to accomplish a certain purpose, you've accomplished that purpose, then to go on with the demonstration doesn't make a great deal of sense. He said, "Well, I've got to get people out of jail. The only way to get my people out of jail (he then had a couple of thousand in jail) is to have demonstrations so that they have so many people who are in jail and such a crisis in Birmingham, that they let everybody out of jail."

This really didn't make a great deal of sense. But if he'd had another day of demonstrations, you would have had great bloodshed in Birmingham and then the Governor who would then start moving into Birmingham, would have taken over the city. So you would never have anything accomplished.

So we were able to prevail upon him to call off his demonstrations, just really in time because I don't think there was any question by that Wednesday night, the Governor would have moved into the city and he would have had complete control of it and you would never have had any of these gains.

So they called off their demonstrations and then you had the Saturday night at ten after eleven, you had one stick of dynamite thrown in Martin Luther King's brother's house and then thirty minutes later, 11:40, you had eight sticks of dynamite were thrown in the Gaston Motel where Martin Luther King had stayed. The Negroes gathered, several thousands, when the police came and the fire department came with their fire hoses. They threw rocks and stones, brought out their knives. They got out of hand.

The local police—the sheriff's office and the police department—by 2:00 in the morning had brought them pretty much under control. Then the Governor sent his people in and his people were game wardens with armbands and alcohol and tax people with armbands and tough [*unclear*]. They had carbines and they got out of their cars with clubs with these guns and the local police asked them to get back, go away, that they had the situation under control, and that they would kill somebody and they said that's what they were here for. So then they started clubbing people, beating them, and then the situation got completely out of control for the next three hours. And it was finally brought under control about 6:00 Sunday morning.

Well, the Negro [*unclear*] felt that they had been betrayed and, so all day Sunday, they indicated quite clearly that that night you were going to have a real war in Birmingham. A number of them were armed. They had knives; they had guns, and that they were going after these people with the armbands. And they felt that the Governor had come in, taken over the city, and that there was no solution as far as they were concerned.

The President then made the determination to send the troops into Alabama and that they would be available to be used in Birmingham if it was felt to be necessary, and he also went on television that night just before Martin Luther King came back and made a speech to the Negroes.

That changed the whole complexion of the situation because Martin Luther King told these people to calm down and stay at home—that the federal government was interested and was going to be active in the situation to protect them. The fact that we moved the troops into Alabama calmed the Negro community down so there weren't any incidents because I don't think there's any question that if that step hadn't been taken that night, that the Negro community would have gotten out of hand and you would have had a tough fight between the governor's people and the Negro community.

We think that the agreement will be kept that was made. And there are problems such as yesterday the school board suspending the thousand students that participated in the demonstrations. The Negro lawyer's going to bring a lawsuit, which we may or may not enter also to try to enjoin the school board from suspending the students. That will have to be worked out, but at least it would appear that the agreement that was made will be kept at least at the present time. We are optimistic about it. We're not out of the woods as yet, but I think we feel that we have a good chance of having that kept.

The lessons that we've learned from it are: First, the importance of having some biracial committee in a community. Each one of these local communities and in the state the Negroes and the whites talking to one another so that they can air their grievances. One of the great problems as far as the Negroes we found in the last two and a half years, is that they feel there is no solution for what they want to accomplish, that nobody will talk to them. And in community after community we find that to be so, that they don't have—the Negroes feel that they have grievances—that there is no place for them to go. Then they want to demonstrate and they can't get a license to demonstrate. And so that they want to walk down the street and they're not given a license, and therefore they're put in jail. That exercises the other Negroes: they don't have anyplace to go, they don't have anyplace to complain, and they can't picket about it because then they're put in jail. So they feel a sense of frustration, and that's what's growing up in the South and really in the northern cities.

The second thing that we learned and which I'd like to take up with you today is when Burke met with these business leaders in Birmingham and talked to them about hiring Negroes, they looked at the government agencies and said, "Well why should we hire Negroes? You don't hire Negroes." And we looked at the situation in Birmingham and found that it's really a disgraceful situation as far as the government departments are concerned—that we really had done a very poor job.

The Veterans' Administration [VA] had done well and there were a number of Negroes who were employed by the Post Office. But by and large, they were of very low grade. There weren't any Negroes that held any positions that anybody could see them, except perhaps somebody to sweep the floor or something like that. Otherwise, they weren't being used as clerks or out front in positions of importance in any of these offices. And so we felt that something needed to be done to remedy that and that you could do it quickly. I talked to a number of you about the situation in your own department and John Macy did a great deal about pulling it all together and I think we helped the situation down there. But sorry, Mr. President, I'd like to have maybe Mr. Macy give a report as to what the situation was in Birmingham and what it is in some of these other major cities, and what's been done about it in Birmingham.

John Macy: Thank you, Mr. President, the facts that we confronted in Birmingham were not at all encouraging, as the Attorney General has indicated. Aside from the VA and the Post Office, there were approximately 15 Negroes employed out of a total employment of 2,000 in Birmingham. We met with the agency representatives in Birmingham last week and endeavored to identify vacancies that were available and moved to hire as quickly as we possibly could. I can report that we do have now commitments for 16 positions since last Thursday: 8 of them in Social Security, 6 in Treasury, 1 in GSA, and 1 in the Post Office.[11] This is just a start. Social Security is particularly helpful. They have indicated that they have about 130 vacancies that must be filled in their payments center there that must be filled by the 15th of July. Work directly with them.

The only other agency that has come up with any vacancies at all as a result of these discussions is the Air Force with four. There is great difficulty in finding qualified Negroes in the Birmingham community. This a product of the poor educational system, the cultural atmosphere that's existed for a long time. We can't be daunted by this. It's necessary that we join forces, work with the Negro community and with Negro leadership to identify the sources of talent that will meet our qualification standards. I'd like to suggest a program of six action steps, which I believe would be helpful with respect to Birmingham.

First, I think it's necessary to reemphasize with our federal representatives in that city that we really mean business. That we can no longer say that because the community does not support this kind of equal opportunity that we are not going to have it in the federal service. Frankly, we found less than a sense of urgency on the part of the federal representa-

---

[11]The abbreviation GSA stands for General Services Administration.

tives when we met with them down there. And anything that can be done from the top down to the local representatives needs to be done. We may even need to change some of our local representatives in that community and others.

Second, there's a need to urge the agency representatives to identify present and prospective vacancies. There's an amazing lack of awareness of any possible vacancies. This was part of our difficulty in trying to determine just what our objectives would be.

Third, we need the assistance of the agencies in recruiting. Generally, the feeling is that this is the Civil Service Commission's job and that's proper, but I think the entire federal community needs to join in the publicity, needs to join in emphasizing the good faith of the federal government at the local level in doing something about [it].

Fourth, I think that in some of the agencies where there are jobs, it may be possible to do a bit of job engineering to change some of the qualification standards so that there will be more doors open to Negroes than has been traditionally the case.

Fifth, I think that we can engage in some strategic placement in view of the fact that there are so few Negroes in these agencies. By that I mean positions that have some visibility in the community: positions that would be judged as leadership models in making it possible for Negroes to be placed.

And sixth, we need to screen in the agencies where there are Negroes to find what talent exists. We found in Birmingham, for example, that there are 50 postal employees—Negroes—who have college degrees. Now, the bona fides of those college degrees may be under question. But this is something that we need to look at. This would constitute a resource for other agencies to draw upon for higher-level jobs requiring a college degree or that level of educational experience.

So that these it seems to me are concrete steps we can take in Birmingham. Now I feel as I have indicated to the Attorney General that rather than wait for these other communities to flare up and then react, that we ought to move in and analyze the employment situation in each one. We started doing that yesterday and we have the first facts. I won't take your time to go into them, but let me say that in Montgomery; Nashville; Memphis; Albany, Georgia; Jackson; Raleigh; and Greensboro, where we ran checks yesterday, the situation isn't any better than it is in Birmingham. And again, it's the VA and the Post Office that have the bulk of the Negroes that are employed and the percentage of Negroes in total employment is very low.

.   .   .

For the next few minutes, Bobby Kennedy and Macy discussed in detail how the federal government could improve its hiring practices. The President had little to say, but as the meeting was drawing to a close, he reflected on what could be done to increase African American employment. Perhaps Kennedy was thinking about the outlines of the bill he had decided to submit to Congress, and it is possible he was mulling over what provisions to include in the bill. The question of hiring practices, which would have to be addressed in any meaningful civil rights legislation, might have piqued his interest.

Clearly, Birmingham had done what nothing else had. It had moved civil rights to the top of Kennedy's agenda. Events in the southern city had been front-page news in papers throughout the country, the news weeklies had highlighted the episode, and the television networks had shone a bright light on the tactics of Bull Connor. The images of black Americans being brutalized by southern policemen and German shepherds and of young men and women having their clothes torn from their bodies by high-pressure water hoses had roused a largely indifferent population. Like so many others, those in the White House had come to realize that something had to be done. The ground had shifted. And on a more practical level, the Kennedy administration would now come under intense pressure from congressional liberals, such as Minnesota's senator Hubert Humphrey, to move ahead on civil rights. Having dithered for nearly two and a half years, Kennedy finally stepped forward and would introduce into Congress a far-reaching bill. But first he had to determine what that bill would look like and how hard he was prepared to work to make it become law.

Chapter 4
The Bill and the March

O n June 11, President Kennedy appeared on national television to announce that he would shortly submit a civil rights bill to congress. Civil rights was "a moral issue . . . as old as the Scriptures and as clear as the American Constitution," he declared. What good is freedom, the President wondered, if an American citizen, whatever the color of his skin, "cannot eat lunch in a restaurant open to the public, if he cannot send his children to the best public schools available, if he cannot vote for the public officials who represent him?" The country had gone too long without redressing such wrongs. And black Americans had waited too long, as well. The time had come, Kennedy asserted, for Congress to address these problems.

According to the historian Carl Brauer, this speech marked the beginning of the "second Reconstruction," a moment when all three branches of government began to work together to help secure the rights of African Americans. And significantly, the President's address to the nation "marked a turning point," which saw Kennedy move from the periphery to the center of the struggle for civil rights.

Throughout May and June, policymakers worked energetically to draw up the outlines of the proposed bill. Not only did Kennedy and his primary civil rights advisers meet to discuss the bill, but they also caucused with key congressmen and civil rights leaders. Unlike previous legislative efforts, including the one Kennedy had recommended in March 1963, this bill would confront the heated issue of discrimination in public accommodations. The Montgomery bus boycott had begun in 1955 over the right to sit where one wanted on a city bus, and few aspects of Jim Crow highlighted so starkly the persistence of institutionalized oppression as did separate eating facilities, separate seating, and separate accommodations. Every day such indignities reinforced the unequal treatment of black

Americans. While the denial of the vote was surely just as consequential—after all, disfranchisement made it even more difficult to change the law—the existence of separate water fountains, lunch counters, and bathrooms was a constant source of humiliation experienced by every black man, woman, and child.

The quest for equal access had driven the Birmingham demonstrations, and the "equal access" provisions of the proposed legislation set it apart from the weak laws of 1957 and 1960. Along with education and voting rights, equal access ranked as the key grievance for the African American population, and, not surprisingly, it would generate intense resistance from southern legislators in Congress.

Four weeks had separated Kennedy's announcement from the end of the Birmingham crisis, a month in which the White House was faced with a crisis in Jackson, Mississippi, and a confrontation with the governor of Alabama, George Wallace. At the end of May, several large demonstrations rocked Jackson as blacks demanded an end to segregation in the schools and at lunch counters, and the employment of more black policemen and crossing guards. Tragically, the unrest in Jackson culminated in the assassination of NAACP field secretary Medger Evers, on June 11—the very evening Kennedy addressed the nation. On that same extraordinary day, Governor Wallace had finally given in to federal pressure and allowed two black students to enroll at the University of Alabama, although he denounced the Kennedy administration for its unlawful usurpation of state power.

It was in mid-May that Kennedy appeared to have made his decision to support far-reaching civil rights legislation, and the meetings he recorded focused on several facets of the legislative process. The first concerned the provisions of the bill. Within the administration, people differed on how far the President ought to go, an issue that was not simply a moral question, but a question of what was politically possible. What kind of bill could the administration get through Congress? Another question concerned goals. Was the aim in fact to change the law or merely to be seen as taking a stand against discrimination, regardless of the bill's political feasibility? Kennedy was under considerable pressure from northern liberals and civil rights leaders to go all out and include a variety of legislative remedies, regardless of whether such a bill could achieve passage. Some believed that in the long run it would be better for an American president to stand unequivocally for civil rights reform, whatever the outcome, at that moment of the legislative process.

But John Kennedy was a pragmatist who would not sacrifice his administration on the altar of civil rights. If he was going to spend political capital on a civil rights bill, he would do so for a bill that he thought was both right and viable, and he would only devote his efforts to a bill he believed had a good chance of becoming law. Public accommodations and voting rights each demanded a monumental battle, and Kennedy was convinced it was prudent to fight for one at a time. Thus, voting rights would be left until a later date.

The first meeting occurred on May 20, 1963. The participants entered the meeting with a variety of shared assumptions and questions, many of which were not stated explicitly. For example, the White House had to contend with legislation that was already making its way through Congress and figure out how best to launch the campaign for a new bill. Should the bill be introduced in the House or in the Senate? Should the administration take the lead or should it find appropriate senators and congressmen to champion the bill in public? What public role should civil rights leaders play? And above all, what separated acceptable risks from unwise ones?

The transcripts suggest that while Kennedy and his advisers supported civil rights reform, they remained suspicious of and resentful toward some civil rights leaders. They were annoyed by Martin Luther King's demand for immediate action and resented having been forced to act, however noble the cause. The meeting begins with a brief discussion of various congressmen and then turns to the question of what to do about civil rights leaders, including the high-profile activist Dick Gregory and New York City's outspoken congressman Adam Clayton Powell. The Attorney General devotes some time to discussing the views of Gregory, with whom he had recently spoken.

Monday, May 20, 1963, 11:25 A.M.

Meeting on Civil Rights

Including President Kennedy, Robert Kennedy, Lawrence O'Brien, Burke Marshall, Theodore Sorensen, Lee White, and Kenneth O'Donnell.

President Kennedy: So I hear you think Gregory wasn't too good yesterday?[1]

---

[1]According to Taylor Branch, activist Dick Gregory met with the Attorney General and Burke Marshall and described tensions among black civil rights leaders (Taylor Branch, *Parting the Waters*, pp. 807–8).

Robert Kennedy: Well, he's on our side. He just thinks we're going to have a lot of trouble. He thinks that there's a complete lack of understanding, and he says the Negroes get mad for no reason at all. He said they want to fight. They want to fight with white people. He says it's true in Chicago. He thinks that that's going to be the big problem area; it's going to be the northern cities. They're just antagonistic and they're mad. You might run a picture with a white boy being chased by a Negro with a knife and they get mad at that because they say that shows the papers are against them and the white people are against them. . . . But I think it's worthwhile keeping in with him because the other fellows aren't reliable. They're all getting tough.

President Kennedy: Negroes?

Robert Kennedy: They're awful tough to deal with now. He says, you can't have a moderate Negro anymore. Because they can't be moderate because all their competitors are not moderate. Everybody's going to be a little bit more extreme than the other one.

President Kennedy: Don't they realize the necessity of maintaining support in the white community?

Robert Kennedy: I think they forget they get us all; like one of them said, yesterday I read in the paper, "We've got them scared now; let's make them run." I think that's what they think. Got the white people on the run. He said these Negroes are all mad and are all over the country. He said I don't know whether it's going to stay that way, but that's the way it looks. He said the place where it's going to come out is in the northern cities.

Unidentified: Adam Clayton Powell made that statement. It's been around. "The whites are running scared now. Let's keep after them."

Lawrence O'Brien: I talked to Powell last week and he says it's very simple. He said, "I'm not going to watch the parade pass me by. I'm going to lead it."

Robert Kennedy: Yeah, Gregory said Powell has got much greater popularity with the Negroes than he ever had before.

O'Brien: Yeah, that's right. And he's the most articulate.

Mixed voices.

Robert Kennedy: They're all mad. For instance, he [Gregory] said that Lyndon Johnson made a speech. They gave him this award Saturday night and I guess he made a speech, and they're [the blacks] all pissed off about that.

President Kennedy: What did he say?

Robert Kennedy: Well, I don't know; he just said what the administration is doing. He said they're all mad at the white liberals because they say they just sit around. They're mad at Weaver because, I don't know quite why they're mad at Weaver exactly.[2] He [Gregory] said Weaver came out and spoke in Chicago and here's a Negro that spoke well and all the rest were mad at that.

President Kennedy: He was a Negro that did what?

Robert Kennedy: Negro that did well and a year ago, this was their proudest symbol. A fellow that had gotten up to this position and spoke well and was articulate, all the rest of it. And was a symbol of a Negro that could be a success. He came out. But they're mad about that. He says nobody could reason with them anymore. It's tough to talk to them. He [Gregory] said he was sitting in a bar where the Negro underworld of Chicago hangs out. Ordinarily, if they hear a police car come down the street, they all run. And a police captain walked in and a couple of the gentlemen told him to get the hell out. They didn't want to see him. He said that's what the riot in Chicago was about. It's because the Negroes are now just antagonistic and mad and they're going to be mad at everything. You can't talk to them. . . . My friends all say the Negro maids and servants are getting antagonistic. She said you don't know how they're sassing me back in my house. [*Unclear*] what you should do. Why don't you fire them?

O'Brien: [*chuckling*] Is this Malcolm X going to play the hill?

Robert Kennedy: He [Gregory] says, "He's nothing!"

Unidentified: Jesus he started having a press conference in the corridor of the House the other day.

Robert Kennedy: Well, that was this week, and he says that because . . . his feeling is that he's nothing. I think he's got somebody in his organization. He's got people all over that he pays. He's putting somebody in down at the university—

President Kennedy: Who? Dick Gregory?

Burke Marshall: Dick Gregory.

Robert Kennedy: He's got a real underworld, underground.

President Kennedy: Is he highly regarded by the Negroes?

Marshall: He's very popular.

President Kennedy: I'll say this. We got a damn good hand in Nashville from the Negroes.

Robert Kennedy: Yeah, I know. That's what John Seigenthaler said.

President Kennedy: When I went through there in the Negro housing thing; Jesus, they're out. I got better applause there than anyplace else in the South, I'll tell you that.

---

[2]Robert Weaver was the African American head of the Housing and Home Finance Administration.

Robert Kennedy: Well, I don't think that they're . . . He says that . . . they surely haven't left us.

President Kennedy: Yeah.

Robert Kennedy: But—

Marshall: Just talking about the summer and the possibility of violence. The race taking place over the problem in St. Louis the other week started just over some white cops arresting people in a crap game.

Robert Kennedy: Turned into a major riot.

Marshall: Yeah. So that's what he was talking about.

Robert Kennedy: He thinks that it's not popularity. Because he says you know these things vary. You probably have to use troops at the University of Alabama, and then you're up to something that they don't like. And that's going to vary. But he says just on the problem of trying to deal with the situation around the country, that's where you're going to have difficulty.

President Kennedy: And [*unclear*] exposure to the dogs.

Robert Kennedy: The dogs. And the Negroes, he [Gregory] said, they're antagonistic and mad, so therefore they're very difficult to deal with. The second point being that you can't get a reasonable Negro leadership because they're competing with one another. Roy Wilkins hates Martin Luther King.[3]

President Kennedy: Of course, they say Weaver's sold out. Any Negro who does well has sold out. Well anyway, what about the legislation? [*Pause.*]

There's a good chance it will be decided against the Negroes. I must say I said to Wallace, I said, "I don't know why they don't take down these signs."[4] And I said, "You've got a lot of the Negroes that are all waiting on everybody at home. Why shouldn't they be, this idea about not hiring clerks." I will say that there has been more progress made, in my opinion, if the Negroes would realize it, by Birmingham for the Negroes because there're a lot of southerners now who are much more ready to accept. I was talking to Smathers the other day and I said, "They can't have these signs saying you can't go into a store. They don't want to go into a store, but they can't. . . . You've got to take all that stuff down."[5] I mean I will say most reasonable southerners say today that you're going to have to . . . you're going . . . the trouble is the Negroes are going to push this thing too far, but they're all going to say he's [*unclear*].

---

[3]Roy Wilkins was the head of the NAACP.
[4]George Wallace was governor of Alabama.
[5]George Smathers was a Democratic senator from Florida.

Marshall: I think, Mr. President, that just judging from my conversation with Gregory, that all the Negro leaders realize that. But the Negro mass in the North, particularly, doesn't see anything except the dogs and hoses. It's all the white cops. But the leaders, I think would—

President Kennedy: Well, that's the idea of the right to demonstrate.[6] What would you do, say an unreasonable limitation on the right to demonstrate?

Unidentified: How about the difficult and unnecessary?

Marshall: Well, Mr. President, I think that's awfully tough.

President Kennedy: Yeah, I don't think—

Marshall: I think that legislation on the whole, if it were passed, would get us in more trouble than it would get us—

President Kennedy: All of it?

Marshall: No, on the right to demonstrate.

President Kennedy: I don't think we ought to touch that one. . . .

.   .   .

The discussion then turned to the wisdom of including provisions in the bill about desegregating higher education. The President was not sure that it was necessary, given that Adam Clayton Powell had already put forward a higher education bill, and he voiced concern that after recent events at the University of Alabama, attaching higher-education provisions to the bill would only raise the stakes of the debate, which were already high, in the House and Senate.

Also discussed was the issue of Title III, a key category from previous civil rights bills (where it was once known as Part III), which provided the Attorney General with the power to file civil rights suits, thus relieving "the black individual in a hostile southern community of the responsibility of filing such a suit."[7] Burke Marshall noted that Title III was critical for black Americans, claiming "it would have a personal impact on their daily lives."

Marshall also spoke about the significance of the public accommodation clause, telling the President that "this business of going in and eating at a lunch counter is . . . one thing that makes all Negroes, regardless of age, maddest." But Robert Kennedy was blind to the issue, claiming that "they can stand at the lunch counters. They don't have to eat there. They can pee before they come to the store or the supermarket."

More broadly, there was continuing uncertainty in the White House

---

[6]President Kennedy briefly raises the idea of limiting African Americans' right to demonstrate in the South.

[7]Robert D. Loevy, *To End All Segregation,* p. 29. As Loevy points out, many African Americans would not have filed suit on their own because the potential danger involved in so doing was too great.

about the constitutional grounds on which the federal government could order desegregation. Eventually, the administration decided to base the law on the interstate commerce clause instead of the equal protection clause set out in the Fourteenth Amendment to the Constitution. While the interstate commerce clause had the advantage that past legal precedent provided (American reformers had used this argument earlier in the twentieth century), it had the disadvantage of being more esoteric and thus less morally compelling than was the equal protection clause of the Constitution.

Lawrence O'Brien, one of Kennedy's closest advisers and a keen student of legislative politics, saw a storm coming. It was impossible, he thought, to predict what Congress would do tomorrow, let alone three months after it had begun debate on the bill. O'Brien was convinced the clash between liberals who favored the legislation and southern conservatives who wished to thwart it would create an impasse, and he saw little chance of avoiding a filibuster in the Senate. He had concluded that the administration was "going to run smack into a straight-out draw that [would] position the extremes on both sides . . . in the Congress."

Bobby Kennedy then presented his wish list, claiming it would be ideal to get a public accommodations law, a school desegregation bill, and a voting rights bill. "If we can get those bills by, it would be damn helpful. Good for the Negroes, relax this thing, and everybody thinks we've been doing something." It would give "us weapons we don't have at the present time. . . ." With these broad goals on the table, the discussion returned to particulars. What about movie theaters? one participant asked. What about swimming pools during the summer? And what about the role of the federal government in enforcing the law's provisions?

Earlier civil rights laws had been rendered toothless because those suits that involved trial by jury virtually ensured that no white person in the Jim Crow South would be prosecuted for violating the rights of black southerners. The President spoke of the recent events in Birmingham and mused that the administration ought to argue that "the people who object to mob actions and unreasonable demonstrations" ought to realize that for southern blacks, there was "no other remedy." His proposed bill, though, "would give another remedy in law." As the Kennedy administration knew, for the reforms to have any meaning, the Justice Department had to have the capacity to bring suits, and Kennedy and his brother knew southern congressmen and senators would fight that provision with every means at their disposal.

O'Brien, ever the strategist, tossed off one of the more consequential suggestions made at the May 20 meeting, which probably did not seem terribly significant to those in attendance. "We ought to get the Vice President in, get him married to this package." And with this, Lyndon Johnson was brought into the process, although nobody knew just how pivotal his role would be. The President considered how Johnson should be used.

. . .

President Kennedy: Yeah. How would we get the Vice President in on this so he's recommending this reasonable action and not cutting us? I think we've got to have a meeting with, we've got to have a conversation with him about this.

O'Brien: I think we can have this conversation in the morning, but my observations of meetings in which the Vice President does participate, which are rare—I've attended a lot of meetings in Mansfield's office where he's present but not participating.[8] But his participation under these circumstances could be helpful as hell. No question about it.

[*Several voices at once.*]

President Kennedy: Just say, we're going to put it in up there ourselves and let you people do it, and I'll say to Lyndon, Lyndon and Smathers, we got to do something.[9] And I'll about a day or so later, I'll have them in and say this is what I think we ought to do. Do you want to get Hubert?

Marshall: Yeah.

President Kennedy: Just tell him, we're going to do it. We're going to hang it on anything and I'm just telling him [*unclear*]. I'm just telling him.

Unidentified: It's a tough thing to do it, too. . . .

Robert Kennedy: Do you want to hear about some of these other things that we think might be [*unclear*]?

President Kennedy: Yeah.

Robert Kennedy: First, when Burke went in with these meetings with these businessmen, one of the major questions they raised was the fact, "Well, you tell us to hire clerks and employ, increase our Negro employment. And look at the federal government here." And we took a look at the federal government in Birmingham—

Unidentified: Just terrible. Just awful.

Robert Kennedy: Except for the Veteran's Administration. But I mean there wasn't, there's hardly anybody above—in the whole of the federal government above GS-6, -7.[10] Clerks all the way down the line.

O'Brien: In the Post Office too?

---

[8]Senator Mike Mansfield was a Democrat from Montana who served as the majority leader.
[9]Senator Smathers was seen as a moderate southern Democrat who might act as bridge to the other, more intractable members of the southern bloc.
[10]A formula used by the U.S. government to rank employees, which determines, among other things, their salary.

Marshall: Post Office is better.

Robert Kennedy: Better . . . HEW: 1,400 people and they work for HEW.[11]

Marshall: In the Post Office, they had a number of college graduate Negroes who were acting as carriers.

O'Brien: I think it's the greatest spot in the Federal Government for us in this area, the Post Office. . . .

Robert Kennedy: Burke said they had quite a number of them who were letter carriers, Negro letter carriers who were college graduates. But in any case, we took a survey and we had a meeting down there—

President Kennedy: It's a pretty good job for a Negro in the South, though, letter carrier. To me it's pretty good pay, a letter carrier, for a southern Negro. But anyway, go ahead.

Robert Kennedy: Well, so we had [John] Macy, and we had all these other people down there. Going to make some real changes down there. And already they have pretty [*unclear*] for a lot of people. HEW's done a lot. A good number of them have already taken some major steps. What we need, what John Macy's prepared to do and what the other government agencies are prepared to do, is make the same kind of survey around the other southern cities. So I thought we might take that up at the cabinet meeting on Tuesday or Wednesday, the fact that this needs to be done. That everybody has to coordinate and assign somebody who would have that responsibility in these major communities so that we start to hire people.

Robert Kennedy is interrupted and there is a quick exchange about which congressmen should be contacted.

Robert Kennedy: . . . One of the great difficulties has been the fact that whites won't meet with Negroes. And if the governors would start giving leadership to this, in their states, what specifically they felt that they could do and then see what ideas and thoughts they might have. And then perhaps at that first luncheon, pick out a half dozen or so governors and then you might do it with some of the other governors, and bring them in in groups and perhaps do it in two different groups and discuss this. See what can be done, and urge upon them, saying that we anticipate you are going to have all these problems. The great thing is they'd set up a biracial committee, which will genuinely want to move on it, and then we think that great progress . . .

President Kennedy: In each state a biracial committee and then to have—?

---

[11]The abbreviation HEW stands for the Deparment of Health, Education, and Welfare.

Robert Kennedy: Yeah, and then also do it at the local level [*unclear*]. After that, there's thought possibly also of having in the mayors of some of these communities like Montgomery, Birmingham. Have Hartsdale [*sic*] in from Atlanta, where he's done it.[12] Have the fellow in from Richmond. We'd pick out twenty, thirty mayors and maybe you'd talk to them also and say that this should be done at the local level and Mayor Hartsfield can talk about how it was handled in Atlanta, where it's had some success. And some of the others . . .

And let them talk about how it was and meet with one another and then say that we've got to have an exchange between the Negroes and the whites. And then just as we were discussing here, that you can't keep opposing any progress and then telling people that they can't demonstrate because you're going to have an eruption. And try to get it started at the local level.

Then the third plan we thought of was to have a meeting here, a White House conference within the next eight or nine days, on public facilities: everybody that owns a chain of restaurants, or a chain of hotels, or a chain of theaters. Any of these groups throughout the southern states. Have the owners and those who run them, and the managers, have them here to the White House and you address them. And speak about the importance of progress in this sphere, speak about the fact this has to be done. And ask them to meet with Negroes and try to work it out on a community basis, and then perhaps have somebody like Hartsfield or somebody else that's already taken a step, but then report once it's done. And that we'd be prepared to help them, that they should be prepared to exchange views with Negroes in the local communities and at the local level.

The advantage of that's a political advantage in the fact that you're taking steps right away as well as sending legislation up. You're trying to do it having the groups do it themselves rather than through legislation so that—

President Kennedy: How many people would we have for this White House conference?

Robert Kennedy: We've been making a study of it for the last five or six days as to who we would have. We've gone over some names who we're going to meet with. Douglas Dillon met some of them today.

Unidentified: There must be oh, somewhere between 150 and 200, Mr. President, who just quickly came out of the Commerce Department's lists of chains that operate in the South. Some of them wholly within the South, most of them national chains with outlets in the South: theaters,

---

[12]"Hartsdale" refers to Atlanta mayor William Hartsfield.

motels, hotels, restaurants, dime stores with lunch counters, and so forth. The thought was, though, that before we let all that mob loose together, we ought to sit down with a few of them to get a feel as to what is possible, what can be achieved, how to set up such a meeting.

Unidentified: [Government meeting] could be done this week. . . .

Robert Kennedy: Don't you think that's a [good] response?

President Kennedy: Yeah. You could have that meeting or the preliminary meeting?

Unidentified: The preliminary meeting first, and I should think that the—

President Kennedy: Okay. Okay.

Robert Kennedy: But we'd like to have the other meeting as quickly as possible. We hope by next week.

President Kennedy: Okay.

Robert Kennedy: Send out telegrams because that's one of the advantages of having it right away.

President Kennedy: Okay.

Robert Kennedy also suggested inviting some local business leaders, from Atlanta and elsewhere. Then he raised the question of which civil rights leaders to bring in.

Robert Kennedy: And then we think that some time this week that you should meet with the Negro leaders. To have in Martin Luther King and have in some of these other people and talk to them about steps that we're trying to take, listen to them, what their complaints—

President Kennedy: I think we ought to have some of these other meetings before we have in the King group; otherwise the meetings will look like they got me to do it. I would think they ought to be next week, that they ought to be notified when they're going to see me.

O'Brien: And also so when you meet with them, you'll have a pretty clear program of what you're going to do.

President Kennedy: The trouble with King is, everybody thinks he's our boy anyway. So everything he does, everybody thinks we stuck him in there. So we ought to have him well surrounded. And I just kind of hate to look like I'm sending for them because then they'll become—

Robert Kennedy: They've asked to see . . . Harry Belafonte sent you a telegram last week.

President Kennedy: Okay. I think we ought to have a good many others. King is so hot these days that if it looks like Martin's coming to the White House, I'd like to have some southern governors or mayors or businessmen in first. And my program should have gone up to the Hill first.

Unidentified: Well we can arrange that.

President Kennedy: Okay.

. . .

As the meeting unfolded, O'Brien continued to express his concerns about the politics of the bill, an issue that would be revisited many times in the days to come. Kennedy had decided to begin the arduous process of cultivating the various interest groups whose support would be crucial for the bill's success, including congressional representatives, southern governors, and civil rights and business leaders. The trick was to strike the right balance. If the administration was seen as being too close to civil rights leaders, it might become more difficult to massage reluctant southerners. And of course, the reverse was also true.

Another key question concerned the legal or constitutional justification for the bill. On June 1, Kennedy met again with his inner circle of advisers. Bobby Kennedy agreed that an argument should be made that American citizens had "a constitutional right to go in and be served no matter what the color of their skin." Unless such a right could be established, however, the federal government would lack the authority to force restaurants or hotels to comply. As of early June, the White House was leaning toward using the interstate commerce clause to make its constitutional case since this seemed the most prudent way to justify federal intervention.

Details mattered. The procedure for involving the Attorney General and the Justice Department in suits had yet to be mapped out, and the White House knew the bill's opponents would try to torpedo its passage by employing any means they could. It was critical that the Attorney General be granted the authority to prosecute violations, and much of that authority would have to be set out in explicit detail. The participants at the June 1 meeting also spent some time debating the question of the proper cutoff level for exemptions from the bill. If a hotel or motel served fewer than five people, should it be exempt from the law, or should desegregation be made mandatory for everyone involved in interstate commerce? This raised an important moral question, namely, if desegregation was right in principle, why should any exemptions be allowed, even one that was politically expedient because it made the legislation more palatable to white southern leaders? That conundrum would not be resolved on June 1 or at any point in the coming months.

Having agreed that Lyndon Johnson should be involved in the discussions, Kennedy invited the Vice President to the June 1 meeting. Johnson, a southerner who enjoyed close relations with nearly every member of the Senate, could be a vital go-between, but Kennedy and his circle were wary of the Texan and uncertain about how to get him to perform the tasks they needed. For his part, Johnson frequently felt snubbed by the Kennedy brothers and, instead of confronting them head-on, tended to sulk and recede into the background. But on June 1, he spoke up, and it was clear he had a great deal to say.

According to the Vice President, the first wave of criticism would come from Democrats not Republicans. And indeed, that was why civil rights was such a dilemma for Kennedy, for it exposed the geographic fault line in the Democratic Party, the rift between North and South. The southerners, Johnson predicted, would "keep talking about dictatorship and freedom and states' rights," just as they had for decades whenever the issue of federal civil rights legislation came up. And given the dynamics of the Senate, it was imperative to get the support of at least some southerners because without it, the bill could be killed in committee or filibustered to death. Since procedural rules of the House gave less power to individual members, it was less of a problem. And so, without the support of some southern senators, Johnson claimed the bill would be "just another gesture."

Kennedy was aware of this; after all, he had served in the U.S. Senate. But if Kennedy understood the problem intellectually, Johnson assumed the White House did not really know what to do about it. Perhaps no one in the country had a better grasp of legislative politics than Johnson did, and he saw trouble ahead for Kennedy's bill, unless the White House shifted its approach. But whether out of deference to the President's office or discomfort with his standing in the administration, Johnson spoke out neither forcefully nor directly. There is no record of Johnson's sharing with Kennedy his full thoughts on civil rights, and while it is possible that such discussions occurred off the record, the evidence suggests that relations between the two were sufficiently strained as to make such candid communication unlikely.

But Johnson did speak with Kennedy adviser Ted Sorensen on June 3, and that meeting was recorded. Over the course of a lengthy discussion, Johnson analyzed the situation, telling Sorensen that Kennedy needed to alter the administration's approach if the bill was to have any chance at all. According to Johnson, Kennedy needed to make a personal push for the bill. He had to travel through the South and appeal to southern leaders, telling them that, while he respected their qualms, as president he was going to do what was best for the entire country. Johnson himself had spent the previous weeks making speeches on civil rights, in the South and at a ceremony commemorating the Civil War battle at Gettysburg.

If the President made an energetic effort in the South, Johnson said, "He'd run some of the demagogues right in the hole. This aura, this thing, this halo around the President, everybody wants to believe in the President and the Commander in Chief. I think he'd make the [Ross] Barnetts and the Wallaces look silly. . . . The President has to go in there without

cussing anybody or fussing at anybody with a bunch of congressmen sitting there listening to him, and be the leader of the nation and make a
moral commitment to them. . . . He should stick to the moral issue and he
should do it without equivocation. . . . I know these risks are great and it
might cost us the South, but these sort of states may be lost anyway. The
difference is, if your President just enforces court decrees, the South will
feel it's yielded to force. But if he goes down there and looks them in the
eye and states the moral issue and the Christian issue, and he does it face
to face, these southerners will at least respect his courage."

Johnson noted, too, that while southern whites and blacks were on
opposite sides, they had one thing in common: "They're not certain that
the government is on the side of the Negroes. The whites think we're just
playing politics to carry New York. The Negroes feel . . . suspicious that
we're just doing what we have to do [politically]." Johnson worried that the
administration was going to have problems with the Republicans in Congress, many of whom would ultimately support the bill, but only after sitting back and letting the two wings of the Democratic Party tear
themselves apart. So Kennedy had to make the same moral appeal to
Republicans, especially from the North and the West, and tell them they
had a duty to fight for the bill. Johnson recommended that Kennedy work
closely with the Republican minority leader in the Senate, Everett Dirksen
of Illinois. Although it is questionable whether Kennedy heeded this
advice, less than a year later Johnson himself would end up cultivating
Dirksen.

The Vice President was blunt in criticizing the administration's
approach to the bill. "You haven't done your homework on public sentiment," he told Sorensen, "on legislative leaders, on the opposition party, or
on the legislation itself." And then there was the question of commitment.
A dog fight was coming, Johnson predicted, telling Sorensen it would
demand a total commitment on the administration's part. When he was
majority leader, he remembered, he'd "slept on this couch I'm looking at
for 37 nights . . . and produced quorums at 2:00 and 4:00 and that's what
you've got to be prepared to do. . . . We've got a little pop gun, and I want
to pull out the cannon. The President is the cannon. You let him be on all
the TV networks, just speaking his conscience, not at a rally in Harlem but
at a place in Mississippi or Texas or Louisiana and just have the honor
guard have a few Negroes in it. Then let him reach over and point and say,
'I have to order these boys into battle. . . . I don't ask them what their name
is . . . or what color they got, what religion. If I can order them into battle,
I've got to make it possible for them to eat and sleep in this country.'"
Johnson also believed not much would happen until September. To be
sure, there would be hearings and jockeying and discussion, but not until

the fall would the debate really heat up. That meant the administration had some time to reorient its legislative strategy.

During the discussion with Sorensen, Johnson displayed his many strengths. He understood the public relations dimension of politics, he understood the Senate, and he understood the South. He was less acute about the House and did not fully appreciate the various pressures on the president. In time, he would recognize that it was less challenging to serve as senate majority leader than as chief executive, that the crosscurrents were trickier in the Oval Office than on Capitol Hill. But Johnson's keen understanding of American politics was unmatched, and by not heeding his advice, the Kennedy administration weakened its prospects for achieving its legislative aims.

But John Kennedy was not naive. As Johnson did, he understood the need to lobby for the bill, and after the June 11 speech, the administration began a multipronged effort. Various administration officials met with congressional representatives, and Bobby Kennedy testified several times before committees that would be considering the bill, including the House Judiciary Committee chaired by New York's Emanuel Celler. The Attorney General did not fare well on Capitol Hill, as he came under attack and responded impatiently to the harsh questions and unpleasant innuendos about the administration's motives.

On June 19, 1963, the Kennedy administration submitted its legislative proposal to Congress. In the words of historian Hugh Davis Graham, it was a "carefully limited" bill, more cautious than bold. The President spoke of the necessity for civil rights legislation and asked Congress to remain in session until the bill was passed. Comprised of seven parts, the bill would make it illegal to require anyone with a sixth grade education to take a literacy test in order to register to vote (Title I); would outlaw racial discrimination in public accomodation such as restaurants, hotels, and swimming pools (Title II); would give the Attorney General the power to file suits to desegregate public schools (Title III); would establish a Community Relations Service to help resolve race-based disputes (Title IV); would extend the life of the Civil Rights Commission (Title V); would stop U.S. government funds to state and local programs that engaged in racial discrimination (Title VI); and would create the Equal Employment Opportunity Commission (EEOC), which could limit discrimination in U.S. government employment (Title VII). Perhaps its most significant omission was the lack of a Fair Employment Practices Commission (FEPC), which liberals and civil rights leaders had hoped for in order to end job discrimination in all public and private places of employment rather than merely in government-related employment as Title VII stipulated.

Throughout June, the President had numerous meetings, in which several hundred people were invited to the White House where they were presented with the administration's civil rights initiative. On June 22, civil rights leaders, including A. Philip Randolph, Roy Wilkins, and Martin Luther King, were called to Washington, where they met with Kennedy. The day before, the plan to organize a March on Washington in August had been announced. The idea, which harked back to Randolph's planned march during World War II, did not please the White House. On June 22, Kennedy warned his guests that the situation was already so tense that such a public demonstration might be counterproductive. "We want success in Congress," the President asserted, "not just a big show at the Capitol. Some of these people are looking for an excuse to be against us. I don't want to give any of them a chance to say, 'Yes, I'm for the bill but I'm damned if I will vote for it at the point of a gun.' It seemed to me a great mistake to announce a march on Washington before the bill was even in committee. The only effect is to create an atmosphere of intimidation— and this may give some members of Congress an out."

Randolph disagreed with the President's assessment of the situation, claiming blacks were already in the streets. In fact, he said, it was best to try to lead them in a peaceful, nonviolent way. But Kennedy was adamant, arguing that the legislative phase had begun and that "the wrong kind of demonstration at the wrong time will give those fellows a chance to say that they have to prove their courage by voting against us. To get the votes we need we have . . . to oppose demonstrations which will lead to violence . . . and give Congress a fair chance to work its will." But the march must go on, King insisted, because "it could serve as a means through which people . . . could channel their grievances under disciplined, nonviolent leadership." King also pointed out that it might mobilize support for the movement in parts of the country which did not "know the problems at first hand. I think it will serve a purpose." And apparently, Kennedy came around, for in mid-July, he spoke of the upcoming march, noting that he looked "forward to being there." And later that summer, the march would go on.

The August 28 event, which drew nearly a quarter of a million Americans to the nation's capital, would be the greatest demonstration in the history of the black freedom struggle, and to this day many who attended the mass gathering consider it the crowning experience of their lives. Held in the shadow of the Lincoln Memorial, the March on Washington saw the capital come alive as black and white Americans—a "gentle army" one reporter wrote—occupied the city and heard the movement's great figures speak about the aspirations of a people. They heard A. Philip Randolph and Roy Wilkins and, finally, Martin Luther King, who, the *New York*

Times reported, touched "all the themes of the day, only better than anybody else." On that late August afternoon, King told the American people about his "dream" for America, a land he hoped would become a place where people would "not be judged by the color of their skin but by the content of their character." He hoped that someday in Alabama "little black boys and black girls [would] be able to join hands with little white boys and white girls as sisters and brothers."

Millions of people in the United States and around the world have listened to King's words again and again since that August day. Children can quote from the address and scholars have analyzed it. Coretta Scott King recalled the moment, observing that it seemed as if "the Kingdom of God had appeared." And a generation later, the Reverend Fred Shuttlesworth, one of the leaders of the movement in Birmingham, spoke of the significance of the speech, noting that good words are spoken every day, but that once in awhile, "God intervenes in such a way that you know only God could do it. That was God preaching the gospel to America through King. It helped change the mind-set of America." And if some scholars have doubted whether the March on Washington had much impact on the Kennedy administration's civil rights legislation, few would question that the event and King's speech captured the attention of America and gave new urgency to the freedom crusade.

After the march, President Kennedy met with civil rights leaders at the White House. Not surprisingly, the two topics they discussed were the march and what the autumn held for the civil rights bill. Several of the participants mentioned the Fair Employment Practices Committee (FEPC), which southerners saw as an insidious device that would allow the federal government to interfere with discriminatory hiring practices. We pick up the meeting with the NAACP's Roy Wilkins telling the President why the march was such a success.

Wednesday, August 28, 1963, 5:00 P.M.

Meeting on Civil Rights

Including President Kennedy, Roy Wilkins, A. Philip Randolph, Martin Luther King, Jr., Walter Reuther, Whitney Young, Floyd McKissick, Eugene Carson Blake, and others.

Roy Wilkins: (*talking to Kennedy*) You made the difference. You gave us your blessings. It was one of the prime factors in turning it into an orderly protest to help our government rather than a protest against our government. I think you'll agree that was psychologically important. And the mood and attitude of the people there today pleased all of us without exception. They came, I said facetiously over the radio, but so truly, I told them you'd be here, but you never told me until the day before yesterday and [*unclear*] didn't tell me until today, when he said, "Did you know I was coming?"

A man said to me, "Now we have fifty people here from Portland, Oregon—NAACP." And I said, "Well, you might tell your next [*unclear*] about it, and he said, "Oh, we were so busy getting here." (*Laughter.*) Well, anyway, I think that's the reason the reports that you had had, indicated it might not be enough. But both our advisers and our inward confidence [*unclear*] told us that we would have a minimum of 100,000 here. And then of course, as you saw some of the television program, I don't have to spend a lot of time on this. In fact, I don't have to spend [*unclear*] time at all because, if you would permit me to say so, sir, you're politically astute. You realize that people there this afternoon were expressing their deep concern from their home communities, from the grassroots, for the enactment of civil rights legislation, yes. But for a change in the climate that will affect their daily lives.

We who come to you occasionally and to the Congress intermittently can say what our people want. I say our people; I stress the interracial character of this because I mean *all* the people who believe in justice and feel that the government should function to bring about justice. Those of us who come to you and say, "Our people want this and we want that and we think so and so ought to be done." Understandably, you might feel, at times, that this is a program dreamed up by the leaders, or at least pushed by them, for some motive of their own with hopes that they have backing.

We think today's demonstration, if it did nothing else, and I think this was the principal thing it did, showed that people back home, from the small towns, big cities, the working people, men who gave up two-day's pay, three-day's pay, paid thirty and forty and fifty and a hundred dollars, who flew from Los Angeles at $300 round-trip to come here. It means that they and not Martin Luther King or Roy Wilkins or Whitney Young or Walter Reuther have dreamed up this civil rights business. They feel it in their hearts enough to come here and show, by their presence, to you and to the Congress that what they hope their government will do.

It fell to my lot, sir, in this afternoon of superlative oratory, to be the one to deal rather pedantically and pedestrianly with the hard business of legislation. And the other gentlemen were free to soar into the wild blue yonder and they did so soar. But I dealt with the legislation and, of course, this must be of concern to you. We would like to see included in your package, which is now being considered by the House Judiciary Committee, an FEPC [Fair Employment Practices Committee] bill for the reasons that all of us outlined in all of our speeches, more eloquently by Walter [Reuther] and by Philip Randolph because they are so familiar with the labor field. But all of us realize that the Negro is terribly underemployed, and while we do not hope and do not believe that an FEPC bill will correct all of this, it will help to relieve some of the tension. It will open up some opportunities, and, best of all, it will arouse a hope that if they do qualify, race, and religion, and nationality will not act to bar them from the job. . . . We have been assured that in the subcommittee of the Judiciary Committee in the House, there are now 6 votes out of the 11 which would include the FEPC bill in the package as reported out to the floor and which would include also the controversial Part III language from the 1957 bill, which was not included of course in that bill.

And today when we talked this morning with Majority Leader McCormack, he reminded us that he had voted for Part III in 1957 as I believe, sir, indeed you did also.[13] And he reminded us also that the House had passed an FEPC bill on at least two occasions and he stressed that he felt that he could assure us, if the committee reported these two items as parts of the package, that they would pass the House. This means that the House would be given an opportunity to pass upon and in his opinion, it would pass and he is a veteran of the House and we don't have to dwell on that. And it would mean that the issue would then be presented to the Senate.

And we believe that both of these houses ought to be given the opportunity to say no on these matters. We do not believe, we do not share the apprehension of some people, that to include these two items would do damage to the chances of the rest of the bill. Now Mr. Dirksen was as frank as he has been with you. He told us he would support all of your package except Title II.[14] And he told us, there was one little word there—and Mr. Dirksen is very good with words. He said, "I have not changed my opinion as yet." Or, "I still have the opinion." I don't think there was any promise there that he might change his mind, . . . [but] he did say his mind wasn't closed. So that this is really the sum total of our conferences with the congressional leaders. Mr. Mansfield was his usual careful and courteous self, restricting himself to his duties as majority leader and being careful not to infringe upon anything else.[15] He did imply on a couple of

---

[13]Wilkins was mistaken. John McCormack, a Massachusetts Democrat, was Speaker of the House.

[14]Title II related to racial discrimination in places of public accomodation like restaurants, motels and hotels, and swimming pools.

[15]Senator Mike Mansfield was a Democrat from Montana and the Senate majority leader who had replaced Lyndon Johnson.

occasions that his personal opinion might not always agree with some of the official acts that he performs.

But nowhere did we get, and I think gentlemen that you'll correct me, nowhere did we get a cold shoulder on this matter, nor even political machine–like consideration, Mr. President. So we are encouraged to believe, sir, that, if the right word could go to the right people who seem receptive to the strengthening measure that we urge, at least it would pass the House. This would be a great encouragement. It would throw the matter straight into the lap of the Senate.

Now, [*unclear*] said that we were going in the other detail, Mr. President. We are in school desegregation, which occupies a lot of our attention. Public accommodations, we take for granted that we'll get something on it. It is spoken of as controversial, but that means only that it's emotional, we feel. It seems to us incontrovertible that citizens of the United States must be accorded this right to go freely and to enjoy public accommodations.

After making a few comments about school desegregation, Wilkins yielded the floor.

A. Philip Randolph: Well, Mr. President, we also want to supplement the statement made by Mr. Wilkins, who is an expert on the legislative situation. That emphasis needs to be placed on the inclusion of the Fair Employment Practice Bill in the package that you presented to the Congress.[16] We feel it needs the presidential backing, the presidential imprimatur in order for it to receive the recognition that it deserves.

This matter of fair employment, we know, must also be linked up with full employment, and we know also that full employment is conditioned by the rate of economic growth. But we also feel that there needs to be, today, because of the incredible position of the Negro worker, whose rate of unemployment is two and a half times that of a white and who represents a disproportionately large number in the so-called hard core of unemployment in this country because of being the first fired and the last hired. There seems to us that something ought to be done to help them get jobs now.

For instance, we have thousands of Negro workers who can't even read and are not in the position to even acquire skills and training, even though we know that today in the job market, you are not going to be able to sell muscle power anymore, to any great extent because of the march of science, technology, industrialism, and automation. Now, inasmuch as the Negro worker is handicapped in selling his labor power through the national job

---

[16]Randolph wanted the bill to include a section banning discrimination in employment practices.

market because of racial bias and because of lack of skills, we feel that some massive public works ought to be developed. Unless that isn't done, they are going to be thrown on relief. Because, as we look at the problem, it just seems almost insolvable, when you have a society which is becoming increasingly mechanized and automated, where skills and training are indispensable, and you have hundreds of thousands and millions of people that can't even be trained because of a lack of the fundamental equipment of being able to read.

Well now, therefore, we need some crash, massive training program, but even this is not going to reach a large segment of the black workforce. In addition to that, and I think that we talked about it some time ago in some of the conferences here, the teenagers constitute a grave problem because they are dropping out of school. It is estimated that 75 percent of Negro [students] now in school will not graduate, will not finish high school. And yet, a high school graduate is necessary to be included in the apprenticeship training program. So that if they're dropping out of school, and they're incapable of going into apprenticeship training programs to get training, well just where are they going? We're up against a terrific problem.

And not only are they dropping out of school and are unemployed, but they're running out of hope. And I come up against the young teenagers from time to time and I may suggest to you that they present almost an alarming problem because they have no faith in anybody white. They have no faith in the Negro leadership. They have no faith in God. They have no faith in the government. In other words, they believe that the hand of society is against them. This is the situation that you find with respect to Negro youth in the various centers of the country.

As we see it, the only way we can relieve this situation is to compel them to take training, to acquire some kind of skill, in order that they may be able to play their role in this automated society. And I know that the trade union people don't want to talk about too much of a crash program with respect to training, that is, getting skills for them and so forth because the old doctrine of a long-term period for the acquisition of skills still obtains in the autonomous unions today. I don't know how sound it is. I ought to question a policy which requires a boy to spend five years to become a plumber, but it only takes four years to become a doctor. This is a situation that seems incredible, but nevertheless that's the position and it's going to be difficult to change the position of the powerful trade and craft union [*unclear*].

But this is one that we need to meet and I hope that it may be possible for these youngsters to be brought into some vast national training program, which will compel them to go through the courses and obtain skills. *Randolph continues to talk about worker training until the President cuts in with a suggestion.*

President Kennedy: I thought we might go into a little discussion of the legislation of how we stand. . . .

Walter Reuther: Well, I'd like to say just two things. First of all, I think, Mr. President, that we're all very appreciative of the great courage that you have demonstrated in recommending one of the most comprehensive civil rights bills that any president has ever recommended. We fully appreciate that.

We feel very strongly that the FEPC thing is a very critical element of the whole total effort because it ties in with the kind of a house a Negro family can have, and the kind of a house they have in the kind of neighborhood and therefore the kind of school. And a job is really basic. And this is why we think FEPC. . . . We've been working very closely with Manny Celler and his committee. And John McCormack indicates that he believes—and we didn't have to twist this out of him—he said this quite freely and openly. He believes that a bill that contains both FEPC, that is, your original proposal, plus FEPC and plus Title III, would clear the House. And obviously, if we could get that kind of legislation through, we'd be in the strongest possible position to start from the strongest point in terms of the Senate.

Now we have put together this March on Washington. If it had just been a march, then I think some people might have said, well, this effort, and the money and the time and the energy that went into that, just a one-day proposition, would not, could not, be justified. But in the process, we've put together the broadest working legislative coalition we've ever had. And we're going to work, not only on the Hill, but we're going to be able to mobilize the grassroots support back home in critical congressional districts where a fellow has to be persuaded.

There's no use working on Phil Hart or people like Paul Douglas.[17] We know where they are.[18] We've got to work in the Midwest where people, where there are very few trade unions, where there are practically no Negroes, and where there's no pressure or there's no sense of urgency. We have to work in those areas. Now we've put together, I think, the best and broadest coalition to do a legislative job.

---

[17]Hart was a Democratic senator from Michigan, and Douglas was a Democratic senator from Illinois.

[18]Both senators had demonstrated that they strongly supported civil rights.

The other thing that I think will come out of this, as I said today in my speech, after we get the legislation, that only means we've got a set of tools to work with. It doesn't mean that automatically this problem is resolved. What we have to do is to develop a broad coalition of men of good will in every community, where we've got to implement this program. And I think that this is what this march has done. It has brought into being an active, functioning coalition around this central question of equality of opportunity and first-class citizenship. And I think if we reflect this by practical work in each community, we can mobilize the community, we can mobilize the men of good will, and we can search for answers in the light of reason by rational, responsible action. Because if we fail, then the vacuum that we create, our failure, is going to be filled by the apostles of hatred. And reason is going to yield to riots and brotherhood is going to yield to bitterness and bloodshed.

So I think that this is really a more significant aspect of what we're doing. We have put together the kind of coalition that can be meaningful at the community level, across this country, after we get the legislation, and it can be effective in mobilizing support for the legislation.

President Kennedy: Very fine, but let me just say a word about the legislation. There's one thing that I, on this question of education. We have this juvenile program, as you know, in New York and a lot, and the Attorney General was out in Chicago on it the other day and was shocked by some of the [*unclear*] crowding of the class, the leaving of the school, the fact that the best teachers [*unclear*] and there's no visiting by the teachers in their homes. And they won't study, and the children won't study unless [*unclear*] what their color or their income level is.

Now, isn't it possible for the Negro community to take the lead in committing major emphasis upon the responsibility of these families, even if they're split and all the rest of the problems they have, on educating their children. Now, in my opinion, the Jewish community, which suffered a good deal under discrimination, and what a great effort they made, which I think has made their role influential, was in education: education of their children. And therefore they've been able to establish a pretty strong position for themselves.

This has nothing to do with what you've been talking about. It seems to me that with all the influence, which all you gentlemen have in the Negro community, if you could emphasize—there's nothing these adults can do about the education they've lost. They really have to concentrate. But I think the Jewish community's done in educating their children, making their children study, making them stay in school, and all the rest. And all the ministers and all the rest can really make that a major effort in the coming months.

After some more discussion about local educational initiatives, President Kennedy continues.

I just thought that, aside from all the things we can do in the government, and if we can get the Negro community to regard the education of their children as really the best way out. I'm not talking about the southern problem or the discrimination, but just making education the same way that it's in the Jewish community and to a degree in . . .

Unidentified: Mr. President, you can almost tie it in with the FEPC; [I remember] twenty years ago, we had Negro college graduates driving garbage trucks in Pasadena, California. You can't blame the younger brothers now. I mean he has no interest; you've got to move the openings. They always were telling us, "We are working on the upgrading," and they were telling us that there wasn't anyone qualified and so on. And the two things just seem to me adequate. I think this will be done if you can get the openings, the assurance of openings, because I think that the Negro community will push as hard as anybody else to educate and get ahead if there isn't that built-in discouragement. . . .

Floyd McKissick: We had a program similar to this in North Carolina, sponsored by the NAACP and CORE. . . . for two years, at which time we had kids being trained on our [*unclear*] and for a number of years and trained some 200 of them and they [*unclear*] any jobs, positions. But we still have a great amount of difficulties because this is not an isolated problem. This is part of a total problem, in that you can send children to school, but if their parents have not been educated, the child, by the time it reaches the sixth grade, can't communicate with his parents most of the time because the parents only finished the fourth.

Now an additional problem is that the parents are not able to stay home to work. I mean they have to work, get out and do some kind of work, and there is a lack of parental control in many of the homes. We've also had volunteer programs in training children to just be quick to transfer to an integrated school, which is a tremendous problem in draining the resources of carrying on tutors for 26 months. Over a period of time, 26 months, to get kids ready to go to an integrated school because they're going to move so fast.

We've been engaged in this program of education. We just concluded a workshop in Durham, North Carolina, sponsored by NAACP, CORE, SNCC. The Student Nonviolent Coordinating Committee just completed a direct action workshop. But in the direct action workshop, mind you, and that's one of the advantages of the civil rights organization. In the direct action, much emphasis was put on training and vocational training and getting into training school with certain qualifications. But neverthe-

less, public accommodations fit entirely into this because without the public accommodations acts in the South, you have killed the Negro child's
chance to aspire. He doesn't aspire to be anything. He believes he's nothing. So these problems are interrelated and interlocking.

.   .   .

At this point, President Kennedy began to go over the names of those who
favored and those who opposed the various provisions of the bill, a process
that required looking at the names of hundreds of congresspeople and
senators. The administration wanted to have at least 220 votes in the
House, and, assuming no southern Democrats voted for the bill, that
meant it was necessary to get 60 Republican votes. One of the most
important House Republicans was the ranking GOP member of the Judiciary Committee, William McCulloch of Ohio, who, while favoring civil
rights legislation, was wary that any bill that passed the House would be
watered down and made ineffective by Senate Democrats. McCulloch
wanted assurances that if he went to bat for civil rights legislation, he
would not be undermined by the Senate.

The Senate presented great problems for the administration. Obtaining a majority seemed likely, but a two-thirds vote was needed to invoke
cloture and thus halt a potential filibuster. Even if the House passed a version of the bill, it was possible that in the Senate it would be killed in committee or never even come to the floor for a vote. As of late August, the
administration had not settled on a strategy for confronting southern
Democrats in the upper chamber.[19]

Kennedy expected that the FEPC provision in the bill would serve as
a lightning rod for the opposition, as had been the case in the past, and he
tried to assess who would vote against any bill that included provisions for
a strengthened FEPC. He worried, too, that as Johnson had predicted, the
Republicans would try to complicate the process and encourage dissension
in the Democratic Party. But Kennedy did not finish the process of vote
counting; others wanted to focus on specific members of Congress as their
names came up, and the conversation headed off into new directions.

The August 28 conversation highlights the nuts-and-bolts character
of the legislative process. It has been said that making laws should be done
away from prying eyes, because lawmaking, even when driven by noble
intentions and moral considerations, can become an unpleasant and con-

---

[19]The filibuster is a senatorial device that allows for unlimited debate and can, in the hands of
skilled and determined senators, stop a bill from coming to a vote. In 1964, to end a filibuster in
the Senate, a two-thirds vote was needed to invoke cloture, which would end the debate.

fusing political exercise. While the meetings on the bill illuminate the legislative process, they can be difficult to follow, as the President's recitation of legislators' names occasionally assumes the character of readings from the telephone book. Yet despite this, an occasional comment stands out because it serves to remind listeners (whether those who were with the President in 1963 or those listening to the tapes today) about the significance of the legislation and how difficult it would be to pass it.

During the August 28 meeting, A. Philip Randolph, one of the twentieth century's preeminent civil rights leaders—a man who had met with presidents for decades—suddenly offered the following observation: "Mr. President, from the description you have made of the state of affairs in the House and Senate, it's obvious that it's going to take nothing less than a crusade to win approval for these civil rights measures. . . . And if it is going to be a crusade, I think that nobody can lead this crusade but you. . . . I think that the people have got to be appealed to over the heads of the congressmen and senators." In essence, Randolph reminded the participants that this was no ordinary piece of legislation and that it would take extraordinary means to pass it.

In the weeks to come, the bill would be under consideration in the committee of Emanuel Celler, a long-serving congressman from Brooklyn, who was a liberal Democrat sympathetic to civil rights. The administration worried that he would yield to the liberal forces committed to the legislation and that his committee would submit a bill that would not survive a vote in the full House, let alone in the Senate. But as it happened, the President was not able to devote all his attention to Congress in September. Instead, events in Birmingham would yet again alter the landscape of race relations in America.

Chapter 5
Bombs in Birmingham

In the summer of 1963, as Birmingham began to desegregate its downtown business district, it seemed race relations might be improving in the Alabama city. In late July, black residents were finally permitted to sit at lunch counters in previously all-white restaurants, and while progress would surely be slow, there appeared cause for optimism. As one participant recalled, "the waitresses were very cordial, while the cooks looked on in quiet amazement." But as was so often the case in the tortured history of American race relations, black hopes for justice would be dashed—this time by an act of unspeakable horror.

On Sunday morning, September 15, 1963, a bomb tore through the basement of Birmingham's Sixteenth Street Baptist Church. Four black girls, dressed in white, were killed by the blast as they were preparing to lead the church service at the annual Youth Day celebration. The reverberations of the event would be felt long after the victims—Addie Mae Collins, Denise McNair, Carole Robinson, and Cynthia Wesley—were pulled from the rubble. Indeed, the church bombing, which transformed the four children into martyrs in the black liberation struggle, remains one of the key events in the history of the civil rights movement. In a few seconds, the hopefulness generated by the March on Washington just two weeks before had been replaced by sorrow, outrage, and despair.

Later that day, two black boys were murdered in Birmingham. Johnny Robinson, 16, was shot by a policeman as he ran down an alleyway after the police had broken up a group of black youths who were throwing rocks at a car filled with taunting white teenagers. (The white teens' car was painted with Confederate symbols and the slogan, "Negroes Go Back to Africa.") On the other side of town, two white boys, both Eagle Scouts, had just finished listening to a segregationist rally. Shortly after leaving the event, they encountered two black teenagers on a bicycle, and without provocation, one of the white boys pulled out a pistol and fired two shots into the head and chest of thirteen-year-old Virgil Ware, killing him. The two Eagle Scouts later told the police they had no idea why they had committed the crime.

In the wake of the church bombing, riots erupted in Birmingham, where tensions had recently been heightened due to a federal court order directing that blacks be admitted to three public schools. (On September 9, Governor George Wallace had sent in the National Guard to stop the court order from being carried out, and just a few days before, vigilantes had bombed the house of a leading black attorney for the second time in two weeks.) The church bombing and the ensuing violence thus marked the culmination of several days of anxiety and disorder, as Birmingham, which earlier that summer had seemed to be making progress on the race reform front, again lived up to its reputation among blacks as the most fearsome city in the South.

On Sunday night, Martin Luther King arrived in Birmingham, and the next day he told reporters the city was "in a state of civil disorder." The U.S. Army ought to come and take over Birmingham, he declared, and "run it because Negroes are tired now, tireder than ever before." To a fellow activist, he observed, "something dramatic has to be done by the federal government to reestablish a sense of hope in the Negro people here." Later on Monday, King wired President Kennedy, hoping that he and several black leaders from Birmingham could meet with the President. Without federal action, he warned, "we shall see the worst racial holocaust this nation has ever seen." In a presidential statement issued on Monday, Kennedy seemed to criticize George Wallace for his intransigence on school desegregation, holding him responsible for the events of the previous day: "Public disparagement of law and order has encouraged violence which has fallen on the innocent." On Tuesday and Wednesday, with thousands in attendance, funerals were held for the slain girls.

On September 19, four days after the church bombing, the President met in Washington with King and a delegation of black leaders to discuss the situation in Alabama. It was an extraordinary meeting, as the President heard in moving detail about the difficulties black Americans confronted every day in the Jim Crow South. After introducing the group, King presented his views on the challenges presented by recent events and offered his suggestions about what the Kennedy administration should do to respond to the situation.

Thursday, September 19, 1963, 5:00 P.M.

Meeting on Birmingham

Including President Kennedy, Martin Luther King, Jr., Dr. Ralph Abernathy, Dr. Fred Shuttlesworth, Dr. Lucius Pitts, Dr. A. G. Gaston, Dr. J. L. Ware, and Bishop Murchison.

Martin Luther King: I would like to just introduce these men once more. Dr. Fred Shuttlesworth is the leader of the local organization there and Dr. Ralph Abernathy, the pastor in Atlanta and has been my close associate in this whole struggle. Dr. Lucius Pitts is the president of Miles College in Birmingham. And Dr. A. G. Gaston is the outstanding businessman in the community in the state of Alabama. The Reverend Dr. J. L. Ware is the president of the Baptist Ministers Conference and also the interdenominational alliance with all of the Negro ministers working with him there in the city. He stands in that leadership position. And Bishop Murchison is bishop of the C.M.E. Church.

We come today representing Birmingham in general and more specifically some 200 business and professional, religious, labor leaders who assembled the day after the bombing to discuss the implications and to discuss the seriousness and the whole crisis that we face there in Birmingham.

And we come to you today because we feel that the Birmingham situation is so serious that it threatens not only the life and stability of Birmingham and Alabama, but of our whole nation. The image of our nation is involved and the destiny of our nation is involved. We feel that Birmingham has reached a state of civil disorder.

Now there are many things that you could say that would justify our coming to this conclusion. I'm sure that you are aware of the fact that more bombings of churches and homes have taken place in Birmingham than any city in the United States and not a one of these bombings over the last 15 to 20 years has been solved. In fact, some 28 have taken place in the last 8 or 10 years and all of these bombings remain unsolved. There is still a great problem of police brutality, and all of this came out in tragic dimensions Sunday when the bombing took place and four young girls were killed instantly and then later in the day two more. I think both were boys, the other two who were killed.

Now the real problem that we face is this. The Negro community is about to reach a breaking point. There is a great deal of frustration and despair and confusion in the Negro community, and there is a feeling of being alone and not being protected. If you walk the street, you aren't safe.

If you stay at home, you aren't safe: there is a danger of a bomb. If you're in church now, it isn't safe. So that the Negro feels that everywhere he goes, if he remains stationary, he's in danger of some physical violence.

Now this presents a real problem for those of us who find ourselves in leadership positions because we are preaching at every moment the philosophy and the method of nonviolence. And I think that I can say without fear of successful contradiction, that we have been consistent in standing up for nonviolence at every point and even with Sunday's and Monday's developments, we continue to be firm at this point. But more and more, we are facing a problem of our people saying "What's the use?" and we find it a little more difficult to get over nonviolence [to them].

And I am convinced that if something isn't done to give the Negro a new sense of hope and a sense of protection, there is a danger that we will face and that will lead to the worst race rioting we've ever seen in this country. I think it's just at that point. I don't think it will happen if we can do something to save the situation, but I do think (and I voiced the sentiment in the evening as well with those that we met with the other day) that something dramatic must be done at this time to give the Negro in Birmingham and Alabama a new sense of hope and a good sense of protection.

On the basis of this we have some specific recommendations, some specific points that have been raised in the meeting, and things that this group wanted us to bring to you. The first point deals with the whole matter of law enforcement and protection of property and lives. We have now, as you know, the state troopers in Birmingham. Governor Wallace sent them in at the request of Mayor Boutwell. Now our experience with [*break in tape*] one of the worst experiences and I followed this in Gadsden and in Birmingham and in other places in Alabama.[1] And the methods they used are just unbelievable and barbaric. Now they are there [*unclear*], and they continue to perpetuate the nightly terror, so that we feel that these troopers should be removed, the state troopers, and be replaced with federal troops to protect the people who—Dr. Gaston just stated he spends 50 dollars a day just to have his house guarded because it was bombed the other night and there are other properties that we mentioned.

So this is the first point, that we feel that there is a state of civil disorder right now and that there is a temporary need, we have a problem in the South that cannot be ultimately solved with federal troops, but these

---

[1]Throughout the summer of 1963, there was unrest in Gadsden, Alabama, as blacks demonstrated to end Jim Crow. The campaign ended unsuccessfully, with the arrests of hundreds of protesters.

states have become so defiant, and unfortunately Alabama has a mad man as its governor who will not yield to reason and we feel that something has to be done.

The second suggestion that we are going to make is that Birmingham, which is an industrial center in the South, would have, to put it another way, that all industries with federal, rather, government contracts would be investigated immediately. And if there is discrimination practiced—and we have evidence that all of these industries practice discrimination against Negroes' employment—that if there is discrimination, that these contracts would be canceled. We feel that this would help the general situation in the state of Alabama.

In short, we feel that there's a need for strong federal intervention and this will give the Negro a new sense of hope and a new sense of protection, which I think can lead us out of this dark moment because there are enough white moderates in Birmingham, I believe, who really want to see the situation solved, but they need help now. The problem is so serious that they need help. So these are the specific things. These men may have one or two others things on their minds concerning the seriousness and the urgency of the situation.

· · ·

After King finished his initial presentation, other participants spoke of the chronic racism and discrimination faced daily by Birmingham's black citizens. Reverend Ware painted a vivid portrait of police brutality and indifference, and Dr. Gaston described how difficult it was for a black family to obtain the most basic services, such as auto and home insurance. Those at the meeting clearly feared a renewed round of riots and violence, which would undoubtedly lead to still more retaliation. But with an almost entirely white police force, it was certain blacks would suffer far more from violence and property damage than whites would.

Ware, ever the preacher, conveyed a story about one of his parishioners. "Just this morning, possibly at 4:30, a lady called me and said, 'Reverend Ware,' she said, 'I see where you and others are going to Washington to talk to the President.' And she was almost in tears, her voice was trembling and seemed like she was frightened almost out of her wits. And she said, 'Please, for my sake and for the sake of the people of Birmingham, tell the President to do *something*.' She said, 'I'm frightened to death here. I have six little children and I don't know what's come up. I'm afraid to send them to school; I'm afraid to keep them here at home. And we just don't know what to do.' And she said, 'Tell the President that if there's any way possible to have somebody to at *least* guard the schools. This, this, this, this is just not an isolated situation in that it's all throughout the city.

And the people are *frightened* and they're even afraid to go to church at night and some of them won't even go to church during the day services. The police are *brutal.*'"

Kennedy wondered if there was any reason for hope in Birmingham, to which Ware replied, "I think that a martial law measure would be their only hope right now." Again, Kennedy pressed the issue: "What is the long-range hope in Birmingham?" King tried to sound a positive note. "I still have faith in the vast possibilities of Birmingham," he said. "There are many white people of good will in Birmingham. They need help. . . . Troops cannot solve the problem, and we know that. This is only temporary. But the problem with the mayor is that he is a weak man. And he's a kind of moderate, as we would call him, I guess, who really doesn't understand the depths and dimensions of this social revolution."

· · · ·

President Kennedy: Does he sit down with you gentlemen?

Several voices: No, No.

King: But if the Attorney General would come to a community like Birmingham, and bring together the Negro community, the leaders of the Negro community and the white political officials, it seems to me that this would mean a great deal in opening channels of communication. . . .

President Kennedy: Let me just say that we've been talking about this question of troops. We haven't any legal ground. At this point, we don't think because . . . but aside from the legal thing, we haven't felt that it was the . . . having been through the Oxford matter, where the troops are in a sense a defeat. Because it finally means that we take over and then everybody then just quits. And the white community just says, "All right, let the federal government have it" [*unclear*]. Doesn't really make them face it. But it may be that we're going to have to come to that. And I have been reluctant to do that, beyond the troops we have there, the federalized Guard. Now as I say, that judgment may change, but up till now that has been our reasoning. And troops, as I say, really do represent a . . .

So what we tried to do . . . these things: First, I think we've got to get the white community to take on this responsibility. Mayor Boutwell has asked if he'd send a group of his people, whoever they are, I don't know, and I'm going to see them on Monday. Then I'm going to see some of the ministers, the white ministerial group on Monday. That's two different groups. Meanwhile, I've asked General [Kenneth] Royall, who used to be Secretary of the Army, a distinguished attorney in New York, and Colonel [Earl] Blaik, who I've known (he's a very fine fellow who used to be in the Army), to go to Birmingham next week, representing me, to see if they can do anything about establishing contact as my representatives, between

the Negro community and the white community. And then come back
and give their best judgment on what the situation requires.

I think we've got two very good men. Royall is an outstanding fellow
and Colonel Blaik is one of the finest men I've ever met. I think they will
be well regarded by the white community in Birmingham. . . .

Now I've announced that this afternoon and we were going to say this
afternoon this statement:

> The tragic death of four Negro children in Birmingham last Sun-
> day has given rise to fears and distrust, which require the cooperation
> and restraint of all the citizens of that city. I have received reports from
> leading Negro citizens concerning the situation this afternoon. Next
> Monday, I will confer at the request of Mayor Boutwell with white city
> leaders who want to give us information concerning the steps which
> the city has taken and plans to take to reestablish the confidence of
> everyone that law and order in Birmingham will be maintained. In
> addition, I have today appointed General Kenneth Royall and Colonel
> Earl Blaik as a committee to represent me personally in helping the
> city to work as a unit in overcoming the fears and suspicions which
> now exist. They will go to Birmingham in the next few days to start on
> this work of great importance.
>
> In the meanwhile, the Federal Bureau of Investigation, along with
> the local authorities, is making a massive effort to bring to justice the
> person responsible for the bombing on Sunday and previous incidents.
> I urge everyone to cooperate with them in this effort and that all citi-
> zens of Birmingham and Alabama will give these processes of law
> enforcement a full opportunity to work. I urge all citizens in these next
> days to conduct themselves with restraint and responsibility.

Now, that's what I propose to put out. Then I will meet with these
people on Monday. I will have Mr. Royall and Mr. Blaik in Birmingham
by Tuesday. I would hope they would meet with you; they're meeting with
the Mayor in an attempt to see if we can make some progress on the local
level. I think their status in the country is such that it will be more difficult
for the Governor to challenge them.

And then if we don't . . . if the situation deteriorates, we will stay in
close touch and then we will consider this final step, which right now I
would rather not take, but it may come to that. I just figure if you ever get
them in, you're going to have an awful time getting them out of there.

Let's just see if we can do, now it's tough for the Negro community.
On the other hand, what the Negro community is trying to do is a very
important effort, which has implications all over the country. And I know

that this bombing is particularly difficult. But if you look, as you know, at any of these struggles over a period across the world, it is a very dangerous effort. So everybody just has to keep their nerve.

If the Negroes should begin to respond and shoot at whites, we lose. I think Wallace has lost. I heard a southern senator with regard to civil rights say to me today, this is what I hear from him: that Wallace has made a bad mistake. Now if you get . . . Wallace is in a bad position. And because you gentlemen and the community have conducted yourselves in the way you have, it's with you. And of course when the police starts going for guns, they'll shoot some innocent people, and they'll be white, and then that will just wipe away all this support that's been built up.

There will be no, in the beginning, you can't get anything. I can't do very much. Congress can't do very much unless we keep the support of the white community throughout the country—as a country. Once that goes, then we're pretty much down to a racial struggle, so that I think we've just got to tell the Negro community that this is a very hard price which they have to pay to get this job done.

. . .

As he had promised, Kennedy met with city leaders several days later. Prior to the meeting, the President was briefed by his aides, including the Attorney General and Burke Marshall. The ripple effects from the Birmingham bombings were still being felt. The city was once again attracting national news attention, and the outrage over the killing of children had led to pressure on the President and Congress to move more quickly to pass legislation. Liberals in the House felt a renewed determination not to make too many compromises with southern conservatives, and the White House was becoming concerned that the bill that Emanuel Celler's committee was about to report might be too strong to pass the Senate.

In the pre-meeting briefing on September 23, Burke Marshall tried to correct the notion advanced by southerners that Martin Luther King had stirred up the situation in Birmingham. Marshall informed the President that King had not been in Birmingham since the events of the previous May and said that attributing the current troubles to King "just did not fit in with the facts." Morover, Marshall noted, in the past week, "King did calm the Negro population. If he hadn't gone down, I think they in fact would have been in much worse shape, and on several occasions he's called off demonstrations, prevented them, that would otherwise have happened."

The tone of the briefing was relaxed, and Kennedy indulged his laconic wit. He remarked that as far as he could tell, in Birmingham, "the Kennedys" were "a great target of wrath." His brother replied, "Yeah, I agree. I recognize that." The President responded dryly, "I guess we're not very popular in Birmingham."

The meeting with the delegation of Birmingham's leading white citizens lasted for more than an hour. Whereas Kennedy had been rather understanding toward, and willing to listen to, the black leaders, he was less patient with Birmingham's white leadership. Not quite angry, Kennedy took charge of the meeting and hammered home the point that the white leaders of Birmingham had little choice but to take significant steps to demonstrate their commitment to progress on civil rights. His goal, he said, was to "lessen the tension" in the city, and he urged the participants to do something toward that end. He suggested that they hire more black policemen, or more black clerks in stores or more workers in city agencies—anything to begin to include the large black population in the life of the city.

Kennedy clearly wanted Birmingham off his back. The legislative fight was heating up, and the Alabama city had apparently become a distraction. Every time something bad happened in Birmingham, the attention of the country turned from the bill that was in the House back toward the city. He wanted the leaders to understand that it was not doing them or the country any good for tensions to continue to simmer.

For their part, the white delegation tried to convince Kennedy that the situation in Birmingham was not so dire and that events there were caused by a few radical individuals and groups who did not even live in the city. They hoped Kennedy would do something about the "outside forces" they believed were aggravating the situation. By "outside forces," they meant, above all, Martin Luther King, but Kennedy was not receptive to their pressure and his tone suggests he was skeptical about the picture painted by the delegation.

The meeting began with the usual introductions, and then William C. Hamilton, the executive assistant to the Mayor, made his appeal.

Monday, September 23, 1963, 12:50 P.M.

Meeting on Birmingham

Including President Kennedy, Landon Miller, Caldwell Marks, William C. Hamilton, Frank Newton, Don Hawkins, and Burke Marshall.

William C. Hamilton: Mr. President, we came here, sir, with no chips on our shoulders. We feel like there was a great deal to be, not so much informed nationally, but we think there's a great deal that has not been said, as well as what has been said about us. And we feel like this business that we're all involved in is too much the nation's business as I know you have said. And that our troubles are not going to be cured, sir, by arguments or by emotions. I think they'll probably be worked out by people, and that's what we are endeavoring to do at the local level.

We honestly believe, sir, that our community, if given a chance to go on with what we started when this new government was elected and put into office, that if we are given a little bit of calm, a little bit of time to put it to work—and by that I don't mean to say we postpone the things that have to be done, I simply mean to create the atmosphere there that will let us go ahead, that we can do it with credit to ourselves and we think, to a credit to the nation. And that is the basis, the premise on which we come, is to try to reach some understanding of your mind as well as to let you understand some of ours.

President Kennedy: Well, I appreciate it. I appreciate the Mayor's suggestion about you coming up and I'm glad to see all of you. This, this, I think it is a major problem of course nationally, which we have in every city and all over the country, which is going to be with us a long time after all of us are no longer in positions of responsibility.

The particular problem in Birmingham is a problem for the city as well as the country. No one, obviously, who lives in Birmingham wants to keep seeing Birmingham get pasted every day or discussed every day. It hurts the life of the community; people don't want to move in there, or do business, and all the rest. So the problem that I'm just interested in is to see what we could do, just speaking as a country and really what you can do in Birmingham, to ease the situation there.

Now I think I've read a good deal about what all of you feel down there in Birmingham, and . . . I think that [*gap in tape*] at least from what I gather, there seems to be some idea that what we're seeking to do is to change the viewpoint of the people of Birmingham in much more basic ways than we can or should.

I recognize that Birmingham is going to, that the desire for a segregated society is going to remain very strong in the minds of the majority of the white citizens of Birmingham. And that's the way they want to live and that's the way, that's the way they feel.

The problem is, however, there are 40 or 45 percent Negroes there and how is the city going to exist as a community? That's all, it seems to me, that's important. Now we've got, Washington has 50–55 percent Negroes; we've got a higher percentage of Negroes than Birmingham. Washington has got a lot of explosive potential here, as you know, and it's a very—it's not a satisfactory situation. It has many advantages which Birmingham doesn't have. It isn't an industrial city with all of the ... And it's, a lot of it's government, which produces an atmosphere which is somewhat different. But we've got a lot of problems here, but there have been, it seems to me, some adjustments made in Washington, which do not provide social integration in Washington, which I really have never seen since I've been here, but which does at least permit, lessen some of the explosion potential. It seems to me some of the things that are done in Washington could usefully be done in Birmingham without changing any of the basic feeling in the city.

Hamilton: A great many, a great many things that have been done—

President Kennedy: I know; I understand.

Hamilton: —Mr. President, and we have not in a great many instances been given credit for them.

President Kennedy: Well, I know that, but it's like all things. We, it's awfully hard to, you have to run very fast to stand still, and on the question of civil rights, the fact of the matter is we had no legislative proposals before the Congress until the events in Birmingham last April and May happened to light off a whole fire around the country, which, as you know, has caused a good deal of action all over the United States. And the situation was such that we felt that it [was] necessary to go the congressional route.

Now, I think the thing is you've got the situation in Birmingham whether you should have it or not, but you do have it, and the question is what you can do to ease it. Obviously you don't want the federal government in there and I don't want the federal government in there. And you don't want federal troops in there, and I don't, because I don't know how you get them out of there.

Hamilton: Yes. It's a problem.

President Kennedy: And, and, so what, that's ... Sooner or later as you know if you get enough trouble in any situation, then everybody comes. As it was even yesterday, I don't know whether you saw the *New York Times* this morning. All these pronouncing by CORE and everybody else and Lee because I haven't done more in Birmingham.[2] We have no plans to do anything in Birmingham, but I'd like to see what steps you could take, even though you may feel that what you've done is enough. The problem is, what is enough, given the situation as it is? Not as it perhaps ought to be or you'd like it to be?

---

[2] The acronym CORE stands for the Congress of Racial Equality, the civil rights organization led by James Farmer.

Caldwell Marks: Well, Mr. President, I think one thing . . . I don't believe that the community feels that it has done as much as it could or should, at the moment. I think the atmosphere in which we find ourselves at the moment is very difficult—

President Kennedy: Of course.

Marks:—to do anything further as long as we have constant agitation from, on both sides of the picture, from outside the community.

President Kennedy: Now tell me why it is you can't get a Negro policeman around there. Seems to me, if you've got 40 percent of the community that's Negro, to keep order really among the Negroes, I would think you'd be much better with Negro policemen.

Unidentified: Ah, I—

President Kennedy: Why is that?

Hamilton: Might I review that? Some years back, that direct antithesis of what we stand for, Mr. Eugene Connor, with whose name—

President Kennedy: Yeah.

Hamilton:—I [*laughing*] presume you are familiar.

President Kennedy: Yeah. He was one of the architects of our difficulties.

Hamilton: He was the architect of this thing and he was the man who was able to intimidate the conscience of the community. As far back as six or seven years ago, actually he himself recognized that that would be a most useful thing, particularly with our delinquent problem. Negro children, for instance, are intimidated by that uniform and by a white man's face. They don't talk to them. Consequently, a large percentage of juvenile delinquency is permitted to grow because the children fear that policeman. And Mr. Connor, for whatever his political views, is a good law enforcement man. He believes in law enforcement. And during, throughout this thing, I must give credit where credit is due. That never once has he tried deliberately to incite civil disobedience. He's opposed to everything you stand for and a great deal of what I stand for, but nonetheless he's a good law enforcement man. He wanted to do it and then he lost his nerve.

When we came into office, that is, this government, we saw that situation and that need. Our police chief, Mr. Moore, is firmly convinced that Negro policemen would be very useful indeed. Here are the steps that we had already taken, prior to this sudden explosion.

In the first place, we operate under a civil service system. Actually, there is no way we could prevent Negro policemen being hired, because we *must* take—say there are ten eligible—we must choose, from that top ten, we must choose only those who are named by the personnel board. And the personnel board, sir, has never been accused of any discrimination where race was concerned. Two men actually were number one and number two on the personnel board's recommendation. If there had been police hiring while those names were there, they would unavoidably have been hired.

Fortunately, or unfortunately—I would say a majority of our police force in its present mood would say fortunately—they found much higher paying jobs than we can afford to pay policemen. They withdrew from the rolls and took a job in industry. At the present moment, there is no eligible man there. It takes approximately thirty days for one to become qualified. If there was a direct step in that direction, there's where it should be taken. Now, as to whether the city will or will not, this is a decision of the council and the Mayor. I do not speak to that. I do not suggest it.

But we have an enormous handicap, sir, in our morale question. The chief is firmly convinced, and I think I share it (the opinion) that the attacks which have been made on our police—now, remember that every man who is presently on our force, with the exception of 10 or 15 that we've hired in the last few days, with that exception, there are approximately 500 men who were hired by Mr. Connor and who were indoctrinated by him. I would say 50 percent of the morning force, when I walk into the city hall and when the Mayor walks into the city hall, if I hold out my hand, they refuse to shake hands. If I speak, they refuse to speak.

We are fairly convinced that at least a third of our police force if, at this particular moment, were forced to share a uniform with a Negro and all the uniform stands for, that they would walk out on us. Mr. President, under circumstances like this, with all the danger that hangs over our community, we can't have that. If we have calm and peace, I think we are all prepared to face the problem: retraining of those men, reindoctrinating them. Yes sir, but it's something that we can't do tonight or tomorrow or maybe the next day. But it is something we're prepared to face; it is something we're prepared to work on. But at this instant, under this enormous pressure, I would say in all honesty it's virtually impossible to do it today or tomorrow. We must have just what I said a few moments ago: we have got to have a few hours or a few days of peace so we can go to work. And that rightly sums up the problem.

And as long as there are people who have—we have no difficulty, Mr. President, in talking to people that live in Birmingham. I worked in a steel plant there for four or five years. Whenever the noon whistle blew, I fell into line to buy sweet milk at the canteen—there was a Negro in front of me, a Negro behind me. And when we sat down to eat lunch, they sat just as close as Frank Newton and I are sitting here. We discussed things in common. When they talked about family, sure colored people got up on one side and I got up on mine, because there was no common ground there. And we talked about the news and the weather and sometimes about you, sir [*chuckles*]. And there was no difficulty there.

Now this sort of personal relationship exists. That there are inequities, sir, we do not for a moment deny it. We realize that there are inequities in education, although our Negro teachers are paid higher than our white teachers and about 65 percent of our educational budget in the last five years has been spent on Negro schools. Actually the best, finest, newest schools in Birmingham are Negro schools, with only one exception of a white high school that has been completed in the last couple of years.

We know there are inequities in hiring. We know there are inequities in their, though this presently does not exist, in voting reception, but we are not turning down Negroes. We are not refusing to qualify them. Many of our industries have already done away with the double standards of seniority. A great deal is being done. That is being done quietly; you don't get [*unclear*] to Birmingham and write that—not at the present moment and under the present atmospheres. . . .

Marks: We had, Mr. President, at the height of the demonstrations, no absenteeism in industry. Almost all of our demonstrators came from the unemployed and from the students who were on the streets at the time. Truly, I'd like to echo very briefly of what Mr. Hamilton has said, and that is if we can just get all of these outside agitating influences on both sides out of Birmingham for a little while, we can sit down and talk to our well-run and well-respected colored people in Birmingham. I don't believe this will be a problem, if the atmosphere is proper for talking to.

But right now, both sides are somewhat leery of [*chuckles*] trying to sit down and discuss this thing because tempers have flared on both sides, and it makes it very difficult to enter into a harmonious, free, and above-board discussion. And I think it would be very difficult under the circumstances to get anybody together to do this.

President Kennedy: Well, you know, I was talking to, there were seven Negro citizens came up the other day to talk to me. As I understand that . . . I suppose what four or five of them you'd regard as natives of Birmingham?

Hamilton: Yes, sir, two or three, four—

President Kennedy: Shuttlesworth, the Reverend Shuttlesworth and Reverend King would be regarded as coming in when you talk about the "outside" versus the "inside." Well now the one of them was president of a school there?

Unidentified: Dr. Pitts.

President Kennedy: Dr. Pitts, and one was a Negro businessman.

Unidentified: Gaston.

President Kennedy: Gaston. And there were two others. . . .

Can't you get to talk to, they seemed to me to be . . . I don't know any-thing about them, except that I just met them. But can't you do anything with them?

Marks: I've been in Mr. Gaston's office on many occasions to discuss his contributions to the United Appeal and things of that kind. I've always found him to be quite easy to talk to.

President Kennedy: Well now then, it seems to me there must be some leadership there that is not regarded as incendiary by the white commu-nity. But I think one of the things that they said to me, this wasn't just Reverend King and Reverend Shuttlesworth, but that they had the feeling about a lack of communication. I know there is a biracial group, but I understand it's rather large; it's not very active.

Frank Newton: Might I speak on that?

President Kennedy: Surely.

Newton: I made a few notes here, because I wanted to make my points. But I am chairman of that committee and there are 250 or thereabouts members of it, and they're from all walks of community life. They're peo-ple in the management group and the labor group, there are ministers, educators, housewives, small businessmen, merchants, and professional men, and they are members of both races. And all of these people have volunteered their service with one interest and that is finding a solution to our problem. And each has indicated a field of action in which their spe-cial interests or their talents are directed, and they've been assigned to sub-committees in accordance with their preferences.

And we have committees including finance and revenue for the city, public schools, group relations, adult reeducation, youth, and so forth. And all of these fields have a prominent bearing on our problems. Now, these people have shown a very obvious dedication to this job. They have a willingness to work and they also are willing to face disagreements with their friends and with their associates over matters of principle.

But much progress has been made, but it has not been adequately pub-licized and I think rightly so. There are many of these things that you don't publicize. The agreements which were made by the Senior Citizens Committee have been carried out in two phases. And there have been changes in the city ordinance which were objectionable to these people. And the present city government made these changes with the idea of improving the relationships in the community. And there have been changes in the work rules and employment practices of industry and com-mercial establishments.

Now, this has not been publicized in the press because it's not customary to do it within a business. It's not a normal process. But these changes are known by the employees of these establishments of both races and they have been communicated to their friends outside of the organization. And the publicity so far as the community is concerned has been adequate, but it hasn't been national publicity.

Now, there's been much agitation, and it's our belief that the stimulus for this has come from outside of Birmingham. From some organizations with special interest to benefit, from certain individuals, and it has produced problems that both races have had trouble meeting. But the leaders of both races feel that these matters can be resolved properly over a period of time if we are left alone, but it's essential that the source of these incidents be removed. And this we think is a national problem. It exists in other places, in addition to in Alabama and in addition to Birmingham. And we believe that if it is not effectively treated, the trend in civil disobedience is going to lead to revolution. Encouragement to violate deeprooted principles can be just as disastrous as encouragement to violate the laws of a civilized land.

Now, there've been charges of police brutality, when in reality we have a well-trained police force and they have acted with admirable restraint in the face of dangerous provocation. Our local government has attempted to deal with law violators and deal equal justice regardless of their race. And if we can have an avoidance of these incidents and a cessation of them, then the local citizens of both races believe that we can work out our problems.

Our long-standing customs [*unclear*] do not yield, however, too well to force, any more than they do on the part of other people. We realize that we stand indicted before the world by press agents, but we have not been convicted of the bombings. We're decent people and we believe we can handle our problems if we are left alone without outside agitation. Pardon the use of notes, but I felt that I wanted to be careful to make my points and to be careful of my choice of words.

Landon Miller: Mr. President, may I add a word or two to this? This new government that came in hasn't had an opportunity to do the many things that they wanted to do. You're right in the middle of the term of office; I'm sure you're familiar with that. The people of Birmingham knew that the old regime was not getting done what it needed to do. And so the Mayor, the whole, the other group did not get to fulfill their terms.

The very day that this group came in, the demonstrations started. Well, I've met with groups of ministers, we've been meeting biracially for months. And I had been meeting before with other groups that were seeking to make improvements and who had to do it in the background because of the temper of the people of Birmingham. There are lots of people we ran into when we left the airport yesterday; there were signs over our heads saying, "These liberals do not represent us." Well, when you have that kind of an incendiary situation, you're on the horns of this dilemma.

President Kennedy: Well, that ought to just give you a taste of what we go through up here. . . . [*Laughter.*]

Miller: Yes.

President Kennedy: No, but I mean the fact that you come and even talk up here, then they charge you and I just appreciate—

Miller: Yes [*unclear*].

President Kennedy:—that, how difficult it is to . . . I understand the problem with Birmingham. Every time [*soft laughter in background*] that you indicate any desire to bring this situation—Burke Marshall told me all about it last spring when there was an effort to see if an arrangement could be worked out that would end the demonstrations—and everybody who tried to get into it was immediately hailed as a traitor to the traditional feelings of Birmingham. So I don't think it's probably, I'm sure it isn't very easy. The difficulty—

Miller: What is important—

President Kennedy: [*speaking simultaneously*] What? Excuse me. What were you saying?

Miller: I started to say, what you have to do, is you have to do it quietly. So the Negro ministers said to us, as I tried to relay to them some of the things that I had found in all of these meetings during the past year, they said, "Why didn't you tell us?" We said, "We couldn't tell you, but didn't the change in government say something to you?" They said, "It didn't say enough."

But the ministers themselves and the people didn't get into this; they were very reluctant to get behind this movement, and stayed out of it. I know that from talking to them, observations, until the school children were brought in and then that did rile them. And naturally it would because I went down, and a lot of ineptness was done in the handling of these school children. I went down to the various places where they were incarcerated; it was a mild type of thing. But we talked to Earl Stallings tonight. He'll be here tonight in the group of ministers that are coming. He said that we said to them, "Do you know where your children are?" He said, "We haven't seen them in three days."

Well, they had to process these hundreds of children and maybe they should have just been sent home or something else. But under the strain of that, when the schoolchildren got in, then all the parents got in, and then the ministers got in behind it, and so it developed into something, but at first they didn't want to.

And that's why we keep talking about outside leadership; it's been so difficult to handle it. The local men are aware . . . It's a very capable man, Lucius Pitts, spoke to our white ministers' conference in the May meeting, which we had had a week early (had it in April), and there's been a real good feeling between them. But all of this has precipitated a feeling that now makes it difficult for us to move out like we need to move out. Our problem is in the web of all these angry feelings that are here. So what's done, as far as people of Birmingham handled it, they handled it quietly. And they're anxious to do something, but to do something fast precipitates worse troubles than if we could move on it gradually.

Marks: We've got to make some move, Mr. President, to get ourselves out of the headlines if we can, so that we can begin to cease drying up industrially because we are losing industry as you can well imagine from this situation that has existed, and we're losing financial support. For example, a couple of New York banks the other day withdrew loan commitments for construction of housing in the Birmingham area. I'm told by some officials of Hayes Aircraft that some military procurement people have been reluctant to place business in the Birmingham district for fear of being criticized.

President Kennedy: Oh, I agree. I think that—

Marks: And this is a terrible problem for us.

President Kennedy: What we'd like to do is to be some help in seeing if the situation could be eased enough to permit some progress. The question of outside agitators, the question really is: How are you going to keep them out?

Hamilton: That's the trouble.

President Kennedy: How are you going to keep them out?

Hamilton: [*Unclear*] is what the Negro leaders say to me and this is the heart and the crux there. There are four groups in Birmingham [*unclear*] and I think Burke will bear out this analysis. We have the political group. There are about 10,000 [*unclear*] well organized. They can deliver about 95 percent of their people; they're a potent factor. Then there is the economic community . . . which is the social business organization. They are considered generally Uncle Toms, "white folks' niggers." I use the expression—

President Kennedy: I understand.

Hamilton:—advisedly. Then there is the—this may amuse you, but it is nonetheless descriptive—there is the messianic group who vow defeat of Dr. King. And then there is the ambitious, the extremely activist, hard-pushing group, which Fred Shuttlesworth more or less . . . [*unclear*]. Now those four, we run into this difficulty, for instance, in naming to the steering committee of Mr. Newton's general committee. There was actually only one Negro in the city of Birmingham who was wholly acceptable to all four of those groups. That was Arthur Shores.[3] Everyone else was suspect.

The problem, sir, is how to develop authoritative leadership in the Negro community that can accomplish something for themselves to establish a sense of responsibility. Unless we can give our local people credit, unless we can, for instance, let Arthur Shores, or let Gaston, or let anybody else (it doesn't make any difference to us). But he needs to be able to stand up in front of his people and say, "You can follow me because look, I'm getting results for you." At the present moment and after the demonstrations, who got the credit?

President Kennedy: King. King and Shuttlesworth.

Hamilton: King and Shuttlesworth. So the next time trouble develops, sir, they do not come to us and seek to work it out. Instead, they call him back again. . . .

President Kennedy: I agree, now let me . . . it seemed to me . . . as I understand it, King left after this agreement of May or June. Why wasn't it possible then or why isn't it possible now, if we're—let's say that Mr. Royall and Blaik go there and we have some days of quiet—why isn't it possible to do something? It seems to me there are two or three things that aren't very difficult to do. You must know the situation, I think you do, much better than I do, that you could do and do it with the local groups. Now, what's happening, of course, is that this thing is becoming more and more radical.

Here's this story from the *New York Times* [*reading*]: "Rallies Are Made in Protest Killing of Six in Alabama. Ten Thousand Cheer Denunciation of Kennedy. [*Unclear*] of Mass Rights Uprising Urged. Ten thousand people here yesterday cheered the denunciation of President Kennedy and called for a civil disobedience campaign that might spread to a hundred cities."[4] And then it goes on to say that, that for those three demonstrators . . . And then it says [*reading*]: "Strong and often bitter statements were voiced at the Foley Square in front of the Department of Justice by such speakers as James Farmer, national director of the Con-

---

[3]Shores was a leading black lawyer in Birmingham.
[4]Only a few days before, there had been a large demonstration in front of the Department of Justice building in Washington, during which James Farmer of CORE, Bayard Rustin, an organizer of the March on Washington, James Baldwin, and others had denounced the passivity of the Kennedy administration in the face of continued atrocities in Birmingham.

gress of Racial Organizations; Bayard Rustin, deputy director of the recent March on Washington for Jobs and Freedom; James Baldwin, author and member of [*unclear*]. The more militant the statement, the heartier the response. Mr. Rustin drew widespread approval, for instance, when he started out with a denunciation of the use of mounted policemen against demonstrators."

Well now, the point of the matter is, what's happening is, we're just talking this morning—we're about to have all the major Negro groups attack our civil rights bill, which you gentlemen, I'm sure, would regard as deplorable and all the rest. They're about to come out against it because it's inadequate.

So he said [*reading*], "If the federal government did not give black men and women and tiny children protection, they would not be men with red blood in their bodies. [*Unclear*] take whatever weapons were at hand. [*Unclear.*] The crowd, with white participants somewhat more numerous than Negroes, was more receptive to Mr. Rustin . . . about massive demonstrations. I call now for uprising nonviolent. Mr. Farmer declared the civil rights leadership offered a very cheap revolution in terms of casualties. They charge that President Kennedy and the Department of Justice could have been active and must share the blame for the bombings in Birmingham. They demand use of federal troops and the use of the Alabama city. . . . The administration will not be moved, Mr. Farmer asserted, and the present administration be replaced."

Well, what that all adds up to is that [*laughter*] it's getting, it's getting, everybody wants to replace the present administration. It's getting hotter—

Hawkins: That's true in Birmingham.

President Kennedy:—and SNCC, which is a very radical group, as you know, very radical, wanted to come in at Birmingham, and I think if they did, you would have, certainly you'd have, which is what they wanted, which was violence, and then you would have some killings and you would have a situation with the demand for federal intervention.

Now, isn't it possible, with everything you say about what you've tried to do and everything—the problem is, we've got a situation here—isn't it possible to do something with either the Negro ministers, or the people who come from the community and do something about the police force or about hiring some people in these stores, which, as I understand, was one of the subjects discussed in May and June, so that there appears to be some progress?

Now, I know everybody hates to look like they're backing down under pressure. But somebody has to do something because otherwise you're going to have another bombing or somebody's going to get shot some night, and 10 people are going to get killed or 15, and that would just about be the end of Birmingham. So it seems to me it's much easier for somebody to have . . .

What we are doing, for example, we're, we're going to have a, just speaking privately here, we're going to have a fight with all these Negro organizations about our legislation because they want to put FEPC in. Well, FEPC in our opinion means that you won't get anything by, you won't get anything by. And you're going to have a *really* turn radical left among all the Negro communities, [*unclear*]. So I think somebody has to break the ice and do something in the next two or three weeks, which gives a visible evidence of movement. Now this whole police force here is integrated in Washington. I don't know why, but I should think that white policemen would be tired of having to go down into the Negro community and arrest—

Unidentified: Well—

President Kennedy:—Negroes in crap games, or drunk, or in everything else.

Hamilton: He's in a peculiar position, Mr. President. He fights white folks by day and Negroes by night.

President Kennedy: I know it. Well, I mean I just see this police force here is integrated in Washington. As I say, I know Washington isn't Birmingham, but it does have 55 percent Negroes and it does have plenty of violence in this city potentially. But I think the Negro police make a terrific difference. A white man arrests a Negro these days, anyplace in the United States, and it's trouble, whether it's Chicago or Birmingham.

I know the difficulty of, how mad they get, but it's just, they, hell, they're integrated in the armed forces, you ought to be able to have them in the police force; you don't have to put them all in the same room, but you can have them [in] different sections of the city and start it out pretty slowly, or get them in some clerks. You have to have two or three things happen, which appears to mean that there's some effort to change the climate. Then I should think the responsibility goes on to the Negro leadership to be more moderate.

Unidentified: More peaceful.

President Kennedy: I think, after all, King did go back, he left in June and I think he left the city then for a while. Now it would seem to me it might be possible, which is after all the object, but you can't argue because we can't win the argument; it's got to be [*unclear*] to Birmingham. Is there anything that can be done?

I can't get the, I think what you were suggesting is, for some reason, I could get these fellows out of town. I can't. As you can see, their view of me is increasingly critical and will be. And that's natural because they always have to be more extreme. But I can't tell people to leave town; others will come up. You'll get the student group in there and you're going to have some real . . . the SNCC group will come in, and they're completely, as I've said, they're very far over to the left.

Newton: Well, we're moving in this direction.

President Kennedy: Can't you get something that would give some appearance?

Newton: Each time we have an incident, it sets a pattern.

President Kennedy: I know, I know.

Newton: There's a reluctance of people to move until the thing settles down. Now, if I may use my own company as an example, we have set regulations with our union. But so far as the racial question is concerned, the union problems have been worked out. Now—

President Kennedy: What company, what do you do?

Newton: Bell Telephone.

President Kennedy: Right.

Newton: But we have now, in other words, entrance jobs for people seeking employment. We have only one job where at the moment it's restricted from Negroes and that's the operator's job. Any other one . . . But we do have this requirement, that they must be qualified, and there are certain employment tests or certain requirements, which we give to everybody, white or black. And the situation is such now that qualified people of either race will be accepted on any job, entrance job, except operator. Now, after their entrance jobs, on entrance jobs, and other jobs open up, then under our union contract we have what is known as bidding. They can bid for a job and then they have to be examined along with other bidders and qualified people. The best qualified person, that's who gets the job. But, we—

President Kennedy: If you do that, why is it that, I'm just trying to think of two or three things might be done that could indicate some movement in the city, which would lessen the tension. Now, nobody can tell, I don't know—maybe there's going to be another bombing; you know, we can only hope that's not so. But aside from that, isn't there some actions that can be—if you can do that in your company and in that union, why is it that they can't do something about the police force and about clerks in these stores, which as I understood, the clerks in stores was something that was talked about last spring.

Newton: There was a clerk recently employed in one of the stores. But when we had a bombing, as you know, a tear gas bombing in one of the department stores, then that slows the whole process down. There's a feeling, well, this is a manifestation of the opposition. And if it happened here, it's gonna happen here. Now, until you can identify the bomber, whoever he may have been, he's still at large. What's to prevent the same thing happening again? And instead of tear gas, maybe they [*unclear*] the church. And there's a reluctance to move, a willingness to move. The president of [*unclear*] called me just before I left, and he indicated that they are willing to move.

President Kennedy: But can't they do it in five stores at once? I understand the problem about it, but I'm just, it would seem to me it would be . . . You're not going to get these fellows to leave. Let's just accept the idea. It may be part of the feeling in Birmingham that this administration can move these people in and out. I'm just telling you flatly we can't do it, and this is only the most limited evidence. Others will come in, and as I say, in my opinion are, they're going to be worse that come in, but that time will only tell that. And I think that when you see Farmer, who's with CORE, which was not the most extreme one, unless he starts to move over, then it indicates they're all beginning to outbid each other. Roy Wilkins and . . . will have to go and they all will. Besides, you can't move them out; you'll have others could take their place. And the Reverend knows for the last, the gospel was spread by outsiders. There's somebody's going to come in there and they're going to talk and they're going to exploit, for one reason or another; there are all kinds of reasons why they do it.

But the problem is, is there anything that you can do now, in this, as you see it in this city in the next month or so that would provide some diminution of tension in Birmingham, and appear to do so publicly so it appears that progress is, while however rocky it may be, it can be made?

Hamilton: Well now is a good time—

President Kennedy: But I tell you, it isn't any use to come at least to say to me to get the agitators out because I can't get them out because I didn't put them in. I think everybody ought to understand that.

Newton: There are a lot of people, though—

President Kennedy: [*Unclear.*]

Newton:—if I may give you a straightforward answer, but a respectful answer. There's a lot of people, though, that think you have given those people encouragement.

President Kennedy: I understand that and I understand that they feel that, but I'm just saying to you what I've tried to do is because I do feel we've got to make progress in this area. And I think that if confidence is lost in the national government by the Negro community as a whole—I'm not talking about these fellows because I don't really think they can deliver. But if it's lost and if there's no support for what I would regard as legitimate requests. Let me make it clear that I regard getting on the police force as legitimate, and I regard people working as clerks in stores as legitimate, and I would do that, and I don't think you can take any other position from the national point of view.

And my opinion is if you can integrate an armed service where you have to live together, eat together, use the same john, and all the rest, you can in these cases work together. The kind I'm talking about. That doesn't mean that I think you can do anything about all the rest of the deeply held principles. We're not talking about that; we're talking about some things which are rather limited.

Newton: We believe—

President Kennedy: So I believe in that kind of progress. Now—

Newton: We believe that your public accommodations goes beyond that, though.

President Kennedy: [*disdainfully*] Oh, public accommodation is nothing. When I think what Harry Truman did in integrating the armed forces—to give you an honest answer, and a respectful one—that was really tough [*laughter*]. That was really tough. In the first place, most of the armed forces is made up of, a good proportion of them are southerners, and traditionally [*unclear*]. Imagine putting them together in a barracks, taking kids out of Mississippi and all the rest, putting them into a barracks, putting them under a Negro sergeant? They did that 15 years ago.

When I look back in retrospect, that was really rough because the public accommodation section, when it finally passes, will say that if you, and it's, if you've got the money, you can go to a hotel or motel. How many Negroes are you going to see in a hotel or motel from one day to another? I've been running around Washington 15 years. How often do you see them in a motel or the Statler Hotel or the rest? And they will have a dollar limit because of the substantial effect on commerce, and in my opinion that's a relatively mild bill and that's why they're finally going to come out against it. The hard part that I can see if I were a southerner is in education, in the schools. That's the tough one—

Newton: [*Unclear*]—

President Kennedy: You've got a population [*unclear*]. That I completely understand: how tough that is, but not in public accommodation or in whether a boy goes or a girl goes down to university. That's nothing, but it's when you get down to secondary education, where you've got 30 or 40 percent Negroes, I appreciate completely what that problem is. I mean nobody up here is naive about it or doesn't understand it.

I've seen what's happened in Washington, which has got 54 percent Negro and it's [the public school system] 85 percent: the whites just running out of Washington. Nobody wants that. Public accommodations are nothing. My God, you can walk into a store or go into a hotel. Of course they could go into the Statler Hotel, but they don't go into the Statler Hotel and they won't be coming into the hotel in Birmingham. They will have the right to, but they won't have the money or the inclination.

So I don't think public accommodation, if you analyze it, is tough at all. I think integrating the Army was tough. I don't think going to the university was tough. I think the secondary school is really tough. I don't think jobs are tough. So that's at least where I, so I'm, we're not, we're not, you know, I can, I understand what the problem is. We're not just sitting up here—

Newton: Let me—

President Kennedy:—unaware of what the southerners are up against. It's very easy. They won't let a Negro in the Metropolitan Club, which is the most exclusive club. All the columnists who write outrageous things about how terrible it is in Birmingham won't even let a Negro ambassador come into lunch. Now they're telling you how to run your affairs. I understand Mississippi, where it's 45–50 percent Negro, where half of them, three-quarters, haven't gone beyond the sixth grade, what it means to try to integrate those schools. That's why, in my opinion, what you're going to get for years and years is a kind of—three or four or five will go in there. That, that's, that I understand, the gut feeling about that, but I don't understand the gut feeling about the police force, I don't understand the gut feeling about clerks, and I don't understand the gut feeling about public accommodation, or about whether a student goes to Huntsville. Now that's my feeling about it.

Now, what we would like to try to do—just, I mean, I don't enjoy at all being in an argument with Alabama. I mean it's a good state and they've been very fine with me, as far as I'm concerned. You've got a damned good congressional delegation, you have very good senators. We don't want to be down in Birmingham and I just think that there must be something— you fellows live there. I don't put these agitators in there. You can say we encourage them or not encourage . . . that really isn't the question.

The fact of the matter is that when they go, when Shuttlesworth and King go, what you're liable to have are people like the SNCC group and others who will be very, or Farmer, who will be very much, who will [be] attacking me constantly, very much against this administration for betrayal and all the rest. You'll still have the same problem in Birmingham. And I think it suggests—maybe we haven't done anything right here, but in the final analysis you've got to settle it. Given the problem as it is today, we would like to be of any help we could, and I would do anything that we can up here reasonably. But isn't there something you can now do, given the problem as it is, that's going to make some difference to Birmingham? You ought to be able to turn that situation around somewhat.

Newton: We think we have turned it around. We think we're moving in that direction, but we continue to get backsets. If and when we can stop these incidents, I think from that point on you'll see continued progress—

President Kennedy: Well, if you can—

Newton:—and substantial progress.

President Kennedy: But what kind?

Several voices speak together.

Miller: Mr. President, that would be wonderful because people are reluctant, really, the timing would be wonderful; they're humiliated now.

President Kennedy: [*speaking over other voices*] But isn't there anything you can do, though?

Miller: If we don't have a reaction that will undo it, you see.

President Kennedy: That's right, I understand that, but isn't there something that can be done that could sort of be a signal, which would give everybody outside of Birmingham and all of us up here and other places, a chance to say, well now, they're trying, they're working this out, it's going ahead? That's why I said something last May about the settlement when it was finally reached. And there was, as you know, a lot of pressure then for a federal intervention. If there's something that could be done now, which you did last May and June, now it got a setback, and I think it's partly because of all the problems in the school situation and that's sort of steamed it up again. But isn't there some action you can take now that will give us a breathing spell? I think Birmingham was pretty well out of the front pages for three months.

· · ·

In response, the Birmingham leaders claimed progress had been made, but they were unable to specify precisely what that progress consisted of, at least not to the President's satisfaction. He continued to press them on particulars and repeated his injunction that they do something concrete and dramatic that would signal to Birmingham's black citizens and to the nation that the situation was being peacefully and energetically resolved.

· · ·

President Kennedy: Can you do anything about the police thing? When these fellows came up here, now, I tell you what they really talked to me about was the police; they made reference to the clerks, and then they had some problem about some insurance and the house, which hasn't anything to do with Birmingham just because the—but the police would seem to me to be the most obvious.

Marks: I would guess the way that could get done would be if they applied to the personnel board and passed the test. That's the only—

President Kennedy: It's tough to go get them, it's tough to get 'em. You have to get them, you have to go get them.

Hawkins: We're working on it. We know from home that this is a problem and we're working on it.

President Kennedy: Can't you get a couple? I know they're going to holler at everybody, the white group, but they're going to say you're giving in to pressure, but it seems to me it's going to make it much more difficult for—

Hawkins: Well, as Mr. Hamilton mentioned a moment ago, we have had in years gone by, and even during Mr. Connor's administration, we have had Negro men that have passed the examination for policeman, have been available off of the personnel board's list. But in waiting until time that we could hire, and goodness knows we didn't hire anybody else, they found something else that was more fruitful so they moved on to—

President Kennedy: I think probably you just have to go out and almost recruit them because there aren't very many that can pass the exam in competition with the whites.

Hawkins: We had just taken another examination and, of course, it was done just as we were leaving, we don't know the results of it, it will be 30 days before we will. But this is in the mill, this is going to work, and we feel like we've got a solution to it.

President Kennedy: I think you, frankly, I think you'll probably have to really make a deliberate effort to get them in. I would think that there isn't anything you could do that would make a—I know it's going to be awfully tough, but it would be more dramatic evidence. Then there would seem to me—I'm sure everybody, outside and in, would make some statement about the progress that's being made there and Birmingham should have a chance to work out its affairs.

Newton: This [*unclear*] can work.

President Kennedy: All it needs is a key that something is breaking, that's all, whether it's reestablishment of some kind of a relationship. In other words, the establishment of the uh, of the uh, I don't know whether you can reform the committee. I'm just trying to think of some actions that could be taken, which would give a sense of communication between the races and a sense of progress that this isn't an increasing cold war. Now, I don't know what it would be—maybe Burke's got some suggestions. What do you think, Burke?

Hawkins: Let me say this, just before you do, Mr. Marshall. Mr. Marshall has been to Birmingham and he's acquainted with our downtown setup. We've got many stores in downtown Birmingham that have got white and Negro clerks, shoe stores, and some of the stores along Fourth Avenue and Twentieth Street. They've got them already. They've been there for years. I'd say 15 to 20 years.

Unidentifed: Some of them were hired last week.

Hawkins: Some of them were already selling side by side. They don't notice these things. We have got in our hospitals, technicians working side by side in the hundreds. We've got in the dentists' and the doctors' offices all through the city, working side by side. They don't think of these things, but we're doing it. We're doing it every day. So when they pick out one thing, now we've got a nice department store downtown, they pick out this one place that they want to clerk. Well, that might be pushing a little bit too far. And certainly the people then boycotted the store because they integrated their restrooms. . . .

Marshall: They shouldn't; they should do it together. [*Unclear*] that's a problem for one store. And I'm sure all the store owners know it's a problem for one store. It's not as much—

Hawkins: It is.

Marshall:—It's still a problem, but it's not as much a problem as 10 or 15 years ago.

Hamilton: Well, that's the way it was on the lunch counters. Now that worked all right.

Marshall: Yes [*unclear*], on the lunch counters.

Hamilton: If all of them had done it at one time [*unclear*], "Katie, bar the door." They persuaded them to—every one, suburban and downtown— do it all at once.

Marshall: I think that the—

Hawkins: This happened without any fanfare.

Hamilton: Yeah, we can get [*unclear*] to do that.

Marshall: The problem of the incidents—having something happen— in part, that's related to the police problem because when you have a bombing, as we were discussing this morning, Mr. Hawkins, half the Negroes, or more than half, think the police had something to do with the bombing. Then the police go out to the house and they fight the crowd. And so there's some, if that happens once more, twice more, I just think a lot of people will get killed—

Unidentified: We would prevent it—

Marshall:—because there's more guns out in that area than there have ever been before. And so the thing simply is a matter of law enforcement. White policemen doing service in that area now is dangerous and every night it's dangerous, every night that goes by.

Marshall then described a recent visit he made to Birmingham.

Marshall: I told you that, Mr. Newton, that Sunday after the bombing, I went out to meet with the Negroes, up in John Drew's house, which is near Arthur Shore's house, up on what they call Dynamite Hill. And I was taken out by Captain [*unclear*] of the civil defense when they put a helmet on me, disguised as one of his civil defense people to get through. There were Negroes with guns armed on every street corner almost. Now that situation is going to continue unless something can be done to restore the confidence of the Negro community at—in large, in the police. And I don't say that they shouldn't have it now. There's no point in discussing whether there's been brutality in the past. The fact is, as Billy says, the police were hired and trained by Connor; they were used as an instrument of suppression and repression for many years. The Negroes haven't forgotten that; they can't forget it.

So that from the point of view of the city and the community and the future incidents, it seems to me that the single most important thing is to do something that restores that confidence. And, as you know, Mr. Hawkins, it's just as bad the other way, because heck, a lot of the whites think the Negroes did the bombing. But I think that that's the single most important thing and that until that's done, you're going to be living on the knife's edge, all the time, on the verge of a real racial war.

Miller: We all had many, many calls, before we left Birmingham, after we announced that the President was going to see us. We all had many calls. A number of them are just what you said, that the whites think the Negroes did the bombing; the Negroes think the police did the bombing. It's all a confused situation. And the people of Birmingham, as a whole, have in the back of their minds that maybe the Department of Justice or Washington knows who did the bombing and will not release the information.

Marshall: Of course, that's why Nathan Weaver made his statement the other day.

Miller: Well, of course, they say—

President Kennedy: Who is Nathan Weaver?

Marshall: He's the United States Attorney there.

President Kennedy: Yeah.

Marshall: He announced that there was a rumor that was quite widespread that Negroes had a cache of dynamite and TNT in the basement of that church. And that the little girl who was decapitated knocked over the TNT thereby setting off the dynamite. And the other rumor was that the janitor in the church had done it and the FBI had spirited him out of town so that no one would find out.

Miller: Oh boy.

President Kennedy: Do they really get so they believe that?

Hamilton: Yes, sir.

Miller: Oh, goodness, sure.

President Kennedy: Why would the FBI, which is not particularly—which has been the object of a good deal of criticism by the Negroes—why would they want to . . . Why would anybody think that [*unclear*] like that? However, the problem is they think it. . . .

· · ·

Kennedy also defended the presence of Martin Luther King in the city. Contrary to the claims of those at the meeting, Kennedy said King was a voice of calm, especially in contrast to SNCC. King "preaches a doctrine of nonviolence," the President reminded them, but others in the black community did not. So it was far better to deal with King and stop griping about "outside interference." The alternatives would be far worse. If King failed, moderate voices would be drowned out. That was the way it always was with protest movements. The moderates eventually get shouted down by those calling for swift, immediate, and violent action. If King lost face over Birmingham, the President said, the shock waves would be felt throughout the country. "The fellow who says, 'Well, let's wait and see,' becomes an Uncle Tom. So I think we're going to have an awful lot of trouble. I'm going to have it up to here, not just in Birmingham but all over the country." Even the civil rights bill would be jeopardized. Taking Kennedy's words to heart, William Hamilton asked, "Where will it end, Mr. President?"

· · ·

President Kennedy: I don't know where it will end. I think that probably we'll get through it, as we do in most . . . But it will take a lot of action by the church groups—Negro and white—and I think we'll get through it. I think this bill, I think is very important because I think it's going to give us a good deal, a breathing spell, for some years. If we don't get it by, there's going to be demands for more legislation next year. And I think you'll find this bill, like a lot of other bills which you dread, that it isn't going to be very bad. That's my view and it will be very helpful. I think we'll get through it, but we're going to have a very difficult time—all over the country, not just Birmingham.

But looking at Birmingham now, I think that if we can leave it, you were asking . . . I think that the press will be after you and I think we ought to try to keep it as . . . I think that if you feel that Mr. Blaik and Mr. Royall coming down there is helpful, I think it would be useful to say that they'll be warmly welcomed, and that you'll be glad to have them come down. They're outstanding Americans, which they are. And that [*unclear*] look at the situation there. And that you came and told me about what you're trying to do in Birmingham, and your concern about the situation in Birmingham, the progress that you've made. . . .

Let me just close by saying I appreciate you coming up here. We're all together in this difficulty, and I do think if you could consider what steps could be taken in the next two or three weeks as quickly as possible, particularly maybe tied into the meetings that Mr. Blaik and Royall might have. . . . We could then call attention to some of the things that are being done down there if you could get something to be done. Now, if you gentlemen could decide what it is that could be done. But I do think something needs to be done just to give everybody a hook to hang it on, and rather than just continue to separate, because the final explosion will be a disaster for Birmingham and the United States.

Marks: That's the reason we're here, Mr. President, because we see such a rapid deterioration of the relationships between the white and colored communities. I mean, we had good relationships with them and now this has been very badly undermined. There's a lot of bitterness on both sides.

Hawkins: Well, as I mentioned a moment ago—

Marks: Somewhat surprised at the rapid deterioration of the thing—

Hawkins:—integration and economical conditions are two of our problems.

President Kennedy: And I think you might point that out to the press, too, about the economic problems in Birmingham as a factor. Because the difficulty is that the people we're trying to—they're off these farms, and they can't do anything except human labor, in a sense, and there aren't any jobs now for unskilled labor. But anyway, I think that is a factor in Birmingham. . . .

I'm sure that some of your, a lot of your calls, and I gather from what you said that there's a strong feeling that if they can get the outside people out, that this could be solved and that the outside people could be gotten out by the Washington administration. I don't really think, it isn't that easy. I don't think I can get them out, but I'm afraid if I got, if I used, if I called King, and said, speaking as president, "I think that you should leave." And Shuttlesworth. Let's assume they did leave. Well, either you . . . We're still going to have the same problem there is the point. I don't think really—I know a lot of people always like to say that if—I don't really think that's probably the answer. I think that—

Hawkins: Well, without them we have to talk with our own.

President Kennedy:—I think if you talk with your own, I don't think it's really necessary to talk to Young and Shuttlesworth.

Hawkins: Well, they think so though, Mr. President.

President Kennedy: I'm sure they do, but they're like everybody. What?

Marshall: They never did last night. Shuttlesworth's somewhat different. King never insisted on it.

Newton: But Shuttlesworth is the real problem, not King.

Marshall: I think it should be recognized that the President noted that. [*Unclear*] I know how much attention is focused on King down there, how much is blamed on him as if he caused these problems. But the fact is last Wednesday was typical of the danger of putting your hopes in the . . . that this will all go away if only he would go away. Last Wednesday at that funeral, King and Shuttlesworth stopped the demonstration which the SNCC workers had started, which would have, I think, led to killings in Birmingham, and it would have been worse than the bombing. Now King and Shuttlesworth did that. The students were in there and they don't care.

President Kennedy: Yeah.

Marshall: They don't care if people get killed.

President Kennedy: They're the ones that [*unclear*]. We got the—

Marshall: King cares.

President Kennedy: King has got a terrific investment in nonviolence and SNCC has got an investment in violence, and that's the struggle. SNCC is the . . . I mean there's no . . . I don't know what will happen there.

Hawkins: Who is heading up SNCC?

President Kennedy: Well, this fellow, [John] Lewis . . . who was on [*unclear*] is one of them. Student what?

Marshall: Student Nonviolent Coordinating Committee.

President Kennedy: They're . . . they're sons of bitches, I'll tell you that.

Unidentified: They really are. They are the ones who are planning to—

Overlapping voices.

President Kennedy: Oh, well they are . . . they're going to get tougher [*unclear*]. They're going to be tough.

Overlapping voices.

Unidentified: Block the airports and block the railroads, and the busses, and everything else. That's a real militant group.

President Kennedy: That's why I don't know whether King is, as I say, I suppose King will be leaving, but I'm not sure if King being out of there—

Marshall: He would not have come back except for the bombing. He came back.

President Kennedy:—[*unclear*] be a mess if you have King out of there. But in any case, if after, whatever Blaik and Royall think is useful, I'll try to do, when they come back, and I appreciate any help you can give them. And, as I said, I wish you'd consider what actions could be taken, whether it's even public relations action, as well as any practical action. But anything that gives a hook, which you can suggest that the prospects are better, which can give those of us who would like to see it get easier, something that we can say about the improvement. When the agreement was made last June, I said something in my press conference about the situation. I think that, and that did—I don't know enough about it—but it seemed to me that until the school situation, which was I think exacerbated in the state which—and then the bombing. At least the situation when King was out of town and it was somewhat [*unclear*]. But I think if we could now get a, some kind of a—and there must be enough brains there to think of it—some actions which could be taken of both the window dressing, if you want to use that word, or the formation of groups, plus some breakthroughs in employment. It would seem to me it would give everybody a feeling that maybe Birmingham was going to move a little.

Miller: May I express appreciation personally for the—I have a feeling more than I did before that you at least are aware of our problems in a greater way than we—

President Kennedy: Yeah, well—

Miller:—perhaps thought you were. [*Unclear*] some of the same problems in your office.

President Kennedy:—Yeah, well, it's a—[*unclear*]. This is, as I say, our most difficult . . . and I never would have guessed that even in February. We thought we were doing pretty well, with this and that. But suddenly this has exploded somehow, and I don't know whether we can get the genie back in the bottle again or not. But I think this sort of story shows where it's going nationally. And within, in my opinion, within a month to two weeks, all of the Negro leadership will be denouncing us. And so we have a problem. That is not a major problem, except that if the extreme leadership gets control of the Negro community nationwide, and you have 10 percent of the population under the control of the most radical leadership, I think you really have a very dangerous situation.

Marks: A very explosive situation.

. . . .

Shortly after this, the meeting broke up. Birmingham would no longer monopolize national headlines, and for Kennedy, at least, it was one less problem to worry about. But the bombings had hardened lines in Congress, and the administration now had to turn its attention to the House Judiciary Committee and its two key representatives, the Democrat Emanuel Celler from Brooklyn and the Republican William McCulloch from Ohio.

Chapter 6
The Bill Moves Forward

In order to get through the House, the administration's bill needed bipartisan support and the backing of a broad array of liberals and conservatives. The liberals, who had been supporting civil rights reform for years, were determined to make sure that this time civil rights legislation would not be merely symbolic. Unfortunately, that strategy also suited the opponents of the bill because the more expansive the draft bill, the more likely it would be defeated, if not in Emanuel Celler's committee, then on the House floor.

In the fall of 1963, Celler moved toward reporting a bill that reflected the demands of both liberals and of civil rights leaders. The bill would ban all discrimination in public accommodations, and in public and private schools; it would also give the federal government the power to bring suits on behalf of citizens claiming violations, and the power to enforce the law in the face of southern resistance. However noble its intentions, such a bill carried a high risk of failure. One of the many challenges Kennedy faced in these months was that of moderating the draft bill's language so as to give the legislation a chance to succeed. That did not mean eviscerating federal enforcement powers, but it did mean shading the language, keeping private associations largely untouched, leaving key voting rights issues out of the bill, and including provisions limiting what the Justice Department could do.

This process involved hours of meetings between administration officials and congressional leaders. Some of the meetings were conducted at the highest level, with the President, Attorney General, and committee chairs working through the bill's language and provisions.

While working closely with legislative leaders to craft the bill, Kennedy also did what he could to gather the necessary Republican support. One of the most influential leaders in the Republican Party was former President

Dwight Eisenhower, who was living comfortably in retirement in Gettysburg, Pennsylvania. If Kennedy could get Eisenhower to press House Republicans to support the civil rights bill, that could be a substantial boon. In an effort to obtain Eisenhower's blessing, Kennedy dispatched Eugene Carson Blake, a distinguished minister associated with the National Council of Churches, to Gettysburg. On September 30, Blake, who had been Eisenhower's pastor in Washington, met with Kennedy at the White House to brief him on the former President's position.

Monday, September 30, 1963, 12:40 P.M.

Meeting with Eugene Carson Blake

Eugene Carson Blake: I took some time to get my appointment; I had an hour and a half with him. He seemed to be very glad to talk. He didn't want me to bring Martin Luther King or [*unclear*]. He wanted to be quiet, so I just went with his pastor and he wanted to talk. I've got some notes here to make sure that I get the order that I want. Number one, he assured me when I left that he would be talking to the congressional leaders, Republican congressional leaders again, and that . . . So far as I was able to tell, he thoroughly agrees that this civil rights ought not to be a partisan matter. He put it that justice to the people ought not to be the credit of any party. I think the most interesting thing that, as far as I was concerned, although I am very much of an amateur in this thing, he did make a concrete suggestion, which, I don't know how it would be implemented, but he said, if both parties could have the same civil rights plank next year, this might help. Now, is that a possible thing to work out?

President Kennedy: Yeah, I think we could think up . . . I think we could talk about it. I don't know whether they would . . . I think it is an interesting idea.

Blake: What he was trying to do is make it that we are for the same thing and therefore . . .

President Kennedy: Well, I think if we could get the same bill this time, then I think . . . If we have a difference in our legislative approach, and of course, it is going to be reflected in the thing. But I wouldn't certainly dismiss that. I have no objection to having the same, but . . . If we could get so we could both support the same bill this year, and write the same thing into the plank, I think it would have merit.

Blake: I will. . . . I report to you what you doubtless remember from the conversation. He told me that he had felt that you were mistaken putting an omnibus bill anyway and that . . . But, I was pushing on the different parts to see what was wrong. The only negative thing I got from him is the interstate commerce on the public accommodations. When he first started talking about public accommodations, he was pretty cold to it in general. I was pushing him on it and he said, well, Fourteenth Amendment, yes.

President Kennedy: But we don't care at all. That's not really involved.

Blake: Well, I thought that you should . . .

President Kennedy: And we do . . . In the language I think they're going to use, they're going to have it covered by both. . . .

Blake: It's both as I understand it. But this was the only negative on the thing; as he talked . . . I came away with the feeling that he was open to trying to do this. But, how much, I mean, I couldn't get him on the line, "Now I will do this," and so on. I did indicate that you had expressed a desire that [*unclear*]; I said that you had said that he was the one who could do it. He is a little bit hesitant about throwing his weight around with the men and so on, and that he was going to see, and is seeing them regularly. I had the feeling that some kind of initiative from your side would probably be necessary for a next step. But I think it would be welcomed, as far as I can see, if it is; I talked to him about the, what I said was the difficulty of the Republicans in the North and what particularly the senators were talking about at the time. Really, if they fight against it, it doesn't do them any good and if they, if it is passed, why it is an administration measure, which doesn't do them any good next year. And he said yes, that's true. But he said, of course, some of the states, on the other hand, in the national situation of course and this is clear to you. I have just come out of the meeting Roy Wilkins is chairing of the people who have been lobbying. Now, they apparently have been successful with the [Celler] subcommittee.

President Kennedy: Yeah, they've gone, my opinion is they are making a mistake, while they are trying to write everything in it. You can't get the Republicans. We are talking on the one hand about bipartisan support. President Eisenhower won't support what they've done up there, and a lot of Republicans, we worked out an arrangement with McCulloch, so we had a pretty good bill, which was going to be bipartisan, but that Leadership Conference, mostly because of Clarence Mitchell, it seems to me, has run away with the situation.[1] Now you are going to end up with a fallout and then I don't think it's going to pass.

---

[1]Representative William McCulloch was a Republican congressman from Ohio; Mitchell was the NAACP's Washington representative.

Blake: Well, this is . . .

President Kennedy: And what good is that? The fact of the matter is, as you know, that a lot of these people would rather have an issue than a bill. But, as I said from the beginning, to get a bill we got to have bipartisanship. The bill they've written in the subcommittee, which is an unrepresentative group, I mean that does . . . You got to get a rule. How you going to get a rule out of that thing? You better get three Republicans on that rules committee to get a rule. Then you got to get it passed on the floor. Well, we had a bill which I understand they thought was unsatisfactory. But once they . . . they ran away with the subcommittee. And now I think, I don't know whether we can get 60 Republicans. And then, so you end up losing and then they'll go around saying, "Oh well. . . ."

Blake: Well, I'm no expert on this aspect of it at all, so I wouldn't do it. I think that they, I mean Roy Wilkins is shrewder than most of them in fact.

President Kennedy: And better judgment, that's right. But he's under pressure from . . .

Blake: He's under pressure. His, what he has felt—that the fatter the bill at the first stage, the more they got to trade with. I mean this is . . .

President Kennedy: I understand that's their feeling. The difficulty, is can you get 60 Republicans for this bill?

Blake: Well . . .

President Kennedy: If they can't get 60 Republicans, they don't have anything. . . .

For the next several minutes, they discussed the difficulty of getting Republican support. Kennedy told Blake that in 1957 Eisenhower had balked at supporting a bill that would have given the Attorney General the power to enter any suit for any civil rights infraction. He then recalled the problems of the 1960 bill.

President Kennedy: But I went through this in '60, when Clarence Mitchell, you see, what has happened is, that nobody wants to say, be a moderate, naturally, particularly in the Negro community—can't afford to be. So we have felt that if we could get the bill we put up there as close to it as possible, that we could then work with McCulloch. We can work with McCulloch for two months on the presumption that we've got to get bipartisan support. Now there is no sense in not having McCulloch's support because if you don't have McCulloch, McCulloch can deliver 60 Republicans. Without him, it can't be done. He's mad now because he thinks an agreement he had with us on language of compromise has been thrown away by the subcommittee, so now he's sore.

So the question is, how many Republicans you going to get? It seems very easy for them to give you the business because they do it all by televotes. Nobody has a roll call. And then there would be a roll call, and then they'd just knock these sections out. Once McCulloch is mad, then it ceases to be bipartisan and then you end up with what you've now got and I think that [*pause*]. But, we're going to try to work with the full committee now. But I think that they're wrong if they think the subcommittee is representative of the House. And I think Clarence Mitchell is the one who's pushing. . . . Clarence Mitchell is the one who has done most of the pushing. What they thought, were satisfied with a month ago, they now are not satisfied with. . . .

Yeah, you see, what I'm concerned about is it will get out of the committee and get to the Rules Committee. Then they won't give us a rule for maybe two or three months, figuring that maybe they can put it over until next year. And then, if they put it over until next year, it is a political year, a campaign year.

So that what you're going to get, the problem it seems to me that we have, is the one which President Eisenhower described. There is a great temptation for the Republicans to think they're never going to get very far with Negroes anyway, so they might as well play the white game in the South. So therefore it is important to bring them along. And if you only bring them as far as McCulloch we'll go, he is the ranking Republican, he is well respected and he can deliver.

Now, if you lose him, which they've done, then the Republicans don't have very much. They'll vote for a bill, but they'll, but you wouldn't even get 60 votes. That's a lot of votes for them. They don't vote with us on much of anything. That's our concern, you see. You won't get the bill out of the Rules Committee for three or four, two or three months maybe, or if you do, you'll lose on the House floor. I think that would be pretty bad, and I don't know whether you've got 60. That's all I'm interested in: how many votes do they have, not telling me what speeches. How many, can they get 60 Republicans because I know all we can get is 160 Democrats.

The other thing is the Senate. We don't see how we can get two-thirds vote for cloture, almost for any bill. And in fact, public accommodations would be close if there were an equal vote.

But to sum it up, I think we, I appreciate your seeing President Eisenhower. He can be very helpful. I think we've got to get the Republicans to go. To get the Republicans, we've got to get McCulloch, and we've got to get as strong a bill as McCulloch can take. And that's the best way to get action, and if the Leadership Conference . . .[2] They have to be dissatisfied.

---

[2]The Leadership Conference was a Washington lobbying group made up of leaders of more than 70 civil rights organizations.

I don't mind what they say, or, you know, they're going to do a lot of complaining, but . . . I'll go as far as I can go, but I think McCulloch has got to come with us, or otherwise it is an exercise in futility.

Blake: Indeed, you've got to have him. In other words, he is . . .

President Kennedy: I think you have to get him. He's the key, and he's a very reasonable fellow. And they had a compromise worked out, but I think the Leadership Section [Leadership Conference] didn't like it. They thought it was too much of a sellout. So now he's mad. . . . And I understand he's mad because he doesn't, he thinks we didn't keep our word. . . . He may vote for the bill, but, on the floor of the House we'll have a tough time.

Blake: Well, is there anything further I can do with the gentlemen?

President Kennedy: Well, I think that what we ought to do with the . . . What I think we ought to do with the . . . I think in this leadership thing you ought to make these people talk about things really and tell you, do you have it? Clarence Mitchell got up there the other day and said that Clarence Brown . . .[3] Well, we checked around that, and all Clarence did was talk to him sympathetically. He didn't say this is what I'll do.

When somebody says this is what they'll do, my experience always is, they'll do it. But they don't usually say it, especially these experienced fellows around here; they say, "Well, I'll give it a good look." Then people walk out, thinking they've got support when they haven't got it. So I think that what we ought to do—is continue to try to emphasize the bipartisan nature, see if this Leadership Conference can get as much assurance, as precise as possible, from Clarence Brown on the Rules [Committee] and McCulloch. As strong a bill as they'll go for, perhaps just a little stronger, is what we ought to finally agree, and I think that we have a good chance of passing. But, if you lose him, then you don't have any bipartisan thing and then we end up with 160 Democrats and you don't get much.

Let me just say, I think you've done a terrific job. The fact that the church . . . You've been so active. And you've been the most active. It made a big difference in trying to get support for this. I notice the poll. While they don't really want to have Negroes living next door to them, nevertheless they do support civil rights, provided you don't have any bad incident. I think we can maintain enough support . . .

Blake: We're still working on this. And it's a long range . . . Because we're trying to really change the pattern of the normal American thinking about the thing, and I think we've made some progress.

President Kennedy: Have you taken a lot of heat in your activities?

---

[3]Clarence Brown of Ohio was the senior Republican on the House Rules Committee.

Blake: My goal amounts to one thing, which is . . .

President Kennedy: How about the elders of your church? Are they . . .

Blake: Well, I would hate to try to get a vote through on most anything that I would be for at the moment, but . . . No, I think that our church, and I don't know if it is typical of the others, I think the . . . Well, I have had more trouble with the lawyers than anybody else. Breaking the law is very bad. This is a very low level of it because they just don't know what is happening with local law in the South, for example. I mean they wouldn't, for a moment. But they've got the idea.

And of course part of it is actually no natural law anymore with the legal profession, not based on any justice idea, just what legislation the court says it is. And, therefore, if you've given your life to support that and somebody breaks it, why, you haven't got any ground. And I think that we need a new theological understanding of the legal profession because they're not being very helpful.

President Kennedy: But I will say that, on the other hand, you don't seem to get much support out of most of those lawyers in a lot of the South for enforcing a court order. At least it is always the federal government who has to do it, but we don't get many lawyers standing up and saying . . .

Blake: No, I think the legal profession is tending to, well this is predicated on the eighteenth-century legal profession where they were really fighting on the whole idea of trying to get at what revolution was, rights and wrongs, and all of this, and I don't get this in my correspondence. These were the only letters that were worth answering in terms of criticism and that we're trying to get . . .

President Kennedy: Well I think, may I just suggest, why don't we at least, if we could, perhaps you could write President Eisenhower in a few days and tell him what the situation is. And that you hope that he could . . .

Blake: All right.

President Kennedy: As soon as we know a little more about this bill, and say the bill looks good, you know, if he could do anything he could with the members of his party. And that you just happened to talk to me and we were very appreciative of whatever he can do would be good. But then in the leadership meeting, I think you ought to make them be very realistic in their head counts.

Blake: Yeah. Yeah.

President Kennedy: Because my experience is that this is a fatal mistake.

Blake: I noticed that, of course, is what you said in terms of when we talked before. And as I say, of course, this is clear, that when you hand in the votes later, it's wasting your time . . .

President Kennedy: And then the difference between the fellow who thinks he's got a vote and hasn't got a vote. If it were that easy, you wouldn't have every candidate going to the national convention under the impression they were going to be nominated.

Blake: Yeah.

President Kennedy: And they'd be able to count. These fellows are too good, you see. These congressmen, senators who have been around. I've talked to these fellows, but they won't ever say the words. And that's what I'm afraid, some of this counting that's going on up the Hill is by people who don't really know. And I've been, we've gotten beaten enough up there to know that, I think it would be a great disaster for us to get beaten in the House.

Blake: Yes, yes.

President Kennedy: You know this fight is going to go on. We're going to have, about two years from now, we're going to have another bill. I would rather take out Title on the . . . Not the Title III, but the Title we have. I would rather take the compromise on the accommodations we worked out with McCullough. And, if they feel they can go stronger, to go for FEPC, rather than I would change the rest of the bill. Because then at least with FEPC, you really get something dramatically important. And that would be a tremendous breakthrough. If I were going to gamble anything, I'd gamble with FEPC rather than tightening up the accommodations section or tightening up the other things.

Blake: The accommodations section of course is the one that really riles them inside more than anything else does.

President Kennedy: I know, but I don't understand why. I had some fellow in here the other day from Birmingham who was saying about your bill. I said, I can understand why integrating schools that were segregated [*unclear*], that's really tough. And if I had a child there, put him in with 30, 40 percent Negro when they're so far behind. I said, that's really tough. But I mean, accommodations is a joke with these fellows fighting that way. I mean, it isn't difficult. I think of Harry Truman integrating the armed services; that was tough. But this, nothing, these accommodations. The fact of the matter is if we didn't have that in it, they'd be picking on another section.

Blake: Yes. Yes. Well, thank you very much, sir.

President Kennedy: Stay at it.

Blake: I'll keep at it.

Inaudible as meeting breaks up.

.　　.　　.

Eugene Carson Blake's determined efforts notwithstanding, the bill remained stalled in the House Judiciary Committee. The problem was with the liberal Democrats and the liberal Republicans. The subcommittee, chaired by Emanuel Celler, but influenced by NAACP lobbyists and civil rights leaders, reported a quite liberal version of the bill, which appealed to civil rights leaders, although it was politically perilous. Even Celler understood there was no way the subcommittee version would ever become law, and it contained enough red flags to keep it from getting through to the House floor.

The White House stepped in aggressively. Robert Kennedy, speaking for the administration, testified in front of the Judiciary Committee and stated boldly that what he wanted was "a bill, not an issue," which suggested the administration was determined to see a civil rights bill that would become law. The President wanted to be able to say that he had changed the law, rather than merely raising the nation's awareness of the problem by proposing legislation that could not pass.

In order to break the legislative impasse, the President needed the support of House Republicans, and that meant convincing McCulloch of the Judiciary Committee. To that end, Kennedy, Lyndon Johnson, Nicholas Katzenbach, Burke Marshall, and House leaders such as Celler, McCulloch, the House Republican leader Charles Halleck, Speaker Carl Albert, and Minority Whip Leslie Arends met several times in October in order to emend the subcommittee bill and turn it into a more workable piece of legislation—one the Republicans would support, the full committee would accept, and the House would pass.[4]

Kennedy taped two of these meetings, on October 23 and October 29. The first was a lengthy point-by-point discussion that considered both the bill's language and who would support or oppose particular sections of the legislation. The October 29 meeting occurred on the same day Celler's committee took a crucial vote on whether to report a less strongly worded bill to the House. The bill the full committee passed on October 29 was more moderate, but still more far-reaching than any piece of civil rights legislation had ever been. While exempting some private clubs and boarding houses, it made discrimination illegal in hotels, motels, restaurants, lunch counters, movie theaters, sports events, and gas stations, provided that these were in some way involved in interstate commerce or that such discriminatory practices were supported by state law or action. It banned

---

[4]Emanuel Celler was a Democrat from New York; William McCulloch, a Republican from Ohio; Charles Halleck, a Republican from Indiana; Carl Albert, a Democrat from Oklahoma; and Leslie Arends, a Republican from Illinois.

discrimination in employment in large- and mid-sized businesses and strengthened the laws against segregated schools. And perhaps most important, it gave the federal government the authority to enforce these provisions.

As President Kennedy realized, the Judiciary Committee was only the first obstacle, and even if the bill had the support of the committee, it would then face a serious hurdle in the Rules Committee, where it would go next before coming to the House floor. Unfortunately for civil rights supporters, the Rules Committee was chaired by an archconservative Democrat, Howard Smith of Virginia, who had already announced his opposition.

These October White House meetings were made more challenging by the competing pressures that pitted civil rights advocates against southern Democrats, and by the need to obtain the support of House Republicans and liberal Democrats. And always the administration had to keep an eye on potential conflicts in the House and Senate, which made it essential to navigate carefully between the moral demands of constructing an effective bill and the pragmatic demands of composing a bill that could pass.

The following excerpts from the October 23 meeting are more heavily edited than were previous conversations. Legislating is often a messy process; it can also be confusing and elliptical. The October 23 meeting was long and not tightly organized. It brought together the most powerful civil rights players in the executive branch and some of the most influential members of the House, and the President assumed the role of first among equals. Had he tried to steer the meeting with a heavy hand, as he would, say, during the Cuban Missile Crisis or as he did when meeting with Birmingham's civic leaders, powerful congressmen such as Halleck and McCulloch might have been resentful and thus less willing to compromise with the administration. While this may have been an effective political tactic, it also made for a lengthy, often unwieldy, meeting, one that lacks coherent flow when reduced to transcript form.

Halleck, the influential Indiana congressman, was accustomed to getting his way and tried to gain control of the meeting's agenda, and the President let him speak a good deal. The session moved in fits and starts toward an uncertain conclusion, and by the end, the participants were clear about which aspects of the subcommittee's bill would go and which would remain. But for the listener, it is difficult to make sense of what was actually decided. In an effort to lend coherence to the meeting, the version presented here has been edited significantly.

Wednesday, October 23, 1963, 6:10 P.M.

Meeting on Civil Rights Bill

Including President Kennedy, Lyndon Johnson, Nicholas Katzenbach, Emanuel Celler, William McCulloch, Charles Halleck, Carl Albert, Leslie Arends, and others.

Vice President Johnson: . . . I think any bill you send over [to the Senate] you'll have some problems with it, but I think the best thing you can do is send over the administration's bill. Maybe that will still be too strong for some of them.[5] They'll want to offer some amendments, but probably you can get your biggest support for the administration bill. You know that if they send over this subcommittee bill, that . . . I think the best thing to do is to take it one step at a time. If I were to give any counsel, I'd try to rally my troops behind the administration bill, and let the people who've already taken the heat for watering it down and modifying the subcommittee bill and all that kind of stuff. Send the administration bill over there, and then let's try to get the votes behind it in the Senate. . . .

Emanuel Celler: Can I say that the delay, that is, the long, long delay has exhausted the patience of the members. They've been working with this thing since May and they're tired. They want to get rid of it. . . .

Charles Halleck: Well, let me . . . just wait. Then I want Bill McCulloch to take over, Mr. President, because he's been sitting in the committee. I said at the beginning that as far as I was concerned, I'd want to vote for a meaningful civil rights bill. Manny has had meetings with his people. . . . We've had some meetings of our people. We had one this morning. I ran around all night to get back for it. We've tried to keep it off the record and so far it's been off the record. I know that from here there will go no word about it. Bill McCulloch opened up the meeting of our guys with a firm statement that we wanted a good, meaningful civil rights bill, and I followed Bill McCulloch with just as plain a statement. . . . And that's where I stand. But we've got guys on all sides of the damn spectrum. We've got southern boys on our side who are . . . want to report out the worst possible bill. Goddamn it, Manny, all of your Deep South boys are going to vote; they'll vote for the Moore amendment.[6]

The participants began an extensive discussion of the divisions within

---

[5]"Them" refers to the senators.
[6]Representative Arch Moore, Republican of West Virginia, had offered a motion that the full committee should simply report the subcommittee's strong version to the House.

the Judiciary Committee, and the desire of southern conservatives to support northern liberals simply to ensure that the bill reported by the committee, as opposed to the original bill proposed by Kennedy, would never be passed by the House. At one point, Charles Halleck interrupted to state, for no apparent reason, that he was committed to civil rights reform.

Halleck: . . . I've been for a meaningful civil rights bill and I said as much this morning—real plain—with our guys there, as many as we could get together. I think it is only fair to say that this damned thing has gotten all fizzled up and fouled up, into where some of the guys on our side who are normally pretty steadygoing—most of them are younger (you probably don't know them Mr. President, because they've been here only one or two, three, four years), but they've got themselves all boiled up. Now, how many votes we could get? I must say that Bill McCulloch and Les Arends and I kind of got our ears beat down a little bit this morning. Isn't that a fair statement?

William McCulloch: That is a fair statement.

President Kennedy: Charlie, I know you get in a mood where they say, "If this is what they want, this is what we'll give them."

Halleck: Goddamn it, I mean—

President Kennedy: But now the point is, therefore, in order to prevent that, we have said this isn't what we want, at least from the administration's point of view, and taken that heat. I thought . . . I'll say we get the Democrats together and say that I think that you're crazy, and that you're going to bear the responsibility for no bill if you follow this course. I think we can pull . . . can't pull them all off, but we can pull some of these fellows off. And need our help. . . . If we do that, it seems to me, you can get your people. Say here's what we can agree on. And I think that if we both do our job, we ought to be able to put together a majority.

Halleck: Well, I want to vote for a bill. I don't think I can vote for the one the subcommittee reported. . . .

President Kennedy: I don't think that's going to pass. . . .

McCulloch: Well, certainly, I can't go for the bill that came out of the subcommittee and so that everyone may know my position on civil rights . . . I had the speaker's help, among many others, in the voting referee section in the '60 bill that . . . I have all along been for a civil rights bill that would be effective and agreeable to not only the subcommittee, but I misguessed, misjudged the subcommittee, the full committee, the House, and possibly the Senate. Long ago I said, as I recall back in January, I was very interested in this cause, not a political issue. That's been my position until today. I have worked, as best I knew how, through the long sessions, which culminated two weeks ago last Wednesday when the roof fell in on our heads. . . .[7]

President Kennedy: Let me say, Congressman . . . we haven't attempted to dump this on you because the Attorney General is one, and I am, and the administration, who are getting the opprobrium for having diluted it in the last week.[8] Now what I think is, I think there's a chance for everybody to come out in pretty good shape.

There are four points, it seems to me, that are in question. I think that if we can get an idea in the next five to six minutes of where we could agree, then we would be able to say, well, we ought to put it off till Tuesday. We have to realize that if we put it off to Tuesday, then every civil rights advocate is going to beat everybody over the head for the next four or five days. . . . But that we might be able to stand, get our fellows to stand, if we could get some understanding of what kind of a bill we would get. Now I know that Nick [Katzenbach] and the congressmen have had a lot of talk. What is it we could do with various sections? Let's just go through them very quickly and see how far apart we are.

McCulloch: Well, I don't think we're too far apart, notwithstanding what the President said about impounding votes.[9] That may be a field in which the administration might have to compromise because there are strong feelings on both sides of the aisle about the necessity of impounding votes when they are cast at certain times and under certain conditions. . . .

Halleck: We got to do some, we've got do a little . . . do a little adjustment on a public accommodations. I have, Mr. President, I have struggled with my damn conscience, and I rode back in an airplane most of the night last night, talking with a bunch of knowledgeable people. And there is an area there where clearly a colored man and his family have got a right to go get something to eat and a place to sleep. In a department store, they got a right to sit down and buy a sandwich if they want to. If they went in and bought a pair of overalls . . . Goddamn it, they can buy a sandwich, too. . . .

The President concluded that there were not major differences on public accommodations and that consensus could be reached. The discussion soon looped back to the more intractable question of voting and civil rights violations.

---

[7]Wednesday the subcommittee voted to report its version of the bill.

[8]The administration was being criticized by civil rights groups for not fighting for the more liberal version of the bill.

[9]One debate had been what to do if complaints were made about ballots. The suggestion that ballots be impounded until a court could rule had created controversy over how much delay was acceptable in determining the results of an election where civil rights violations were alleged.

President Kennedy: . . . The voting question, it seems to me, the only objection to the impounding is the time that it takes. [*Unclear*] a procedure by which this thing can be done, make a decision on these ballots immediately. We don't want to have an election for a governor, senator, or president that goes . . . maybe a governor of Minnesota can go for three months, but we don't want to be sitting around February, March, April, May, and June trying to determine who won a presidential election.

McCulloch: But if I might interrupt, Mr. President, neither do we want votes cast for president that later are invalid by reason of the fact that there is no pattern or practice ever found and it turns on the fact that there were *x* number of votes cast that were not really eligible to be cast.

President Kennedy: Well, I completely agree with that. All I would say is that I think that we ought to have a procedure where this determination would be made before an electoral college meets, which would be about five or six weeks after the election. But I think you drag the presidential election through, the Constitution says he has to be sworn in in January. . . .

Unidentified: This refers to congressional elections, too.

President Kennedy: I mean, you can't have the Congress, the House, the Senate, and the president all not knowing whether some people are going to be elected until the spring. So I think we ought to have a procedure by which you could be . . . I have no objection to the impoundment; we ought to establish a procedure so that the electoral college when it meets will be able to make a judgment before it meets. . . .

Celler: [*interrupting*] Now look, look. . . . Forgive me for taking the devil's advocate here. It is one thing for Bill [McCulloch] and I to agree. One thing for you gentleman to agree, but it is another thing to get the members to agree. We've had this before. I tried to whip my men in line. I got some; I couldn't get the others. Bill couldn't get his. . . .

Apparently on the verge of settling matters a few moments earlier, the participants suddenly became more contentious. Kennedy kept trying to nudge the various leaders to work it out, exclaiming at one point, "You're not very far apart. My God! I could sit . . . we could do this thing." The House leaders were not so sanguine.

Halleck: . . . The whole picture, Mr. President, here's the dilemma we're in. We've got guys up there . . . that want to keep this bill so damn bad that they kill the whole damn thing. I don't subscribe to that view and I've said so, very, very plainly. I want to get a bill that's good, help in the situation, and assure a lot more rights to the colored people and the other people, but it's got to be one that can pass. But here we are with certain boys, John Lindsay, on our side: Christ, he thought he'd vote for anything.[10] . . . As far as I'm not playing this thing for political advantage. And I want to say this also, that when the Attorney General came up there, he said we want a law, a bill, and not an issue.[11] I publicly said to the press, "I applaud that statement." And I thought what he said and did up there was very commendable. . . . And as I say, hell, you see, Mr. President, there's been a feeling among a lot of our guys, Manny's subcommittee—and I don't know whether he is responsible or not—but they loaded this thing up, way beyond anything you asked and way beyond anything we ought to do. And then the feeling got abroad that we were supposed to be the goats. We are supposed to go ahead and emasculate the damn thing, and . . .

President Kennedy: No, we've done that. We're the goats.

Halleck: That's right. I said a moment ago, and I stand by it, that you and the Attorney General have been most courageous through this whole damn operation. Now then, as far as I am concerned, I want to carry it forward. But I think actually, with all the conversations we've had, Nick [Katzenbach] (I haven't had as many with you as Bill McCulloch has), but I think there is a pretty general feeling as to what the areas in which there is substantial agreement.

President Kennedy: Right.

Halleck: Now then, we could undertake to have a meeting and formalize it and then probably it would make it more difficult for us, Manny, to get votes on our side to be against the Moore motion. In other words, if they thought that there's been some hard and fast deal made, maybe without consultation with them . . .

Celler: Folks, without defeating the Moore motion, we're lost. . . .

President Kennedy: The understanding would be, as I understand it then, Charlie, you would talk to your people and say that if the Democrats were prepared to vote for a bill roughly like this, we'd have to agree to them [unclear]. But, if the Democrats (at least a reasonable number of them, we can't deliver everybody), but if they were prepared to go and the administration was prepared to endorse it, would you fellows be prepared to go for the same bill and make that the committee bill, the bipartisan bill?

The President had asked a direct question but received no direct answer. The Republican leaders were not prepared to make the commitment Kennedy was requesting, and they spent several minutes tactfully avoiding saying yes or no. But Kennedy was persistent. He wanted to

---

[10]John Lindsay was a liberal Republican congressman from New York City.

[11]The reference was to Robert Kennedy's testimony before the Judiciary Committee in October.

know where the Republicans stood before he tried to convince the recalcitrant Democrats to vote with the administration, and he wanted to know that he and the Republicans had a deal before he attempted to sell it to the Democrats.

President Kennedy: ... I think that what we ought to try to do is make sure that we've got an understanding, so that when I talk to the Democrats, I say, "Here's what I think is a good bill."

The minority whip, Les Arends, confessed that he thought some Republicans would be skittish about supporting the bill without knowing first that the Democrats supported it. He gently implied that if there was going to be criticism, he and the other Republicans preferred that the Democrats received the brunt of it.

I think you'd have difficulties, if the mood is as Les has just described, selling them anything, unless they understood that the administration, the President, and the Democrats were signed off. Then you were giving them a proposition, should we go or shan't we go? If you go in and say well maybe the President is going to try to sell the Democrats if we agree, then the initiative has to be taken in a sense by the Republicans, rather than by the Democrats. And then they'll say, "Hell, let the Democrats take the heat." I would think you'd sell it to them better, if you understood that what the Democrats were ready to go ... Therefore, I would say, and I think we could get the Democrats to go, once we get an understanding of what kind of a bill. And I'm not ... that's why I want to know what it is on the four or five critical points, which I think we're in general agreement on, and which I'm sure you and Nick can get to complete agreement in a half hour. Then I can say to the Democrats, "Here's the best we can do, and my judgement is, we ought to try to do it." Then if I can get them to agree, the numbers it requires, I'm confident we can get the Republicans.

Even this did not fully mollify the Republicans, but Kennedy kept pushing. Halleck hemmed and hawed about timing and the difficulty of assembling a coalition within the committee, let alone the full House. Kennedy did not agree, and nudged Halleck. "Charlie," he said, "You're a pretty shrewd politician, and I've looked at this thing myself. ..." "You aren't bad yourself," Halleck interrupted. As he had several times, Halleck then tried to steer the meeting.

Halleck: Well, as a matter of fact, Mr. President, when we were talking down here at the outset of this damn business, you said, very correctly, that no matter what we do, we are going to have some people think we've gone too far and others think we haven't gone far enough. It is a complex, difficult problem that runs the whole doggone range of human emotion.

President Kennedy: But you know, let me just say this, Charlie, I had a conversation [*unclear*] with a fellow I know who has got responsibilities with the Republican Party. He thinks, "Well, we'll report this bill out. It's a lousy bill, and it may even get defeated." Now then, if that's so, I'm in the position of being able to say, "Well the Attorney General went up there and told you that's what's going to happen." So, I'm in a pretty good position. . . . Now, if you report a bill out of the kind we want, I'm going to catch a lot of hell because they're going to say that the Attorney General recovered . . . who got the compromise and who made them water it down and they're the ones who sold out. So to be frank with you, if I didn't think we needed the bill, and if we can't come to an agreement, I'm not going to drop dead because the fact of the matter is I can report out on Moore's thing and we can't lose, to be honest with you.

If you defeat the bill finally in the House, the House wasn't going to say we told you it was a lousy idea. And if you pass it, well then we'll just negotiate it over with the Senate. So it isn't that it's that much . . . we're not in that much of the hot seat. Republicans haven't this much to gain. I think we're both better off, if we got together, particularly when I think we'll bear the heat for the compromise. And I don't think, therefore, it seems to me we're meeting our responsibility. . . . Now, why don't we agree on this procedure? If we could get Nick, Manny, and Congressman McCulloch together in the morning, let's say at, I don't know, at 9:00 or 9:30. Let them come to an agreement on all of these provisions, which they know much more about it than I do. They will then call and tell us that they have come to an agreement. Then I will ask the Democrats to come down to the house, down here, and I'll ask them if they'll go for it. If I can then get enough of them to go for it, I will call you. Why don't you then get your people in? Now it may be that you can turn it around right then. If you can't, we'll go over till Tuesday.

Halleck: I don't think we can do it that fast. . . . As far as I'm concerned, Mr. President, I have felt from the beginning, and since we had the meeting in the Speaker's office, that there was pretty substantial agreement among most of us on the details of this legislation. I've had a little trouble in my own thinking about public accommodations, but I've reached a conclusion in my mind that with reasonable limits on it and restraints, with limitations, that I can buy it. Now, our principal trouble over there has been the conviction that got abroad, after Manny's subcommittee blew this thing up to be hell, that the whole purpose of that was to put the Republicans in the position of emasculating the bill.

McCulloch: And can I interrupt there, Charlie? And that I had been taken for a ride. . . .

Halleck: I think Bill McCulloch and I have both, out of this whole damn operation, the bill that you've been talking about, Mr. President, with some modifications of public accommodations, and I have seen a little of the language, Nick. Nobody else has seen it but me, as far as I know. But I've got to the point where I want to vote for a bill and I said as much this morning and I've been saying it all up and down our side. So I don't really see a hell of a big problem there.

I think, we've had three or four meetings of our boys on Judiciary Committee, one place or another around the place up there. And when this thing began to develop, the whole pitch was, "Well, who in the hell is going to have to take some burden on?" And the Attorney General and you, Mr. President, have certainly stepped up and taken your share of the load. There is no question about that. And hell, I've said as much to our people. But, I've got guys, that . . . you've got some yourself and you're in a damn sight better position to work yours over than I am to work mine over [*laughter*].

A shift had occurred, and Halleck signaled that the Republicans were ready to deal. The problem of timing remained, and much of the remainder of the meeting was consumed by a discussion of exactly who would meet with whom and when, down to hour, time, and place. President Kennedy wanted to make sure that everyone coordinated their actions and that he did not speak to certain representatives before Halleck, McCulloch, or Celler had.

Celler: Let me ask one more question I want to get clear in my mind. Let's assume we've got an agreement that we're going to kill the Moore motion, and we got an agreement as to what we want in the bill, the final bill.

President Kennedy: Yeah.

Celler: Then I take it that a motion will be made to report out the . . . bill, with amendments, which were the amendments we'd agreed upon.

President Kennedy: Right

The meeting then began to break up, with some participants leaving and some final discussion about the appropriate venue of subsequent meetings. At the very end, Kennedy and Johnson have a short exchange about the potential pitfalls ahead. Johnson worries about delaying over the weekend, as it will give opponents of the compromise an extra few days to put pressure on committee members.

Johnson: I'm afraid that if you let them go over the weekend . . . they're going to get this pressure in the home district and by the time you talk to them, you'll be at their mercy. If you get them in the morning, they'll be at yours. You can say, "Now listen, I've had some talks here and here is going to be our position. And this is the only sound Democratic position, and fellows you can this one, we won't have the bill and it is up to you. Now please help me. . . ." If they don't go, why, there's no use of having the committee. If they do go and you've got your position fortified, you can stand. Then you say I want you to hold this, and as soon as I can get these other folks, we'll put it together.

President Kennedy: They're going to string us out, of course.

Johnson: That's what he's trying to do.[12] And he wants you, what he plans for, if I don't miss my bet, they're hoping the Clarence Mitchells and the Negro crowd will put the heat on you where you will lose control of it.[13] Then, he can come to us and say, "Well, we're trying to help, but heck, your own crowd is the one that messed this up. They messed it up in the subcommittee and they messed it up again." I think he might get them in here and keep . . .

President Kennedy: [*Unclear.*] Let's say I haven't met with the Democrats, and the assumption being, you can't get them all. And Charlie says to me, "If I can get my fellows tomorrow and now you can't deliver the Democrats." Do you want to wait until after Charlie's here? He's going to give me a vague answer, anyway.

Johnson: I would suggest get them all . . .

. . .

It took almost a week of delicate negotiations before the committee was ready to vote on the new, less ambitious version of the bill. While this draft was surely more aggressive than Kennedy's initial bill, the version taken up by the Judiciary Committee weakened the enforcement powers of the Justice Department and permitted more exceptions to the equal access provisions in public accommodations. Kennedy himself was intimately involved in the last-minute politicking, including a telephone call to Mayor Richard Daley of Chicago, who was the patron of Democratic Representative Roland Libonati. Kennedy wanted Daley to make sure Libonati voted for the bill. "He'll vote for it," Daley promised. "He'll vote for any goddamned thing you want." Daley's assurances notwithstanding, Libonati would vote no.

The day of the vote, October 29, Kennedy called a final caucus with many of the same participants of the October 23 meeting. Most of the discussion involved a vote count of each of the 34 committee members. The participants were certain of 17 votes, but that proved pessimistic. When the vote was taken later that day, the amended bill passed 23 to 11.

A major hurdle had been cleared. Kennedy called Halleck to thank the Republican leader for his support. "You did a great job," he told Halleck. "I

---

[12]"He" is probably Halleck.
[13]Lose control of the debate and of the bill.

got a lot of mad people up here," Halleck replied. "I got a lot of them too," the President reminded him. "I got a lot of mad Negroes that are ready to come and throw rocks at me."

That was an exaggeration, but the bill that passed the committee was certainly less than ideal, at least from the perspective of civil rights advocates. Kennedy had tried to split the difference between the demands of the civil rights leaders and congressional liberals on the one hand, and the moderate Republicans on the other. He knew the version that passed the Judiciary Committee on October 29 was imperfect, but he also knew that federal legislation rarely achieved perfection. Kennedy believed it was essential to make a choice between incremental reform and ideological purity.

Though it is true that he had dedicated his administration to progress on civil rights only after the shift in public opinion in the wake of the events in Birmingham in the spring of 1963, Kennedy was not suddenly backing down in the face of congressional opposition. Instead, he was doing what he felt could be done within the context of the American political system. Morality demanded a meaningful bill, while pragmatism demanded that some compromises be made. The legislation the Kennedy administration now supported would go farther in addressing the problem of racial discrimination than had any bill since the nineteenth century. That it did not go as far as some wished was seen as a regrettable necessity by Kennedy and his advisers. For the administration, it was not a choice between no bill and a symbolic bill; it was a choice between no bill and one that was reasonably good. From the perspective of the White House, that made the choice easy.

With the bill in hand at the end of October, the administration turned to the complicated process ahead. The next obstacle was the Rules Committee, and after that, the House, and then the more difficult problem of the Senate. Each stage had the potential to end the process and hand Kennedy a stinging defeat.

We will never know how John Kennedy would have managed these next phases of the legislative process. We will never know if the bill would have become weaker as it went through each stage or if Kennedy would have used his considerable influence to make sure the bill was not fatally weakened. We do know that Kennedy's dedication to civil rights had won him few friends in the South, and for that reason, among others, he was warned by friends and advisers that he would receive a cool reception when he traveled to Texas. On November 22, 1963, Kennedy arrived in Dallas expecting to face some tough questions about civil rights and about his policy toward Cuba. Before he could answer those questions, he was assassinated.

Chapter 7
Johnson Takes Over

Although Lyndon Johnson assumed the presidency in unenviable circumstances, the former senator was widely respected in Washington and throughout the country, and few questioned his qualifications for office or his political skill. Millions of Americans were in shock and the days following Kennedy's death were chaotic and confused. Johnson needed to assure people that the assassination was an isolated event and not part of a plan to destabilize the country. It was also essential to allow the nation to experience a full measure of collective grief. At the same time, the new President had to allay the country's concerns by demonstrating that he could assume office with the same degree of competence his predecessor had possessed. But he had to tread a fine line. If it was crucial to appear competent, it was also critical not to appear too eager. Johnson had to take control of the government while appearing suitably moved by the young President's assassination. It is likely that Johnson was both genuinely devastated and utterly prepared to take the reins, and to his credit, he managed to strike the right balance in these first days. As a result, given the circumstances, the transition was smoother than anyone could have imagined.

Within hours of receiving the news on Friday afternoon, November 22, Johnson began working the telephones. Throughout his career in the Senate and then in the White House, the telephone was one of Johnson's favorite tools. He had always used the telephone to contact allies, to cajole adversaries, and to ruminate. As president, he immediately took advantage of the taping system to record his phone conversations, and in his first months in office, he taped almost everything. In later years, he would become more selective, but initially, he clearly wanted an official record of what he had said and to whom. That raises the question of how much this influenced what he said—or chose not to say—but judging from the transcripts, the taping system did not significantly interfere with his candor.

Johnson brought years of experience to the presidency. He had spent decades in politics and had been elected to the Senate in 1948 after a hard-fought, extraordinarily close contest with the governor of Texas, Coke Stevenson. For the rest of his life, Johnson was shadowed by allegations that he had stolen the election from the taciturn Stevenson, a charge many who knew Johnson would not have found difficult to believe. He wore his Texas identity on his sleeve, and this child of the hill country west of Austin had known poverty.

Unlike the Kennedys, Lyndon Johnson was a self-made man, and it is clear he suffered from feelings of inadequacy when faced by those who were more polished and privileged than he. If he lacked the distinctive self-confidence that is often found in those born amidst great wealth and power, he possessed more than enough bluster and political acumen. When the Democrats retook control of the Senate in the 1954 midterm elections, Johnson became majority leader. A master manipulator and a seducer, he used the power and prestige of his position to bully people of lesser intelligence or weaker will. His vulgarity was legendary, his lack of decorum unsurpassed. Something of a populist, Johnson believed in the New Deal notion that government possessed the authority and had the responsibility to help those who were less fortunate.

Intensely ambitious, Johnson became one of the most formidable majority leaders in the history of the U.S. Senate. With a preternatural feel for the legislative process, he understood that in Congress, all was personal. Johnson knew legislation was not an impersonal creation but the result of myriad relationships, late-night conversations, and drinks imbibed in the offices of friends and foes away from the glare of public scrutiny. It was horse-trading and handshakes and giving to get.

As majority leader, Johnson developed thumbnail sketches of every senator. He knew their likes and dislikes. He knew their peccadillos and to whom they were beholden. He knew what their predecessors had stood for and what their constituents expected. As president, he was every bit as acute, and not just about the Senate but about the House, as well. He also understood the inherent tension between Congress and the White House, even when both were controlled by the same party. He recognized he could not tell Congress what to do. Because he was a southerner and because he had cultivated his personal relationships over many years, he enjoyed more congressional support than Kennedy ever had, but he still had to massage and wheedle and, in public, act deferential. If there was one thing his years in the Senate had taught him, it was that the House and the Senate demanded deference from the president in the legislative arena.

Forceful personality that he was, Johnson rarely behaved rudely toward senators or congressmen, but instead, flattered and seduced. In person, he was known for applying the "Johnson treatment," which often involved standing nose to nose with his listener and using his bulk and his voice to bend a person to his will. But the telephone transcripts present a somewhat more reserved Johnson, who, without benefit of his physicality, had to rely on the power of his office and his words to win over the person on the other end of the line.

Perhaps the most frequent recipient of his calls was Senator Richard Russell of Georgia, although the two men did not often discuss civil rights on the phone. As a junior senator, Johnson had looked to Russell as a mentor, while Russell, perhaps recognizing that Johnson was a rising star, cultivated the Texan. As majority leader, Johnson relied on Russell's counsel, and on the Georgian's links to the more conservative wing of the Democratic Party. Johnson was identified with the party's southern wing, but ideologically he shared more with the liberals of the North. Russell, however, was a southerner of the old school, and that meant he was a staunch segregationist.

As vice president and later as president, Johnson split with Russell on civil rights, but he never ceased to turn to him for advice. Russell, for his part, fought against civil rights legislation, but nonetheless maintained a close relationship with Johnson. Their telephone conversations reflected a relationship built on mutual respect, and Johnson rarely tried to nudge the Georgian, understanding that they were worlds apart on the issue of race in America. On civil rights, Johnson knew that Russell would never budge.

To many, Johnson's passion for civil rights came as a surprise. Within the Kennedy administration, he had become a point man in the summer of 1963, but most of his work was done outside the public eye. When he suddenly assumed the presidency in late November, many civil right advocates were dismayed. They assumed that Johnson, a Texan, would be antagonistic to civil rights and considered his record as majority leader to be decidedly mixed. Yes, he had gotten the 1957 and 1960 bills through the Senate, but he had also allowed the southern bloc to reduce those bills to little more than hollow gestures. By late November, civil rights leaders had come to believe that they had the Kennedy administration actively on their side, but they had no idea what to expect from the new President.

To their surprise and delight, Johnson did more than stay the course. Instead, he made civil rights the fulcrum of the new administration. His motives were a blend of conviction and expediency. As a senator from Texas, Johnson could only have gone so far on civil rights without fatally damaging his career, and as vice president, he had played second fiddle to Kennedy. But as president, he was no longer beholden to the voters of

Texas, and civil rights enjoyed wide and deep support outside the South. The Judiciary Committee had voted for the bill just two days before Kennedy's death, and the events of that fall had placed civil rights legislation at the forefront of national politics. The only other major piece of legislation that had been put forward by Kennedy that year was a tax cut plan. Quickly discerning that the surest path to public acceptance was to link himself to Kennedy's legacy, Johnson decided to make the tax cut and civil rights the sole objectives of the coming months.

Johnson had reached that conclusion with astonishing speed. Less than a week after Kennedy's assassination, Johnson set the agenda for the new White House, and judging from his numerous telephone conversations with civil rights leaders, he probably made the decision within two or three days after becoming president. The only way to account for his alacrity is that Johnson had an instinctive sense for what would ease the transition and a profound belief that civil rights reform was both necessary and just.

Johnson knew that the first weeks of his administration would set the tone for what followed and that a failure to solidify his position quickly would spell his doom come the 1964 election. It was necessary to reassure and connect with the American people, and also to take a stand as leader of the Democratic Party. As he would observe later, if he did not "get out in front on the issue, the liberals would get me. They'd throw my background against me, they'd use it to prove that I was incapable of bringing unity to the land I loved so much. . . . I had to produce a civil rights bill that was even stronger than the one they'd have gotten if Kennedy had lived. Without this, I'd be dead before I could even begin." Johnson saw civil rights, more than the tax cut, as the path to party leadership and as the way to claim the presidency in his own right.

But one ought not underestimate the moral dimension of Johnson's support for civil rights. As Johnson adviser and soon-to-be presidential assistant George Reedy would remark, "Mr. Johnson is one of the least prejudiced or biased or intolerant or bigoted men I have ever met. He has many shortcomings and many failings, but I don't believe there is any racial prejudice in him whatsoever; and this is the thing that became very apparent to most of the Negro leaders when they had a chance to know him personally." Having decided, almost immediately upon assuming the presidency, that he would make civil rights one of the two priorities of his administration, Johnson asked those leaders for advice and support.

Knowing he would be viewed suspiciously, Johnson employed his considerable charm to win over skeptics like James Farmer of CORE and Roy Wilkins of the NAACP. In an interview years later, Farmer admitted that he feared "a President from Texas might change the civil rights bill," but that these fears were quickly allayed by Johnson himself. Roy Wilkins had a similar experience, recalling that Johnson "was asking us if we wanted [the civil rights bill], if we would do the things required to get it enacted. He said he could not enact it himself; he was the president of the United States; he would give it his blessing; he would aid it in any way in which he lawfully could under the Constitution. . . . In effect he said—he didn't use these words—'You have the ball; now run with it.' He gave unmistakable notice that you had a friend and not an enemy in the White House for this legislation." Johnson conveyed the same message to other leaders, especially Clarence Mitchell, the NAACP's legislative point man who would play a crucial role in lobbying Congress for passage of the bill. Mitchell later recalled his astonishment at Johnson's attention to detail; he had never dealt with a president who telephoned him the moment a bill was reported out of a congressional committee or who seemed to know exactly where the vote count stood.

It took Johnson less than five days to prepare his agenda and announce it publicly. On November 27, the day before Thanksgiving, he made a nationally televised address delivered to a specially convened joint session of Congress. He urged Congress to pass the tax cut and the pending civil rights bill. "All I have I would have given gladly not to be standing here today. The greatest leader of our time has been struck down by the foulest deed of our time." He called on all Americans to continue what the late President had begun. "No memorial oration or eulogy could more eloquently honor President Kennedy's memory than the earliest possible passage of the civil rights bill for which he fought so long. We have talked long enough in this country about equal rights. We have talked for one hundred years or more. It is time now to write the next chapter, and to write it in the books of law. I urge you, as I did in 1957 and again in 1960, to enact a civil rights law so that we can move forward to eliminate from this nation every trace of discrimination and oppression that is based upon race or color."

One speech did not put to rest all concerns and suspicions, and many black Americans, having been frustrated by unfulfilled promises in the past, welcomed Johnson's words but waited for them to become deeds. Many southerners believed that Johnson was simply honoring the late President, and were convinced that he lacked the stomach for a civil rights fight and would quickly abandon the controversial public accommodations sections of the proposed bill. But Johnson demonstrated he was serious about the bill, and during his first days, he worked behind the scenes to rally civil rights leaders.

On Sunday, November 24, Johnson called Whitney Young, the executive director of the National Urban League. Young was one of the more aggressive advocates of civil rights legislation and stood in the forefront of those calling for additional protests and demonstrations that were intended to force Washington's hand. Though not as prominent as some other leaders, Young had worked with Johnson on the Committee on Equal Employment Opportunity, which LBJ had chaired as vice president, and that may explain why he was the first person the President called about civil rights. The first moments of the call bounced between Young, Johnson, and Johnson's secretary.

Sunday, November 24, 1963, 5:55 P.M.

Whitney Young

Begins in midconversation.

Whitney Young: I just happened to be talking to the *New York Times*, and made the point very clear that Negroes, if they didn't, I was going to see that they had 100 percent confidence in you.

President Johnson: Well, you're mighty—

Young: And I've been saying this on television and radio, and I'm quite sincere about it.

President Johnson: I know that. You've been wonderful. I want you to come in [in] the next few days when we get this [President Kennedy's funeral] behind us. But in the meantime, I want you to be thinking. Of course, I'm going to urge the Congress to go ahead and act now. But I don't know what we're going to get out of them in the way of taxes and civil rights—

Young: Yeah.

President Johnson:—in the next three weeks. They're going home Thanksgiving and they're coming back, but we're just beginning to fight.

Young: Yes.

President Johnson: But I want you to give some thought to what our approaches ought to be, and who we ought to talk to, and how we ought to organize, and how we ought to really move ahead with what we're going to do, and let's all try to go in the same direction, kind of like we have done with the Equal Opportunity Committee.

Young: Marvelous.

President Johnson: And I want you to do some heavy thinking on it and statesman-like thinking and, then come in to see me. I'm going to call Roy [Wilkins] as soon as I hang up talking to you.

Young: Good.

President Johnson: And I don't know who else to call. But if you wouldn't mind—

Young: We'll pass the word on.

President Johnson:—If you don't mind giving a little thought to that maybe I ought to call one or two more. And if you do, why maybe you can give me—

Young: [*Unclear*] I'll give you Mr. [James] Farmer's.

President Johnson: All right. Give me that.

Young: Ah, just a minute. [Speaks to someone in room] Mr. Farmer's number is B-E—

President Johnson: He's CORE, isn't he?

Young: Yes.

President Johnson: All right.

Young: Three.

President Johnson: B-E?

Young: B-E-3.

President Johnson: B-E-3.

Young: Zero-5-

President Johnson: Zero-5.

Young: Three-6.

President Johnson: Three-6.

Young: I think it might be good strategy. Now we're—

President Johnson: All right.

Young:—we're going to meet tomorrow—

President Johnson: What about Phil Randolph?

Young: Phil is in Chicago.

President Johnson: Would you call him if you were me?

Young: Yeah.

President Johnson: All right.

Young: I think this is so strategic—

President Johnson: All right.

Young:—All it's really doing is reconfirming, because Jim Farmer and I were together yesterday, and he feels the same way I do.

President Johnson: Well, I just want to get the benefit of your thinking, and your approach, and let's try to not move with that ball until we know where we're going. Then let's go, and go right on through to that goal line, and then not ever . . . We might get run out of bounds a time or two, but we'll keep coming, and, ah . . . Kind of like the fella [who] said, "What's the difference between a Texas Ranger and a Texas sheriff?" [He] said, "Well, when you hit a Ranger, he just keeps coming."

Young: [*Laughs heartily.*]

President Johnson: [*Joins laughter*] So—

Young: Well I—

President Johnson:—so that's the kind of a fight we want to get in. We want to just keep coming when we start, and—

Young:—Well, I've got some ideas and I'd be happy to sit down and talk with you—

President Johnson:—And—

Young:—and I think the sooner, the better—

President Johnson: Uh-huh—

Young:—as far as I—

President Johnson: I got to get this funeral behind me, and I got all these heads of states coming and I got this—I've got to say something publicly. I'm going to a joint session [of Congress] and I think I'll just tell them we're carrying on and ask for the passage of his [President Kennedy's] civil rights bill and his tax bill. Then I got to sit down and we got to devise the strategy to get it done.

Young: Yeah.

President Johnson: [Hubert] Humphrey told me yesterday that they're all going home for Thanksgiving. They're not going to come back to taxes until December the 10th, and said everybody's so worn out, and mad, and tired, [that] they're not going to pass anything between now and December the 18th, when they quit for Christmas. So, I've got to get in behind them pretty quick.

Young: Well, let me make a quick suggestion here.

President Johnson: All right.

Young: Ah, I think if you got to make a date for that, it's good to point out that, ah, that for the good of the civil rights thing, that the death of President Kennedy points out, that hate anywhere that goes unchecked, doesn't stop just for the week, and the killing of—at Birmingham. The people feel that they can react with violence when they dissent. Then it's a bad situation. So this thing is now bigger than just—

President Johnson: I dictated a whole page on hate. Hate internationally, hate domestically—

Young: Right. [*Unclear.*]

President Johnson:—and just say that this hate that produces inequality, this hate that produces poverty—that's why we got to have a tax bill—

Young: That's right—

President Johnson:—The hate that produces injustice—that's why we got to have a civil rights bill—

Young:—That's the top.

President Johnson:—This—it's a cancer that just eats out our national existence.

Young: Right, sir. That's *wonderful.*

President Johnson: All right.

Young: [*Unclear.*]

President Johnson: God bless you, and I was thinking of you, and, well I—

Young: [*Unclear*] one thing. Roy [Wilkins] and I haven't heard anything about . . . we had sort of expected an invitation to the funeral. How are they handling that?

President Johnson: I have no idea—I have no idea under the sun, but let me inquire on it, and I'll . . . I'd sure—I'm taking my family and I'd almost take you as my guest if I can get an extra ticket. Let me see about it. I don't know—Bobby's [Kennedy] handling it. But I'll check it—

Young: Well if—

President Johnson:—get right in.

Young: If you would. I think it would be good that—there's six of us and I'd be happy to be with you.

President Johnson: Well, I'll just check it and see what happens and I'll get back to you—

Young: All right.

President Johnson:—sometime tomorrow.

Young: Thanks so much.

President Johnson: Bye . . . bye—

Young: I'll be right here.

President Johnson:—Bye.

Young: Thanks for bothering.

.   .   .

Later that evening, Johnson did call Young back, telling him to get in touch with presidential assistant Bill Moyers for the invitation to the state funeral. After getting off the phone with Young for the second time, Johnson then called Farmer. There is no tape of that conversation, but it was clearly effective because Farmer remembered it years later. In an oral history interview, Farmer said, "He called me at home. And I was astonished. I'd never been called by a president before. It was impressive." Johnson asked Farmer if the administration could count on his help in gaining passage of the civil rights bill and invited him to come discuss strategy at the White House in the coming weeks.

Two days before his planned speech to a joint session of Congress, Johnson called Martin Luther King, whose support in the months ahead would be essential. Unlike Kennedy, Johnson had no history of tense relations with civil rights leaders, but he did not have a close relationship with them either. The Equal Employment Opportunity Commission had conducted its business away from public scrutiny, and its role was mainly advisory. In this setting, Johnson had met many civil rights leaders, but he had not tangled with them during the crises of the previous two years as had Kennedy. And though Johnson had worked assiduously for the passage of the two earlier civil rights acts, he had not made many overtures to black leaders in his years in the Senate.

Newly installed in the White House, Johnson approached King and the others deferentially. Whether he did so by conscious design or political instinct is unclear, but Johnson's approach was brilliantly effective. Civil rights leaders were accustomed to banging on the doors of the White House and gaining a few grudging minutes here and there, unless a crisis like Birmingham made it expedient for the president to pay more attention to them. They were not used to being wooed, and the experience of a president coming to them in this way was unfamiliar. Black leaders were both disarmed and charmed by the President's methods.

Monday, November 25, 1963, 9:20 P.M.

Martin Luther King, Jr.

President Johnson: . . . interest and your cooperation, and your communication, and a good many people told me that they heard about your statement. I guess it was on TV, wasn't it?

Martin Luther King: Yes, that's right—

President Johnson:—I been locked up in this office, and I haven't seen it. But I want to tell you how grateful I am, and how worthy I'm going to try to be of all your hopes.

King: Well, thank you very much. I'm so happy to hear that, and I knew that you had just that great spirit and you know you have our support and backing—

President Johnson: Well . . .

King:—because we know what a difficult period this is. [*Unclear*]—

President Johnson: It's a—it's just an *impossible* period. We got a budget coming up that's—we got nothing to do with it, it's practically already made. And we got a civil rights bill that hadn't even passed the House. And it's November, and Hubert Humphrey told me yesterday everybody wanted to go home. We got a tax bill that they haven't touched. We just got to let up—not let up on any of them and keep going and . . . I guess they'll say that I'm repudiated. But I'm going to ask the Congress Wednesday to just stay there until they pass them all. They won't do it. But we'll just keep them there next year until they do, and we just won't give up an inch.

King: Uh-huh. Well this is mighty fine. I think it's so imperative. I think one of the great tributes that we can pay in memory of President Kennedy is to try to enact some of the great, progressive policies that he sought to initiate.

President Johnson: Well, I'm going to support them all, and you can count on that. And I'm going to do my best to get other men to do likewise, and I'll have to have you-all's help.

King: Right.

President Johnson: I never needed it more than I do now.

King: Well, you know you have it, and just feel free to call on us for anything.

President Johnson: Thank you so much, Martin.

King: All right. Give my—

President Johnson: Call me when you're—

King:—regards to the family.

President Johnson: I sure will. And call me when you're down here next time.

King: I certainly will, Mr. President.

President Johnson: Let's get together. And any suggestions you got, bring them in.

King: Fine, I certainly will do that.

President Johnson: Thank you so much.

King: Thank you for calling.

.   .   .

By the end of his first week in office, Johnson had decided to push for civil rights even if it meant a delay in the passage of the tax bill. He needed to pass both by the summer if he was to claim the party's mantle for the election of 1964, but unlike Kennedy, he felt that civil rights, while riskier than the tax cut, promised more benefits, moral and political. He asked Congress to remain in session longer than usual so that the Rules Committee and Chairman Howard Smith of Virginia could vote and send the bill to the whole House early in the new year. He explained this strategy to a large number of people, including Dave McDonald, the president of the United Steel Workers' Union. McDonald was a party loyalist and adept lobbyist, and Johnson fully expected him to go along with the push for civil rights.

Smith presented a formidable hurdle. He was one of the senior members of the House, and as chairman of the Rules Committee, he could single-handedly kill almost any bill by simply refusing to allow it to come to the floor of the House for a vote. In the early 1960s, committee chairs had almost dictatorial powers, and Judge Smith, an old southerner with no enthusiasm for civil rights, was about as autocratic as they came. He had called the 1957 bill the civil "wrongs" bill and made no secret of his animus toward the new bill. As of late November, civil rights advocates, including Johnson, were worried that the only way to prevent Smith from torpedoing the bill was to obtain a discharge petition passed by the full House. That would have forced Smith to send the bill to the floor. But even some of the bill's supporters opposed a discharge petition, a dramatic step rarely taken and one that would have been a snub of the still powerful Smith.

Johnson called McDonald on November 29 to discuss ways to get the bill through Smith's committee. "We're gonna have to get a discharge petition," he told McDonald, "and I think if there's ever a time when you talk to every human you could . . . you oughta do it. I don't think that oughta come from me, but . . . if we could possibly get that bill out of the [House] Rules Committee. . . . They've got to petition it out. That means we got to get 219. We'll start at about 150 Democrats; that means we gotta get 60, 70 Republicans. . . . They'll be saying they don't want to violate procedure. . . . [O]ur answer, it'll have to be, 'Well, a man [who] won't give you a hearing at all—that's the way they treated [Lee Harvey] Oswald in Dallas.' They just shoot him without a hearing. And . . . a man's entitled to a hearing."

Having compared Smith's refusal to hold hearings to Jack Ruby's assassination of Lee Harvey Oswald, Johnson urged McDonald to lobby for a discharge petition and, failing that, to pressure his congressmen to make sure Smith agreed to hearings. That afternoon, the President met with Roy Wilkins at the White House to discuss how to proceed. In a memo to Johnson prepared for the meeting, legislative aide Larry O'Brien suggested that the President ask Wilkins to get as many religious leaders as possible to exert pressure on congressional leaders, calling on them to move the civil rights bill for the moral good of the country. After an hour with Wilkins, Johnson went back to the phones and called A. Philip Randolph to make essentially the same points.

Friday, November 29, 1963, 4:17 P.M.

A. Philip Randolph

Office Secretary: Mr. Randolph?
A. Philip Randolph: Yes.

Office Secretary: Thank you. Just a moment, please.

President Johnson: Phil?

Randolph: Hello. Mr. President?

President Johnson: Phil, this is Lyndon Johnson.

Randolph: How are you, Mr. President?

President Johnson: I'm just doing fine. I wanted to call you, and just tell you that I hope the first time you're down here, you'll give me a ring. I want to visit with you some about our program. Will you give me a ring?

Randolph: All right. I'll be very glad to do that. I'll be down there Wednesday.

President Johnson: You give me a ring, and don't say anything about it. But, I don't want to stir up the folks on the Hill until we get ready to see the whites of their eyes.

Randolph: Surely, all right.

President Johnson: But I want to talk to you, and have a little visit with you. And you just call my girl when you get in town, and be thinking about the general picture. They're not going to give us a rule. I have had the Speaker [John McCormack] go to the chairman [of the Rules Committee, Representative Howard Smith]. He [Smith] said, nothing this year.

Randolph: I see.

President Johnson: And I think if we wait until next year, and get it out of the House, by the time it gets to the Senate they'll be debating the tax bill, and then the [1964] primaries will be coming on, and they'll talk us to death. I think we've got to move now.

Randolph: I see. All right, Mr. President. I'll give you a ring and I'll come by.

President Johnson: My judgment is—we probably ought to try to get this petition signed up and get every single vote that's available in the House of Representatives, particularly both sides, and get them on that petition the first day.

Randolph: Very good. Surely, I see. Very good.

President Johnson: So you be thinking about that, and thinking about what forces we can bring to bear to talk to every single Republican and just [say,] "You're for civil rights or you're not."

Randolph: Very good. All right.

President Johnson: And the whole test's going to be is whether they give us a hearing. Now [the] Rules Committee won't give us a hearing, so we'll have to get a hearing on the floor itself by discharge.

Randolph: I see.

President Johnson: And, I haven't talked to anybody but Roy Wilkins about this. But—and I don't want you to quote me because . . .

Randolph: Oh, no.

President Johnson: . . . you know, it's mighty easy to get—for the President to get in the paper, and then we'll destroy all we're doing.

Randolph: That's true.

President Johnson: But this ought to be your-all's strategy, and I want you to be thinking about it. But I just think we ought to have every friend to sign that petition the moment it's laid down.

Randolph: Surely. Very good. All right, Mr. President.

President Johnson: Thank you, Phil.

Randolph: Thank you for calling.

President Johnson: Bye-bye.

Randolph: Bye.

· · ·

Johnson's great concern, which his adversaries on the Hill recognized, was that he was competing against the clock. It was not simply a matter of passing a civil rights bill; it was imperative that it pass by the summer of 1964. As Johnson explained during a telephone conversation with Treasury Secretary Robert Anderson on the afternoon of November 30, it was not necessary for Smith to vote against the bill. Slowing it down would itself be fatal. Smith's plan, Johnson told Anderson, was:

> that he'll run it [the Civil Rights Bill] over until January. And then January, they'll be late coming back, and he'll piddle along and get into February, and then maybe they won't get it out until March. And then in March, the Senate [will] be able to filibuster it until it goes home, and there'll be nothing done.
>
> Now this country is not in any condition to take that kind of stuff . . . and that's going to hurt our section, and it's going to hurt our people. And it's going to hurt the conservatives. I was talking yesterday, and Roy Wilkins said, "Now we're willing to do anything reasonable. We don't have to have every *i* and every *t*." But he said, "Jack Kennedy was killed in Dallas, and we had some people killed in Mississippi. And there's all this stuff going on, and we've been talking about this for 100 years, and looks like about time to stop talking." And I . . . I just think that we're going to have them out in the streets again if we don't make some little progress. . . . But Howard's just gone to his farm and tells the Speaker, "I won't even give you a hearing on it." . . . I'm going to lay it on the line, if I get to. [I'm going to] say to the Republicans, now you['re] either for civil rights or you're not—you're either the party of [Abraham] Lincoln or you ain't. And let's—by God, put

up or *shut up!* This is it. If you are, you sign the petition to consider it. If you're not, why just get over there, by God, with Jim Eastland and Howard Smith and stay.[1] And I believe that we can dramatize it enough that we can wreck them. . . . But I don't want to do that way. I don't think you ought to do that way. I don't feel that way about the Con[gress]. But when a man won't even give you a hearing, that's just getting too damned rough. It's been heard, you know, for—since May . . . in the Judiciary Committee. Now it comes [to the] Rules Committee, and all he [Smith] got to do is report a rule. But he won't even give you a hearing on reporting a rule. Just says, "Hell, no. Go eat cake. Goddamn it—and don't mess with me till next year."

Johnson's anger at Smith was partly the result of frustration. He knew Smith had the advantage, and he hated that. Until he could find a way to make an end run around the chairman of the Rules Committee, the best Johnson could do was to brainstorm and vent. Though the Democrats had 257 seats to the Republicans' 178 in the House, more than 90 of those Democrats were from the 11 Confederate states, including the powerful Howard Smith of Virginia, and none would support a discharge petition. That meant the administration needed 60 to 70 Republican votes. And as much as the majority of the Republican Party supported civil rights legislation, they were not going to make things easy for Johnson or the Democrats.

After getting off the telephone with Anderson, the President called Senator George Smathers. Smathers, a Florida Democrat, was something of a maverick, and Johnson counted on his support for civil rights if and when the bill reached the Senate. Florida was unique, a bit like Texas in those years in that it was, at once, part of the South and not part of the South. On race relations, Smathers preferred the status quo, although he was more liberal than most in the southern bloc. He advised Johnson that the southern bloc would be far more malleable with Johnson in the White House than they had been with Kennedy. Though he did not explain why, both he and Johnson understood that Johnson, a Texan and former majority leader, could more effectively apply pressure to the South and that the longer they resisted on civil rights, the more harm they would inflict on themselves. They would never support the bill, Smathers said, but they would not lay down their political lives to impede it.

Over the coming days, Johnson continued to fume. On December 2, he met with Whitney Young, and while Young was still in the room, he

---

[1]Senator Eastland was also a steadfast opponent of civil rights legislation.

called G. Mennen Williams, the Assistant Secretary of State for African Affairs. After discussing some outstanding business, Johnson revealed his frustation with Smith.

Monday, December 2, 1963, 9:51 A.M.

G. Mennen Williams

President Johnson: I want to get any ideas you got on what we can do with our Negro community, too, and additional things in the field of equal opportunity, and what our goals ought to be. We've got to have new plans, new programs, new ideas of our own, and you have operated in Michigan so long that you're bound to know some things that you've done there that would be good in Mississippi.

And we're going to go all out on this civil rights bill. We're going to give our blood, sweat, and tears. But the President did that from May to December and they hadn't made any progress—and the tax bill from January to December, so I don't know what we'll do. Now, I think we'll win, but Howard Smith refused the Speaker even an opportunity to be heard. He said, "I'll see you in January." And we've got to go the petition route and that's a mighty hard route, as everybody knows. But we got to put the Republicans on the spot. [Charles] Halleck put it on yesterday, saying, [*mimicking, in a whining tone*] "Well, we've got to have hearings, and the bill was rushed through."

Rushed my ass—it was there from May till November. But he was telling how it rushed. [Everett] Dirksen was on explaining why *he* couldn't quite get the job done. So we've got to find some way, somehow that those people either go with us or they're anti–civil rights. And I want you to give some thinking to it and talk that over with me, particularly in our goals. Now, I'll take care of that bill itself, but we'll all work on it. Everybody will have his assignment. But I want some new fresh things and I want to rely on you to do it. . . .

G. Mennen Williams: Yes sir, I appreciated the fact that you've been most loyal to the ideals of the [1960] convention, and I'm with you all the way.

.   .   .

A few hours later, Johnson called Katherine Graham, the publisher of the *Washington Post,* and complained about what was happening in the Rules Committee. He wanted to shape coverage in the *Post,* to put public pressure on those legislators who might try to sabotage the bill. Johnson lambasted Smith and described those who refused to sign a petition for a vote as little better than Hitler. While the hyperbole might have been unfair, it was effective. After the conversation, the *Post* began to criticize Smith and those Republicans in Congress like Charles Halleck who were allowing Smith to play games on civil rights.

The conversation ranged over a variety of issues; we pick up in midstream when Johnson turns to civil rights.

Monday, December 2, 1963, 11:10 A.M.

Katherine Graham

President Johnson: [*continuing*] But I've got to ask you this: Howard Smith said to the Speaker of the House, that I quietly and judiciously asked to go talk to him about civil rights, that you will have to come back and talk next year, January. And we'll all be late coming back in January. They want to have the holidays. And we won't even give you a hearing on a bill that has been up there since May, that they have had hearings on from May to November, that's reported several days ago, that they don't need any more hearings on, but that we would be willing to spend all the year on hearings if they would give them, but he won't even give them a hearing. He won't even call a meeting. He just said, "I'm out at my farm and I can't have any hearings."[2] Now, I don't want him lectured on account of it. I want to give you my factual situation. So we have no alternative when you won't give a man a hearing. We thought [Lee Harvey] Oswald ought to have a hearing. We are upset. That's why we've got a commission because we thought even Oswald ought to have a hearing. In this country, that's not in keeping. So they are going to try to sign a petition that will give them a hearing in the House, so they can discharge the Rules Committee and bring it out.

Katherine Graham: Right.

President Johnson: Now, every person that doesn't sign that petition has got to be, fairly, regarded as being anti–civil rights, because he is even against a hearing. I don't care if he votes against the bill after he gets a chance to vote on it, if he says it goes too far, if he says that public accommodations ought to do this or that. We've got the votes to pass it. But I don't think *any* American can say that he won't let them have a hearing

---

[2]Smith had an apple farm in northern Virginia, to which he regularly retired when he sensed that he lacked sufficient support on the Rules Committee.

either in the committee or on the floor. That is worse than Hitler did.

So we've got to get ready for that. And we've got to get ready every day, front page, in and out, individuals, [asking,] "Why are you against a hearing?" Point them up, and have their pictures, and have editorials, and have everything else that is in a dignified way for a hearing on the floor. This matter has been there since May and if the committee won't . . . Judiciary has already given it a hearing. And supposedly they are the greatest lawyers in the House, so they ought to know it. But Rules Committee, which is a pure procedural thing, and they don't have any hearings on procedure at all in the Senate. But they usurped their power through the years.

Graham: Mm-hmm.

President Johnson: And because George Norris set them up to protect them an arrogant speaker, they have set themselves up, and they protect their own selfish interest from a popular vote.[3] So they won't let it be voted. They won't give a hearing. So our position has got to be that we are entitled to a hearing. Not the merits of the bill, but we are entitled to a hearing. Once we get that, then these cowards will all vote for the bill. But we have got to try to appeal to the southerners, a few of them in border states, to sign that petition. We've only got 150 Democrats; the rest of them are southerners. So we've got to make *every* Republican [sign]. We ought to say, "Here is the party of Lincoln. Here is the image of Lincoln, and whoever it is that is against a hearing and against a vote in the House of Representatives, is not a man that believes in giving humanity a fair shake." Vote against it if he wants to. Let him do it. But don't let him refuse to sign that petition! Now, if we could ever get that signed, that would practically break their back in the Senate because they could see that here is a steamroller that could petition it out.

Graham: Yes.

President Johnson: And they will put cloture on and the psychology would be just like Texas [football team] won every game this year, that they are a going outfit.

Graham: Right.

President Johnson: Otherwise, now, they are saying Johnson is a great magic man—well, I'm not. But you want to bear in mind Mr. Kennedy was able and he was popular and he was rich and he had young giants helping him—much more enthusiastic in helping him than they are me.

---

[3]In a 1910 revolt against the autocratic rule of Speaker Joseph Cannon, led by Norris, a progressive Republican, then just beginning his career, the House had stripped from the Speaker the simultaneous chairmanship of the Rules Committee.

And he had the newspapers helping him. And he had everything else, but his tax bill. . . . The last conversation I had with Phil [Graham], he said he had asked the President to make me take charge of the tax bill and pass it because it would never be passed until I did. . . . That's the *last* thing he said in a conversation to me, and it's almost unbelievable how prophetic he was, that I'm sitting here today, and that tax bill [remains]. He came and got me and just was real ugly to me—

Graham: I know it.

President Johnson:—And said *mean* things to me. But he was trying to drive me into action on the tax bill. But the President has tried for a year and *he* hasn't been successful in 12 months. Now I *hope* in 12 months I *can* be. But he tried since May on civil rights and he hasn't been successful, so they'd better not be too quick to judge it. If this Mickey Mantle, that's got a batting average of .500 and is the star of the Yankees, if he couldn't do it, how do you expect some plug-ugly from Johnson City to come in and do it pretty quick? [*Graham laughs.*] But we are working on it, and that's part of the effort right now, so you can tell your editorial board—

Graham: I sure will.

President Johnson:—that this Rules Committee has quietly said they are not going to do anything. And somebody ought to be asking these leaders. I can't do it. . . .

.   .   .

The conversation continued for several more minutes, as Johnson talked a bit about the commission he was assembling to investigate the assassination of President Kennedy. But the signals Johnson had sent were unambiguous, and Katherine Graham understood them. In the coming weeks, her newspaper would put pressure on Smith and on House leaders to hold hearings on the bill or to vote on a discharge petition that would move it through the House.

Toward the end of a busy day, Johnson talked to Richard Bolling, a Democratic congressman from Missouri who was a member of the Rules Committee.

Monday, December 2, 1963, 6:56 P.M.

Richard Bolling

President Johnson: [*softly*] . . . a little run down . . . I want to keep this secret. I don't want them to be thinking I'm going around them or anything. But I just want to get your . . . You just keep this confidential, but give me our ideas about what are your prospects up there?

Richard Bolling: Well, I think with the position that you're taking and the Speaker's taking that we will get our maximum Democratic signatures pretty quick. What the Republicans are going to do us, I don't know. There's some mumbling and grumbling. I am to meet with Brown— Clarence Brown—tomorrow morning as soon as he is in his office.[4] I arranged that on last Wednesday when I told him I was going to put this resolution in. Brown has been more or less cooperative, but he doesn't give us a "when." He tried to push [Howard] Smith into having hearings on civil rights before Christmas, but didn't get anywhere. And that really was the thing that convinced me that we absolutely had to go this route or we wouldn't have any lever at all. We would just be whistling in the breeze.

President Johnson: I think you can *really* make a point of that. Just say that the humblest man anywhere has got a right to a hearing. In the first place, there is no real necessity for having hearings. They have been hearing it from May till November. . . .

Bolling: Right.

President Johnson: . . . But if the procedural committee in the House has to have a hearing—they don't have them in the Senate, but they have to have them on this subject—they oughtn't to be extensive. And if they are going to be extensive, they ought to begin them. But you have been denied any opportunity to be heard at all, and the only way you *can* be heard is on the House floor itself.

Bolling: That is right.

President Johnson: And anyone that is for civil rights is going to be signing this petition. If they are not for civil rights, all right. But don't hide behind a procedural thing, because it is well known they want to wait until they get back in January, and then they want to start hearings and maybe run it into Lincoln's Birthday, and then they want to go into Washington's Birthday, and then they want to go into Easter . . .

Bolling: Right.

President Johnson: . . . And then the Senate thinks it can kill it, and that's what the play is. Anybody that wants to be anti–civil rights, that's their right. You've got no objection to that. They can do what they want to. They vote their convictions. But they can't pretend to be for civil rights and then say that they won't even allow them to have a hearing. Let them sign the petition and then vote against the bill.

---

[4]Brown was a Republican representative from Ohio and the ranking minority member on the House Rules Committee.

Bolling: Mm-hmm. I think that kind of pitch ought to come out of the Speaker's mouth when he leaves the White House tomorrow. Something very like that.

President Johnson: Mm-hmm.

Bolling: I think we've got to put them on the frying spot, but I don't think it's appropriate for you to do it, at this stage.

President Johnson: No. No.

Bolling: But I *do* think it's appropriate for him to do it. Just to lay it on the line. When I talked to him on Tuesday last, he told me to go ahead, but to do it on my own, and then when I put it in, he approved it in public. So he's got every right to make a statement like that. It ought to be said sort of gently and low key, but so that it . . . I'm sure there will be lots of coverage. This will be the first leaders' meeting, and I'm sure there'll be *lots* of coverage, and that this will make the point and put the pressure on them. Then next week, I'm organizing an inside group. I'm also working with—as I know you have been—with the various people on the outside that are for this bill, and I probably will talk to them on Wednesday afternoon when they have a meeting describing the technical aspects of this, so they'll understand what they're dealing with. I think we can get, you know, in the order of 160 Democrats pretty fast for this kind of goal.

President Johnson: Are you going to get any from Texas?

Bolling: Well, I don't know. I had a sort of surprise this morning: Albert Thomas called me up and wanted to know what the score was on Rules Committee, and made it very clear that he was going to be helpful.[5] At least that's certainly what I got from him, and I assumed that was out of loyalty to you.

President Johnson: I called Jack Brooks this afternoon.[6] He was off down in the Marine Camp, and said he'd be back Tuesday.

Bolling: I get the impression that Albert is going to be helpful. Now whether he's going to want to be—whether he's going to want to sign a petition or not—I don't know. But we could, it seems to me—you know them a lot better than I do—but there are a number of fellows down there that could.

President Johnson: Yes. Yes. There are a half dozen that could.

Bolling: That's right. And I think it would be extremely impressive if the day we get that petition on the desk, which I hope—

President Johnson: The more you get to sign it the better.

---

[5]Thomas was a Democratic congressman from Houston.
[6]Brooks was a Democratic congressman from Texas.

Bolling: That's right.

President Johnson: Now, you think any Republicans are going to sign it? Twenty?

Bolling: Well, that's up in the air. They've been sending me messages, and I've refused to talk to them, until I talk to Brown tomorrow, because he's the real key in the Rules Committee. . . . Brown has always dealt with me in good faith, both in '56, '57, and '60. He's a tough old boy, but he's always been fair. He's never crossed me. I've never *quite* been able to get him to, you know, say how hard he would push, and that's the purpose of the meeting tomorrow. His situation is complicated by the fact that his wife is dying in Ohio, and he has a number of other personal problems that are of very substantial and tragic proportions.[7] So I don't feel I can shove him too hard; all I can do is just go with him.

President Johnson: Mm-hmm.

Bolling: But I'll take to him in the morning. I don't think he's going to shove the Judge [Howard Smith] hard enough to cut his people loose on this, but the four civil rights Republicans, the ones out of the East and out of the West, have been sending me messages, as we did in 1960, that we ought to get somewhere between 40 and 50 signatures pretty easy. Now, the trick we pulled on them in '60 is that we got a flock of signatures that included only about ten Republicans, and then the rules of the House were violated and the *New York Times* had a complete list. And I think they're obviously scared of this. I think the fact that they're scared of this means that the more pressure we put on them, the better.

President Johnson: Well, I think it's got to go. I'm going to ask them in the morning to really get their teeth into this and taxes too, because . . . I don't want to tell them about procedures, what ought to be done, but I did tell [John] McCormack what I thought about it before it started.

Bolling: Mm-hmm. Well, this is the only lever we've really got in our arsenal.

President Johnson: I agree with you. I agree with you. I think it would be a mistake for me to be quoted now, but . . .

Bolling: I agree with that.

President Johnson: . . . But I think you're doing a good job, and I'll be seeing you.

· · ·

The next day, Johnson invited congressional leaders to breakfast at the White House. Taxes and civil rights occupied much of the meeting, and

---

[7]Brown was terminally ill and died in 1965.

yet again, Johnson expressed his ire that Smith was refusing to hold hearings. Press coverage was increasingly favorable to Johnson, and he was winning accolades for his overtures to civil rights leaders. But the congressional leadership did not like the idea of a discharge petition because that had wider implications. Whatever the merits of the bill, a discharge petition could undermine not just Smith but the entire committee system, which gave chairmen such power. That was why discharge petitions rarely succeeded. McCormack, the Speaker of the House, told the President that "a lot of members don't like the discharge petition as a matter of policy." He said that he never signed discharge petitions but assured Johnson he would "sign this mighty damn quick." House Majority Leader Carl Albert seconded McCormack and seemed supportive of the petition route. But along with Hale Boggs of Louisiana, they both warned that the votes were not yet there and that they would be hard to find.[8]

After breakfast, Johnson began another frantic day, in which civil rights was never far from his mind. He met with Martin Luther King at the White House and impressed on King his committment to passing a meaningful bill, saying that with such staunch opposition, it was vital that they cooperate. Johnson also talked about how the White House could work for improved employment opportunities in the South. For Johnson, civil rights and southern poverty went hand in hand.

Not only was Johnson confronting an uphill struggle on obtaining enough votes for a discharge petition, but he was also facing the traditional holiday adjournment, when congresspeople went back to their districts for the remainder of the year. He was worried the issue would remain unresolved during the recess, which would strengthen the position of those who wanted the bill to die. Johnson began to speak more frequently to Carl Albert, the House majority leader from Oklahoma, who had pledged to fight for the President and for civil rights.

Some of the discussion was relatively arcane, as the two men delved into a who's who of the various people in congress and where each stood. But that was a key to the legislative process, not just in early December but throughout the next several months. The act of passing a bill is complicated and involves endless hours of conversation about the prejudices and predilections of individual legislators. And civil rights was as controversial as any subject Congress had considered. If Johnson wanted the bill to pass, he had to attend to every possible contingency. That meant going

---

[8]Notes on the First Congressional Leadership Breakfast, December 3, 1963, Presidential Appointment File, Lyndon Baines Johnson Library.

over each and every vote. But Johnson had been an adept majority leader precisely because he loved that process, and understood its importance. His conversation with Albert is a snapshot of a moment in the life of a bill, albeit a bill of unusual moral and political significance.

Tuesday, December 3, 1963, 3:00 P.M.

Carl Albert

President Johnson: Carl, how are you?

Carl Albert: Fine. How are you?

President Johnson: Pretty good. I wanted to talk to you. I didn't get a chance to individually this morning a little more about the situation up there. I gather you're getting some static and backfire. Tell me about [Charles] Halleck's conversation last night.

Albert: Well . . .

President Johnson: [*continuing*] On adjournment and all that stuff.

Albert: . . . He just said that [*mimicking Halleck*] by God he was going to raise hell if we didn't adjourn by the 14th, that there wasn't any use going around here, and that he was going to fuss about this Civil Rights Bill. And if they wanted to get it up quicker, if they go the normal route, and have a reasonable hearing, well, his boys would go with us. . . . But I don't know. The truth of the matter is he's wanting to get a little bit of an anti–civil rights aura around him himself because his right-wing group *really* chewed him when he went down to the White House there and agreed with President Kennedy to get that bill out.

President Johnson: Yes.

Albert: You know.

President Johnson: Yes.

Albert: But, oh, I'm catching from all sides, because I said on the TV Sunday, on the program *Face the Nation*, they asked me would we have the bill on the floor by the end of the year—have it up on the floor this year. And I said, "Well, as a matter of practical, parliamentary fact, I think it is almost impossible," and the other wing of the Republicans are chewing me for saying that, you know. [*Both laugh.*] . . . Halleck is threatening to do anything he can. . . . Of course, he and [Howard] Smith are going to get together and we have to go to Rules Committee, and [if] Smith wouldn't call Rules, they could lock us up here. But if they do, we'll just stay here through the Christmas holidays. But he is, he's in bad shape. He's hitting the bottle *too* much—too early in the day, you know.

President Johnson: Mm-hmm.

Albert: But, I'll tell you, we'll do anything you want to. I'm going to work hard for that Civil Rights Bill. It might beat me, but I'm going to try to help you out.[9] I really am. I'm going to help put it over. And that's going a lot further than a lot of people would on other issues, you know.

President Johnson: Yes. Yes.

Albert: It is going to be a little tough for me, but . . .

President Johnson: I thought Charlie [Halleck], that night the leaders met with me, he talked very cooperatively.

Albert: Yes, he did.

President Johnson: Was he drinking a little last night?

Albert: Yes, drinking too heavy. But he's been smarting. He told us to quit bringing up, that he's getting tired of these things being brought up named after the President, that there's a limit to all this business, that there's a limit to what we should do.

President Johnson: I hear a good deal of that, Carl, a good deal of it.

Albert: I do too. But the thing . . . Where he's playing it wrong, Mr. President, is for *him* to say it. If these people overdo it themselves, *they* are the ones that will get hurt, but if he criticizes them for it, *he's* the one that's going to get hurt.

President Johnson: That's exactly right.

Albert: And, well, he even said, "It is time for Lyndon Johnson to move into the White House." You know, well [*unclear*], you know.

President Johnson: [*Laughs ruefully.*] That's right.

Albert: But you want me to find out anything?

President Johnson: Yes, I want you to get the lay of the land and find out what they're thinking. I don't know of any choice we've got here if Smith won't have a hearing, except just try to get the petition signed.

Albert: Yes. I think we *will* get it signed. We may not get it signed by Christmas, though.

President Johnson: No, but we ought to get as many the first day as we can.

Albert: That's right. Absolutely.

President Johnson: George Meany said labor is going to bat on it. Dave McDonald called me, told me he had 33 men on the Hill.[10]

Albert: Well, Dave's brother was up here just now. I saw him.

President Johnson: He told me he had 108 that have agreed to sign it.

---

[9]Albert was exaggerating the risks. He represented a district in Oklahoma that did not send a Republican to Congress until 1994.

[10]McDonald was president of the United Steelworkers Union.

Albert: That's right, 108. He showed me his list.

President Johnson: And 45 that said no.

Albert: Yes, sir.

President Johnson: Of the Democrats.

Albert: And I think we will . . .

President Johnson: Can we make a little poll of our own and just start going down them by whips?

Albert: Yes, sir.

President Johnson: And just say to each whip, "Now, we've got to know and this is it."

Albert: All right. We may not do it by whips—may do it by . . .

President Johnson: States?

Albert: Yes. And I by people I can count on, you know.

President Johnson: Yes. What about—

Albert: Let it come from somebody besides a leadership official. It might be better to let them do it, but let us be behind it. You don't want the [Democratic] Study Group to do it.

President Johnson: No.

Albert: [*continuing*] That's already created a lot of mad, because [Richard] Bolling filed a resolution on [Emanuel] Celler's bill, and some of them wanted me . . . Homer wanted me to file a discharge motion.[11] I can't file a petition. It's not, Celler would never forgive me if I took the bill away from me. You know.

President Johnson: Mm-hmm. I believe it would be better though if you talked to him and just said, "Now, this is going to be all or nothing." We can't . . . We ought to . . .

Albert: He'll be ready. He'll be ready on Monday. Next Monday he'll be here to discharge that bill.

President Johnson: I know. But wouldn't it get more votes if you filed it?

Albert: I don't know. I asked Lew about it—because I don't mind filing it—I asked Lew about it, but Lew says it would be the worst thing in the world for leadership to file that petition.[12] He says you're just admitting that you can't lead, and you're doing something that no leadership has ever done in history, and that you'll do yourself more harm than good on everything that comes along. You'll get this one just as quick. Now, his judgment is pretty good on this sort of thing. I admit he's a little conservative, but his judgment's good. I don't mind filing it.

11Homer was Homer Thornberry, a Democratic congressman from Texas.

12Lew was Lew Deschler, the House Parliamentarian and a close adviser of the House leadership.

President Johnson: Does he think that you can get a rule out of Rules? Is that where he's at?

Albert: No, no. No, no.

President Johnson: He thinks we've got to go the discharge route, doesn't he?

Albert: He doesn't mean that. He thought we might eventually get one out of the Rules Committee. But he has no views on the discharge petition. He does about me filing it. And he doesn't even think the Speaker and I should sign it until the very last word, until we have to. I'm going to think that over, whether I sign it early or not. Normally they don't sign it early. What do you think?

President Johnson: I'd lead them into it if that were me, but I don't know. I don't want you to take my judgment. I think that we've got to make choice whether we want to go the Rules route or the petition route. Once we make the petition route, we ought to go all the way, the quicker the better, with all the steam we've got. It's just like if we say, "Well, we're going to pass. We're going to try a 100-yard pass—

Albert: I agree with you.

President Johnson:—And you say, "Okay, but don't let the best passer pass. Just get him out and let's let somebody else do it." Now, there's not as many men going to be in on the petition that Celler signed or Dick Bolling puts up as they will if it's the majority leader. And I think you've got to take the position that "I'm against short-circuiting committees. I don't want to go around any committee. We've asked for hearings. This [is a] procedural question. We're willing to have hearings. The Speaker *begged* for hearings, but they won't give us hearings, and we just can't wait till it is too late to pass a bill and delay it in the Congress and kill it. And therefore I'm going to ask the House of Representatives itself for a hearing in the Committee of the Whole, and if its agent won't function and can't function, then I'm going to ask the whole House to function, because we just can't have stand-still do-nothing government." It seems to me that that would be more effective than having Celler do it or anybody else, because then a fellow like Homer Thornberry and Albert Thomas and Jack Brooks and some of them could walk up there and sign it, and say, "Hell, the Democratic leader . . ."

Albert: Yes. Let me check this out with the Speaker, will you?

President Johnson: Yes.

Albert: He's already talked to Celler. He may be committed to let Celler do it, you know?

President Johnson: Yes. Yes. Well, I thought old Celler wants success, doesn't he?

Albert: Sure he does. He wants success.

President Johnson: Well, now, don't you think that between you and Manny Celler that you can . . .

Albert: We can probably work it out. I'll find out, and then I'll let you know what we can do. I don't want, you know, as a matter of helping you down the line, first of all, we've got to pass the bill. This is it. If we don't pass this one, we're going to be blamed and you're going to be blamed. They're going to say, "Well, it could have been here." They're going to say any darned thing.

President Johnson: Sure. Sure they will.

Albert: The Republicans will say that. There's no question about it: this is it. This bill and the tax bill.

President Johnson: Why have they got a story today in the paper that says I'm trying to get rid of McNamara and McNamara is going to run against me on the Republican ticket?[13] He's the best cabinet member I've got. And Charlie Bartlett, the President's [Kennedy] best friend, wrote it.[14]

Albert: Is that so?

President Johnson: Yes. I just can't understand it.

Albert: Well, that kind of stuff. They're always doing that to me—that sort of thing. The other thing about this is that maybe we ought to take a poll before we decide. And we ought to take it between now and tomorrow or the next day, about what we're going to do and how far we go. If we *can't* get this out by a discharge petition, we may have to be at the mercy of the Rules Committee. What do you think?

President Johnson: Yes, you'll have to.

Albert: Well, I mean, we might do ourselves more harm than good if we start pushing it too hard unless we know we can do it. See what I mean?

President Johnson: Mm-hmm. I'd take that poll and I think the bridge is pretty well burnt. I think you might near got to do it, but I think I'd take that poll and see.

Albert: All right, we'll do it.

President Johnson: I wouldn't tell them I talked to him, but you call me back later in the afternoon. Let's keep in pretty close touch.

Albert: All right. Okay.

. . . .

The following day, December 4, Johnson talked several more times with Albert about trying to squeeze out votes. Toward the end of the day, he

---

[13]Robert McNamara was the Secretary of Defense.
[14]Charles Bartlett was a journalist and had been a close personal friend of the late President.

had a brief discussion with legislative aide Larry O'Brien. The two went over the vote count; it was still an uphill battle. Looking for ways to break the impasse, Johnson had begun to toy with the idea of hinting to civil rights leaders that he would not mind a demonstration or two. Perhaps a few highly publicized protests would step up the pressure, if not on Smith than at least on those Republicans like Halleck who were questioning the need for the discharge petition. Already, prominent Republicans were making noises that a discharge petition was a terrible precedent, and William McCulloch, one of the most ardent Republican sponsors of the bill in the Judiciary Committee, made strong statements to that effect. Johnson was disgusted, "Hell. He [McCulloch] told Kennedy in my presence he was for this bill, and as soon as Kennedy dies he runs like a damned [*unclear*]." O'Brien agreed. "If that's the way they want to play it," he told the President, "I'm sure we're capable of playing it hard."

The next few weeks saw the first stage of a protracted game of chicken. Public opinion polls showed that support for major civil rights legislation was growing. Fifty percent of the country had not favored rigorous action on civil rights in the early fall of 1963. By the end of the year, that number had fallen to about 30 percent, while the percentages favoring Johnson's stance rose accordingly. But opposition remained substantial in the South. The shift in public opinion gave Johnson an advantage, and the fact that a majority in Congress supported reform also helped the cause.

As of early December, Johnson could not be sure that he could get a strong bill, complete with a ban on discrimination in public accommodations and with provisions for federal enforcement of local violations. For generations, the internal dynamics of both the House and the Senate had allowed southern representatives to block the passage of civil rights bills, and Johnson respected and feared this reality. Although the atmosphere favored the passage of a bill, the perils were evident, and Smith and the Rules Committee were merely the first of many dangers.

Though the bill had not even passed the House, Johnson began to lay the groundwork in the Senate. He tried to use the tax bill as leverage for the civil rights legislation, and vice versa. Johnson was genuinely concerned about the prospects for both bills, but he was also careful about the way he discussed each of them. When talking to a southerner whom he knew would oppose civil rights, he pointed out that quick passage of the tax bill was imperative because if it failed to pass soon, it would be overshadowed by civil rights for the next six months and then never passed at all. In speaking to someone who favored civil rights, Johnson stressed how important it was to get the bill moving through the House because otherwise it would be slowed by the tax bill.

For example, on December 13, Johnson talked with Democratic senator Harry Byrd of Virginia. "See," the President explained, "what I'm afraid of is, every businessman in the country wants to figure this on January, and I think if we pass it in January, we can do it. But if you got a civil rights bill over there, and it took four or five months discussing that thing, and your tax bill got behind it, why, all of our work would have been done in vain."

Judge Smith was no fool. By mid-December, he made a tactical retreat and agreed to hold hearings on the civil rights bill, beginning in early January, after the President's State of the Union address. That took the steam out of the discharge petition and ensured that at least another six weeks would pass before the bill was brought to a full House vote. It was a hollow victory for the bill's supporters because time remained a problem. In addition, Johnson had gotten a break when congressional leaders agreed to extend the session until closer to Christmas.

As of late December, Johnson's mood was grim. Part of what made him an effective legislator was his capacity to see the potential clouds behind every silver lining. On December 20, in a particularly sour mood, he vented to Jim Webb, the National Aeronautic and Space Administration (NASA) head and a longtime ally of the President. "If you don't pass the civil rights bill, and you don't pass the tax bill, you can't do it. And I don't see any hope for passing either one right now. That's my honest judgment. I'm just *so* disappointed that . . . Kennedy worked for the tax bill for a year, and it's in worse shape than anything I ever saw, and I can't do it in a month. Harry Byrd and Everett Dirksen and them are not the slightest interested in doing anything about it.

"And the civil rights bill is going to be out of the House, and we'll have to intercept it, and they'll start filibustering. Dick Russell's got the votes where you cannot put cloture on. So the tax bill'll get behind the civil rights bill. And your civil rights'll be defeated, and by that time, it'll be too late for taxes. And I'll go to the country with nothing."

Given the advantage the Democrats enjoyed in the House and the Senate, as well as the good will toward Johnson and the fact that he had presented his legislative agenda as a way of honoring Kennedy's legacy, going before the country in the middle of 1964 with nothing to show was an unlikely possibility. But Johnson took little for granted, and that would prove an asset during the next six months.

Chapter 8
Through the House

Hearings were not scheduled to begin until January 9, 1964, and Christmas was coming up, but Johnson hardly paused for breath. The country remained disoriented, and the flurry of activity in Congress was matched by the ongoing investigation into John Kennedy's death and the slow adjustment to the shock of the event.

In mid-December, Johnson was still trying to woo his doubters, when unexpectedly, he was attacked in the pages of *Jet* magazine, the widely read black weekly. The highly influential journalist Simeon Booker penned a harsh description of Johnson's record on civil rights. Booker claimed that many blacks were dismayed to see Johnson in the White House because they doubted that a southerner would ever endorse anything but Jim Crow. Booker also charged that as vice president, Johnson had refused to meet with black reporters, having used the flimsy excuse that Kennedy was the president and hence the architect of the administration's policy.

Johnson was incensed. Booker had gotten under the new President's skin, and as usual, Johnson let everyone know it bothered him. He had two responses. First, he complained bitterly that he was being treated unfairly, and then he proceeded to hire a black secretary whom he paraded before the world in an effort to suggest he was no bigot. The woman's name was Gerri Whittington, and she was working for Johnson's assistant Ralph Dungan. Without anyone on his staff informing her beforehand, Johnson called her at home on the evening of December 23. Not expecting a call from the President of the United States, the young woman was understandably surprised and assumed it to be a crank call.

Monday, December 23, 1963, 9:50 P.M.

Gerri Whittington

President Johnson: [*to operator*] How long does it take me to get her?
After a delay, Whittington comes on the line.
President Johnson: Gerri, where are you?
Gerri Whittington: I'm at home. Who's this?
President Johnson: This is the President.
Whittington: [*taken aback*] Oh!
President Johnson: What are you doing?
Whittington: Oh, I think someone's playing with me.
President Johnson: No, no, you're not. I want to talk to you about our work, honey. Where are you—at home?
Whittington: Oh, yes, I am.
President Johnson: Are you busy?
Whittington: No, I'm not.
President Johnson: Can you come down here immediately?
Whittington: Oh, I'd be glad to.
President Johnson: Come on down. I've got Jack Valenti here and we want to talk to you about a little reassignment.[1]
Whittington: Oh, yes, sir.
President Johnson: I'm in my office, and you grab a cab and come to the Southwest Gate, and I'll tell them to let you in. If you need a car sent out for you, I'll get one, but you can get a cab quicker, can't you?
Whittington: Well, usually I can, Mr. President, but inasmuch as the weather is so—
President Johnson: I'll get one now. Give me your address.
Whittington does so.
President Johnson: How far are you away from the White House?
Whittington: Oh, I guess about 25 minutes.
President Johnson: Twenty-five minutes?!
Whittington: Yes.
President Johnson: Hell of a long way. Do you walk to work?
Whittington: [*Laughs.*] No, sir, I don't.
President Johnson: All right. Okay. 399-6293, Mayfair Apartments, 3807 J Street, NE.
Whittington: Yes, it is.

---

[1]Valenti was a presidential aide.

President Johnson: Okay, get ready now and get your walking clothes on.

Whittington: I certainly will. Thank you.

.   .   .

Less than 20 minutes later, with aide Jack Valenti in the room, Johnson called Andrew Hatcher, who was the assistant press secretary and, more important for the business at hand, one of the few black men on the president's immediate staff. He asked Hatcher whether Gerri Whittington was competent, but he kept forgetting her name. The conversation with Hatcher was followed immediately by calls to Whitney Young and Roy Wilkins. Johnson was in damage-control mode, and he wanted to make sure neither Young nor Wilkins believed the *Jet* story.

Monday, December 23, 1963, 10:15 P.M.

Andrew Hatcher

Jack Valenti: Maybe you ought to have one of these Negroes meet you—I don't know, Philadelphia had some racial strife there. I don't know enough about it to know.

Hatcher then comes on the line.

President Johnson: Andy, I read your stuff you sent me here on Simeon Booker, and I don't know. It looks like he's awful rough on us.

Andrew Hatcher: Yes, he is, uh, not the kind of things I'd like, but . . .

President Johnson: Well, now, I was under the impression we had a picture with every leader. Is that wrong? He said that we wouldn't have a picture made with a single one of the Negro leaders, and I thought we had them with every one.

Hatcher: Well, I got on him about that, and I told him that was incorrect, and, you know . . . And that we had them of all of them. And I sent him—

President Johnson: I called five of them in here and had everyone I could think of. I've called them all on the telephone separately. I had Bob Weaver go up with me to the United Nations. I had Mrs. [D'Jaris Hinton] Watson ride in the car with me along with the mayor [Robert Wagner of New York City], and I had to throw out even his wife to get room, and I took them to the United Nations.[2] I don't know what more I can do.

---

[2]Weaver was the administrator of the U.S. Housing and Home Finance Agency. D'Jaris Hinton Watson was the wife of Johnson's friend, African American judge James Watson. She served as a member of the EEOC.

Hatcher: Yes, well, I wouldn't worry too much about that, Mr. President, on that—

President Johnson: Well, I mean, why doesn't he give the facts? He says that I wouldn't let one pose with me, and all of them posed with me. So what do we do about this?

Hatcher: I called him up just as soon as I saw that. He's just trying to test us out. We were getting good and bad reports from him before. But, overall, we're winning on this thing, and we're just going to keep at it. You see, the story is written out of Chicago. Larry Stills, the writer out of Chicago, is writing the other stories, and they're pretty good stories.

President Johnson: But Simeon Booker says that we wouldn't pose with a Negro, and we posed with all of them. Now, what do we do about that—nothing? Can't we ask, write him a little note, and say, "Here are the pictures? Why would you write this if it was untrue?" Is he working for [Nelson] Rockefeller or somebody, you reckon?

Hatcher: [*laughing*] No, no, no. No, sir.

President Johnson: Or you reckon he just doesn't know?

Hatcher: No, he knows. He knows. Because when I saw that, I mean, I . . . I—

President Johnson: Now, what southern guests are he talking about? When I get Harry Byrd here to talk the tax bill—is that what he's talking about?

Hatcher: Yes, that's what he's talking about?

President Johnson: Well, should I just not mention and talk to any of them?

Hatcher: I wouldn't do anything on that. We're going to win on that. He has to write this type of column that's supposed to be a smart-alecky type of Washington column, and that's—

President Johnson: But he doesn't talk about all of them that I've seen. I'm catching more hell for seeing [James] Farmer and Melman and all that group than I ever caught from anybody.[3]

Hatcher: I guess that's right.

President Johnson: And I put them out in front. I had Mrs. Watson riding in the automobile with me and Mrs. Johnson. I had Bob Weaver—I called him and asked him to go with me. I called the congressman, Dawson, and asked him, and asked him to investigate the whole department.[4] I've

---

[3]Seymour Melman, professor of international relations at Columbia University, was known as a critic of defense procurement policy. Johnson had met with him on December 4. He had met with James Farmer on December 6.
[4]William Dawson was a Democrat from Illinois.

asked the five Negro congressmen to come in here.[5] I don't know what the hell else I can do. I put civil rights first in my State of the Union message: it's my first priority. They tell me they've got enough votes to never allow cloture. They've got 70—they say that they can never get the 70 votes we need—but I'm still fighting. And I just don't understand, for them to just . . . [reading from article] "While Johnson's conducting the civil rights thrust, opposition from Democratic lawmakers threatens to weaken the bill." They do—but I'm not going to weaken it. I'm not going to agree to a goddamned amendment. They're going to beg me before I ever let them touch it. I don't think we'll pass a bill without something, and Kennedy didn't either! He said we'd have to give on two things, but I'm not going to give.

Hatcher: Well, we have a good—we have a great start on it. And actually, even though I saw these others, I wanted you to see the kind of feature stories that we were getting. Everybody recognizes that this is sort of a controversial type of column that this fellow writes, and everybody who reads it knows how inaccurate he is most of the time. But we're winning on the overall story.

President Johnson: I wonder if you couldn't get Martin Luther King and Farmer and [A. Philip] Randolph to tell them that everyone had their picture made, and they were published. We sent them copies of them.

Hatcher: All right. I'll take care of that, and—

President Johnson: I'd just get them, and [forcefully] call them, and just say I invited them. They didn't invite me. I guess I'm the first President who just went out of my way to have every one of them come in and have a picture made, have coffee, and sit down and talk to them, and then go to bat for them. I've talked to them all over the phone three or four times since.

Hatcher: Of course, you know, also, that we've sent out the pictures— every one that you've had taken. So, I mean, the newspapers will have had—

President Johnson: Well, I wish you'd get me tomorrow . . . I wish you'd get me tomorrow over your signatures the pictures that I had made with the popular leader, Dr. King. I'm just autographing one tonight here to him.

Hatcher: [quietly] Yes, sir.

---

[5]William Dawson, Charles Diggs (D-Michigan), Adam Clayton Powell (D-New York), Robert Nelson Cornelius Nix (D-Pennsylvania), and Augustus Hawkins (D-California) were the five black congressmen in the 88th Congress.

President Johnson: I just autographed one to Martin Luther King, A. Philip Randolph, and James Farmer. Get those plus Roy Wilkins and plus Whitney Young—five of them. I'd just get them . . . and send *every* goddamned one of them to Simeon Booker, and say, "Please print a retraction. Here they are. And this is not so." And just say when I went to New York, I had Mrs. . . . I had Bob Weaver. I called him up at 11:00 at night, and got him away from testifying before the budget—made him quit his job to go with me. I got Mrs. Watson and her husband to come and meet us at the airport. I don't arrange the arrangements committee up there.

Hatcher: Yes.

President Johnson: [*continuing*] That's up to the mayor.

Hatcher: No, next week they'll have something in there about Mrs. Watson.

President Johnson: Well, this is December the 26th date here.

Hatcher: Yes. All right, sir.

President Johnson: I think I'll take this girl if I can get her—used to be in Ralph Dungan's office—and just put her in my personal office. And I think I'll furthermore get a Mexican and bring him in here, put him on the staff in the White House. I've already got a good Italian, Jack Valenti.

Hatcher: Yes, sir!

President Johnson: I wish you'd point that out to all the minority groups—that the first man I hired was Jack Valenti.

Hatcher: Yes, I noticed that in the story the other day. That was a good ride.

President Johnson: Well, I think I'll get this boy Cornavo [Dan Luevano]—what's the California, the man who's finance commissioner, the Mexican that's Pat Brown's finance commissioner out there?[6] He's a damned good fellow. Do you know him?

Hatcher: Uh, no.

President Johnson: [*teasingly*] Well, you're a Californian, getting ready to run for Congress.[7]

Hatcher: I've just forgotten about that.

President Johnson: Cornavero or Cuernavo, or something like that. . . . Anyway, what's this girl—do you know this Wilkinson girl?

Hatcher: Gerri Whittington.

President Johnson: Whittington. Is she any good?

---

[6]Brown was governor of California.
[7]Johnson was referring to the seat of Congressman John Shelley, who had been elected mayor of San Francisco.

Hatcher: Yes, she's very good.

President Johnson: Well, now, why don't we just put her outside here and be my secretary?

Hatcher: [*softly*] That's very good, sir.

President Johnson: Huh?

Hatcher: Yes, sir.

President Johnson: She's got good character?

Hatcher: She's good.

President Johnson: Good ability?

Hatcher: She's good.

President Johnson: Respected by all her employees?

Hatcher: Yes, sir.

President Johnson: Okay. I'm just going to offer her a job here and put her out in my office, and you watch these things. Get me those pictures, though, and you write a letter over your signature, and let me see it.

Hatcher: Yes, sir.

President Johnson: Okay. If I'm not here, you go on and send it anyway. Just say that you like him, and you enjoy the magazine, but you think he ought to see the pictures because I've autographed one five minutes ago I'll find for you, and you can send it, to Martin Luther King.

Hatcher: Yes, sir, I'll do that.

President Johnson: Okay.

. . .

Monday, December 23, 1963, 10:30 P.M.

Roy Wilkins

President Johnson: Lyndon Johnson.

Roy Wilkins: How are you, Mr. President?

President Johnson: Fine. I'm still signing mail. I had three or four things before I left the office to go to Bill Green's funeral and then to Texas I wanted to talk to you about.

Wilkins: Yes?

President Johnson: One is the Civil Rights Commission. Did Lee White talk to you about that?

Wilkins: No, he didn't talk to me about that.

President Johnson: Would you mind looking into it, and seeing who we think that might be real good for it?

Wilkins: Very good.

President Johnson: Number two, the State of the Union message.

Would you mind giving me some suggestions as to what we ought to do about that?

Wilkins: Very good, sir.

President Johnson: Number three, do you know this Gerri Whittington here in the White House? This Negro girl that's been working for Ralph Dungan.

Wilkins: No, sir, I don't know her.

President Johnson: Well, they tell me she has good character, and good ability, and I'm thinking about just moving her in as my secretary.

Wilkins: I know of her, and they say she's a good worker, but I've never met her, and don't know her.

President Johnson: Well, I think we probably ought to do it. Now, did you go to California?

Wilkins: I went to California, and was only there to turn right around, and tried to get in touch with Mr. [Lloyd] Hand and could not do so.

President Johnson: Well, I want this—what's this Mexican boy's name out there? Cuerno?

Wilkins: Dan Luevano.

President Johnson: Dan Q [*Struggles with name.*]—

Wilkins: Luevano. It's L-u-

President Johnson: Dan Luevano is the finance director out there for Pat Brown, a Mexican. And I rather think we ought to bring him in and put him in the White House, too. I've got Andy Hatcher, this girl Whittington, and I rather think we ought to give them a *little* attention, because they've had nobody. I checked him out, and he seems to be pretty good. I don't know whether I can get him or not, but I want to talk to you before I offered him a job.

Wilkins: I agree with you 100 percent about giving them a chance.

President Johnson: I guess the first man I hired on my staff was Jack Valenti, who's an Italian boy, and I think that he's doing a good job in *that* field. But I just think we ought to be sure we've got some minority groups. Now, didn't I have my picture made with you when you were in here?

Wilkins: You certainly did.

President Johnson: *Jet* magazine said I refused to be photographed with you leaders. And I had it made with every one of them.

Wilkins: No. No, Mr. President, you not only had it made with me, but it was carried in all the papers.

President Johnson: Well . . .

Wilkins: It was carried in a number of the southern papers I saw, on page one.

President Johnson: What do we do with . . . What do we do with . . .

Wilkins: *Jet*, I think, made the statement, Mr. President, that you had not had your picture taken with two of them, I believe.

President Johnson: No, they said, "A more serious breach came during Johnson's welcoming to the White House of the Negro leadership. By some unexplained action, the direct action leaders were denied the opportunity to pose with LBJ in his office."

Wilkins: That was—they're referring there to [Martin Luther] King and [James] Farmer.

President Johnson: Well, I had my picture made with every damn one of them.

Wilkins: I'm pretty sure you did, sir. I know—

President Johnson: [*agitated*] I just autographed one to A. Philip Randolph and one to Martin King. I've got them in front of me.

Wilkins: Well, this is—if you will permit me, I'd be glad to speak to the editor of *Jet*.

President Johnson: I wish you would, now—

Wilkins: The publisher.

President Johnson: Now, "the southern leaders," I don't know what he's talking about. He may be talking about Harry Byrd because I called him down here on the tax bill.

Wilkins: Yes.

President Johnson: But Harry Byrd called me, and I want to get that tax bill out of his committee.

Wilkins: Of course. Of course. And this is a matter that everybody understands. But I will undertake to speak to him.

President Johnson: I called these people on my own. They didn't call me—none of these leaders.

Wilkins: I understand.

President Johnson: And I had a wonderful meeting with them, and I just caught hell about the Farmer conference from everybody. But I had a good meeting. And this fellow that was with him didn't do anything wrong.

Wilkins: Yes.

President Johnson: But they all jumped on me about it.

Wilkins: Yes, I know. I know. I think I'll speak to the *Jet* publisher *and* to the editor in Washington.

President Johnson: I don't know. I'll do anything that I ought to do. If you'll tell me what I ought to do, I'll do it. If you've ever had a friend in this place, you've got him now.

Wilkins: So far, sir, you haven't made any mistakes.

President Johnson: Well, you tell me about the State of the Union, and you call Simeon Booker and tell him that his December the 26th article in which he says that policy was denied these people, that that's not true, that I have pictures of every damn one of them.

Wilkins: Very good. I'll check with him. Now, Mr. President, may I say just a word to you?

President Johnson: Yes.

Wilkins: I hope you're going to have, first, a Merry Christmas.

President Johnson: Thank you.

Wilkins: As merry a Christmas as you can.

President Johnson: All right.

Wilkins: I hope you get away, down in Texas. And I'd like to say this to you: please take care of yourself.

President Johnson: I'm going to. I'm going to.

Wilkins: Please take care of yourself. We need you. Now, I'm in your corner. I can't get out on the housetops—

President Johnson: I know that. I know it. I don't ask you to. I'm not embarassing you. But Roy, tell me this: did I make a mistake in taking a woman that's as close to me as my mother and my wife to hear me speak [before the United Nations]?[8]

Wilkins: No.

President Johnson: I didn't take her because she's a Negro. I took her because I took my wife and my children.

Wilkins: This is a very good thing, and, believe me, it made a hit with the rank and file. I don't know what the intellectuals might have said, but you don't have to worry about them.

President Johnson: Well, she's in charge of forty people [*unclear*]. She's the chief of staff of the whole operation. She's a college graduate. And I don't know how in the hell people would be objecting to her. When I had my heart attack, she stayed with me every day and every night. . . .

Wilkins: Yes. Well, this is the type of the thing that I think you're going to have to expect, but I think [among] the rank and file, all the comment I've heard has been favorable. Everything I've heard has been favorable. And I think you've got this minority group well on the way. Everybody that's commenting, the newspapers and others and I've gotten around a little bit. I was in a group last might, and Minnie, my wife, made a campaign speech for you in a little dinner party up here in Westchester County [New York].

President Johnson: Well, bless her heart. You bring her down here to

---

[8]The woman was D'Jaris Watson.

see us, now. You tell me what I ought to do if I'm not doing it right. Because if I don't, it's a mistake of the head, and not the heart.

Wilkins: I know that. I know that. I saw you yesterday in the candlelight service. I was up here with Bob Wagner at the armory, and we saw the telecast of what happened at Washington, and I thought it was wonderful.

President Johnson: Thank you, Roy. Now, call me, Roy, and don't wait until I call you.

Wilkins: All right, Mr. President. Thank you so much. Remember, Merry Christmas. And remember, *please* take care of yourself.

President Johnson: I'll do that. Don't worry about that. I'll be going strong, and you just let me know. And write me that note on civil rights. And right me that note on the State of the Union.

Wilkins: The State of the Union, and on the Civil Rights Commission.

President Johnson: That's right.

Wilkins: [*continuing*] And I'll get in touch . . . I got a list from your office today about the Latin American leaders in California.

President Johnson: That's right. Well, Lee White, in my office, is going to stay here, and he has nothing to do except stay on top of this thing. And if he doesn't, you let me know.

Wilkins: Very good. I'll be in touch with him.

President Johnson: Okay.

Wilkins: Thank you.

President Johnson: And you come on and you meet this woman [Gerri Whittington] the first time you're in this White House.

Wilkins: Very good, sir.

President Johnson: Good night.

.   .   .

Monday, December 23, 1963, 10:35 P.M.

Whitney Young

President Johnson: Give me that drink over there.

Jack Valenti: You were going to talk to Martin Luther King, too.

President Johnson: Yes.

Valenti: I think he's, King, is the real spiritual leader of this group.

A pause ensues before Young comes on the line.

President Johnson: Whitney?

Whitney Young: Yes. How are you, Mr. President?

President Johnson: Fine. I want you to write me a note about what you think ought to go in the State of the Union [address].

Young: When would you give this?

President Johnson: On the 7th or 8th of January. I've got to go to press with it about the 28th or 29th [of December].

Young: So you ought to have this by . . .

President Johnson: I ought to have it just as quick as you can get it—tomorrow or the next day.

Young: All right.

President Johnson: Number two, I want you write me if you've got any real, top people, anywhere, on the Civil Rights Commission. I'd like to look at anybody you've got.

Young: What do you need by way of—

President Johnson: [*irritated*] Appointment to the Civil Rights Commission.

Young: I know it. But, I mean, does it have to be a white person, or from the North?

President Johnson: No, it doesn't have to be. It could be anybody. I'd like to have some real, able leader from the South.

Young: That's what I wondered: did you need a southerner?

President Johnson: Yes. Yes. Yes. I'd rather have an able leader—somebody, if you've got a white man that you'd recommend that would really do a better job, I'll have him, or anybody else. I just want to look at several of them.

Young: All right. I remember there was a fellow from Texas or somebody, who resigned not long ago. I know they lost one person. And they lost Nick. Nick left them.[9]

President Johnson: Yes, they've lost everybody, nearly. They've got two vacancies on it.

Young: Well, I'll get busy on this.

President Johnson: Now, I see where the *Jet* magazine says that, number one, I didn't have anybody meet me when I came to New York for the funeral. I didn't have Adam Clayton Powell with me. I made [Robert] Weaver go with me when I came up there to the United Nations, and I made Mrs. [D'Jaris Hinton] Watson meet me and ride down with me. Then they say that "by some unexplained action, the direct action leaders were denied the opportunity to pose with LBJ in his office." Now, I've got pictures with you, with Roy Wilkins, with Martin Luther King, and A.

---

[9]This may be a reference to Nicholas Katzenbach, although he was not on the commission.

Philip Randolph, and James Farmer. They were all taken. Now, where did that damn fellow get the idea I wouldn't have my picture made with them?

Young: I wouldn't pay any attention to this. This magazine just is *known* for—

President Johnson: [*agitated*] No, but I don't want them lying on me, Whitney!

Young: Well, I think they were talking about inside, now.

President Johnson: Well, didn't you have your picture made with me?

Young: I did, sure! It was in there.

President Johnson: Well, what did they say—that I wouldn't pose with you?

Young: Well, no, they were talking about Martin Luther King—

President Johnson: But he had a picture made! I just autographed it right now. I got it right in front of me. I'm sending it.

Young: [*laughing*] I don't know. They're so inaccurate. But I'm glad you're telling me.

President Johnson: I just signed one to Martin Luther King and A. Philip Randolph, too.

Young: Is that right? And it was right inside.

President Johnson: Right inside my office sitting here talking to me, like you and Roy Wilkins.

Young: They've been wrong so many times, there's not a person—

President Johnson: Now, what's wrong with [*unclear*] a woman that's as close to me as my mother and my aunt, she was sitting together with me, when she rode with me, and she's a college graduate. And she's chief of staff. And she's running [*unclear*], and has got more sense than anyone in it. What's wrong with that—because she's black?

Young: Well, there's nothing wrong with it. [*calmly*] Jesus, they're just inaccurate; that's all.

President Johnson: Then they said that he brought his cook with him, and that's an old Dixie tradition. And the cooks and the VIPs mixed, but JFK never permitted his maintenance help to be exposed.

Young: Well, that's typical of them. They do it. They've done stuff on me. But I think you're doing very well, and everybody else is saying that.

President Johnson: Well, JFK was a wonderful fellow, and we all love him. But he didn't have a chief of staff like I've got that's been with me 25 years, and graduated from college. I've got a lot of Negro people working for me. I haven't got any Irish folks.

Young: [*Chuckles.*] Well, don't let that worry you.

President Johnson: Well, I just, damn it! I don't like to be lied on and Whitney, I want you to tell them that you had your picture made with me.

Young: I will. I'll talk to them.

President Johnson: Just call them tomorrow and say that's unfair.

Young: I'll talk to him. I know him well. I'll talk to him. You know him.

President Johnson: Yes, I know him, but I don't know why he would tell that story on me.

Young: Well, you see, Johnny doesn't really see that thing half the time.[10] He leaves that up to some other people.

President Johnson: This is Simeon Booker that wrote this.

Young: That's right. I'll talk to him.

President Johnson: Will you do that?

Young: I'll straighten it out. You said that Martin never had that picture taken in the room there with you?

President Johnson: I said that Martin Luther King and A. Philip Randolph and James Farmer—every damn one of them had every photographer attached to the White House come in. And I just autographed pictures to A. Philip Randolph and Martin Luther King tonight.

Young: Okay. I'll take care of it, Mr. President.

President Johnson: I can send you copies of pictures if you want them.

Young: No, I don't need those!

President Johnson: Well, I just want him to quit lying on me.

Young: Okay.

President Johnson: And he said that they were having southerners down here on the balcony as my guests. The only southerner I had was Harry Byrd. I had him down here on the tax bill, and told him if he doesn't get that tax bill out, we're going to have hell. [*Young chuckles.*] I guess I ought to talk to him, oughtn't I?

Young: No. Let me handle it.

President Johnson: I mean, I have to talk to the chairman of the committee, Byrd.

Young: [*correcting himself*] Oh, I thought you were talking about Booker. You don't need to talk to him.

President Johnson: No, I'm not going to talk to Booker. I'm just talking about how can I get a tax bill passed if I don't talk to the chairman of the committee?

Young: Yes. Well, you've got to do that. We understand it. We understand that. You're doing all right, now.

President Johnson: Okay. Well, you write me, now, and tell me what I

---

[10]"Johnny" is John H. Johnson, publisher of *Jet*.

ought to know. And if I'm doing anything wrong, you let me know.

Young: I'll do that. I'll keep in touch with you.

President Johnson: All right. Now you write me on civil rights and State of the Union.

Young: All right.

President Johnson: Good night.

Young: Merry Christmas.

President Johnson: Same to you.

. . .

Shortly after ending the conversation with Young, Johnson had a call placed to Martin Luther King, but either King was not available or Johnson decided not to tape the conversation. A short while later, a bewildered Gerri Whittington arrived at the White House and sheepishly apologized for not taking his initial call seriously.

Johnson passed the holidays still working the telephones and canvassing various staff members and people in Congress about the dual challenges of the tax bill and civil rights legislation. By early January, it was beginning to look like the chances for passage of the civil rights bill were good, at least in the House. Smith had yet to hold hearings, but Johnson's vote counts indicated more than enough support for the bill to pass both the committee and the full House.

But problems loomed in the Senate, where there was a near certainty of a filibuster. That prospect was also creating problems for the House bill. In both 1957 and 1960, the bills passed by the House had been significantly altered by the Senate, which had led to the anemic bills that eventually became law. The backers of the House bill, especially Republicans like McCulloch, were understandably anxious that the same fate might befall the current bill. If that happened, the supporters of the legislation in the House would have taken a political risk for nothing, and McCulloch and other Republican leaders made it clear to the White House that they would not support a Senate bill that compromised on the major points, such as public accommodations.

When Congress returned in early 1964 after the holiday recess, Smith convened nine days of hearings on the bill. During that time, more than 30 witnesses testified before the committee about the merits of the proposed reforms. Smith still had not agreed to let the bill come to a full House vote, but while support for a discharge petition had all but evaporated, support for the bill had grown. Smith remained recalcitrant and during the hearings clashed frequently with his opponents on the committee. Finally, on January 30, Smith allowed the committee to vote, and the bill passed by 11 to 4.

The White House followed these developments closely. As of early January, Johnson and his team were fairly confident the bill would be passed by the full House, but it was not yet a done deal. Larry O'Brien kept careful track of the vote count, and Johnson further cemented his ties with civil rights leaders. While attending to the fate of the bill in the House, Johnson was already anticipating the battle in the Senate. The President knew that compared to the Senate, the House was a cakewalk, and he wanted the bill's Democratic backers to be prepared to challenge the southerners who would fight tooth and nail to kill the legislation before it went to the Senate floor. On New Year's Day, the President called Everett Dirksen, the powerful Senate Republican, and Mike Mansfield, the Senate majority leader. No mention was made of civil rights, but Johnson was too crafty a politician to have called these two particular men simply to wish them happy New Year.

While all this was unfolding, Johnson continued to be fixated on the *Jet* magazine story, and Gerri Whittington had assumed a temporary importance that had little to do with her actual job. Just before the hearings began, on January 6, Johnson talked to Whitney Young and Carl Sandburg and asked them to spread the word that Johnson had hired a black secretary.

Tuesday, January 6, 1964, 3:55 P.M.

Whitney Young

President Johnson: Well, we had some good meetings down there, and I think they did all right.

Whitney Young: Yes, I was just very pleased. I just talked with Lee White.[11] He mentioned to me about what you're thinking about doing today, and the two people, as far as the judgeships are concerned.

President Johnson: Yeah.

Young: And I think this is excellent. I think both of them are good men.

President Johnson: I want to do it if your people want me to do it. I don't want to do it just because they serve them up and got no one else, because I've got forty men that would like to have a judge. But if these are the best ones in the community, and we can give them some recognition, and our people will understand it, and you-all can do something about let-

---

[11]White was associate counsel to President Johnson.

ting them know that I'm not a hater, and a bigot. You-all, you know that, but most of the—a lot of them don't. They keep saying I have all this trouble in the Negro community, and I've never heard a Negro say that.

Young: I haven't either. I don't . . .

President Johnson: I've got a new secretary here. Do you know this little [Gerri] Whittington girl?

Young: I heard about that. That's written—

President Johnson: Well, she's in my office, and she's my personal secretary, and I took her to church with me yesterday in Stonewall, Texas. She stayed in my home down there for two weeks, and [was] the most competent person in the world. But . . . We're just doing fine. I've got to get two good civil rights commissioners. I want to appoint these judges. But I keep reading in the columnists where they don't quote you, and they don't quote Roy Wilkins, and they don't quote [James] Farmer, and they don't quote Martin Luther King, and they don't quote Phil Randolph, because every damn one of them knows that I'm stronger for them than nearly anybody around this place, and have been all these years.

Young: Well, now, you know, last night, in the TV film—I don't know whether you saw it—the duties of the president and the job facing you and all of this . . .

President Johnson: No, I didn't.

Young: Well, they quoted again from us, and showed pictures of our meeting with you.

President Johnson: Well, that's good.

Young: And this was awfully good visibility—

President Johnson: Well, but *Jet* magazine—

Young: What *Jet* did, well now, *Jet* this past week talked about Miss Whittington, and I think their whole tone has changed after I talked with you.

President Johnson: Well, that's good then. That's good. I hadn't seen it. I just see it when it's bad.

Young: They have a beautiful story on Miss Whittington [*unclear*] be in there—

President Johnson: I didn't know that. I didn't know that.

Young: But you see, some of these people they figure their role—just like they were with JFK—they figure their role is to stick pins in him. But I wouldn't get too concerned about this if you—

President Johnson: Well, I do want to get concerned, [*Young attempts to interject*] because I want them to know that I'm their friend.

Young: Well, [if] you make moves like you're fixing to do today, you won't have any questions on this.

President Johnson: Well, but I'm afraid they just think well that's because that somebody recommended him that was with Kennedy.

Young: No, this won't happen.

President Johnson: All right now. If you want it, it'll be done.

Young: I want it.

President Johnson: Now, the President [Kennedy] wanted it, and he would have done it. I feel like I've got an obligation to it. But I don't want to do it unless the whole Negro community knows that I'm doing it, and the Democrats are doing it. This damn *Jet* and the rest of them quit cutting us up and saying we hate the Negroes.

Young: Yes. Well, no, you won't have that to worry about. This is what we want done.

President Johnson: All right. It'll be done.

Young: All right.

President Johnson: Thank you, Whitney.

Young: Thank you—

President Johnson: You be my ambassador, now, and talk to them about it.

Young: Okay.

President Johnson: Bye.

Young: I'll do it. Bye.

Monday, January 6, 1964, 4:55 P.M.

Carl Sandburg[12]

Before placing the call, the President asks an aide in the room to make sure that information of his hiring of Whittington gets circulated to the African American press.

President Johnson: Sandburg?

Carl Sandburg: Mr. President.

President Johnson: I understand today is your birthday, and I wanted to call and tell you how fortunate I thought America was to have you with us. [*Sandburg laughs.*] I hope when I am your age that I will just [have] contributed half as much to our country as you have.

Sandburg: Well, it's good to talk with a president of the United States. I guess this is the only time on such an occasion. . . . I've talked with pres-

---

[12]The distinguished poet Carl Sandburg.

idents over the telephone when I was a reporter with the *Chicago Daily News*—

President Johnson: Yes.

Sandburg:—but this is the first time the White House has called me.

President Johnson: Well, we're mighty thankful for you and I just hope you have many happy returns of the day.

Sandburg: This is an event. Will you write me a one-sentence letter and autograph it? Sign it.

President Johnson: I—

Sandburg: I want [*laughs*]—

President Johnson: I'll be delighted to. It'll be a great honor to me, Mr. Sandburg. I'll do it today, and you'll get it in the morning. I hope you have many happy returns and many more birthdays.

Sandburg: Well, you're doing pretty good, and you're . . . you make more friends, I think, from month to month.

President Johnson: Well, I appreciate your encouragement and the strength that comes from it. I'll drop you that little note this afternoon and—

Sandburg: [*Unclear.*]

President Johnson:—I hope everything goes well with you.

Sandburg: Next time in Washington . . .

President Johnson: You do come in to see me.

Sandburg: Yes, I hope to have five or ten minutes with you.

President Johnson: I hope that won't be long.

Sandburg: [*chuckling*] All good luck to you.

President Johnson: You do it just as soon as you can, and I'll be waiting for you.

Sandburg: All good luck to you. We include you in our prayers.

President Johnson: Please do, I need them.

Sandburg: It's a terrific job

President Johnson: Well . . .

Sandburg: A wearing job. You have our prayers. Please know that.

President Johnson: Thank you so much.

Sandburg: [*Unclear.*]

President Johnson: Good-bye.

Sandburg: All good luck.

President Johnson: Good-bye.

.   .   .

A short while later, Johnson talked to Roy Wilkins about two important judicial appointments and about the progress in the House. The President wanted to make sure that the NAACP would maintain its pressure on the House and also start strategizing for the Senate. As usual, Wilkins was polite, but the subtext was clear. The NAACP would not sit quietly and watch the civil rights legislation evaporate. Wilkins had made it known that at the first sign the bill was being gutted, demonstrations would be organized and official Washington would have to contend with a new wave of unrest. Johnson reiterated his position. He had no desire to compromise and wanted to assure Wilkins and the rest of the civil rights community that unlike past presidents, he was behind civil rights 100 percent.

After talking with Wilkins, Johnson called Senator Eugene McCarthy of Minnesota. The state's junior Democratic senator, McCarthy had been elected in 1958, and though a staunch liberal who was firmly behind the bill, he was less important to its passage than his colleague, Hubert Humphrey, who would assume the major responsibility for getting the bill through the Senate. The conversation with McCarthy was one of many that Johnson had in January and February to discuss the obstacles the Senate presented. McCarthy was on the Senate Finance Committee, and thus was intimately involved in the negotiations surrounding the tax bill. Johnson stressed to McCarthy that the tax bill had to be passed soon or else it would delay civil rights, which would be fatal for the administration's program and for Johnson's 1964 election strategy. McCarthy was also up for reelection, and Johnson insinuated that the fate of the tax bill and civil rights would affect all Democrats running in the fall. Much of the conversation covered the strategy for moving the tax bill, but for Johnson the bills were two pieces of the same legislative puzzle.

Monday, January 6, 1964, 5:12 P.M.

Roy Wilkins

President Johnson: [*to staff, in background.*] Who are these names of these judges now?

[*to Wilkins*] Roy?

Roy Wilkins: Yes.

President Johnson: How are you doing?

Wilkins: Mr. President, I'm fine, thank you. I'm sorry to keep you waiting.

President Johnson: Well, I hope that you had a good Christmas and a good New Year.

Wilkins: I did, sir. And I read about yours—every little bit of it.

President Johnson: When are you going to get down here and start civil rights?

Wilkins: As soon as I get rid of my board of directors and my annual meeting, which is winding up now.

President Johnson: Well, you tell them that I think that they've got a mighty good head man.

Wilkins: Thank you, sir.

President Johnson: I don't know of a better one in the United States— and a fairer one or abler one.

Wilkins: Well, that's very kind of you.

President Johnson: Now, you tell that NBC and CBS that you want some equal time, and you get on that television a little bit.

Wilkins: [*Chuckles.*] I don't know whether you were—I know you didn't—but NBC had a—

President Johnson: They had it last night. I heard about it.

Wilkins: Yes, they had one, and I put in a word.

President Johnson: What I want you to do, though, is to get on this bill now, because . . . unless you get 25 Republicans, you're not going to get cloture. Russell has already said that—this cannot be quoted—but Russell says he's got commitments that they can't get cloture.

Wilkins: Yes.

President Johnson: Now, I talked to [Mike] Mansfield for an hour and a half this morning. He's not a fellow that likes to go past 4:30, and he all went right out. I told him I thought the only way to do it is like we did it before. Either go around the clock or get 67 people and start working on both. I can't be too much of a dictator, but I'll help him any way I can.

Wilkins: Yes, sir.

President Johnson: However, I stimulated him as much as I could. He went out and told the press he'd have two sessions. He'd have to adjourn for the convention and come back. That's terrible. We ought not to come back. We ought to go on and get through. But he didn't mention that to me.

Wilkins: Yes.

President Johnson: But I think that you all are going to have to sit down and—maybe not Clarence Mitchell. Clarence is a good fellow, but maybe he irritates them a little bit

Wilkins: I know.

President Johnson: But you're going to have to persuade Dirksen on why this is the interest of the Republican Party. I think the Republican [that] goes along with you on cloture, that y'all ought to tell him that you're going to go along with him and help him. I'm a Democrat, but I think that—

Wilkins: Oh, you have to do it. [*Unclear*] do that.

President Johnson:—if a fellow will stand up and fight with you, you all can cross party lines.

Wilkins: That's right.

President Johnson: Let them know that you're going to go for the presidential candidate that offers you the best hope and the best chance of dignity and decency in this country, and you're going with a senatorial man that does the same thing. Then you're going to have to get busy and do something about it, because they say I'm an arm twister, but I can't make a southerner change his spots any more than I can make a leopard change them.

Wilkins: That's right.

President Johnson: You know it and I know it. [*Wilkins agrees*] I'm no magician. I'm going to be with you, and I'm going to help in every way I can, but you're going to have to get these folks in here and the quicker you get them in the better.

Wilkins: Very good. Now, I talked to—

President Johnson: If we lose this fight, Roy, we're going back ten years.

Wilkins: I know, I know. I talked to the House—Mr. Albert—[13]

President Johnson: Yep.

Wilkins:—he called me.

President Johnson: Yep.

Wilkins: He said he wanted me to come down sometime after Christmas, after New Year's. He wanted to talk with me about pushing this bill through the House. I told him I'd be down and I will, just as soon as I get these people off my neck. This is my corporation meeting—membership, stockholders, annual reports, and gripe session and everything all rolled into one. As soon as I get them off, I'm going to be on this bill.

Mr. President, we appreciate everything. We know what your attitude is, and we know that the work has got to be done here with us. We're going to do it.

President Johnson: Yes. I'll help you, and I'll confer with you, and you can come in every day and talk to me about it. I'll do everything that I can, but I don't want anybody to get any illusions that I'm a magician, because I'm not.

Wilkins: I think they all understand that. If you agree—If you will indulge me one more minute, you would be surprised at the number of

---

[13]Carl Albert was the House majority leader.

people I ran into over the holiday—among my own folks, I mean, who said to me, "Look, don't you think that Lyndon Johnson is going to be even better than the other man?" Now, they are beginning to swing, Mr. President, and I've been surprised and gratified at their willingness to be fair. I don't mean this holds true all down the line, every single one of them. I can't say that. But I'm talking about the ones that I've come in contact with. They have surprised *me,* and I thought I knew them.

President Johnson: I'm going to put 500 million [dollars] in this budget for poverty, and a good deal of it ought to go to your people, but we ought to have some better ideas about how it can go. How we can have adult education, how we can give extra school training. I wish you'd give a little thought on that and maybe get with Whitney Young or some of your other people—

Wilkins: I'll do that.

President Johnson:—and give me a little direction. These boys are pretty theoretical down here, and if I get it passed, I'm going to have to have more practical plans. So you give a little thought to that.

Now, the third thing is: I don't want to appoint these folks to judges unless you all want them appointed. I've got 100 Johnson men that were for me for Congress, for the Senate, for president, vice—when I got defeated, for vice president and everything else, but I want to be fair to your people. Now, are these the best people that are available, and do you want them appointed? If so, do you recommend them?

I'm not asking for a pound of flesh. I'm just being damned sure that it's who you want. If you don't, I want to appoint somebody else.

Wilkins: Yes . . . Yes. You got my wire, didn't you?

President Johnson: Yes, but your wire was kind of . . .

Wilkins: [*Unclear.*]

President Johnson: You just said that you feel that I would want to. Well, I don't want to. I don't know them at all.

Wilkins: Well—

President Johnson: I never met either one of them.

Wilkins: I'll tell you, Mr. President. Briefly, [Spotswood] Robinson is a top-notch man, Spotswood—top-notch.

President Johnson: Yeah . . .

Wilkins: He's a former dean of the Howard University Law School. He's a practitioner of the law, a student of the law.

President Johnson: Well, am I going to get any credit if I name him?

Wilkins: Certainly will. I'll see to that.

President Johnson: All right. Now what about [Leon] Higginbotham?

Wilkins: Higginbotham made his mark at the Federal Trade Commission. He's a young lawyer, out of Philadelphia, not too young at that. Excellent training, fine background and upstanding young fellow and a 100 percent Democrat, I'm sure [*unclear*], uh, Green would have said something to you if he could have about this.[14]

President Johnson: Yes.

Wilkins: I'm sure of that.

President Johnson: And you want him appointed?

Wilkins: I would count it a favor.

President Johnson: Well, it'll be done—period. Now, and then don't be so damned modest. Make them—

Wilkins: The only reason I'm modest is because I never . . . I'm breaking my rule with you. You are a salesman, out of this world.

President Johnson: No, I'm not.

Wilkins: I break my rule because—

President Johnson: No, I just want—

Wilkins:—I've never asked a president—pardon me sir, I never ask a president for a favor.

President Johnson:—I just want, judgment's all I want.

Wilkins: I'm trying to give you a judgment, that's it.

President Johnson: All right. Okay.

Wilkins: I don't want to, but for you, I said yes.

President Johnson: All right. It's been done. It'll be signed in the next five minutes. And good-bye, and come and see me.

Wilkins: Thank you so much.

President Johnson: Bye.

Wilkins: Good-bye.

Monday, January 6, 1964, 7:46 P.M.

Eugene McCarthy

President Johnson: Gene?

Eugene McCarthy: Hello.

President Johnson: Why do you cancel this party when you hear I'm coming for [it]?

McCarthy: Welcome back to Washington!

---

[14]William Joseph Green was a Democratic congressman from Pennsylvania and a Democratic city chairman in Philadelphia.

President Johnson: Why do you cancel this party when you hear I'm coming for it?

McCarthy: Well, I'll tell you, my office called. I think there's a breakdown between you and your wife's staff.

President Johnson: No. My wife's staff told me that there was no party.

McCarthy: That's right.

President Johnson: My staff told me there was, and I always think my staff's better than my wife's.

McCarthy: Oh. That's the trouble. I figure it the other way at my house.

President Johnson: They tell me they had a wonderful midwestern conference. They say you're going to be elected without any opposition.

McCarthy: Well, that would be a good way to have it.

President Johnson: When are you going to get my tax bill for me?

McCarthy: I just talked to Joe Barr today and told him anytime, anything you want done, I'm right ready.[15]

President Johnson: Well, I want you to get a hold of Joe, ... Paul Douglas, and Clint Anderson and give me some leadership.[16] Make them meet morning, afternoon, and evening. Don't let them talk and mope and move to table, and get me that bill so I can have it out of the way when the civil rights [bill] comes over, and I can intercept civil rights.

Now, I talked to Roy Wilkins tonight. All the nigras are going back to the streets and we're going to have chaos in this country if we don't go on and pass the tax bill and get to debating civil rights. But if you haven't passed the tax bill, and I have to take up civil rights first, then you won't get to the tax bill until May or June.

McCarthy: Well, I'll take hold of those fellows.

President Johnson: Now I don't think you ought to tell them that I'm calling a junior member, but I think you ought to just reason with them. Just say to Paul Douglas that after the election, we'll get some good reforms if he's got to have reforms. For God sakes, let's get rid of it so we can intercept the House bill when it comes over. I think I can get the House bill out by the end of the month. If I can do that ... Well, Dick Russell's hoping that they can get the House bill out and the tax bill will still be pending, he and Harry Byrd.

McCarthy: Sure.

---

[15]Barr was the Treasury Department's liaison to the Senate Finance Committee.

[16]Douglas was a Democratic senator from Illinois and Anderson was a Democratic senator from New Mexico.

President Johnson: Therefore taxes will get behind civil rights.

McCarthy: Yeah.

President Johnson: That just ruins us. We have nothing to go to the country on, and besides we'll have a damn good depression.

McCarthy: They can play one against the other, that's right. Plus the depression.

President Johnson: Now, what you do is just take those Democrats— ten Democrats. You can't get Harry Byrd, but you *can* have a lunch or something in your office or somewhere. Get Anderson and get Douglas— you can't get [Albert] Gore—[17]

McCarthy: No.

President Johnson:—but you ought to get everybody else. They ought to just go to that committee and make a quorum, morning and afternoon and evening. They don't have a damned thing to do. They've had two weeks off [for] Christmas.

[Everett] Dirksen announces tonight that nobody'll be here to do anything this week and that he wants to go home before the convention, and he doesn't want to ever come back.

McCarthy: Mm-hmm.

President Johnson: It's to their interest for us to do nothing. If we can do nothing, they can say, well, we had no program.

McCarthy: That's right.

．　．　．

On January 8, Lyndon Johnson gave his first State of the Union address. Beyond urging Congress to pass the civil rights bill, he called for a national "war against poverty," which would evolve into the various programs known as the Great Society. Public hearings began on January 9 and lasted for nine days. During that time, White House aide Larry O'Brien kept careful track of the vote count. By month's end, it seemed there were enough votes to ensure passage of the bill, provided that Smith allowed it to be released from his committee. In the meantime, Johnson continued his charm offensive, calling regularly on civil rights leaders and impressing on them his commitment to the bill's passage. As James Farmer of CORE later recalled in an oral history interview, "He certainly fought for the bill, and he fought to get it through without emasculation." Johnson said repeatedly he would not allow the bill to be watered down and claimed any piece of legislation without a public accommodations section was unacceptable.

---

[17] Albert Gore, Sr., was a Democratic senator from Tennessee.

The President also continued to make symbolic gestures. In mid-January, he nominated Carl Rowan to replace Edward R. Murrow as the chief of the U.S. Information Agency (USIA). Rowan, an African American, was then ambassador to Finland, and Johnson clearly wanted to hold Rowan up as a symbol of his administration's commitment to civil rights. During the Cold War, the head of the USIA occupied an important policy-making position, with responsibility for enhancing America's image overseas. The turmoil over civil rights had become both an international and a domestic problem, which was undermining America's claim that it stood for freedom against Soviet oppression. As Johnson explained in a phone conversation with Roy Wilkins on January 16, appointing Rowan would be a "master stroke" for the country's image abroad. Wilkins agreed, but warned Johnson that Rowan was somewhat compromised in the "Negro" community because he had a reputation as being "too much on the white folks' side." The concern was that Rowan might be seen as something of an Uncle Tom. Still, Wilkins supported Johnson's decision to appoint him.

Having cleared the nomination with Wilkins, Johnson then called Senator John McClellan, the Arkansas Democrat who chaired the Government Operations Committee. McClellan was the key to funding USIA, and Johnson wanted to make sure the notoriously anti–civil rights senator would not try to cut the agency's budget just because it was headed by a black man. McClellan complained that civil rights leaders were harming the United States. He said that foreign countries had used doctored pictures of the March on Washington in an effort to "show the worst side of America" and that civil rights leaders had been willing collaborators. Johnson acknowledged that the United States had an image problem but promised McClellan that Rowan's appointment would help. "I don't want you to say," he scolded McClellan, " 'Well, Johnson sent me a Negro up here. He's a Tennessee Negro and a good one.' I didn't want you to say we sent him up there and you send him one day without his peter." McClellan laughed good-naturedly, and replied, "I wouldn't do anything like that." Of course, the discussion about Rowan was also a veiled conversation about the coming Senate fight on civil rights legislation, during which McClellan could be expected to be one of the harshest opponents.

The next day, on January 17, Johnson talked with the influential black political insider Louis Martin, who had served as a publicity man on the Democratic National Committee. Johnson sounded out Martin on various appointments, including Rowan and several potential nominees for the Civil Rights Commission. The President again touted his hiring of a black secretary. "I've got me a good Negro secretary," he told Martin, "this Gerri Whittington. Do you know her?" Martin said he'd heard about her.

"They want to put her on a show," Johnson continued, "*I've Got a Secret*. And her secret is that she's a secretary to the President of the United States. Would that be exploiting it?" Martin said no, it wouldn't be. "You think it would be all right?" Johnson pushed. "Nothing wrong with it because the girl's with you already. That's a good way to break it," Martin assured the President.

On January 18, Johnson invited civil rights leaders to a meeting at the White House. Addressing Martin Luther King, James Farmer, Roy Wilkins, and Whitney Young, Johnson once again affirmed his staunch support for civil rights reform. As Wilkins recalled in a later oral history, Johnson reminded them that as president, he could not lobby excessively for the bill. He knew the Senate would be especially sensitive to any infringement of their legislative prerogative. But he would continue to fight for passage of the bill, "without a word or comma changed."

While Smith continued to hold up the bill for as long as he could, Johnson maintained his busy schedule of meetings. On January 21, he met with Clarence Mitchell, the NAACP's point man on Capitol Hill, and with another group of civil rights leaders on January 22 to discuss an idea for voluntary desegregation that had been floated by a group of Atlanta businessmen. The bill remained stalled in the Rules Committee and Johnson was getting impatient. Talking on the telephone with close friend Abe Fortas on January 27, he let off steam. He blasted Tom Wicker, a *New York Times* reporter, for asking softball questions of Smith, but swore he would not release a public statement because he did not want to give the press or his opponents any fodder. Finally, on January 30, Judge Smith let his committee vote on the bill, and as expected, it passed, by a vote of 11 to 4.

That set the stage for a debate on the House floor, in anticipation of a full House vote. For the next week, countless amendments were proposed to every section of the complicated bill. Celler and McCulloch supervised the floor debate, and almost all attempts by the southern bloc to dilute the language of the bill were defeated. Johnson monitored the progress in conversations with Wilkins, and though pleased that the bill was on the verge of passing, he was not about to celebrate. "We've got to figure out how we can get that bill past the Senate," he told Wilkins during a phone conversation on February 6. "We're just halfway through."

On February 8, as the debate was drawing to a close, Smith stood and offered a frivolous amendment meant to derail the bill's progress. During the debate over Title VII, which covered equal employment, Smith rose to propose altering the phrase that banned discrimination against "any individual because of his race, color, religion, or national origin." The change was simple. "After the word *religion*," Smith said, "insert the word *sex*."

Smith had come up with the idea because Congresswoman Martha Griffiths of Michigan had suggested it. She was dismayed that there was no consideration of discrimination against women in the legislation, but Smith hoped that this one little word might derail the civil rights bill or at least hold it up indefinitely.

The subsequent debate over the proposed amendment ranged from the serious to the absurd. As reported by *Time* magazine, Emanuel Celler rose to oppose the change, saying that in his household there was no tension between the sexes. "I usually have the last two words," he said, "and those words are *Yes, dear.*" But the dozen female representatives were not taking the amendment lightly. Republican Katharine St. George of New York rose to support the change. "Nothing could be more logical," she said to her male colleagues. "We outlast you. We outlive you. We nag you to death. We want this crumb of equality. And the little word s-e-x won't hurt the bill." Edith Green of Oregon dissented. "At the risk of being called an Aunt Jane, if not an Uncle Tom, let us not add any amendment that would get in the way of our primary objective."

By a vote of 168 to 133, the proposal was adopted by the House after several hours of frantic maneuvering. Hearing the final tally, a woman in the gallery started shouting, "We made it! We made it! God bless America." In a case of unintended consequences, Howard Smith, in his tendentious attempt to stall the civil rights bill, had helped advance the cause of equal rights for women.

With that bit of theater at an end, the bill moved to a final House vote. On February 10, H.R. 7132 was approved by a tally of 290 to 130. There were 152 Democrats and 138 Republicans who supported the bill, while 86 southern Democrats from the 11 states of the old Confederacy opposed it. But the House had never really been in doubt. It was the Senate that presented the true hurdle, and as of early February, no one—not even the master legislator sitting in the Oval Office—knew how long it would take or how the bill would survive the filibuster that stood in its way.

Chapter 9
Into the Senate

The day after the House vote, 10 inches of snow fell on Washington. The city was covered in a blanket of white. It was nothing compared to the storm that was coming.

In previous decades, the Senate had been a graveyard for civil rights legislation. The power of individual senators far surpasses the privileges enjoyed by individual representatives in the House, and one recalcitrant senator can delay legislation for weeks, either in committee or on the floor. Committee chairmen have the power to hold up a bill indefinitely, and when a block of senators opposes a potential bill, they can, as a last-ditch strategy, stymie passage by filibustering. Senators are allowed extensive opportunities to speak on the floor, and unless they yield their time, no action can be taken until they are finished speaking. In short, senators can effectively talk a bill to death.

The filibuster was only the most dramatic device that the opponents of civil rights could use. Over the years, numerous mechanisms had been perfected to prevent a bill from passing, including objecting to each clause, proposing countless amendments, and calling for constant quorums. Unless 51 senators, or half the chamber, responded when their names were called, the Senate might have to recess until the next day.[1] Normally, assembling a quorum presented a challenge, as most senators were in their offices or at meetings. In order to challenge the filibuster and meet the quorum calls, the defenders of the civil rights bill would have to be effectively organized.

The task fell to Senator Hubert Humphrey of Minnesota, the majority whip. Humphrey was appointed by Senate Majority Leader Mike

---

[1]Without a quorum, a motion to adjourn would be in order but not mandatory.

Mansfield to be the floor manager for the bill. Mansfield, the pipe-smoking Montana Democrat, chose well, for Humphrey had been an ardent advocate of civil rights reform even before he was elected to the Senate in 1948 and had attracted national attention when he called for an end to racial discrimination at the 1948 Democratic Convention. Sixteen years later, Humphrey, a leading contender for the vice presidential nomination, was widely admired on Capitol Hill and possessed unmatched energy and enthusiasm for the bill.

Humphrey was aided in his task by his Republican counterpart, Thomas Kuchel of California, who had been chosen by the Senate minority leader, Republican Everett Dirksen of Illinois. Because of the dynamics of the Senate, Dirksen was the key to the bill's passage. The Democrats enjoyed a 67 to 33 majority, one of the largest margins any party had ever held, but on civil rights, that was meaningless. The southern bloc, composed of Democrats, would fight the bill, and to assemble enough votes to end a filibuster, the supporters of the bill needed at least 67 (two-thirds) of the members. To gain the votes necessary for cloture, the technical term for bringing debate or filibuster to an end, the Democrats needed between 10 and 15 Republican votes. And the person who would release those votes was Dirksen, the minority leader.

While the Illinois senator supported civil rights reform, he was also a party loyalist. It was in Dirksen's interest not just to see civil rights reform pass, but also to humiliate and weaken the Democratic Party in the process. In many ways, Dirksen, whose clothes were unkempt and who smoked excessively, was the opposite of the courtly Richard Russell of Georgia, who was the leader of the anti–civil rights phalanx. The Illinois senator was known as The Wizard of Ooze, a sobriquet derived from the mellifluous speaking voice he had perfected after years of gargling with a blend of Pond's cold cream and water. He had worked closely with Johnson during the latter's years in the Senate and had a healthy respect for the President.

Although Dirksen supported the general contours of the bill, he had some concerns. He was a Republican from the state that had produced Abraham Lincoln, but he was a conservative who had never sanctioned an activist government. He endorsed the principle of equal opportunity and nondiscrimination in public accommodations but wanted compliance to be voluntary, without the stringent enforcement the House bill proposed. He had genuine, ideological concerns about the extension of federal power and the creation of new enforcement agencies to police civil rights infractions. And significantly, he was the spokesman for those conservative Republicans who shared his worries.

Whether his opposition was based more on conviction or on tactics mattered little to the Democrats. Dirksen had to be won over, one way or another. Humphrey understood that without Dirksen's Republicans, there would be no civil rights act, and he knew this not just because he understood the Senate but because he had an excitable President hammering the message home. As Johnson told Humphrey, "The bill can't pass unless you get Ev Dirksen. You and I are going to get Ev. It's going to take time. We're going to get him. . . . You get in there to see Dirksen. You drink with Dirksen! You talk with Dirksen! You listen to Dirksen!"

The opposition in the Senate consisted primarily of southern senators led by Georgia's Richard Russell, who was in the uncomfortable position of being Johnson's closest friend in the Senate. Moreover, he had served as a confidant of the President during Lyndon Johnson's first term. Johnson and Russell talked frequently by phone, and the President valued the Georgian's advice. But on civil rights, they were opponents. Both understood this and did not allow it to disrupt their relationship. Russell knew that the tide had shifted and that much of the country supported civil rights legislation. He saw that Johnson could no longer pursue sectional politics at the expense of national imperatives and probably recognized that opposing civil rights in the spring of 1964 was as desperate a battle as that waged by the Confederacy in the spring of 1865. But his constituents were adamantly opposed to the legislation, as was he, and he intended to use every strategy he could to delay, impede, and perhaps fatally undermine the proposed bill.

Russell was aided by diehards like James Eastland of Mississippi, who as chair of the Judiciary Committee presented a serious threat to the bill; Allen Ellender, Democrat of Lousiana; John Stennis, Democrat of Mississippi; and the Republican John Tower of Texas. The bill's opponents were outnumbered, but Senate rules would enable them to create interminable snarls and thus prevent the bill from moving through its labyrinthine stages in a timely fashion.

Time was not unlimited, however. The Senate was scheduled to recess in mid-July for the Democratic Convention to select a presidential candidate. Johnson had staked his prestige on the passage of the civil rights bill, and if he went into the convention with the bill stuck in the Senate, his prospects would be considerably less bright. His Senate opponents knew that; thus, it was not necessary to defeat the bill, only to delay it. Once Congress recessed and the 1964 electoral campaign got underway, attention would shift from legislation to politics. No matter how much support there was for civil rights legislation, if it remained tied up come summer, no one could say for sure when it would be taken up again. From Johnson's perspective, delay beyond July would be a stinging defeat.

The President had already laid the groundwork for the Senate fight. Even as the bill was being debated in the House, he had reflected on the problems in the Senate with friends and advisers. He was concerned that unless his forces were prepositioned, the bill would make its way from the House floor to the Senate, where it would languish in the Judiciary Committee. "You got to intercept it when it comes to the door," he told Congressman Wilbur Mills (D-Arkansas) during a phone conversation on February 7. "It goes to Jim Eastland's committee and you never get it out of committee. . . . That's the way we passed the others [Civil Rights Bills of 1957 and 1960]: just when they message it over, [you] receive it at the door. . . . You don't send it to conference; you don't refer it to a committee. You just take it up right then."

For that reason, the minute the bill was passed in the House, Johnson had Clarence Mitchell and Joseph Rauh (one of the bill's chief lobbyists) rush over to the Senate. As Mitchell later recalled in an oral history interview, "To show you how closely Johnson was following the situation, when we got the bill through the House, Joe Rauh and I were in a footrace over in the Senate to start work there. . . . The phone rang in one of those booths over there in the House wing and to our amazement it was the President calling—I don't know how he ever managed to get us on the phone, but he was calling to say, 'All right, you fellows, get over there to the Senate and get busy because we've got it through the House and now we've got the big job of getting it through the Senate.' Well, that was the really fascinating thing to me, that the chief executive of a country could have followed this legislation so closely that immediately on the passage of it by the House, he knew how to get the fellows who were working over there on a pay telephone." Mitchell also credited Johnson with supplying the necessary energy for the bill's movement through the Senate. "You really had to have a force working for you that the members of the Senate would respect. The President supplied that force." And Johnson knew how to apply the pressure. As Mitchell remarked, "I don't think it's a kind of pressure of threats or anything of that sort because I'm sure having been a member of the Senate, the President would know that wouldn't work. But I think it was just that constant persuasion and argument and keeping in touch that turned the trick. I have seen it work a little, and it just makes a person feel like a real heel if he doesn't do what the President asks you to do."

The challenge for Johnson was to be intimately involved in the process without appearing to infringe on the Senate's prerogatives. During the four and a half months between the bill's passage in the House and its final passage in July, Johnson frequently talked with Humphrey, Russell, and other ranking senators, including Dirksen. Though his relationship with Robert Kennedy continued to be strained, he also kept close tabs on the Justice Department. Rather than dealing with the Attorney General, Johnson often dealt directly with Nicholas Katzenbach, the Justice Department's point man on the Hill, who provided crucial support for Humphrey. The President also continued his outreach to civil rights leaders, and his advice was often heeded. But in public, Johnson kept his remarks about the legislative process to a minimum. While relentlessly urging the Senate to pass the bill, he knew the best course of action was to let Humphrey and, to a lesser degree, Katzenbach handle the implementation of the administration's policy.

At times, Johnson became frustrated, worried that his lieutenants might mishandle the bill and play into the hands of its adversaries. He had a complicated relationship with Humphrey, who was also the leading contender for the vice presidential slot. Johnson thought Humphrey had a tendency to say too much, too soon. He also questioned the Justice Department's decision to push for a vote of cloture. In fact, Johnson questioned whether it was best to confront the southern filibuster, and in late February, he communicated his qualms to his aides.

From his experience as majority leader in the 1950s, Johnson doubted that a vote of cloture was possible. No civil rights filibuster had been ended by cloture before, and Johnson believed that unless some of the southern demands were met, the filibuster would continue indefinitely. Skeptical of cloture, Johnson toyed with the idea of compromise, but after vehement objections from Katzenbach and Humphrey, he realized compromise was not an option. The bill's supporters in the House would not accept a diluted Senate bill. In a heated discussion with Katzenbach (which Katzenbach recounted later in an oral history interview), Johnson expressed concern that there were not enough votes for cloture. By his count, 58 would vote for cloture, 9 short of the required number. "Now where are we going to get the others?" Johnson asked Katzenbach. Katzenbach estimated that there were 14 possible supporters among the remaining senators, and lobbying them would be the administration's principle task in the coming weeks. But to get them, Katzenbach warned, Johnson would have to express nothing but confidence that the votes were there. "If you do anything publicly but indicate that we're going to get cloture on this bill," he told the President, "we can't possibly get cloture on this bill."

Johnson evaluated the situation and decided he would opt for the confrontational strategy of cloture rather than the conciliatory approach that had worked in the past. This meant the bill's supporters would need to be superbly organized and prepared to wear down their opponents. For the next months, Mansfield, Humphrey, Kuchel, Mitchell, Katzenbach, Burke Marshall, and Larry O'Brien would work together, pressuring wavering senators, lobbying Dirksen, and making sure quorums were met. And behind it all stood the President, urging, cajoling, and maintaining the pressure.

Though the bill went to the Senate right after passage in the House, due to the continuing debate on the tax bill, it was not taken up by the Senate calender until February 17, and it was not introduced for debate until early March. Russell's filibuster did not begin until March 9. But during these weeks, when Johnson was not monitoring the progress of the tax bill, he was taking the pulse of the civil rights bill.

On the evening of February 10, shortly after the House vote, Johnson made a round of congratulatory calls to Carl Albert, Charles Halleck, John McCormack, and Emanuel Celler. He also talked with the Attorney General about the looming fight in the Senate, and he discussed the press release for his official statement with Larry O'Brien and press secretary Pierre Salinger.

Tuesday, February 10, 1964, 6:30 P.M.

Robert Kennedy

President Johnson: . . . Pretty good. Looks like you're going pretty well on the Hill.

Robert Kennedy: Yeah, I think it is going along well.

President Johnson: [Mike] Mansfield is out here waiting to see me, and he wants to talk about what they're going to do with this bill, when it gets to the Senate. Have you talked to him?

Kennedy: No, I have not.

President Johnson: Wonder if it's not advisable? [*Unclear.*]

Kennedy: I'd be glad to.

President Johnson: I have the impression that he's going to . . . First of all, I think that [Richard] Russell and [Everett] Dirksen have got a deal on cloture. . . .

Kennedy: Yes.

President Johnson: And I don't think we can get Dirksen to take with him 25 Republicans out of the 35 that will be necessary to get cloture. So we're stopped there. Now, I have the feeling that Mansfield may want this thing to go to a committee, the Judiciary Committee. I don't think it will ever be reported if it goes there.

Kennedy: Can they send it up there for a period of time, or something?

President Johnson: Yes, they could send it up there with instructions to report it back at a certain period. Or they could report out the public accommodations from the Commerce Committee without any trouble, and they could amend that. I think that's something, though, that your people that handle all this strategy, and handled it very successfully in the House, ought to give some thought to before he decides. I think it's something you ought to have your organizations together on pretty well, because if they get the impression that they've lost a big round, it may affect their morale. In other words, if they . . . I had always thought that the best way to handle it would be to intercept the bill when it comes over, put it on the calendar, move to take it up, and never set it aside for anything except the tax conference report, which shouldn't take over a day or two.

Kennedy: Well, Mr. President, could we meet with you? You know, this is an area that we don't [*unclear*].

President Johnson: First, I think it would be good if you'd have Burke [Marshall] take the feeling, take the temperature of the people who are very interested in this from the outside, who have been fighting the battle for 10 or 12 years. That's the [Roy] Wilkinses and the Joe Rauhs and the others that are pretty familiar with all the parliamentary ups and downs, and they all have ideas on it. Then, I think it would be good, before Mansfield decided, you can call me on the phone and we might get together and see that we agree. I think I'd be inclined to agree with what these groups feel ought to be done, because if they think we short-circuit them in any way, why, they'll be suspicious.

Kennedy: Yes, because if we'd done what they wanted to do in the House, we'd never had the bill.

President Johnson: That's right, that's exactly right. But that was a question that went to the merits of the bill, wasn't it?

Kennedy: Well, no, really to strategy. I think basically to strategy.

President Johnson: I thought they wanted more substance in it than—

Kennedy: Yeah, if they follow that procedure, they thought you get it on the floor of the House and then amend it on the floor of the House and then you could get your bill out.

President Johnson: I don't think there's any question but what the strategy in the House has proved itself. It's successful. What we want to be careful about it is we know we are going up against a more difficult task. I'd never been able to see my way through it, and I want to do *everything* that I possibly can, but I don't want anybody to think that there's any disagreement among us, or that there's any sabotaging taking place and we have to be very cautious about that. So what I'm going to do is listen to him and I want to suggest he talk to you. Then you touch whatever bases you think in your wisdom are indicated. Then get back to me with your ideas.

Kennedy: I'll call you tomorrow.

President Johnson: Fine.

Tuesday, February 10, 1964, 8:37 P.M.

Pierre Salinger, with President Johnson and Larry O'Brien

Pierre Salinger: Mr. President, let me read this to you: "The overwhelming passage tonight of the civil rights bill marks an historic step forward for the course of human dignity in America. It represents the culmination of months of hard work by men of good will in both parties. I congratulate them, particularly the Speaker and Congressman [Charles] Halleck, and the leaders of the Judiciary Committee, Congressman [Emanuel] Celler and Congressman [William] McCulloch. Now the task is before the Senate. I hope the same spirit of nonpartisanship will prevail there to assure passage of this bill, assuring the fundamental rights of all Americans."

President Johnson: All right, that's good. Now, one thing about Carl Albert.

Larry O'Brien: I was going to say—

President Johnson: He said it damn near beat him. He got a bunch of wires today. Reckon he wants to be congratulated?

O'Brien: I would think that if you said the leadership of both parties *and* the chairman of the Judiciary Committee, and the ranking minority member, Manny Celler and Bill McCulloch. Well, you don't have to. You say "the leadership of both parties."

Salinger: I think naming Halleck is an advantage, in that it puts the arm a little bit on our friend Ev Dirksen.

President Johnson: I think so, too.

O'Brien: Yes, but you're going to have to tie in, not the Speaker and Halleck, be better if you're going to go that far. See, the trouble is that Hale Boggs didn't participate in this damn thing.[2] You have to name the Speaker, and then you name [Carl] Albert, and then you have to go to Halleck and then Les Arends, or you're in a jam.[3]

---

[2] Boggs, a Democratic congressman from Louisiana, was the House majority whip.
[3] Arends, a Republican from Illinois, was the House minority whip.

Salinger: I see.

O'Brien: So . . .

President Johnson: Well, if Hale didn't participate, how can you say the leadership?

Salinger: Say "men of good will in both parties. I congratulate them, particularly the Democratic and Republican leaders."

President Johnson: Why? We don't have to congratulate Arends.

O'Brien: No.

President Johnson: I'd put in Carl Albert's name and leave it as you got it. What's wrong with that?

Tuesday, February 10, 1964, 8:38 P.M.

John McCormack and Emanuel Celler

President Johnson: Congratulations. I'm proud of you.

John McCormack: Thanks, Mr. President—a historic event.

President Johnson: It certainly is. You had great leadership. I'm going to put out a statement commending you.

McCormack: Thank you, Mr. President.

President Johnson: We're calling Carl Albert now. You reckon we ought to commend him? I don't know whether it will hurt him or help him.

McCormack: Well I don't know why not. I've got Manny Celler here with me.

President Johnson: All right, we're commending Manny too, and I got in a call for him. Let me talk to him.

McCormack: Yeah, he's right here.

President Johnson: Let me talk to him.

McCormack: Yeah, wait a minute, Mr. President.

President Johnson: You tell Miss Harriet I think you did a wonderful job.

Celler then comes on the line.

Emanuel Celler: Hello?

President Johnson: Manny, I want to congratulate you. You did a good job.

Celler: Thanks very much, Mr. President. We did it in part, you know, for you, as well as for the country.

President Johnson: No, well, you did a wonderful job, and the vote was magnificent, a tribute to your leadership.

Celler: Thanks very much. How are you?

President Johnson: I'm just doing fine. I'm mighty proud of you, and hope you get my immigration bill out now.

Celler: I spoke to Larry, and I'd like to talk to Larry about that. I'm having some trouble there. I'll work on it.

President Johnson: Okay.

Celler: I'll get to work on it.

President Johnson: Thank you.

Celler: You want to talk to John?

President Johnson: Yeah.

McCormack then comes back on the line.

McCormack: I'd give McCulloch credit, too.

President Johnson: I'm going to call him.

McCormack: I mean the bipartisan effort.

President Johnson: I will. I'm congratulating the Speaker and Leader Albert and Leader [Charles] Halleck. I want to put the little touch on Everett Dirksen over in the Senate. [*Laughs.*]

McCormack: This is a historic day, and the debate was on a high level.

President Johnson: That's good.

McCormack: It helped the cause throughout the country. And in between ourselves, it didn't bring any bitterness around, which is important in the South, as I see it.

President Johnson: Surely is, surely is. Well, that's a wonderful job.

McCormack: You could have had a debate of bitterness up here, which would have been very harmful, could have been harmful all around. I'm very, very happy.

President Johnson: I'm proud of you. Tell Miss Harriet I'm proud of you.

McCormack: Thank you. Give our love to—[*Long pause.*]

President Johnson: Lady Bird.

McCormack: Lady Bird.

Tuesday, February 10, 1964, 9:07 P.M.

Robert Kennedy

President Johnson: Congratulations.

Robert Kennedy: Yes, it was very nice, wasn't it?

President Johnson: I thought it was wonderful, 290 to 130. You can't do better than that.

Kennedy: I would think that would put a lot of pressure on them in the Senate, wouldn't you?

President Johnson: Yes. Now, you get with Larry [O'Brien] and Mike Mansfield in the morning and work out procedure. I really think that they ought to put that on the calendar, and then take it up the first day that they can, and then go on and debate it a while before we take up our tax conference report. We might put a little pressure on them that way, might have a few businessmen, a few withholding people, help us a little bit for four or five days. I think it would be dramatic, anyway.

Kennedy: Yes.

President Johnson: You talk to Larry.

Kennedy: Will we be able to talk to you tomorrow?

President Johnson: Yes, sir.

Kennedy: Okay.

President Johnson: You talk to Larry and Mike Mansfield in the morning. I told Mike—he was in here—I talked to Larry O'Brien, too, and they both have ideas. You get with them, then you all agree on it. Whatever you want, I'll be for.

Kennedy: Bye, now. I'll get back in touch with you.

President Johnson: That will be good.

Tuesday, February 10, 1964, 9:45 P.M.

Nicholas Katzenbach

President Johnson: [*picking up in midconversation*] . . . So my inclination would be to start with civil rights just the earliest minute you can. They oughtn't to give them this holiday, but we're weak sisters up there and we did. And I'd get on it Thursday by sure. Then they can't debate it but one day, and then come back Monday and be right on it, so they'll be meeting on taxes on Monday, and then Tuesday go right on it. [Have a] long session Tuesday and still be on the tax conference report. Maybe the House will pass it Wednesday, if we're lucky. Then we just say, "Well, boys, we're going to wait and see how civil rights comes out for a few days."

Nicholas Katzenbach: Well, you're the fellow that knows the Senate, Mr. President.

President Johnson: I don't know it, I don't. But that's something to . . . Anyway, I'd get them on civil rights as soon as I could. Then we can make the decision whether we want to pull it down. We can always pull it down and take it up, but your job is to get the Attorney General and them to agree with [Mike] Mansfield to get it up as soon as you can. I know they can object to it when it comes over tomorrow. I know it can go to the calendar. I know it can be moved up Thursday morning. Now, he may have made some damn fool agreement that he won't do anything Thursday. If he does, why, just let him make a pro forma motion to take it up, and let somebody start debating and then adjourn.

Katzenbach: I haven't had a talk with Mansfield in some time. I know he's very good at this.

President Johnson: I know this: you did a superb job. Everybody I talked to just said that you were hiding around the corners, drafting amendments, passing on them, and I'm really proud of you.

. . .

A week and a half later, Johnson talked with Mike Mansfield, with presidential aide Bill Moyers present. Johnson was still attempting to tie up the loose ends of the tax bill, as well as some remaining issues on the farm bill that was making its way through the Senate. The immediate reason for the call was a story being written by *Washington Post* reporter Mary McGrory. Talking with Mansfield, Johnson betrayed his suspicion that Bobby Kennedy's Justice Department had its own agenda and that Kennedy would try to undermine him. The President was sure that McGrory's leaks were coming from Justice and that the people over there wanted to make trouble for the administration. The conversation with Mansfield was followed five days later by a similar discussion with Humphrey about handling the media.

Thursday, February 20, 1964, 5:28 P.M.

Mike Mansfield, with President Johnson and Bill Moyers

President Johnson: I'm going to put Bill Moyers on, and tell you what Mary McGrory just called here and said to him, so you can call her.

[*to Moyers*] Get over there.

[*to Mansfield*] I would imagine it's a leak from some of her friends over at Justice. But I told him to get with you, and for you all to arrange the strategy, because I knew that if I got into it, they'd say that I was bossing the Senate, and directing it. Now, she's raising hell, because I imagine Justice has told her that I'm not directing it. So listen to Bill, see what he says, so you can call her and give her the facts.

Mike Mansfield: Okay.

Bill Moyers: Senator, she says that she has been on the Hill for the last two days trying to do a story on the strategy of the civil rights bill, particularly the pro–civil rights bill and the Democratic majority. She finds no plan, and no strategy, and no one has had any instructions from the White

House, that she can find no evidence of any strategic or tactical decisions that have been made, and that there is a great deal of confusion, and that no one seems to know what the other person is doing. She went to the Republicans, she said, and asked them if the Democrats had appointed a liaison with the Republican liberals and pro–civil rights senators to try to work out some strategy, and they said no, that there had been none of this.

Mansfield: Well, she hasn't been around to see me. She hasn't been around to see Hubert [Humphrey]; I don't know. Is this article out?

Moyers: No, sir. She's writing it.

President Johnson: She's writing it, and she wants somebody to inform her on it. I thought it would be good if you said to her that you understood that she called the White House about this, that you discussed it at breakfast the other morning what the plans for the leadership were, and that they're satisfactory to the White House, but that you make those decisions yourself, that you and your policy committee have decided that you'll put it in the hands of four people—Humphrey and whoever they are—that you're going to be in constant touch with [Everett] Dirksen on the matter.[4]

Moyers: Incidentally, she said that the committee of four had apparently fallen apart, and that she understood the President himself had said that you can't run a government by committee.

Mansfield: He didn't. I didn't hear him.

Moyers: He didn't.

President Johnson: You see, Justice, I imagine, Mike, is starting this. She's got awfully close sources over there. So I think you'd better just tell her what you have done and tell her that it's going very well, and you're very happy with it, that you think that you've made more advance planning than you have ever known to take place before.

Mansfield: Shall I just tell her that the White House informed me?

President Johnson: Just tell her Bill Moyers has.

Moyers: We could have her call you. I could have her call you.

Mansfield: Why don't you do it, Bill?

Moyers: If she doesn't call you in the morning, let me know, would you?

Mansfield: She could call me right now.

Moyers: All right, I'll have her call you right now.

---

[4]Mansfield had appointed a committee of four Senate Democrats (Humphrey, Warren Magnuson of Washington, Joe Clark of Pennsylvania, and Philip Hart of Michigan), each with responsibility for coordinating debate on different sections of the bill.

President Johnson: I'd tell her that you've got a liaison with Dirksen, that you've agreed to have a liaison with Dirksen—

Mansfield: Mr. President, I've even met with Dick Russell, but I didn't give it any publicity.

President Johnson: And just tell her that you've also got four people, you've divided up the pro-senators. It might be 60—where each one of them have about 15—and you're right on top of it.

Mansfield: Yes, sir.

President Johnson: Tell her furthermore that you've had the Attorney General up, talked to him about it. Had Katzenbach up, arranged for him to go with each individual member. That you had announced at the leadership meeting, after the House had told what they'd done, that you are doing very similar, the same thing that worked so successfully over there, and that you announced it at the leadership meeting, and it was agreeable · to everybody.

Mansfield: Right.

President Johnson: She's just a troublemaker, and they want to start the trouble.

Mansfield: [*to Moyers*] Okay, Bill, will you call her?

Moyers: I'll go call her right now.

Mansfield: Call me back and give me the number. Okay, Mr. President, and good luck on your trip.

Tuesday, February 25, 1964, 11:00 A.M.

Hubert Humphrey

After discussing other matters, the President turns to civil rights and to the administration's farm bill.

President Johnson: Now, on your civil rights thing, Hubert. I think that you've got to be awfully careful that you don't leave that at the White House because they'll say that it's a plot of the cotton South.

Hubert Humphrey: No, I'm taking full responsibility—

President Johnson: So, I'm just thinking that it had better be a leadership decision. When they ask you what the White House says about it, I'd just say, "We make those decisions up here; the White House has never told us how to handle procedures, and we gladly discuss them with them, but they tell us it's a matter for the Senate to decide." Then, if I were you, I'd surely call Nick Katzenbach and tell him that you think that you'll modify the southerners' opposition a little bit, and they won't be near so mean to you if you get their bill through for them. That you believe you can get it through in a week to ten days. That you've got to do something for the agricultural people. If you don't, you can't get their vote for civil rights. There's already a good deal of agitation about that—they're about to repeal this damn Crawford Act in California. You've got to do something for somebody besides civil rights and the House has spent all year on it. And for that reason, you think that this is wise, and be sure to get their consent, because—

Humphrey: Yes, I have them coming in at 12:00.

President Johnson:—they'll clip you if you're not *awfully* careful. And there's a good deal of stuff like that going on. Then I would try to get on television, some of these question and answer programs this Sunday—the *Today* show. Or get some of our men to leak it that this farm thing, they just say that the radio and television networks don't ever give the farmer any shake at all. They just cuss him, and you can show if the figures are right, that this bill really saves $400 million.

Humphrey: You bet.

President Johnson: And appeal to consumers that way too. But I'd try to get it on, so that I could get a little sentiment for my farm thing.

Humphrey: Yes, sir.

President Johnson: And then, I think you've got to be on that television anyway. I think that these group speeches are wonderful, but the fellow that's on there, they see him. I'd try to get on it this week.

Humphrey: May I say this? When I had this chance, I was on this California trip, I covered the entire Rocky Mountain area over CBS, NBC, and ABC. I had some good interviews that I think were most helpful to our cause here.

President Johnson: That's good.

Humphrey: And you're going to see on the Steve Allen show there was about 30 minutes, in which we discussed the poverty program, what your administration is attempting to do here, and I think that it's going to be good. I really agree with you. These meetings are just little tidbits compared to one shot on that TV.

President Johnson: That's right.

Humphrey: And the TV reports that we've got out there were, if I may say so, were very good.

President Johnson: That's good. Okay. Now, I'm very anxious—I don't want to say this to anybody—but I'm very anxious to get this tax bill. So you keep 'em there tonight if you can to get it and see that it's messaged on down to me.

Humphrey: All right.

President Johnson: Because they mess around, you know—five days engrossing the bill in the House, and God knows how long it will take them to carry it down here.

Humphrey: We'll push it past.

President Johnson: All right.

. . .

In terms of taped conversations on the Civil Rights Act, March was a sparse month. The Senate did not begin deliberations on the bill until March 9, and for the next two and a half weeks, Russell successfully prevented the bill from coming to the floor for debate. Mansfield, Humphrey, and dozens of other senators and staffers were busy countering Russell's moves, and by month's end, they had engineered a vote to bring the bill to a full floor debate. But many senators were sticklers for senatorial rules. Wayne Morse, the liberal Democrat from Oregon, insisted that the bill first go to Senator James Eastland's Judiciary Committee, which was the proper course for a piece of legislation of this type. Eastland had already fulminated that the bill owed more to Stalin and Hitler than to the U.S. Constitution, and Morse knew full well that Eastland would try to use his powers as chairman to kill it. On principle, however, Morse introduced a motion to let the Judiciary Committee debate the bill, which would have ended matters then and there. To stop Eastland from preventing the bill from coming to a vote, Mansfield introduced a procedural motion that would require the bill to be brought to the floor directly. Mansfield prevailed by a vote of 50 to 34.

Johnson watched these maneuvers closely but did not become directly involved. He communicated regularly with Humphrey and with legislative aide Larry O'Brien about what was transpiring and had regular meetings with leading lawmakers. But in the taped conversations that survive, he did not talk extensively about what was happening in the Senate, perhaps because he knew that once the ball was rolling, he could no longer play a day-to-day role.

For Johnson, March was also devoted to Vietnam and the farm bill, and to intensive meetings on the recently launched War on Poverty, headed up by Sargent Shriver. Johnson wanted the public to see the War on Poverty as the hallmark of his election campaign, and he also viewed the Civil Rights Act as essential to improving the economic plight of black Americans.

Given these concerns, and the delays in the Senate, only a few of the recorded conversations are of interest, and many are largely tangential to the legislation. They do indicate, however, that civil rights was rarely far from Johnson's mind. Early in the month, he tried to appoint William

Mitchell to the Civil Rights Commission. Mitchell, a southern lawyer from Arkansas, was meant to round out the regional balance of the commission, and Johnson needed the approval of leading southern senators. He called both senators from Mitchell's home state, John McClellan and William Fulbright, but did not directly broach the topic of civil rights with either. The very fact that he was making a civil rights appointment while the civil rights bill was being debated is intriguing. Both senators knew where the President stood, and Johnson, of course, knew their position.

The conversation with Fulbright includes a long digression on Vietnam, which had held most of Johnson's attention that day. Though much of the following transcript has little to do with civil rights, it suggests how even in the midst of this key legislative fight, the President had other issues of equal significance that demanded his attention. This was one of many such discussions Johnson would have with Fulbright, the chairman of the Foreign Relations Committee. After that, Johnson talked with McClellan and then with Mitchell himself. Mitchell later declined the appointment.

Monday, March 2, 1964, 8:50 P.M.

J. William Fulbright

President Johnson: Bill, who was that fellow that introduced me down there at Hot Springs when you were in such great distress and danger of being defeated and didn't get but 92 percent of the votes?

J. William Fulbright: Will Mitchell.

President Johnson: I want to appoint him on the Civil Rights Commission. You reckon he'd take it?

Fulbright: He might. He's a good fellow. He's been . . .

President Johnson: I want a man that will be a southerner, that is able, and can take care of himself, but just won't be a damned vicious, like the governor of Alabama.[5]

Fulbright: Oh, no! He's a very moderate, intelligent fellow.

President Johnson: Intelligent. That's the best introduction I've ever had.

Fulbright: Yeah. He's been president of the Arkansas Bar [Association]. He's a prominent lawyer there.

---

[5]The governor of Alabama was George Wallace.

President Johnson: Has he got any flies on him, or troubles or anything, with [John] McClellan or anybody else?

Fulbright: Well, now, not that I know of, but I can make a little inquiry. I mean he hasn't taken a really strong partisan position, you know, out in front. If he does, it would go way back beyond my knowledge. I don't think so. I could make inquiries about him.

President Johnson: Well, I just wanted to be sure he was all right with you, and I'll call John, because I just don't want to appoint anybody on something like that, but I want a southerner on it, and he impressed me.

Fulbright: He's a very solid, you know, moderate fellow, and I support him. That's a difficult position. Now whether or not he'd want to do it or not, I don't know.

President Johnson: Well, he probably wouldn't want to, but we've got to have somebody. Dick Russell didn't want to sit on that commission with [Earl] Warren either.[6]

Fulbright: [*laughing*] Say, you know, I thought Dick's performance on television was more, what shall I say . . .

President Johnson: Understanding than you could . . .

Fulbright: Yes, than I would have thought.

President Johnson: Well, I didn't see it, but everybody here has bragged on it all day, and I could just kill him for not telling me about it.

They then had a brief exchange on Panama and Cuba.

President Johnson: Well, tell Betty [Fulbright's wife] I love her and I'll see you.

Fulbright: Well, you take care of yourself. How you feeling?

President Johnson: I couldn't feel better—couldn't feel better. I think we're doing all right. I think we've got a *good* thing working for us economy-wise—our tax bill. I think we got prosperity, and our market hit over 800, and I'm rather pleased, and the thing I'm worried about now is they tell me that some of our boys are afraid our unemployment is going to get down under 3 percent and we may have inflation. I don't believe it, but I guess a little inflation is good for you in an election year, isn't it? [*Chuckles.*]

Fulbright: Yeah, I wouldn't worry about that yet. I'd worry more if—

President Johnson: Well, the report I got tonight from my economist was that it hit below 3 percent, unemployment. Hell, all of them . . . the boys in New York say that the capital investment is going to be over 20 percent, and they estimated 10 percent. Everybody believes in the govern-

---

[6]The Warren Commission was assembled by Johnson to investigate the assassination of John Kennedy.

ment and they not harassing them, and not investigating them too much; they're getting ready to go to town.

Fulbright: Good.

President Johnson: So maybe if we can just get our foreign policy straightened out. Now, of course—

Fulbright: Yeah, get that damn Vietnam straightened out. Any hope on that?

President Johnson: Well, we got about four possibilities there.

Asks aide to get him his memo on Vietnam.

Fulbright: That's the most difficult one, I think, at the moment.

President Johnson: The only thing I know to do is do more of the same, and do it more efficiently, and effectively. We got a problem out there that I inherited with [Henry Cabot] Lodge. I wire him every day and say, "What else do you recommend?" But I want to take one minute here to read you what I think is the best summary of it we have, because I had it this afternoon for some folks I talked to. [*reading*]

> In Southeast Asia today the free world is facing an attempt by the Communists of North Vietnam to subvert and overthrow the non-Communist government of South Vietnam. North Vietnam has been providing direction, control, and trained cadres for 25,000 Viet Cong guerrillas and 60[,000]–80,000 irregulars engaged in harassment, systematic terror, and armed attacks on the people of South Vietnam.
>
> Two, our objective: Our purpose in South Vietnam is to help the Vietnamese maintain their independence. We're providing the training, the logistic support which they cannot provide themselves. We will continue to provide that support as long as it is required. As our training missions are completed, certain of our troops can be withdrawn. In December, 1,000 men came home. This group included two military police units whose airport guard duty had been taken over by Vietnamese that we had trained for that purpose. Therefore, there's no reason to keep our police there when we had Vietnamese that we had trained for that purpose.
>
> Three, the current situation: In the past four months, there have been three governments in South Vietnam. Each of them has appointed its own cabinet members, its own provincial governors, its own senior military leaders. The Viet Cong have taken advantage of the confusion resulting from these changes by raising the level and the intensity of their attacks. They have been using larger forces and more powerful weapons. This increased activity has had a good deal of success. Strategic hamlets formerly under government protection have

been lost to the Viet Cong. Roads formerly open to free movement have now been closed.

On the other hand, the Viet Cong fatalities have been very high. The unfavorable rate of three or four Viet Cong killed for every Vietnamese has continued. Although 20,000 Viet Cong have been killed during the past 12 months, their strength has remained approximately level through the receipt of cadres from North Vietnam, and recruits from South Vietnam.

Now, in other words, we've killed 20,000; they've killed 5,000 in the last 12 months.

Fulbright: Well I–

President Johnson: [*continuing to read*]

At least four alternatives are open to the United States tonight. We can withdraw from South Vietnam. Without our support, the government will be unable to counter the aid from the north to the Viet Cong. Vietnam will collapse, and the ripple effect will be felt throughout Southeast Asia, endangering independent governments in Thailand, Malaysia, and extending as far as India on the west, Indonesia on the south, the Philippines on the east.

That's number one.

Number two, we can seek a formula that will neutralize South Vietnam a la [Mike] Mansfield, [Charles] de Gaulle, but any such formula will only lead in the end to the same results as withdrawing support.

Fulbright: Yes.

President Johnson:

We all know the Communist attitude that what's mine is mine, what's yours is negotiable. True neutralization would have to extend to North Vietnam as well, and this possibility has been specifically rejected by the North Vietnamese and the Chinese Communist government, and we believe if we attempted to neutralize, the commies would stay in North Vietnam; we would abandon South Vietnam, and the Communists would take over South Vietnam.

Fulbright: Yes.

President Johnson:

Three, we can send the Marines—a la Goldwater—and other U.S. ground forces against the sources of these aggressions, but if we do, our men may well be bogged down in a long war against numerically superior North Vietnamese and Chi Comm forces 10,000 miles from home.

Four, we continue our present policy of providing training and logistical support for the South Vietnam forces. This policy has not failed. We propose to continue it. Secretary [Robert] McNamara's trip to South Vietnam will provide us with an opportunity to again appraise the future prospects of this policy, and the further alternatives that may be available to us.

Fulbright: I think that's right. That's exactly what I'd arrive at under these circumstances, at least for the foreseeable future.

President Johnson: All right. Now, when he comes back, though, and we're losing what we're doing, we've got to decide whether to send them in or whether to come out and let the dominoes fall. That's where the tough one's going to be. You do some heavy thinking, as the little Jewish boy said. Do some heavy thinking, and let's decide what we do. Okay.

Fulbright: Righto.

President Johnson: Give Betty my love.

Fulbright: Sure will. How's Lady Bird standing up?

President Johnson: Yes, she's just . . . She and my two daughters are against the White House. They want to go back to Johnson City—they say it's too much strain.

Fulbright: I don't blame them. I would agree with them.

President Johnson: Well, I'm going home and eat dinner now. I'll talk to you. Good night.

Fulbright: Okay. Bye.

Monday, March 2, 1964, 9:00 P.M.

John McClellan

President Johnson: Hello.

John McClellan: Hello.

President Johnson: John?

McClellan: Yes, sir.

President Johnson: Lyndon Johnson. Will you pardon me for calling you at home at night?

McClellan: That's perfectly all right.

President Johnson: I had a fellow introduce me down at Arkansas at a bar association, and I wanted to try to get him to take a job, and I haven't talked to him, and I know he'll tell me to go to hell. It's an ugly job and a mean one, but I didn't want to ask him if he wasn't a friend of yours, or if he'd ever done anything against you: Will Mitchell.

McClellan: Oh, it's perfectly all right. I don't know how Will was, but he's all right. He's a very good fellow, I think. Feel free as far as I'm concerned.

President Johnson: All right. Well, I didn't want to do it. It's a non-paying job and it's an ugly job but I need some southerner to do it, and I wanted to call him, but I didn't want to call him unless he's—

McClellan: Well, he's not an enemy. Other than that, I don't know. He probably supported me. I mean he's not one of those that I call a *close* friend, but he's all right. If you want him for anything . . . I think Will's a good man.

President Johnson: Well, you're mighty fine and mighty friendly.

McClellan: I think he's a good man, and whatever it is—

President Johnson: Civil Rights Commission. That's unpleasant as it can be.

McClellan: [*laughing*] I don't know if he'll take it or not.

President Johnson: I think he'll tell me to go to hell, but I've *got* to get some southerner that will stand up that's able, and talk to them. And I thought he made one of the ablest introductions of me I ever heard.

McClellan: Well, Will's a great fellow, and I'll say this to you: I think he'd be a credit to you.

President Johnson: I know damn well he will. You're my lawyer in the Senate, but I don't imagine you'll take this job, will you?

McClellan: Well, I don't know about that now—I've no idea whether he'll take it.

President Johnson: I say, I don't imagine *you* would. You remember when I was sworn in I told you to stay there until I got in. I wasn't sure they were going to let me be sworn in.[7] Do you remember that?

McClellan: Yes . . . I remember all of that.

President Johnson: I heard you thunder over in the House two or three times, and I like what you said and the way you did it.

McClellan: Yes, I do that when I get scared.

President Johnson: No, you just do it when you're protecting your rights, by golly. I came and asked you in the cloakroom to please stay here until I got sworn in—well, that was 1949. Now, that's a pretty long time ago.

---

[7]In his 1948 Senate campaign against Coke Stevenson, Johnson had triumphed by 87 votes in an election characterized by widespread vote fraud.

McClellan: I remember that cloakroom.

President Johnson: I had Dick Russell and I had a lot of friends, but I thought they were a little gentle, and I wanted somebody, by God, that could really stand up and let them have it if I had to have it because [Arthur] Vandenberg had indicated he was going to keep me standing aside there unless old [Homer] Ferguson was sworn in.[8] I asked you to stay, and you said, all right, and you kept wanting to go to your office. I kept . . . I was scared to death. I was a kid, and I made you stay.

Now, I can't get you to be my lawyer on the Civil Rights Commission, but I got to get some southerner.

McClellan: Well, I couldn't . . . When was that thing created?

President Johnson: Oh, I don't know. . . . It's been a long time—

McClellan: Well, I'm opposed to it anyhow.

President Johnson: I know you're opposed to it!

McClellan: So I couldn't serve on it.

President Johnson: You couldn't serve on it—you're in Congress, but if I can't get you, I'm going to get somebody else, and I'm going to ask this fellow, and he's going to . . .

McClellan: Will, I think, would be a nice fellow.

President Johnson: Yes, I just want some southerner that'll stand up with his hind legs, and say, "By God, wait just a minute." You know Mr. Rayburn used to say that.[9]

McClellan: I think it's gone so far now nobody can put on the brakes for you.

President Johnson: No, they're pretty good—they're pretty good. They're not bad. I've got the dean of Yale on it, and I got a Republican out from Michigan. They're not too bad. As a matter of fact, I've asked them to lay off of everything and not do a damn thing until we get action on the [civil rights] bill. I'm handling them pretty well, but I just wanted to have—

McClellan: How many is on that commission?

President Johnson: Five.

McClellan: Just five. Do they all have to be appointed at once?

President Johnson: No, no, they're already appointed. There's just one vacancy, but I want a southerner. We had Dean Storey, the head of American Bar from Dallas.

McClellan: Yeah, I remember that he was on it.

---

[8]Vandenberg and Ferguson had both been Republican senators from Michigan.
[9]Sam Rayburn of Texas was the former House Speaker.

President Johnson: Then we had John Battle before him, from Virginia, and I want to get a good southerner that's not regarded as too mean, and at the same time would kind of look after us if we had to have a little looking after.

McClellan: Will is not a radical.

President Johnson: No. I think . . . I'm going to try him if it's all right with you.

McClellan: It's certainly okay with me. He'll be all right as far as I'm concerned.

President Johnson: Tell Norma that I'll love her and I wish you'd let her come around once in a while and quit hiding her out.

McClellan: [*chuckling*] Okay.

President Johnson: Good night.

Monday, March 2, 1964, 9:10 P.M.

William Mitchell

The President calls the wrong William Mitchell about the appointment to the Civil Rights Commission.

Monday, March 2, 1964, 9:15 P.M.

William Mitchell, with President Johnson and Wilbur Mills

President Johnson: Hello. Mr. Mitchell?

William Mitchell: Yes sir.

President Johnson: This is Lyndon Johnson.

Mitchell: [*excitedly*] Yes, sir . . . President Johnson!

President Johnson: How are you doing?

Mitchell: Fine sir, and you, sir?

President Johnson: Are you the Will Mitchell that introduced me up there at Hot Springs?

Mitchell: I am.

President Johnson: Well, I've got a very ugly job I want you to do for me.

Mitchell: I'll be delighted to if I can, sir.

President Johnson: Well, you can do it, and you've got to serve your country. Were you in the service?

Mitchell: Yes, sir.

President Johnson: Well, what . . . Navy, Army, or Air Force?

Mitchell: Army.

President Johnson: Well, this is just another service job. I'm here talking to Wilbur Mills, and we've got to have a southerner, a man that's got ability and a man that's got composure, a man that's got judgment. We've got to have Robert E. Lee to sit on our Civil Rights Commission and give our viewpoint—tell them what's right and what's wrong.

I've got Dean [Erwin] Griswold of Yale University. I've got Dr. [John] Hanna of Michigan University. I've got Father [Theodore] Hesburgh, the President of Notre Dame, but I've got to have a southerner. I had John Battle, and John Battle served his term out under President Eisenhower. Then we got another southerner, Dean [Robert] Storey, the head of the Law School at Southern Methodist University, at Dallas. He served his term out.

We *cannot* be unrepresented on that commission, but we can't have a man that's just wild and that doesn't reflect credit on us. I've looked over the whole South. I've gone to Atlanta. I've looked at some of my top lawyers in Texas. I've gone to Baton Rouge and New Orleans. I considered a couple from Alabama. But time comes when you got to enlist, and I've just got to have you.

Mitchell: Mr. President, may I call you in the morning, sir?

President Johnson: Now, if you think about it over night, you won't want to do it. [*Mitchell laughs.*] And I just got to have you because I fell into this job and I don't ask you to endorse anything. All I ask you to do is follow your conscience, and come to a meeting once every month or two, but we've got to have our viewpoint presented and represented. And I've just got to have you, and I don't want anybody else. And I never met you but once, but I heard you that day when you introduced me, and that's the best introduction I ever had in my life. I'll go with you on this thing and help you any way I can. You don't have to do anything that'll embarrass you. You just have to follow your convictions. I don't want any commitments. I don't want any special pleas. I just want you to do what your good horse sense tells you. But I want somebody that I can depend on.

Mitchell: Here is my problem. I want to help you and I am *highly* flattered by this call, sir. I have partners in this law firm, and we have made an agreement that we would not take on any outside jobs without first telling the others—

President Johnson: Well, you just tell them in the morning that you've got to do this, because your President got his tail in a crack. Then you call me back in the morning.

Mitchell: I'll do that, sir.

President Johnson: But we've looked the whole South over, and this is the trouble spot, but there'll be others that are good ones. I've got to have somebody that's got the capacity, and you've got it because I sat there and listened to you. Here's Wilbur, who wants to say a word to you.

Mitchell: All right, sir.

Wilbur Mills: How you feeling, Will?

Mitchell: [*laughing*] How do you think I feel?

Mills: Well, I know how you feel: you're honored.

Mitchell: Very much so.

Mills: He's got the same high opinion of you that I have, and that everybody I know has, of you. I think you can do a good job on this. You're not going on as a patsy. You're going on there, the full intention is, to represent the viewpoint which you have, which is the viewpoint of all of us down there.

Mitchell: You know I'm highly honored, Wilbur. I would like to be able to say yes now, but our law firm just has a rule that we won't take on work that's going to take us out of the office without first touching base with the others.

Mills: I understand that. And the President understands that, of course. But . . .

Mitchell: Could you give me some idea about what time we're talking about?

Mills: Well, what is the time, Mr. President, of this appointment? How long would it be?

Mitchell: No, I'm not talking about that—I mean, out of the office.

Mills: Oh, about once a month. You'd just be up here for a meeting and back home.

Mitchell: I see.

Mills: Maybe once every two or three months.

Mitchell: I see.

Mills: I understand five or six meetings a year. It's not going to take you away from your work, if that's what you're concerned about.

Mitchell: That's what I'm concerned about.

Mills: No.

Johnson is talking to him in the background, giving him the names of the commission members.

Well, you know Dean Griswold of Harvard and Father Hesburgh of Notre Dame and John Hannah of Michigan State: they're all outstanding men.

Mitchell: I assure you I'm flattered to death.

They then discussed the tactics for Mitchell to call the President the next morning, and Johnson returns to the line.

President Johnson: Will?

Mitchell: Yes sir.

President Johnson: I've got Dean Griswold at Yale, Dr. John Hannah of Michigan State. These are men that have served before. I've got this vacancy. But I want the vacancy to go to a southerner that understands southern life, that understands our viewpoint, that can say to people, "I think you're making a mistake. Here's what you ought to do." That [will] dissent if they need to. But I want somebody that I can be proud of as my appointee, that just won't be a plain damned idiot and want to eat a little Negro baby for breakfast, but, at the same time, will understand how to approach this thing as best they can. Now, these are the top men of the nation, and I just don't want the South to show up with a bastard child. That's that simple.

Mitchell: Well, I . . .

President Johnson: And I know it's not something that's going to reward you, except the satisfaction of doing the duty that you did in the Army and serving your President, and maybe I can find something better as a result of it. But I want somebody that I can depend on, and I know what I think of you because I make my judgments of people.

Now, I've already talked to Senator Fulbright. I've already talked to Senator [John] McClellan. Wilbur Mills is sitting here talking to me. We're talking about your introducing him down there at the dam, and I was talking about your introducing me. I think that there's not a man in Washington that I've got more respect for than Wilbur. I just decided that I ought to clear this out tonight, and I've just got to have you represent the South.

Now, you just get Robert E. Lee out. He left West Point, you know, and said that he'd have to get out of the Federal Army and go home and look after his people. That's what you've got to do because we've got this problem. We've got to have somebody that's got judgment, got eloquence, got ability, and that can sit in a room with people and disagree with them, and still without being too disagreeable. And that's what I'm having to do every day.

Mitchell: Well, I'm certainly 100 percent for you, too, sir. You're doing a *wonderful* job.

President Johnson: Well, you just come to help me, and you'll never be sorry of it. I'll guarantee you that. You just tell your partners in the morning that your President drafted you last night, and you had your agreement . . . But you call me tomorrow and tell me that you're going to do this, because if you can't come to some of the meetings, that's all right. But when you're here, I want somebody I can be proud of.

Mitchell: Well, I certainly appreciate it, and I'll call you first thing in the morning.

President Johnson: Thank you.

Mitchell: Than you very much. [*Hangs up.*]

President Johnson: Well I think it may be Harvard. Well, that's where it is. I thought it was Yale. No.[10]

.   .   .

A few days later, talking by phone with Larry O'Brien on March 6, Johnson again voiced his suspicion of the Attorney General. While he seems to have had faith in Katzenbach and Burke Marshall, his distrust of Bobby Kennedy did not wane. He was worried Kennedy might try to alter the strategy then being worked out between the White House, Humphrey, and two high officials from the Justice Department. He was also doubtful that the bill was being handled properly. As he often did with O'Brien, he let off steam and sounded the petulant note of a former majority leader. He bemoaned the helplessness that came with the Oval Office. The power of the presidency was his, but he could no longer get down in the trenches in the Senate. While he had once reveled in personally handling all aspects of a major piece of legislation, now he had no choice but to let others do the fighting for him.

In sharp tones, he instructed O'Brien to talk to Katzenbach, Marshall, and Humphrey: "You be damned sure the Attorney General agrees to the procedures they follow . . . I just want to be sure the Attorney General approves of this. . . . You be sure that you explain to them . . . I want them to handle this bill and I'll work with them any way I can, and if Hubert and them work it out, that's their business. They ain't damn sure going to put it on my lap, because I'm for civil rights—period. Just as it passed the House—period. And that means all night, every night. I'll stay here all night, every night to do it myself. I've passed two of them [Civil Rights Acts of 1957 and 1960], and I never passed them on any 9-to-4 business." Yet as much as Johnson wanted to micromanage the process, he could not. His earlier battles over civil rights had given him a wealth of experience, but his position as president limited what he could do with it. Though he kept his concerns out of the public eye, his aides bore the brunt of his frustration.

---

[10]The President and Mills were apparently discussing the affiliation of Dean Griswold. Griswold was dean of Harvard Law School.

Still, Johnson's advice was heeded, especially by Humphrey. On March 8, the senator from Minnesota appeared on *Meet the Press* to discuss the bill's prospects. Expressing optimism that it would pass before the summer, he gave a good performance. He spoke highly of Dirksen, calling the Republican leader "a man who thinks of his country before he thinks of his party." Johnson called to congratulate Humphrey. "Boy," he began, "that was right. You're doing just right now. You just keep at that." He then offered Humphrey the unsolicited counsel to "get in there and see Dirksen." Humphrey later confessed that he did not always like the tone Johnson used when talking to him; the President often acted as if Humphrey was a political naif, although he had entered the Senate the same year Johnson had. But Humphrey wanted to be selected as the vice presidential nominee, and so he accepted the President's counsel graciously.

As the Senate remained deadlocked, Johnson came up with new ideas. Ever attuned to the personal dimension of politics, he suggested to O'Brien that all administrative assistants working on the civil rights bill should be invited to the White House. "If you want to have them in for tea," he said during a phone call on March 11, "you can always deliver me. Just ask and I'll show up—the White House, the East Room, any of those things that you want in your legislative program. Plan them, now, because then you can deliver me. I'll show up. You can just say, 'I want you to come to the White House, and, confidentially, I think the President will come by, but I want you as my guest.' And maybe their wives." In legislating, Johnson had learned that little things mattered, including nurturing a warm relationship with administrative assistants.

On March 26, with no warning, the Senate voted 67 to 17 to send the bill to the floor for debate. Richard Russell was not finished with the filibuster, and if anything, March had been a warm-up, a period of spring training before the real season began in April. With the mid-July recess looming and the nominating conventions a barrier to further debate, Johnson needed the bill to pass some time in the next three and a half months. No filibuster had ever gone on that long. But this one would.

Chapter 10
The Final Fight

The Senate fight lasted the better part of three months. It was an arduous enterprise. The southern opponents of civil rights knew public opinion was overwhelmingly in favor of a bill. They also knew a substantial majority of the Senate would vote for a bill along the lines of the one passed by the House. Although outnumbered and fighting the current, the southerners knew the rules of the Senate gave them an outside chance of turning back the bill. Richard Russell and fewer than two dozen other senators were tightly organized, disciplined, and determined. They knew how to use and bend Senate rules, and how to mount a filibuster. And most of all, they understood one thing: a majority of the Senate might endorse civil rights reform, but senators also treasured their privileges.

In essence, that was the key to the opposition strategy. To end the southern filibuster, the Senate would have to vote for cloture. During all previous civil rights debates, as far back as the 1930s, cloture had never been successfully invoked. To vote for cloture meant to end debate, to cut off the filibuster. In a way, it represented a mild vote of censure, a sign from the Senate as a body to a few recalcitrant colleagues that it was time to allow business to proceed. Over the years, senators had routinely voted against cloture, regardless of how they felt about the issue being debated. In essence, senators were inclined to defend their parliamentary privileges even at the expense of principle.

The legislative history of the Civil Rights Act was a chess game of moves and countermoves, of traps laid and avoided, of taking risks and making strategic retreats. It was a game played by several key characters, including Richard Russell, Hubert Humphrey, Everett Dirksen, Thomas Kuchel, and Mike Mansfield. Between late March and mid-June, much of the Senate's business was consumed with civil rights, and at one point or another almost every senator was involved. Neither side could be sure what the outcome would be. For those southerners who opposed the bill and feared its passage, their Confederate heritage demanded that they not go down without a fight.

This drama rarely made its way into the telephone conversations Johnson recorded in these months. The trend that had begun in March continued, for there was little Johnson could do once the filibuster was underway. His position was clearly understood by the Senate, and the lines were so firmly drawn that even the "Johnson treatment" would not have achieved much. Johnson saw little point in haranguing Russell or James Eastland or Dirksen and seemed to have sensed that however strongly he desired to see the bill pass, pressuring individual senators would do little good.

Although Johnson could not do much to change the outcome in the Senate, he had staked his reputation and that of his administration on the bill's passage. Accordingly, throughout these months, he continued to speak passionately about the bill in public forums and to massage civil rights leaders. Already, he was thinking ahead to the fall presidential campaign, and with public support for civil rights legislation climbing throughout the spring, he recognized that it was politically prudent to remind people that he was deeply committed to ending racial discrimination.

On March 25, Johnson met with more than a hundred representatives of the Southern Baptist Convention at the White House. He used the occasion to admonish them gently that being a genuine Baptist demanded certain choices, one of which was to do what was right and moral. Civil rights was an unambiguous cause, he claimed, making it incumbent on the ministers to use their influence at home to help pass the bill. Ultimately, the Southern Baptist Convention refused to endorse the civil rights bill, so perhaps Johnson's efforts were fruitless. Yet, while Johnson rarely lobbied senators directly in these months, by making such appeals, he did his best to maintain the pressure.

The leaders of the pro–civil rights forces in the Senate also took their case to the public. That meant forging close working relationships with civil rights leaders and their organizations, as well as with religious leaders. In the civil rights struggle, ministers, priests, and rabbis made up one of the most energetic sources of support. Humphrey and others urged religious leaders to mobilize their congregants to write to their congressional representatives, and the result was a steady stream of mail to Washington in favor of civil rights. But letters alone were not sufficient. From April 19 through the end of the month, interdenominational groups gathered at the Lincoln Memorial and marched peacefully through Washington to express their support for the legislation. While Russell and the southerners fulminated in the Senate, outside, the wind was blowing the other way.

For two reasons, Humphrey was determined to keep the issue on the national radar screen. Not only would it help ensure the bill's passage, but it would also enhance his prospects for becoming the vice presidential nominee in the fall. Humphrey was an eloquent spokesman on behalf of the bill's virtues, and he shared the prevailing sense that reform was a moral, even a religious, imperative. On March 30, he announced on the Senate floor that the purpose of the bill was "to give fellow citizens— Negroes—the same rights and opportunities that white people take for granted. This is no more than what was preached by prophets and by Christ himself. It is no more than what our Constitution guarantees."

During these weeks, Johnson turned his attention to the fight over the farm bill that was making its way to the Senate, and to preparing the next phase of his domestic program, which would culminate in a May speech at the University of Michigan. In Ann Arbor, he would announce his goal of mobilizing America's wealth "to move not only toward the rich society and the powerful society but upward to the Great Society." Preoccupied by other matters, he only occasionally discussed civil rights on the phone.

For most of April, the contest in the Senate was between Humphrey and Dirksen. While the southerners conducted their filibuster, Dirksen and the other 32 Republicans proposed numerous amendments. That presented a severe problem for Humphrey, for if the eventual Senate bill departed too much from the House version passed in February, the gap between the two bills would be impossible to bridge in the subsequent House-Senate conference. The defenders of the House bill had made clear that they would not agree to yet another watered-down Senate version and that this time, it was essentially all or nothing.

As Johnson kept tabs on these developments, he may well have had off-the-record meetings with Humphrey about strategy. From the phone records, however, and from the records of White House meetings, it seems that having impressed his views on Humphrey in March, he let his lieutenant manage the matter in April and May.

Of course, Johnson was concerned about his own reputation during this period, and he watched his poll numbers closely. Having made civil rights the cornerstone of his administration, and staking his election on the issue, he had a strong interest in how he was being perceived. He also wanted to use his own popularity and the civil rights issue as a cudgel against his opponents. In a conversation with Senator George Smathers on April 7, Johnson reminded the Floridian about a recent poll. "Our popularity jumped up Gallup four points this month," he told the senator. "It's now 78 . . . jumped up from 74." Smathers did not respond directly, but instead relayed a conversation he had just had with newspaper publisher Jack Knight. "I had a nice visit with Jack Knight Sunday to play golf," he told the President. "He kept saying, 'Everybody wants to like Johnson; I do, except for those extreme things.' I said, 'What extreme things?' He was talking about civil rights. I said, 'Well, he's got a problem there, Jack. He just inherited this problem. He wouldn't be any more extreme than anybody else.' And he said, 'Then, well, I intend to be for him, et cetera,' which is good, because he's got, you know, the Akron paper, the *Detroit Free Press,* plus the *Times Herald,* the *Charlotte News and Observer.* But I'm sure he's going to be for you." This exchange was characteristic of the conversations Johnson had with senators opposed to civil rights: gentle banter with a pointed subtext.

A few days later, on April 10, Johnson talked with Senator Robert Byrd of West Virginia, the patrician Democrat who in his youth had been a member of the Ku Klux Klan. The reason for the conversation, a superb example of Johnson-style lobbying, was a questionable judicial nomination Byrd had put forward. Johnson thought the nominee was too old, had "meddled in politics," and had too many enemies. The conversation, a classic case of political horse-trading, saw the President insinuate that he would hold up a senator's judicial appointee unless there was a quid pro quo. In this case, Johnson wanted Byrd to soften his opposition to the civil rights bill, but he knew how unlikely that was. Byrd demurred. Johnson had another request: he wanted to force senators who had been lawyers to disclose the amount they received in legal fees. It was purely a public relations ploy for Johnson, a tactic designed to make some of the more affluent senators squirm when the public learned how profitable their legal practices had been. Of course, Johnson would have preferred a Byrd declaration of support for the civil rights bill, but they both knew that was not going to happen. After the two men had jousted on civil rights, Byrd turned to the controversial nomination of Judge Sidney Lee Christie. The President wanted to know how important the nomination was to the West Virginia senator.

Friday, April 10, 1964, 4:55 P.M.

Senator Robert Byrd

Robert Byrd: Well, Mr. President, I'd rather have Judge Christie than anybody in West Virginia. That's the reason I submitted his name.

President Johnson: I know, but we want somebody down there to try us and he'll be dead before we get old enough to be convicted of anything.

Byrd: Well, no, no he won't. The reason I submitted his name was because of his competency and judicial demeanor and the fact that it would be acceptable to other members of the bar. And then too I did it because I thought he deserved it as a working Democrat and so I have no reservations on his appointment at all. I'm a thousand percent for him. If I can't have him, why, I just wouldn't submit anybody else.

President Johnson: Oh, now, you wouldn't do that. . . .

Byrd: No, that's right, no, I mean that.

President Johnson: You can have anybody you want.

Byrd: I know that, but you know when I go for a man, Lyndon, as I went for you, I don't take any second best, and that's the way I feel about Judge Christie.

President Johnson: Well that's the way I feel about them. I just don't know of a man I have a better friendship than I got with you.

Byrd: I took all kicks coming, in the back and in the teeth, for Lyndon. And that's the way I feel about a man when I pledge him my support. I go all for him. There's no halfway business about it.

President Johnson: Well, how is he doing down there now? Are they going to hurt you on account of it?

Byrd: Well, no . . . on account of his appointment?

President Johnson: On account of me.

Byrd: No. Why would they hurt me on account of you?

President Johnson: Well I just got some enemies, I guess. . . .

Byrd: Oh well, hell! Everybody down there is for you now. People who were kicking my butt four years ago for being for you are all out waving your flag now. I get a kick out of the SOBs. By golly, I say, where were you four years ago when I was for Lyndon Johnson?

President Johnson: All right. When they get through whipping me up on that Hill though, don't you let them do it.

Byrd: The only thing that I won't go along with, Mr. President, you and I have already discussed, and that's the civil rights bill.

President Johnson: Well, you don't have to go along on that, but make them vote on it. Don't let them keep [*unclear*] the vote . . .

Byrd: No . . . No . . . No sir, I wouldn't make them vote on it because I know if they vote on it, they're going to get it. And if a man starts to come in my house, if I can't beat him with my fist, I'm going to take a poker to him. The only way we can win here is to not let them vote. You know I'm honest with you, and you always get an honest answer with me.

President Johnson: Well, I don't want you fighting too hard now. I can't be here. I've got to pass that bill.

Byrd: I know, but you're going to be here. You're going to win without—

President Johnson: Well I can't do it. I can't do it at all, and you know I can't. Me and you tried that once, didn't we pardner?

Byrd: That's all right. Nobody in the United States can beat you this time.

President Johnson: Oh yes, they . . . if I don't pass that bill, they'll beat me. Anyway, I'm not going to argue with you about that bill. I know how you feel about that bill and I expect you to vote against it. Of course, I might send you off on a tour or something, some of these days, before they vote cloture. I don't want you to—

Byrd: I wouldn't leave this [*unclear*] for all the tours in the world.

President Johnson: [*laughing*] I might make you stay at home, and nurse me, and give me a thermometer. I'm going to be so sick and I'm going to have somebody put cold packs on my head.

Byrd: No, Mr. President, when I'm with a man, I'm with him.

President Johnson: Well that's what I'm talking about, I want you with me [*laughing again*].

Byrd: I'm with [Richard] Russell in this fight.

President Johnson: You're with me, you're with me. You've got to be with me.

Byrd: No, Mr. President, my convictions are against that bill.

President Johnson: Yeah, I know it, I know it. And I don't blame you, and I wouldn't quarrel with you there, but I don't want you to help the [*unclear*] too much now.

Byrd: Well, when I'm against something, I fight it with everything that is in me, and I'm against this bill, just as when I was for Johnson, by God.

President Johnson: When you were? You mean you still are! Hell, don't go talking like that.

Byrd: I was with you when the going was rough.

President Johnson: That's right, and it is going to be rougher if I don't pass this bill.

Byrd: No, it won't either.

President Johnson: Yes it will. You all going to beat it?

Byrd: I hope the hell we beat it. . . . We're going to do all we can for Lyndon Johnson, but we don't need that bill.

President Johnson: [*Laughter.*]

Byrd: You know there's ways to beat it.

President Johnson: I know that.

Byrd: You remember? Well, I'm not going to bring up another item that you and I both [*unclear*] recently and I did what I could.

President Johnson: What was that?

Byrd: Well, you know I'm on a certain—

President Johnson: Oh, yeah that's right. You don't need to be talked to. You do what is right. I would, though, tell those sanctimonious bastards that have all these law practices and so forth, you'd think all these people get fees and all these people that make speeches and practice law ought to report their earnings or something.

Byrd: Well, I'm not against that.

President Johnson: I'd go pretty strong on that if I was you. You're a poor boy and you haven't got a great big law firm, making millions of dollars, and these fellows like Scott raising hell.[1] I'd just say, "I think that is good; let's recommend that they all report it to the Senate. All the employees report it." They haven't proved anything that's wrong anybody has done.

Byrd: All right, I'll go on that.

President Johnson: I'd just tell my boys. I'd just outdo them. I'd be more virtuous than they are. I'd be more holier than they are. I'd just say I think every penny of income ought to be reported and let's let the people know, make it public.

Byrd: I'm for that and I'll say so.

President Johnson: File it in the Rules Committee. I'm going to send Judge Christie up there, and I assume he's going to keep me out of jail.

Byrd: Keep you and me both, out of jail [*laughing*].

President Johnson: I'm going to try to sign it this afternoon and, I don't know, when are you all in session tomorrow?

Byrd: Yeah.

President Johnson: I guess tomorrow then.

Byrd: When can I announce this?

President Johnson: You can announce it now. Just tell them that you've just talked to the President and the President said he was going to nominate Christie on the recommendation of the Department of Justice and Mr. Robert L. Byrd.

Byrd: I will announce it in the names of the two West Virginia senators, and I'll say we've been informed by the President. How's that?

President Johnson: That's all right. Say the White House . . . is what I'd do, so they won't think we're talking about other things.

Byrd: Exactly.

President Johnson: But I'm for it and it will be up.

---

[1]"Scott" was probably Republican Senator Hugh Doggett Scott of Pennsylvania.

Byrd: All right.

President Johnson: God bless you and I love you and come see me.

Byrd: Thank you, Mr. President. Bye.

President Johnson: Bye.

. . .

The conversation with Senator Byrd epitomized how little Johnson could do at this juncture. Indeed, Johnson rarely engaged in lobbying while the filibuster was underway; the forces were already set in motion. There was an almost inverse relationship between the amount of time Johnson was devoting to discussing the bill on the phone and the amount of attention the filibuster was receiving in public.

With Johnson's standing on the sidelines, the various religious groups that had descended on Washington attracted prominent media attention. The daily intrigues in the Senate were covered assiduously by the major daily papers, the weekly news magazines, and the television networks. At times, the attention was perhaps excessive. On CBS, Roger Mudd reported several times each day from the steps of the Capitol, keeping Americans informed about which senators had done what. In April and throughout the next two months, civil rights and the filibuster was a major story, which Americans followed closely.

In mid-April, two sticking points engaged the Senate. Dirksen proposed dozens of amendments, most of which simply altered the language of the House bill, but not its substance. But the Illinois senator still had serious reservations about Title VII, which extended federal power by establishing an Equal Employment Opportunity Commission. An additional issue was an amendment proposed by Senator Herman Talmadge, the Georgia Democrat. Talmadge opposed the entire bill, but his amendment addressed a provision in the House version that even its supporters were unsure about, namely, the absence of jury trials for criminal contempt of any portion of the bill. Talmadge wanted to add a Title XI to the bill that would provide for a jury trial. Given the constitutional sanctity of trial by jury, this amendment garnered wide support in the Senate. The problem, though, was that civil rights jury trials in the South were almost certain to involve all-white juries, which had almost never been willing to convict white defendants in cases of racial discrimination.

The Talmadge amendment had the unintended effect of accelerating negotiations between Dirksen and the Democratic leadership. Dirksen started sending signals that he was prepared to compromise on his slate of amendments. He would demand the acceptance of some of his amendments even if they were substantively the same as what was contained in the original bill. But he would be flexible on amendments that proposed dramatic changes to the House bill. Slowly, he began inching closer to Humphrey. While these movements seem clearer in retrospect than they did at the time, by late April, Dirksen, Humphrey, Mansfield, and Kuchel, along with Nicholas Katzenbach of the Justice Department, were actively seeking some sort of consensus about the shape of the bill. Once that consensus was reached, the bill's supporters would be able to proceed toward ending the filibuster.

At the end of April, Dirksen and Humphrey were still trying to outmaneuver each other, not on whether the bill should be passed, but on who was to receive the most credit for its passage. Dirksen got Humphrey to agree to bring the Talmadge amendment to a vote, but Humphrey needed Dirksen to withdraw most of the other amendments or at least to begin serious negotiations on them.

Johnson watched their contest with great interest and did what he could to bolster Humphrey. One of his most reliable sources of information continued to be Larry O'Brien, and on April 28, the President talked at length with his legislative aide about the Senate morass. The conversation began with a lengthy discussion about a House transportation bill before O'Brien turned to civil rights.

Tuesday, April 28, 1964, 5:50P.M.

Larry O'Brien

Larry O'Brien: [*picking up midconversation*] . . . I was up in that civil rights meeting. . . . I just came from there. . . .

President Johnson: What happened there?

O'Brien: Well, Bobby [Kennedy] was up there, and Hubert [Humphrey] and Mike [Mansfield] and we went over all this stuff again, and the question was . . . Hubert said that he talked to you this noon about the thing, and of course, the question was whether we should follow the road of trying to invoke cloture on the jury trial amendment in the event that [Richard] Russell doesn't come to agreement on the vote which is apparently [Everett] Dirksen's stated position to the press now. Hubert is a little concerned. He'd rather try and zero in on cloture on the overall bill, and I said to them that Christ, I could see them crossing paths here, if it didn't seem to me that Dirksen had it met now bipartisanly that they were to discuss all the Dirksen amendments, and why the hell couldn't they get the Dirksen amendments discussed and see if there was an area of agreement with Dirksen on his various amendments by Thursday night? And if that were the case . . . I said, I know that's probably a rosy glow, but it's certainly worth a real stab on the part of the leadership to get this done. Katzenbach has redrafted language on Dirksen's 11th amendment you know . . . on that Title VII . . . that seems to be the one in greatest controversy . . . and that language is in the hands of Cliff Case, who is trying to sell it to their side, and so we decided that they'd work as hard as they could along those lines to see if they could get to any agreement with Dirksen, which would mean that they might head the first of the week toward a straight cloture overall rather than one on the jury trial amendment.[2]

Now Hubert said that in his candid view—I guess Dirksen is scheduled tomorrow to make a presentation to you at 12:00 noon—and he said that the impression that he has gotten is that Dirksen feels that that would present him an opportunity to discuss this directly with you. So I said to Hubert, well, hell, I would think, I don't know, but it would seem to me the President would say to Dirksen, "Well God, whatever my leadership and my department head agrees to is fine with me."

President Johnson: That's right.

O'Brien: And I said that I think we can go on that basis, and Hubert said, "Well, I hope that's the way it works out," and I said I don't blame Ev [Dirksen] for trying to move it a little bit . . . a notch above the . . .

President Johnson: How does he want to move it . . . on the . . . ?

O'Brien: Hubert would like to get the sleeves rolled up totally with Dirksen on the Dirksen amendments overall, try to work out an agreement with him in the next three or four days and then aim for overall cloture rather than shooting for cloture on the jury trial amendment. Now that may possibly not be something that can be worked out, but it's worth taking a stab at. Now Hubert has told the press—you know Hubert and the press: he tells them something, and then if he'd walk away from them he'd be fine, but I was standing in the background up there; he, you know, told them pretty much that everyone concerned wanted to resolve this thing at the earliest possible moment, but that all amendments that were involved in this bill should be put on the table on block and reviewed item by item, and that an agreement be worked out, and he didn't feel it was possible to do this until all amendments were on the table like a deck of cards, and that's fine. And then he said, his personal view in answer to an inquiry from a member of the press, his personal view was that cloture has to be invoked and he felt it would have to be invoked before this bill could be enacted. It should be invoked on the overall bill. But that was his per-

---

[2]Case was a Republican senator from New Jersey.

sonal view, and his mind was open and the leadership generally had their open minds on any kind of suggestions.

President Johnson: Wasn't that about what you and Bobby and Hubert agreed to?

O'Brien: Yeah, that's where it stands and it isn't bad because I think it puts a little heat on Dirksen and hell, if it's our judgment by the weekend that we've got to go on cloture on the jury trial amendment, you can always make that determination, but what I wanted to be sure that Hubert didn't do today . . . was to come to an agreement along those lines with Dirksen on the jury trial amendment, and he has not and will not, and his views . . . understanding is, unless we advise him otherwise, I told him to leave it that way unless after I talked to you there was something else that when Dirksen tries to press you into a position of a straight negotiator with him, which is what Hubert suspects he may try to do tomorrow, that you simply throw the ball back through Dirksen to the leadership.

President Johnson: All right.

The conversation then returned to the transportation bill in the House.

•   •   •

That evening, Johnson prepared for a meeting with Dirksen the next day and for a reception with a group of religious leaders who were in Washington to support civil rights. With his speech-writing staff out of the office, he called presidential aide Bill Moyers in New York for last-minute help on preparing remarks for the meeting. "We need a speech for religious leaders tomorrow at noon," he told Moyers, "150 of the top, what do you call them, the civil rights religious leaders. Now, you get your Bible coming back tonight, and get in one of those hotels up there, and get us some good quotations on equality, all of God's children." Moyers interrupted to say that he was actually flying back to Washington that evening, implying that he would not be in a hotel. Johnson shifted gears. "You can mark," he told Moyers. "Go buy you a Bible, and I'll pay for it. . . . And mark yourself, with a lot of good quotations, and get a central theme, with a good lead."

The next day Johnson went from the sublime to the mundane. He addressed the civil rights leaders with his usual stirring rhetoric about equality and God's justice, and then met with Dirksen. Dirksen's posturing was starting to annoy Johnson. Just before that meeting, he called Mike Mansfield to sound him out on how he should handle the Wizard of Ooze, and to let the Montana senator know he was growing impatient.

Wednesday, April 29, 1964, 11:32 A.M.

Mike Mansfield

President Johnson: Mike?

Mike Mansfield: Yes sir.

President Johnson: What should I tell Dirksen when he starts trying to put me on the spot down here on this civil rights thing? Did they just work it out with the leaders?

Mansfield: That's right. Tell him that I gave a report to you yesterday, that I told you that we, Dirksen and I, were in constant contact and working together agreeably, and that it would be your suggestion that he and I just keep working together and it is our responsibility now.

President Johnson: I'm going to tell him that I support a strong civil rights bill. He gave out a long interview of what he's going to tell me today, before he comes, which is not like him. I don't know what is happening to him here lately. He's acting like shitass!

Mansfield: Yeah.

President Johnson: First thing he said, he wouldn't treat his dog like I treated mine.[3]

Mansfield: Oh, I didn't know he said that.

President Johnson: Oh yeah. Said "I wouldn't treat my dog that way," and its none of his damned business how I treat my dogs. I'm a helluva lot better to dogs and humans too than he is.

Mansfield: [*Laughs.*]

President Johnson: I stand my damned dog up and hold him by the ears so AP photographer can get a picture, and another little guy that didn't know what he was doing, he writes a story that it is cruel to the dog, and hell, I know more about hounds than he ever heard of. But they've got every dog lover in the country raising hell thinking I'm burning them at the stake—all just a big play about nothing 'cause that's all they can get and Dirksen is right in the middle of it trying to stir it up and it is too little a thing for a big man like Dirksen. But I gathered from Larry O'Brien that Humphrey wanted us to tell him that we want to get cloture on the whole bill, but I gather from the paper that you are going with cloture on the jury trial.

Mansfield: Well, I raised the question with them after this meeting yesterday and he wouldn't go along with it.

---

[3]Dirksen had publicly criticized the way Johnson treated his two pet beagles.

President Johnson: On the bill?

Mansfield: On the bill, and I would rather go on the bill but we've got to get those 23–25 votes there, and if we can get cloture on this, at least we'll break the ice and we'll get enough committed. It might be in our favor this way.

President Johnson: Yeah.

Mansfield: I would far rather . . . for the bill . . .

President Johnson: Well then what I'm going to say to him is this: I'm going to say, "Now these details can't be decided down here in the White House, legislative-wise. I have the Attorney General and he's in constant contact with Senator Mansfield and Senator Humphrey, and whatever you all work out, I'm sure will be agreeable."

Mansfield: Yes sir. Put it back on us and stroke his back.

President Johnson: That's good.

Mansfield: Okay. Bye, Mr. President.

President Johnson: Okay.

. . .

When Dirksen appeared at the White House, he met with a cool reception. As planned, Johnson did not want to discuss civil rights at any length. If Dirksen had come looking for validation that he was the central player, Johnson refused to give him the satisfaction. Instead, the President brushed him off, saying in effect that he was not the one to appeal to, Humphrey was. That was exactly the strategy Humphrey had urged, and it forced Dirksen to drop his posturing and turn to the arduous task of hammering out a workable compromise with Democratic leaders.

That same morning, the President talked with William Fulbright of Arkansas. Fulbright, the chair of the Senate Foreign Relations Committee, had planned a brief speaking tour in Europe and Johnson asked him to extend his stay for several days in order to attend meetings on Vietnam, Cuba, and Cyprus. Johnson was thinking ahead to the fall election and assumed, as did many others, that Richard Nixon would be the Republican nominee. Nixon had been traveling abroad, criticizing Johnson's foreign policy at every opportunity. Johnson wanted Fulbright to do some damage control in Europe. Fulbright, however, was part of the southern bloc then filibustering against civil rights, and he was concerned his trip would be misinterpreted by Senator Russell.

Wednesday, April 29, 1964, 11:55 A.M.

J. William Fulbright

After discussing Fulbright's agenda in Europe, the conversation turned to civil rights.

J. William Fulbright: You know, one thing that bothers me is our mutual friend, Dick Russell. Would it be possible . . . you know what he's going to say. I think you know what he's going to say, that I'm being taken away because of the pending cloture vote.

President Johnson: Well, I wouldn't do that. You're going to be away anyway.

Fulbright: Well, I was only going to be a couple of days.

President Johnson: Well, you won't have to be but a couple more.

Fulbright: Understand what I mean [*unclear*] . . .

President Johnson: I don't want him [Russell] to think I'm doing it 'cause I wouldn't do it for that at all, and I don't know when it is going to be.[4]

Fulbright: Well, I'm not objecting to it; it's just about my relations with him. You know what I mean.

President Johnson: Well, I don't want to cause that. I'd rather lose the government than to have you and Dick falling out and I don't want to be charged with being the instrument for trying to get a vote away because I'm not doing that at all. I don't want to do that.

Fulbright: I don't think you are either. I was going to be away but only, see, over the weekend. Now I'm going to have to tell Dick. I can't just go off, you know, and leave him without telling him that I've got to be away, and I wanted to clear it with you. What I told him, you see . . .

President Johnson: Well, I don't want him saying that I'm trying to plot through to beat him this way. Don't you tell him. What I'd do is just tell him that I was going to go over the weekend and that you've got to make a couple of extra stops and that you'll be back on the [*unclear*] for him to figure out what day that he needs you.

Fulbright: Well, the paper says they're about to have a cloture vote.[5] I can't just go off and leave him. You know what I'm saying.

President Johnson: Well that's right, but I don't want you to leave him blaming me, because I'd resign before I'd hurt his feelings.

---

[4]Johnson was probably referring to an upcoming key vote on the jury trial amendment.
[5]That report was premature. A cloture vote was still more than a month away.

Fulbright: I agree. I don't want you to, but you can see the possibilities. The way, at least, according to the paper, it is building up. If that cloture vote comes while I'm away, you know it might make quite a difference, the way I understand this thing. Now, personally, if I've got a good excuse, I'm not going to cry about that, but on the other hand, I don't want him to think . . . I'm just asking your advice. You know him as well or better than I do.

President Johnson: I'd tell him that I was going on this trip, that I'd planned it a long time, and not to have this cloture vote the day you're gone, and that you've got to go to Paris and London. It will take you one day there, and that you got to go—where was it you're going, Geneva?

Fulbright: No, I was first going to The Hague. That's the first speech; it's the 15th anniversary of the Exchange Program, you see. They asked me a long time ago. And Denmark. That's the 50th anniversary of the Denmark-America Association, which was the first exchange program, one of the first, started 50 years ago, you see. That was what has been set for a long time and I would have been back on Tuesday; this will probably take a week. Now, I've got to tell him. I can't just leave town and not show up, I think . . . I don't think that would be right.

President Johnson: No. I'd tell him but I wouldn't tell him that Johnson has called because he'll think it is a trick. . . .

Fulbright: Well that's just what I was afraid of.

President Johnson: So I'd just tell him that I was going to have to have these two speeches and I'd sandwich one day in on these others if I could. If I didn't, well, we'll give it up and go some other time but I just thought it would help. I thought number one, it would make it easier for you to make your trip and you can make it quicker and more comfortable. Number two, I thought it would give you a little participation in what was really happening, that was awfully important and I thought that you with your good offices could have some influence. I think that if you were a good salesman, talked a little tough, I think that it could cause them to close things down from now till the end of the year and make us easier to beat Nixon.

Fulbright: Well, God knows, you know I'm all for that. I don't want to embarrass you, God knows, at all. I'm not so concerned about my own thing, other than Dick's [Russell] relationship. These silly statements, you know Novak's and others, that I was going to trade my vote on cloture.[6]

---

[6]The journalist Robert Novak had reported a rumor that Fulbright wanted to be secretary of state in the next Johnson administration and that he was willing to trade his vote on cloture in order to get the appointment.

President Johnson: Yeah . . . yeah . . . yeah . . .

Fulbright: Goddamned press will find out I'm gone, and this is what I'm anticipating. And I hope to minimize that. You know damned well I don't want to be secretary of state, and all that. I just don't want them to say [*unclear*] . . . I'm just counseling with you, that's all.

President Johnson: Well I'd be awfully careful. I don't think I'd tell him that I was going to do this administration stuff 'cause he'll think it is a slick trick of Johnson's.

Fulbright: That's just what I'm afraid of.

President Johnson: I'd just tell him about the other two and if he doesn't want you to go, then that's your decision. I don't know what I'd do but . . .

Fulbright: Well, I'm so committed; hell, they've got the whole thing set up. My God, that ambassador at The Hague [*unclear*] he's got me visiting with, the Queen, and all that crap. You know these things, and you know these people abroad take these things very seriously, and Bill Blair up at Copenhagen is in a very similar program . . . and I positively, I don't care if I did miss it.[7] I can't back out on those, and it's not likely to, you see being gone so little there. The only problem is: it is going to take me out the whole week, and practically into the following week, and I didn't want this happening.

President Johnson: Well I'd just tell Russell I had these two speeches and how long it is going to take you and tell him to arrange his schedule accordingly and if he needs your vote, why, he'd better do his talking, and if he doesn't, why . . .

Fulbright: I can't afford to let him talk me out of the other. . . . I can't be talked out of that.

President Johnson: That's right. Well, I wouldn't mention ours, 'cause he'll think ahead . . .

Fulbright: No, what I mention is one thing. What the damned press is going to say, that's another. You can't go into these places without being picked up. The press is . . .

I've got to speak, Lyndon; I've got to speak on this damned thing. This is my day.[8]

President Johnson: Well, do it in the morning.

Fulbright: [I'll] do it tomorrow.

President Johnson: Good. Call them and tell them. Have one of your

---

[7]William Blair was the U.S. ambassador to Denmark.
[8]It was Fulbright's day to filibuster on the Senate floor.

secretaries call 'em and tell them to come to your office at 10:00 in the morning or whatever time you can get free.

Fulbright: . . . See, this is my day. Just got a meeting with the southern senators at 2:30, right after that when it is over I'm going to have to tell him [Russell] this because. I don't want [*unclear*]. It is a kind of embarrassing thing for me, as you know, goddamn it. I'm never very enthusiastic about . . .

President Johnson: I know it. . . . I know it. . . . I know it.

Fulbright: Christ, I'm really over a barrel on this thing. I wish to hell I could vote with you, you know that.

President Johnson: I know that. I know it.

Fulbright: I hope to hell I can get this thing out of the way, but I feel like a traitor, you know. Arkansas had all these damned people from chamber of commerce here last night, about 300 of them [*unclear*]. John McClellan makes a rousing speech about the civil rights bill and I didn't say a damn word about it, but you know it puts me in a hell of a position.

President Johnson: Sure does. I know it does. Well, I've got to . . .

Fulbright: The only thing really concerns me is my relations with Dick. I don't want him to think that I'm welching on him. That is what really bothers me. The fact that I am out of the country and [*unclear*] my constituents, I'll say, well hell, I was on government business. But Dick, well, he's a little different from my constituents in that connection. I'm awfully afraid of what his reaction is going to be.

President Johnson: Well you just . . . I'm like Sam Goldwyn, with you and Dick. I love him so much and you, too. Include me out.

Fulbright: That ain't easy with him.

President Johnson: I know it but I've got to do it and don't you let me ask you to do anything that would interfere with him. But if you go [on the trip to Europe] anyway, I sure want to make you a little more comfortable, give you a little sense of really helping to do this thing. And I think with these two men giving you some support there, that when you went in that you could lay it on the line. I think that you could stop this trading until we get rid of Nixon.

Fulbright: Uh-huh.

President Johnson: That's my judgment.

Fulbright: I want to do anything I can to help you.

After a few more pleasantries, the conversation came to an end.

·   ·   ·

Ultimately, Fulbright would vote with his constituents and against his conscience by siding with the southern bloc. But Fulbright's dilemma on civil rights would pale in comparison to what he experienced over Vietnam. An early supporter of Johnson's Vietnam policy, Fulbright would become an outspoken critic of U.S. policy in Southeast Asia.

Meanwhile, though Johnson brushed off Dirksen at the White House on April 29, the machinations continued. Humphrey needed to get Dirksen to sit down and commit to a compromise bill, and the jury trial amendment was the key. Only with Dirksen on board could Humphrey move the Senate to the next phase, cloture. From late April until mid-May, the Senate leaders (minus the filibustering southerners) hashed out a workable draft bill, which included a considerable amount of Dirksen's language, while not straying radically from the House version.

During this period, Johnson was frequently in touch with other senators on matters like Vietnam, the farm bill, and a food stamp bill that was integral to the War on Poverty. But when talking with southern senators such as Allen Ellender and Richard Russell, Johnson avoided civil rights, though he often made veiled allusions to the filibuster. It is not clear, though, whether these allusions were designed to needle the recalcitrant senators or were simply an outgrowth of a natural tendency to discuss what was transpiring.

Johnson's communication with Humphrey was different, due in part to the fact that Johnson was not only president, but also the bill's strongest supporter and the leader of the Democratic Party. But perhaps more important, Humphrey sought Johnson's counsel on civil rights because he was, in essence, auditioning for the vice presidency. Humphrey certainly had the right to manage the bill as he saw fit, without prior consultation with Johnson. But that would not have been wise politically. Instead, Humphrey approached Johnson deferentially and let the President tell him what to do.

Thursday, April 30, 1964, 12:11 P.M.

Hubert Humphrey

President Johnson: Hubert, I don't believe you ought to be quoting me on what I'm ready to do on these amendments. Just go on and tell what you all are doing.

Hubert Humphrey: Mr. President, that was not my quote, and I'm very sorry.

President Johnson: It was on all the tickers though and they're raising hell about it, and they're saying . . .

Humphrey: Well, I just was asked in the Senate, and I said now, the President of the United States . . .

President Johnson: Don't quote me unless you talk to me and unless you know I want to say it. Because I can say it down here, and I've been saying it at every press conference since I came in here, and they would like very, very much to say I weakened the bill and I'm not going to . . . That's not my position. I'm against any amendment . . . going to be against them right up until I sign them. Now you all can take whatever you want to on the advice of Attorney General.[9]

Humphrey: That's what I said here this morning. I said the President of the United States wants the House bill, and I said the President of the United . . . Our job in the Senate is to legislate. The President of the United States is not going to tell us what to do, and that he's a reasonable man. We will do what we are required to do here, and then the President will have to decide if he wants it.

President Johnson: That's good. That's the thing to do, and that's the way to handle it.

Humphrey: One of these reporters last night came out after Dirksen had talked and said to me, "Well now, will the President accept . . ."

President Johnson: They're trying to jockey us into that position, and we just must not be caught in it now.

Humphrey: I won't say a word.

President Johnson: I'm against any bill except the House bill, and the only bill that I'll sign is one that you and the Attorney General both recommend in writing I sign.

Humphrey: I understand that.

President Johnson: And let's don't get divided on it, because [Richard] Russell says this morning that he thought there was some significance in Johnson's willingness to accept amendments. When the debate started eight weeks ago, he said everyone was saying we had to take the House bill without changes. Nobody has ever said that anybody has to take anything. We just said we're going to pass a bill and we favor the House bill.

Humphrey: I'll go over exactly what I said.

President Johnson: Well, you just tell that damn UPI [United Press International] to correct that impression they put out.

---

[9]Johnson is saying that his public position is that he is opposed to any amendments to the House bill. However, he also knows some compromise will be necessary. He wants Humphrey to take the public position that while the President is opposed to any amendments, Attorney General Robert Kennedy may not be. If Humphrey accepts any amendments, whether offered by Dirksen or anyone else, Johnson wants Humphrey to say or to imply that the Attorney General had agreed. That way, Johnson could deflect potential criticism of the bill's failing to Bobby Kennedy.

Humphrey: I gave it to Bill Theis just a few minutes ago and gave him the devil.[10]

President Johnson: Well, I just don't want the farmers and the rest of them coming in and saying I've changed my position because I haven't.

Humphrey: I understand that.

President Johnson: And you tell them . . . and you know they can do that mighty quick.

Humphrey: I know that.

President Johnson: Okay, pardner.

Humphrey: Yes sir.

. . .

Word of this exchange with Humphrey leaked to the press, and the *Baltimore Sun* reported that Johnson had given Humphrey a tongue-lashing. Johnson wanted to make sure that his press secretary, George Reedy, set the record straight.

Friday, May 1, 1964, 11:50 A.M.

George Reedy

Picking up in midconversation.

George Reedy: Now, the other thing, sir, I'm always almost certain to be asked, whether you called Hubert Humphrey and "dressed him down" as the *Baltimore Sun* story went this morning.

President Johnson: Well, I'd say . . . I'd call Hubert and ask him what to say about that. Tell him that we never said anything to anybody. I didn't dress him down, but I just told him that I wouldn't be making statements about the White House position. I'd just take one position. I didn't dress him down at all.

Reedy: If they ask me to take a position, shall I just refer them to previous statements, shall I just say you were . . . you believe it's a good bill, or something like that?

President Johnson: I'd say that I have made my recommendations, and that obviously from time to time proposals come up that would be considered. I haven't been asked to pass on any. That's a matter for the Senate, and I'm not going to comment on legislation at this stage.

. . .

---

[10]William Theis was a Washington reporter.

That was, of course, not accurate, but Johnson wanted to prevent any public impression that he was meddling in Senate business. He also wanted to allay concerns that Humphrey was the President's yes-man. It would be awkward come the general election if Humphrey had gained a reputation as Johnson's lapdog.

May was a busy month for Johnson. He went on a brief speaking tour of the South, where he was greeted warmly. He was occupied with the antipoverty bill then making its way through the House, and he was squeezed by an uncomfortable scandal involving the financial misdeeds of his former Senate secretary, Bobby Baker. Civil rights may have been the most important issue on his agenda, but it was hardly the only thing he had to contend with during this period.

Johnson did play a behind-the-scenes role during these weeks. As Humphrey and Dirksen worked to assemble a coalition for the upcoming cloture vote, it was necessary to persuade senators from the West to break with the southerners. Traditionally, western senators had voted with the South on civil rights issues in return for southern support on federal aid for irrigation projects, which were vital to the economic health of states like Arizona and Utah.

Impatient with the glacial pace of developments, Johnson started to worry about the looming summer recess. He had factored in a good deal of delay for the Senate fight, but July was still a drop-dead date if Johnson's strategy for the fall election was to hold. As of early May, there was not a bill even Dirksen could support, and the cloture fight had not yet begun. Until cloture was invoked, there would be no floor debate on the bill, and until there was a floor debate, there would be no Senate vote. And only after both the Senate and the House had passed the bill could the President sign it into law.[11] Each of these steps might take many weeks, which meant the bill would carry over into the fall. And that the President could not allow.

On May 4, at a White House breakfast, Johnson met with Democratic Senator Carl Hayden of Arizona, along with Mansfield and Humphrey. Hayden, like many western senators, had never voted for cloture and was on record as being against cloture on the current civil rights debate. According to Charles and Barbara Whalen, authors of *The Longest Debate,* an account of the history of the 1964 Civil Rights Act, on May 4, Johnson offered Hayden a quid pro quo: in return for Hayden's vote for cloture,

---

[11]From early on, the goal was to have the House agree to all the Senate's amendments, thus making a conference committee unnecessary.

Johnson would make sure that Congress authorized funds for a major irrigation project that would help Arizona's economy and Hayden's political career.[12]

Johnson also had to contend with his persistent "Bobby problem." The Attorney General was intimately involved with the ongoing Senate discussions, but relations between the two men remained cool at best. With the question of the vice presidency still unresolved, Robert Kennedy remained hugely popular in the Democratic Party, and there were murmurs that Kennedy, not Humphrey, should be the running mate. But Johnson was deeply suspicious of Bobby Kennedy, just as he had been suspicious of his brother Jack. In direct dealings with the Attorney General, though, Johnson was always polite, and while fuming privately about the Kennedys, he respected their popularity and influence. In the midst of the civil rights imbroglio, Johnson called Joseph Kennedy, who was in Hyannisport with his niece, Ann Gargan, who was helping him recover from a stroke. At this time, Edward Kennedy was beginning to make a splash as the junior senator from Massachusetts.

Monday, May 11, 1964, 12:45 P.M.

Ann Gargan and Joseph Kennedy

President Johnson: Ann?

Ann Gargan: Oh yes, Mr. President.

President Johnson: How are you?

Gargan: Oh, fine, thank you . . . and yourself, sir?

President Johnson: Fine, how's my friend?[13]

Gargan: Well, he's doing pretty well, sir. . . . He . . .

President Johnson: I saw in the paper where he had come back home and I just wanted to say a word to him and tell him we were thinking of him and wishing that he was down here.

Gargan: Oh, fine. Wonderful. Well, I'll put him right on, sir.

President Johnson: Fine.

Joseph Kennedy: [*very faint*] Hello.

President Johnson: I'm so glad to hear you and I'm so glad you're back

---

[12]As it turned out, at the very end, Hayden's vote was not needed, and he voted no on cloture. Had it been necessary, however, he would have voted with the majority.

[13]The friend was Joseph Kennedy.

home. And I just wanted to tell you that Teddy and Bobby are doing a wonderful job, and we're so proud of them, and I hope you're feeling better.

Kennedy: [*Makes noises of assent.*]

President Johnson: You've got so much to be proud of because Teddy is just burning up the Senate. He's the best thing they've got up there. Bobby is doing a wonderful job with the civil rights bill, and I know you must be awfully proud of the training you gave those boys.

Kennedy: I know . . .

President Johnson: And I sure do want to see you, and I hope you're feeling better.

Kennedy: [*Inaudible.*]

President Johnson: And I hope you enjoy Hyannisport, and maybe I'll get to come to see you before too long. And if there's anything I can do, you please have Ann call me.

Gargan: Hello, sir?

President Johnson: Yes, Ann?

Gargan: Well, thank you very much.

President Johnson: Ann, I told him—if he didn't understand it—that Bobby and Teddy were doing a wonderful job, that Bobby works day and night on civil rights, and he's going to get a good bill, and Teddy is just the most popular thing in America.

Gargan: Well, thank you, sir.

President Johnson: Every place he goes . . . he was down in Georgia, and he was over in Maryland. He was up in New York, and every place they're just crazy about him. And every member of the Senate . . . both sides—Democrats and Republicans—just think he's . . . he's more popular than Jack or Lyndon or everybody ever was in the Senate.

Gargan: Oh, that's great, thank you very much. Uncle Joe has been very good, but he was a little stunned by your call.

President Johnson: Well, you explain to him how proud I am of both of them, and what a wonderful job they're doing, and how much training and how much time I know he spent on them and how proud he ought to be.

Gargan: Fine. Thank you very much, sir.

President Johnson: Bye.

Gargan: Good-bye.

President Johnson: Let me know if I can do anything, Ann.

Gargan: Oh, thank you. Thank you very much, Mr. President.

President Johnson: Bye.

·   ·   ·

May 13 was a pivotal day. Finally, Dirksen, Humphrey, Mansfield, and

Robert Kennedy (along with dozens of staff members who had scrambled to get a draft ready) settled the unresolved questions about the bill. One of the main sticking points had been the form of the jury trial amendment. Rather than accepting Herman Talmadge's version, Mansfield and Dirksen offered an alternative one. An amendment sponsored by both the majority and minority leaders of the Senate is always in a strong position, and this was no exception. That compromise paved the way for settling the remaining unresolved portions of the bill.

Even with evident progress, Johnson was nervous and unsure about what would come next. Congressman Jack Brooks of Texas asked Johnson on the telephone what he thought about the bill's chances. "Goddamn if I know," he told Brooks, and then moved on to other matters. Late in the afternoon on May 13, a concerned Johnson was on the telephone with Robert Kennedy, Dirksen, and, finally, Humphrey to assess the next moves and the challenge of assembling a coalition to vote for cloture.

Wednesday, May 13, 1964, 4:05 P.M.

Robert Kennedy

President Johnson: Hello.

Robert Kennedy: Mr. President, we had a meeting all day today and . . . with Senator Dirksen on the civil rights bill . . .

President Johnson: Good.

Kennedy: . . . and feel that we have an agreement with him and Senator [George] Aiken [R-Vermont] and Senator [*unclear*].

President Johnson: Congratulations . . . congratulations! Now, what does he think . . . does he think he can get the votes for cloture?

Kennedy: Well, he's hopeful. He's going to have to go back. . . . They're going to have a meeting of the Republicans on Tuesday morning.

President Johnson: Did you . . . are you in pretty good shape with the folks that are interested in the bill?

Kennedy: Well, we're supposed to meet with them at 4:30. . . .

President Johnson: You think that you . . .

Kennedy: Yeah, you know, they're not going to be happy, but nothing makes them happy and so we just have to accept that.

President Johnson: Well, I don't know. You did a good job making everybody happy on the House side.

Kennedy: Well, you remember we went through in October? They weren't happy when we did it.

President Johnson: Yeah, I know, but they saw the wisdom of it after you did it.

Kennedy: After it was over. . . . But Senator Humphrey did a fine job, I must say. Senator Dirksen was terrific. You might just . . .

President Johnson: Should I call them?

Kennedy: Yeah, I think it would be nice. And senators . . . Shall I give you the names? Senator [Leverett] Saltonstall [R-Massachusetts] and Senator [George] Aiken, and Phil Hart [D-Michigan] was damned helpful and Senator Warren Magnuson [D-Washington], very helpful.

President Johnson: All right. All right.

Kennedy: And, of course, you've got Dirksen and Senator Humphrey.

President Johnson: Okay. Dirksen, Saltonstall, Aiken, Humphrey, and Hart.

Kennedy: Yeah, and Magnuson.

President Johnson: Magnuson. All right. Thank you, Bobby. . . . Bye.

Kennedy: All right. Thank you, sir.

Wednesday, May 13, 1964, 4:30 P.M.

Everett Dirksen

President Johnson: Everett?

Everett Dirksen: Mr. President, how are you?

President Johnson: The Attorney General said that you were very helpful and did an excellent job and that I ought to tell you that I admire you, and I told him that I had done that for some time.

Dirksen: That's very kind.

President Johnson: And I'd repeat it, and I hope that you go on and let the others . . . get the folks together and let's do the job.

Dirksen: Yeah, well, we set the conferences for next Tuesday morning.

President Johnson: All right.

Dirksen: And as soon as those are out of the way, we are then . . . see what we do about procedure, to get this thing on the road and buttoned up. I talked to Dick [Russell] this morning. He gave me no comfort. I said, "Now I thought we were going to vote as of Wednesday," meaning yesterday, but I said, "What are you going to do?" Well, he said, "You're not going to vote this week because we're going to keep the show going." I said, "Well, what about next week?" "I can give you no commitment because we'll have a caucus of our members Monday morning." Well, I said, "Dick, you're going to have to fish or cut bait, because I think that we've now gone far enough, and I think that we've been fair."

President Johnson: Well, you've got . . .

Dirksen: So, that's about where it stands.

President Johnson: You've got that exactly right. That's what you've got to do; you've got to take care of your own people, and you're doing that, and I saw the other day . . . We don't want this to be a Democratic bill; we want this to be an American bill. And if these schools are out—they're coming out at the end of this month—and if they're out and we haven't got a bill, we're in a helluva shape and we're going to be in trouble, anyway.

Dirksen: Well, we're going to try . . .

President Johnson: I saw your exhibit at the World's Fair, and it said, "The Land of Lincoln," so you're worthy of the "Land of Lincoln."[14] And a man from Illinois is going to pass the bill, and I'll see that you get proper attention and credit.

Dirksen: Oh, thanks.

President Johnson: Bye.

Wednesday, May 13, 1964, 7:25 P.M.

Hubert Humphrey

Picking up in midconversation.

Hubert Humphrey: I had a little trouble on the civil rights, my groups up there, the leadership conference people are just up in arms as they generally are over anything. And I must confess that ol' Joe—goddang it, I thought we had Joe all wired.[15] He was in there and I stepped out of the room here when I answered the phone for your call, and I went into another room, and while I was away five minutes, why Joe gave them a lecture about them being sold out on Title VII.[16] But I talked with Bob Kennedy about it and I told Bob, I said—now he and I, we've got a contact—and I said, "Now, look, we're sticking together, I mean, you're in on this and I'm in on this." There isn't anybody moving or wiggling around and with Everett Dirksen, the whole bunch, before we left that room today . . . Joe, I will say, walked out before then; he said, "Look I'm not going to cause you any trouble, but I don't want to be here because I'm not sure I want to agree yet, you see." And I . . . but before the rest of us went

---

[14]Johnson had recently spoken at the opening of the 1964 World's Fair in New York City.

[15]Joe was either civil rights lobbyist Joseph Rauh or Senator Joe Clark of Pennsylvania.

[16]Title VII refers to the bill's fair employment practices provisions.

out, which included Mans-, [Phil] Hart of Michigan—who is great—
Maggie [Senator Warren Magnuson] and myself and Dirksen and
[George] Aiken and [Leverett] Saltonstall. I said we've got to have not
only a little understanding here, but if we're going to *be* for this, what
we've done, we're going to *be* for it. And we're going to resist everything
else.

President Johnson: That's right. That's right. That's right.

Humphrey: And we're going to go to our own caucuses and we're
going to sell it.

President Johnson: Now can Dirksen get the votes for cloture?

Humphrey: Yes sir, he can get 25 votes. I had dinner with him last
night and, Mr. President, we've got a much better bill than anybody even
dreamed possible. We haven't weakened this bill one damn bit; in fact in
some places we've improved it. That's no lie; we really have.

President Johnson: Well, now what you've got to do is tell these leadership people this one thing: The thing that we're more afraid of than anything else is that we'll have real revolution in this country when this bill
goes into effect. I've got to go onto television in a fireside chat and say to
them, "Now, it took us ten years to put this Supreme Court decision into
effect on education.[17] But we have got to appeal to all of you to come and
put this law into effect, and unless we have the Republicans joining us in
helping putting down this mutiny, we'll have mutiny in this goddamn
country. So we've got to make this an American bill and not just a Democratic bill.

Humphrey: That's right.

President Johnson: And they've got to be glad that the Republicans
have participated like [William] McCulloch and like Dirksen, because it
doesn't do any good to have a law like the Volstead Act if you can't enforce
it.[18]

Humphrey: That's right. Now, Andy Biemiller was here, and I had
Clarence Mitchell . . . Andy Biemiller, Tom Harris, the AF of L [American
Federation of Labor] attorney, Joe Rauh, [Arnold] Aronson, all these guys
in. I've been trying to keep in touch with them.[19] God almighty I'll tell you.

---

[17]Johnson was referring to the 1954 landmark school desegregation case, Brown v. Board of Education.

[18]The Volstead Act was passed in October 1919 to enforce the Eighteenth Amendment, prohi-
bition. It proved to be so unenforceable that it became a byword for futile legislation.

[19]Andrew Biemiller was a Wisconsin Democratic Party activist with strong ties to organized
labor. He was a leading civil rights advocate and an ally of Humphrey. Aronson was a civil rights
activist who worked for a group called the Leadership Conference, and Harris was counsel for
the AFL-CIO (Congress of Industrial Organizations).

President Johnson: I know it.

Humphrey: Andy sat there and shook his head, you know, and [said] this is awful and so on, and I just said to him very frankly, I said, "Well now, goddamn it, lets just settle down to business. You know damn well you can't pass the bill up here that we've got." If anybody thinks he could, I ought to. I'm more for it than you people ever thought about being. I'm the guy who's going to catch hell for weakening the bill, as you fellows say. But Andy, I've got to talk to George Meany and tell George Meany, "Look here, this is as far . . . by God we're going so far on this bill that it'll be the greatest advance in a hundred years."[20]

President Johnson: Of course it would, of course it would.

Humphrey: And I . . . if for chance you see Meany for any way . . .

President Johnson: I will do it, I will.

Humphrey: . . . just touch him up a bit.

President Johnson: I will and you ought to get Bob Kennedy to call him, too.

Humphrey: Yes, I will. I told Bob that he had to get on that telephone; I just talked to him here about twenty minutes. I said you have got to use your influence now. I'm putting myself on the line. . . . You're gonna check me and I'm gonna check you.

President Johnson: Now, Dirksen thinks he can get the Hickenloopers and the votes like that?[21]

Humphrey: Yes sir, Dirksen feels he can get 25 votes for cloture.

President Johnson: Now how many have you got? Forty?

Humphrey: I've got 42 or 43. We've got 41 for sure, Mr. President. And that means that we got cloture.[22] And we can put this bill out and we can then . . . it'll take us a little time; we're not going to rush anybody here now. But the truth is that Dirksen said today to our group that he contemplated about the first week of June.

President Johnson: Do you know they think they are going to win with Wallace in Maryland?[23]

Humphrey: Yes. Well, this is what they're all waiting for. And I'll tell you the tragic . . . By the way I called the national committee today; they haven't given any money for the goddang campaign in Maryland. I told the [*unclear*]; I said, "What in hell is up?" I said you people have got the fight of

---

[20]George Meany was the president of the AFL-CIO.
[21]Senator Bourke Hickenlooper of Iowa was a conservative Republican who eventually voted for cloture but against the bill.
[22]Humphrey needed 67 votes for cloture.
[23]George Wallace, the Alabama governor, was running for president.

your life over here. First of all, our candidate is not a good candidate. Let's face it. I mean, [Senator] Brewster . . . God almighty, he just . . .[24]

President Johnson: I was amazed. I thought he was . . . I thought he was . . . I didn't know that boy was as dumb as he is.

Humphrey: Well, I just figured it wasn't very smart for a fellow like me to get involved in it. I'd love to but I . . . It's all a matter of judgment whether carpetbaggers in this sort of thing are helpful.

President Johnson: I think you ought to get some reporter, though, to write and Pearson or some other people that you can contact.[25] Everything I say they immediately label it; you ought to say that all these years that southerners have resented people coming into their states and they talk about the do-gooders in the North. Yet now it's the South that's going in stirring up this trouble and these tear gasses; Alabama's coming into Maryland, and Alabama's going into Indiana, and Alabama will be going into New York. They're fine ones to be talking; they've been raising hell about it all these years. It's a pretty good point.

Humphrey: Yes sir.

President Johnson: He's . . . he's just divide and conquer, that's what he is.

Humphrey: And he's clever

President Johnson: Yes he is.

Humphrey: I watched him on the radio, on television.

President Johnson: Yes. I saw him.

Humphrey: Even these commercials are no damn good.

President Johnson: That's right, and 6:30 tonight he had a lot of stuff on Huntley-Brinkley, nationwide. All the crowds are applauding him and the kids are applauding him and all that.

Humphrey: Oh it just makes me sick.

President Johnson: Well, you're doing a wonderful job though, and I think . . . stay on this one though, in the morning and try.

Humphrey: This is number one and we'll handle this.

President Johnson: And make Mansfield get some guts in him and make him get up there and say something about this, and let's kill this off because we can make this a party thing and hold together on it.

Humphrey: Yes, sir.

President Johnson: All right.

Humphrey: All right.

---

[24]Daniel B. Brewster was a Democratic senator from Maryland.
[25]Pearson was famed Washington journalist Drew Pearson.

. . .

The May 13 compromise was announced with some fanfare during a press conference that featured Humphrey, Dirksen, and Robert Kennedy. Speaking for the administration, the Attorney General announced that he was satisfied with Dirksen's emendations to the bill. There were few significant changes. In the House version, the Justice Department could bring suit in individual cases of discrimination in employment or public accomodations. In Dirksen's revision, federal action could only be taken if there were a number of such cases that pointed to a pattern of discrimination. Also, complaints about public accommodation would have to go through state agencies first, and only after that had been exhausted could the federal government intervene. In addition, there was the new jury trial amendment. However, the sponsors of the bill in the House, Emanuel Celler and William McCulloch, had been apprised of the changes and had agreed that though not ideal, they were not deal breakers.

Now it was up to Dirksen to lock in his Republican colleagues. He had done what he had set out to do, which was to make the Democrats squirm. He had solidified his position as a power broker. Now, he shifted to the role of statesman and, borrowing the words of Victor Hugo, announced that civil rights was "an idea whose time had come."

Predictably, that process took several weeks. Humphrey gently nudged Dirksen, who met with senators such as Hickenlooper of Iowa and Carl T. Hayden of Arizona who were willing to support the leadership only in return for a favor, a pet project, or some sort of political cover. By late May, Humphrey was nearly certain he had the 67 votes needed for cloture. But it was no sure thing. Russell and the Democrats continued their filibuster, and by the end of May, it had surpassed all previous records for longevity. Much of the business of the Senate had effectively been halted for two months by a few dozen senators bent on preventing federal civil rights reform.

Outside Washington, the civil rights struggle continued. Martin Luther King, confident the Johnson administration needed no further prodding in the legislative arena, returned to the grassroots activism that had been so successful in raising public consciousness during the past several years. He headed to St. Augustine, Florida, the oldest European settlement in North America, where civil rights activists would engage in a lengthy, violent, and not terribly successful campaign to abolish segregation. Elsewhere, leaders like Malcolm X, who were unwilling to work with white officials and refused to treat the debates in Washington as meaningful, became more determined than ever to challenge racial discrimination throughout the country.

The continued unrest in the South, along with the filibuster, weighed on Johnson. He had always known that supporting civil rights would not win his administration any support below the Mason-Dixon line, and he had gambled that his political losses there would be outweighed by gains elsewhere. Still, he fretted that come the general election, southern antipathy would weaken his chances for victory.

He could not have been cheered, therefore, when he talked with Senator George Smathers of Florida on June 1. Johnson and Smathers were in the midst of an ongoing repartee about Johnson's poll ratings. Several months earlier, Johnson had bragged to Smathers that his Gallup numbers were up. Now, opposed to Johnson on civil rights, Smathers needled the President about the numbers going down. He wanted Johnson to worry about the political fallout, and when asked what he thought about the prospects of the upcoming cloture vote, he did his best to make Johnson worry that things were about to spin out of control. To make matters worse, as the final confrontation in the Senate drew near, the situation in St. Augustine, where the Reverend King was hard at work, was becoming increasingly volatile.

Monday, June 1, 1964, 2:48 P.M.

George Smathers

Picks up in midconversation.
George Smathers: Well, everything else is all right. We took a poll in our state [Florida] which we've had three now, and unfortunately, your popularity is still of course, strong, but while this civil rights thing is going on, it will drop. It's come down eight points since we took the first one, which was just about now two months ago. But I'm not at all worried about it, and I don't think anybody else is. I think when we get through with the damn civil rights . . .
President Johnson: What's going to happen to civil rights?
Smathers: Well, I think that a bill will pass. I hope that. Mike [Mansfield] announced today that he was trying to file a petition for cloture on Saturday and we'd try to vote on Monday. Now, I hope that he's done his counting and has got the votes.
President Johnson: Do you think he has?
Smathers: I don't know, and Hickenlooper, just between us, told me that at this stage of the proceedings unless some other amendments were adopted, he had a little group that ranged between, he figured, between six and ten who would not vote for this present bill unless it was further amended. Now, I don't know. Then I said, well, Bourke, are you going to

offer additional amendments yourself? And he said that he was. Now I don't know how they're counting him, but he told me this this past Friday. So, I presume that Mike and Hubert [Humphrey] know what they're doing.

President Johnson: I would doubt it. I would doubt it. It's mighty hard to figure out these things.

Smathers: It may be the strategy is that they want to lose the first cloture vote to establish the fact that they have to give more. That may be their strategy; I don't know. If it is, why then, I would think, why, in that case, I would file the damn cloture petition on Wednesday and get the vote on Friday and move it along. And then they could give some more and file the next one a week from Wednesday and maybe get the thing voted on the following weekend and they'd really finish the thing up in about three weeks. But I think they've got to start taking some action.

President Johnson: What about Saint Augustine? They're giving me unshirted hell on that, and we've called down and talked to the Governor, and he says that he's watching it very carefully, but they say they're shooting into King's white-man's house down there. This assistant to King, and a lot of trouble like that.[26] He's demanding we go in. We talked to the Governor. He thinks he's got it. He's watching it, pretty alert to it.

· · ·

Smathers was not far off in his estimation of the amount of time it would take to vote on cloture, debate, and then pass the bill. It took just under three weeks. The cloture vote came on June 10, after a feverish period during which both the Democratic and Republican leadership tried to assemble the 67 votes needed. Each day brought some new twist, and a new count. Most of the senators were unalterably committed one way or another. Sitting on the fence were a handful of undecideds like Bourke Hickenlooper and Carl Hayden. But it was not simply a matter of lobbying the undecideds. Some of their demands, if met, would have a domino effect and would push other senators to vote against cloture. Putting together the cloture coalition required deft balancing by Humphrey, Dirksen, Mansfield, and the rest.

In early June, Johnson had to deal with another potential crisis in Mississippi, as well as simmering tensions in St. Augustine. The Student Non-Violent Coordinating Committee had announced its plan for the Mississippi Freedom Project, the so-called Freedom Summer, which would consist of flooding the state with black and white volunteers intent

---

[26]This assistant was probably Harry Boyte, a white SCLC aide to King, who was the target of an unsuccessful murder attempt at a St. Augustine motel. The cottage King was staying in while in St. Augustine was also fired on.

on registering black voters. The Freedom Summer was certain to trigger violence and a police reaction in Mississippi, and as of early June, Johnson was already preparing himself for a rough few months in the Deep South. If the Civil Rights Act did not inflame passions among southern whites, then the Freedom Summer surely would.

On June 4, Johnson had a telephone conversation with White House aide Lee White about a black student who had been admitted to the University of Mississippi. Johnson feared this would lead to a replay of the Ole Miss situation of 1962, and he wanted to prevent that. Burke Marshall had already been dispatched to start negotiations with the school's chancellor and the governor of the state who had replaced Ross Barnett. White assured Johnson that if anyone could head off the crisis, it was Marshall. White told Johnson that Marshall was well known and respected by officials in Mississippi and that he had the added advantage of having been in a key position during the Ole Miss crisis in 1962. As it turned out, the situation remained under control, but the calm would be short lived. Just a few weeks later, the situation in Mississippi took an ugly turn, and nearly overshadowed the victory on civil rights that Johnson and the leaders of the civil rights movement had fought so hard to achieve.

The cloture vote was scheduled for June 10. Until the very end, the exact count was uncertain, though Humphrey was confident they would just squeak by. Shortly before the vote, some senators finally made a decision, while others were mollified by the passage of the jury trial amendment. The evening before the vote, Republican Karl Mundt of North Dakota, a fiery anti-Communist who had been on Capitol Hill for decades, called Johnson to let him know that he was going to vote with the majority. But during the conversation, he also acknowledged his relief that Johnson had not pressured him. Mundt knew Johnson, and he knew the President was inclined to be aggressive when he was pursuing votes. But Johnson's instincts had been correct. Taking a less interventionist approach toward the Senate during the filibuster had been the proper strategy, and as Mundt's call showed, it was now paying dividends.

Tuesday, June 9, 1964, 4:58 P.M.

Karl Mundt

President Johnson: Yes, Karl.
Karl Mundt: Hello. Lyndon?
President Johnson: Yeah.

Mundt: Thanks for calling back. I just thought I'd call you up as an old friend and tell you that I'm going to vote for your doggone cloture motion tomorrow.

President Johnson: Well, good, Karl, good.

Mundt: You're the first one I've told, so I thought I'd tell it to you.

President Johnson: Well, thank you, my friend. Well, I appreciate that.

Mundt: Yeah, I appreciate that you didn't call me up and give me the old Texas twist, so I just up and tell you myself. That's better.

President Johnson: I haven't called a human, Karl. I haven't called a human.

Mundt: Haven't you really?

President Johnson: No. I don't do that. I just talk to my friends once in a while about general things, but I'm not calling anybody to ask them to vote for anything. I saw Dirksen said I was an arm twister one time, but I hadn't really done that.

Mundt: Devilish, ticklish issue for a state like mine, but I figure, holy cow, if I believe in majority rule, some time I got to face up to the votes.

President Johnson: Well, fine. I appreciate your calling me, my friend.

Mundt: Just thought I'd let you know.

President Johnson: Thank you.

.   .   .

But the count remained fluid and Johnson caucused with Humphrey to get a sense of where things stood. Humphrey believed they had enough support, but he was not completely sure about who was going to do what.

Tuesday, June 9, 1964, 7:03 P.M.

Hubert Humphrey

President Johnson: Hubert . . . tell me . . . do you have a reliable count on your cloture?

Hubert Humphrey: Yeah. I think that my reliable count shows a minimum of 68 votes, and I'm just going to go over it here again with one of the staff fellows, because we're going to be in session practically all night. I guess we got some boys who are going to hold us in session. We had a little parliamentary snafu here but we got it all cleared up. So I think we're all right. I'm going to be here for some time; can I call back one of your men and let you know?

President Johnson: Yeah. I'm going. Call Lee White. I'm going to have to be at dinner at 7:40 to meet the prime minister, but I'll . . . you call Lee

White.[27] How are you counting Hayden? Against us, aren't you?

Humphrey: Yes sir. I'm counting him against. I was hopeful that he . . . well he gave us a couple of good votes today. I'm counting we got some Republicans that come in that sound pretty good. Mundt.

President Johnson: Mundt called me and told me that he was going to do it. [Have you] counted [Ralph] Yarborough [D-Texas]?

Humphrey: Yarborough, counted him, yes.

President Johnson: Well, I know what the steel workers told you, but our information is that they weren't quite that sure.

Humphrey: Well, I'll put the arm on him again. He told me he was going to go.

President Johnson: Yarborough told you . . .

Humphrey: Yep.

President Johnson: Today?

Humphrey: Yep.

President Johnson: Well, that's all right then. I thought that was what he'd do, but if he told you . . .

Humphrey: Yep. I haven't got any commitment out of [J. Howard] Edmonson [D-Oklahoma] yet, but the boys tell me that it looks good. I've asked some of the people to contact his brother. I've been after Edmondson two or three times, and since that jury trial amendment got in, I thought that might pull him through, and I think it does because he was so anxious about it.

President Johnson: But you think we're safe?

Humphrey: Yes sir.

President Johnson: Okay.

Humphrey: That's my . . . I'm just pawing around here for some papers but as I see it now, we have 68 votes.

President Johnson: How many of those are Democrats?

Humphrey: 42.

President Johnson: Well, the Republicans are doing a little better than we are, aren't they?

Humphrey: Yes sir. Dirksen tells me he's got 28 votes, but I don't think he has. I think he's got 26.

President Johnson: And how many they have, 36?

Humphrey: They got 33 members of the Senate.

President Johnson: Thirty-three.

Humphrey: Yep, he's losing seven.

---

[27]President Johnson was meeting the prime minister of Denmark.

President Johnson: I know three of them is [Edwin] Mechem [R-New Mexico] and [John] Tower [R-Texas] and [Barry] Goldwater [R-Arizona].

Humphrey: Mechem, Tower, Goldwater, [Milward] Simpson [R-Wyoming], and let me see . . . those are the four . . . one more . . .

President Johnson: What about [Wallace] Bennett [R-Utah]?

Humphrey: Bennett is wobbly. That's the fifth one that we counted out, but he's wobbly. It looks like a possibility, but Mecham, Tower, Goldwater, Simpson, Bennett, and let's see, who the hell was the other one . . . possibly, yeah, the other one I had was [Bourke] Hickenlooper, and . . .

President Johnson: And [Roman] Hruska [R-Nebraska]?

Humphrey: No. Hruska is with us. [Peter] Dominick [R-Colorado] is with us. [Karl] Mundt is with us. B. Everett Jordan of Idaho is with us. The other possibility I saw was John Williams of Delaware. So that would leave 26. I . . .

President Johnson: I believe Williams will go with us.

Humphrey: I think he will. I think Williams and Bennett will go. That's what Dirksen is planning on giving him 28, which he thinks he's got. I think he's got 26, just to be a little gun shy and careful.

President Johnson: Okay. All right.

The conversation then turned to other matters.

.   .   .

Shortly after this conversation, Robert Byrd of West Virginia made one last attempt to keep the filibuster going. He stood up just before 8:00 in the evening and spoke for 14 hours, not stopping till the morning of June 10. In addition to reading the entire text of the Magna Carta, he rehashed the old arguments against federal civil rights reform by warning that the bill would be a new form of slavery, an unconstitutional imposition of federal power on the states. He was speaking in 1964, but his words echoed what southern segregationists had been asserting for generations, and behind him stood the ghosts of John C. Calhoun and his secessionist brethren. Less than an hour after Byrd finished his defense of legal discrimination, the Senate voted 71 to 29 to bring the longest filibuster in Senate history to an end.

Forty-four Democrats were joined by 27 Republicans. Dirksen did indeed have the votes—and some to spare—which allowed Carl Hayden to vote no. Johnson was elated, and his exuberance extended even to Robert Kennedy, whom he hailed as a hero that day in the White House. Richard Russell did not take defeat graciously and complained that the South had been the victim of a legislative "lynch mob." He threatened to delay the debate on the floor with hundreds of new procedural motions, but without the acquiescence of the majority, he was overruled. Humphrey, Mansfield, and Dirksen scheduled the full vote on the Civil

Rights Act for June 19, and after the last version of the jury trial amendment was passed on June 17, senatorial speeches were scheduled prior to
the final vote. These were not meant to alter the outcome because by this
point almost all the senators had decided where they stood. Instead, the
speeches were meant to record their positions for posterity, and some of
the rhetoric was memorable.

Mansfield offered high praise for his Senate colleagues, especially
Dirksen and Humphrey. He also invoked the name of John F. Kennedy,
including the valediction, "This indeed is his moment, as well as the Senate's." On a more disturbing note, Barry Goldwater, the conservative
Republican from Arizona who would soon become his party's nominee for
president, rose to explain why he was voting against the bill. He called the
provisions outlawing race bias in employment and public accommodations
unconstitutional. He argued the case for states' rights and claimed the act
was a dangerous usurpation of state power. He warned that it posed a
threat to the entire system of government, and though he spoke against
racial discrimination, he announced that he could not in good conscience
support the act. Reporting on the speech, *Newsweek* said Goldwater had
"astonished nearly everybody by the depth and harshness of his position."

On the verge of a significant victory, Johnson was worried. He feared
the bill would cause an outbreak of violence in the South. The Freedom
Summer, the scuffles between police and civil rights protestors in St.
Augustine culminating in the arrest of Martin Luther King, and the general feeling of resentment in the region appeared to Johnson to be potentially explosive. On the afternoon of June 19, he explained his concerns in
a telephone call with Dr. George Taylor, who had been Johnson's delegate
during a recent railroad strike.[28] Johnson wanted Taylor to serve as his
"conciliator" with the governors of the southern states, to work to implement the provisions of the Civil Rights Act. Without effective communication between the White House, the Justice Department, and the
southern governors, Johnson believed there would be "bloodshed."

What was needed was a process of conciliation, which would allow
infractions of the Civil Rights Act to be handled gradually, case by case.
There was considerable concern that as soon as the bill passed, civil rights
leaders would mobilize and flood the courts and the Justice Department
with thousands of complaints, and that this would provoke southern
authorities to stiffen and refuse to enforce the bill's provisions, even in the
face of federal power. Johnson imagined a nightmare scenario of hundreds

---

[28]George W. Taylor was a professor of industrial relations at the University of Pennsylvania's
Wharton School.

of simultaneous crises, each on the scale of Ole Miss or Birmingham. Understandably, the President wanted to prevent that at all costs.

On the afternoon of June 19, the Senate passed the bill by a vote of 73 to 27. Six Republicans joined 21 Democrats in opposing the legislation. Uncertainty about what would happen when the revised bill reached the House, as well as apprehension about violence in the South, did not dim Johnson's satisfaction. One of the first people he called was the head of the NAACP, Roy Wilkins.

Friday, June 19, 1964, 5:20 P.M.

Roy Wilkins

President Johnson: Feel pretty good?

Roy Wilkins: I do feel pretty good. I haven't got the official news yet. I've been at a . . .

President Johnson: 73 to 27.

Wilkins: 73–27. Mr. President, that's very good news.

President Johnson: Well, you're a mighty good man. You deserve all the credit. I sure do salute you. And I'm mighty proud of you. Our troubles are just beginning. I guess you know that. . . .

They spend several minutes discussing Johnson's speech in San Francisco before turning to the question of whom to appoint as conciliator.

I talked to Bobby [Kennedy] yesterday, and we think that a good deal of the success of whether we get this thing going or not is going to depend on getting the right man for conciliator.[29] And we thought of a lot . . . and the first thing we decided is that we probably ought to get a southerner that had the confidence of our organizations, and maybe we could bring the two together that way and give some leadership.[30] But every time we run into one, why, we run into one that either wouldn't have your confidence or wouldn't have the other side. So we finally . . . I concluded that maybe we ought to try to get a professional. So I called Dr. Taylor, George W. Taylor, who settled the railroad strike for me; he's professor up in Pennsylvania. He was the head of the War Labor Board during the war under Roosevelt.

Wilkins: Yeah, I know his name. He has a very good reputation.

President Johnson: He's a wonderful man. Bobby said he had checked with a good many pople and that they all thought that he would be mighty

---

[29]"This thing" refers to the implementation of the the Civil Rights Act.

[30]The two main sides were the civil rights organizations and the southern state authorities.

acceptable, if we could get him. Now they don't know him in the South, but he's a fair man, and he's got a judicious temperament. And he's kind of like you all, he doesn't shoot . . . he sees what he's doing before he moves, and he's quiet and humble, modest. I saw him handle these tough railroad boys pretty well. . . .

They then go over several other names, including the mayor of Atlanta, William B. Hartsfield. Wilkins responds enthusiastically to that idea, though he says that if Johnson cannot get a southerner, then Taylor would do.

President Johnson: I want to take some leadership. I'm just afraid of what's gonna happen this summer, like I saw yesterday at St. Augustine. I talked to that governor two or three times, and our people, Lee White, says that he moved in a hundred people and then he moved in another hundred, and that he was given reasonably good protection there.[31] And I thought from the result we got there maybe I ought to call each one of the individual governors. Then I decided it would be too many. There's 19 states that don't have an accommodation law. So I'm gonna write 'em all a letter. I'm a little afraid to call 'em to Washington 'cause I'm afraid the local demagogues will say that they're selling out to Hubert Humphrey and Bobby Kennedy and Lyndon Johnson.

Wilkins: Yes, yes, yes. You're right about that.

President Johnson: And we get 'em up there and [George] Wallace and Johnson would probably take the lead and start ranting and the other fellas would be afraid not to outdo them.[32] So if you think of anything we can do. I thought maybe we ought to get one or two men representing, maybe kind of have their viewpoints that would carry my message and go around and see these governors. And just tell them that you've got to call meetings now of all your people and we've got to have observance instead of enforcement. If they'll observe the law, then we won't have to take pistols and enforce it.

Wilkins: That's right. That's right. Well, this is the thing . . . I'll think about that and I'll do whatever I can to help. I can't . . . nobody can think of as many ideas as Lyndon Johnson. I say that in all honesty. But I'll do whatever I can.

President Johnson: [*laughing heartily*] We've come a long way in six months.

Wilkins: You've come . . . Did you happen to see that . . . you must have seen that cartoon of the big Texas boot and that little fellow looking

---

[31]He presumably refers to Martin Luther King, who was relatively peacefully arrested there.
[32]Paul Johnson was the governor of Mississippi.

up there, the Republican, saying, "I know they grow them big in Texas, but this is ridiculous!"

President Johnson: [*Laughs.*]

Wilkins: I thought about that, and one other thing, if I may keep you one more second.

President Johnson: Sure, I got plenty of time.

Wilkins: That speech of yours in Ann Arbor . . . I mean, I'm supposed to be interested in civil rights and I am interested in civil rights, and that's my first business. But I'm interested in my country, too. And I think that speech in Ann Arbor was simply magnificent. . . .

President Johnson: Why thank you so much.

Wilkins: A magnificent speech.

President Johnson: We got a lot of nice compliments on it, but you remember when we were talking when we had to get that petition signed to try and get it out of the Rules Committee?[33] And we finally had to get 185 and now we've gone the hard way, every bit, cloture and everything else, but we've done it.

Wilkins: It was absolutely magnificent and of course, [Richard] Russell put his finger on two things. First, he said it was Lyndon Johnson. And second, he said it was the clergy. He hasn't been wrong much. [*Both of them laugh.*]

President Johnson: I just hope that we can get through the summer. You give me your ideas, and I haven't heard from you. Pick up that phone and call me once in a while.

Wilkins: Thank you, sir.

President Johnson: You talk to Whitney [Young] about this, will you?

Wilkins: I'll talk to him right away.

President Johnson: And anybody you-all can think of down South.

. . .

Though he had asked Wilkins to get in touch with Whitney Young of the Urban League, Johnson ended up speaking to the civil rights leader that evening at about 8:00. "I want to congratulate you," he told Young. "It was a good day for all of us." Young told the President that while he knew Johnson was working on the southern governors and businessmen, he did not want "to see King and Farmer and everybody talking about how they're going to insist on immediate compliance." In Young's opinion, since Johnson was trying to get the governors to agree in principle to the bill, civil rights leaders should not threaten to test it.

---

[33]Johnson was referring to the arduous attempts to get a discharge petition passed by the House in December and January.

Young also suggested that they ought to pay more attention to Mississippi. Both men agreed that if a fire was going to flare up, it would happen there first. They would have been dismayed to know how prescient they were. The civil rights bill passed the Senate on June 19. Then it went back to the House, where Howard Smith once again threatened to prevent its passage. This time, however, it was a hollow threat, for he lacked the necessary support. Public opinion was overwhelmingly in favor of the legislation, as was sentiment in the House. Indeed, the House leadership in both parties had agreed to pass the Senate's version of the bill, and then send it straight to the President for his signature. There would be no further amendments in the House.

But two days after the Senate vote, on the night of Sunday, June 21, three volunteers working for the Mississippi Freedom Project disappeared. Michael Schwerner and Andrew Goodman were white college students from New York. They were accompanied by James Chaney, a young black man from Mississippi. Their disappearance became a national story and seemed to confirm Johnson's worst fears. Two days later, FBI director J. Edgar Hoover called the President and told him that their burned-out car had been found outside Philadelphia, Mississippi. He also told Johnson it was his opinion that the three had been murdered. It would be some time, however, before their bodies were found. The search for the three young men became a major FBI investigation, overseen by a reluctant Hoover, who was convinced this was just the beginning of a wave of violence. He did not want the FBI to be put in the position of enforcing order in the South.

Johnson reacted swiftly. He did everything in his power to prevent the incident from igniting the South. For the White House, June 23 was a frantic day spent trying to contain the situation. Johnson had dozens of telephone conversations, with Hoover, Katzenbach, Burke Marshall, Senator Eastland (who said the whole thing was "a publicity stunt"), Bobby Kennedy, and others. In the late afternoon, to his profound annoyance, Johnson learned that Roy Wilkins, who had been so supportive just four days earlier, now planned to mobilize the NAACP to protest what they took to be the slow response of the Johnson administration to the dangers facing civil rights workers in Mississippi. Informed that the NAACP planned to picket the White House to demand protection for the Mississippi volunteers, Johnson told Lee White, "I think you ought to try to get a hold of Roy Wilkins and ask him what in the hell we've done. I've been on the phone all day long. . . . Ask him what else he wants us to do. . . . I don't see what good they think they can do by picketing the White House. They think they can do something."

Johnson had staked his political future on the passage of civil rights legislation, but whatever satisfaction he felt was tempered in these final weeks by his recognition of the real dangers that lay ahead. And in late June, Mississippi continued to occupy the attention of both the President and the nation.

It was not until July 2 that the House approved the Senate version of the bill, which it did by a margin of 289 to 126. Anticipating the bill's passage on that day, Johnson had prepared a signing ceremony at the White House for late afternoon. But even that did not go smoothly because of lingering anxieties about what might happen once the President signed the bill into law. On the one hand, there existed the potential for public defiance in the South, which Johnson discussed by phone with Robert Kennedy that morning. At the same time, there was a risk that southern blacks would celebrate and demonstrate, and that this might provoke a violent response by whites in the region. The last thing Johnson wanted was for the historic occasion to be marred by social unrest in the South. Kennedy even suggested it might be best to wait until after July 4, so that supporters of the bill could not take advantage of Independence Day celebrations, combining the usual parties with civil rights victory parades.

In several conversations on the morning and afternoon of July 2, Johnson discussed the potential pitfalls of signing before the Fourth. Lingering in the background was an even greater concern that southern whites would rise en masse against the bill and that blacks would in turn challenge and provoke local authorities to retaliate. Of course, there was little Johnson could do at this juncture to prevent the worst from happening. After a long fight, the bill was ready for the President's signature, and Johnson had to take a leap of faith, hoping that when the bill became the law of the nation, it would be respected even by its opponents.

Thursday, July 2, 1964, 10:25 A.M.

Clare Booth Luce[34]

President Johnson: Hello.
Clare Booth Luce: Oh, good morning, Mr. President. How are you? Clare Luce here.

---

[34]Clare Booth Luce was a former Republican congresswoman from Connecticut and a former ambassador to Italy. She was married to Henry Luce, founder of *Time*.

President Johnson: Fine thank you.

Luce: I'm sorry I'm wasting your time. I called up because I heard yesterday that you were going to sign the civil rights bill on the 4th of July, and it seemed to be such an appalling idea that I placed a call yesterday, and they just put it through and I just read the newspapers that you aren't, thank God; forgive me for wasting your time.

President Johnson: No, no, I never had any thought of doing that.

Luce: Well, it was in all the papers.

President Johnson: I know it, honey, but [*laughter*] I don't want to be critical of the press [*laughter*].

Luce: I know, do you mean to say they put that in without asking?

President Johnson: I mean no human being has ever discussed it with me, and I have never given any indication that I would do anything except sign it the first moment it was available, which would be Thursday. It's very much like the great war speeches we make all the time you know. I made a speech out in Minneapolis the other day, for ten minutes a thousand words on peace, but I said in order to have it sometimes we have to risk war and we have to be strong and they took half of a sentence [*laughter*] and the peace went by the wayside and the headlines were all that I was launching a new war.

Luce: I know, it's terribly difficult. I don't know what's happened to the papers; they pick up this something and the other. Well I was—

President Johnson: You take my word there's not one person out of 190 million that ever mentioned the 4th of July to me, and I have not mentioned it to one.

Luce: Well, this was given in the *New York Times*—

President Johnson: That's right—

Luce:—and I thought no, no, I mean this can't be because—

President Johnson: I think what happened, I think what happened, Mr. [Charles] Halleck wanted to take off a week before the San Francisco meeting so that some of his members could go and work on the platform. And I think that in the discussions on the Hill, they decided they'd try to get through this week, and it happens that . . . I think the 4th must be on Saturday. And that that would be the end of the week when they would normally adjourn so they would have to pass it by that time, and therefore it would be available. So the story is, I've watched them and I'd say in fairness to the press they've all originated on the House side of the Congress, and I think that's because it just happens that they will be adjourning, but they're not going to be adjourning Saturday; they'll be getting through Thursday. They moved faster than they thought, you see. So I plan to sign it tonight as soon as it's available.

Luce: Oh well, that is very good news, it would have been quite improper to inject racial struggle into the 4th of July. Well, I'm sorry to have bothered you. How is Lady Bird?

The conversation continued, but now Luce and Lady Bird discussed Luce's proposal to conduct an interview with the First Lady.

Thursday, July 2, 1964, 11:19 A.M.

Robert Kennedy

The first few minutes of the conversation covered Kennedy's trip to Poland and a discussion Kennedy had with a reporter about his potential candidacy.

Robert Kennedy: Could I just take a minute. . . . I talked to Jack Valenti, and I don't know whether this has gone too far about the signing of the bill; this is a . . . you know if it's signed today, we are going to have a rather difficult weekend, holiday weekend anyway . . . and . . . whether . . . I'm encouraging . . . whether that Friday and Saturday with the 4th of July and firecrackers going off anyway, with Negroes running all over the South figuring that they get the day off, that they're going to go into every hotel and motel and every restaurant. Whether if it's possible, and again I don't know how far it's gone, whether it would be possible to postpone until Monday and sign it so that it's in the middle of the week. The other problem of course is that I've met with Governor Collins this morning and he really hasn't got any appropriation; he hasn't got his machinery set up and so he won't be able to move in on any of these situations.[35] There is an advantage . . . if everything was equal . . . there would have been a great advantage in signing it at the beginning of the week, but, as I say, I don't know whether it's gone so far that you feel it's necessary to sign it today.

President Johnson: No, I don't think so; here were the considerations that entered into it. They all announced . . . we got to stop that, you tell your publicity man over there don't say a damn word about what I'm gonna do. There have been all these stories come out about who I'm talking to in the South and what I'm doing and the kind of thing we discussed but didn't carry out. And there have been two or three columns written about it. Well, the House did the same thing on me. Some of their people up there planned on what the President is going to do. So they all got it

---

[35]LeRoy Collins was governor of Florida.

pretty well scattered over the country that he was going to wait until July the 4th to sign it, so that he'd tie it in with the Declaration of Independence and that was pretty well accepted and generated all over the country before we could stop it. We never mentioned it, never opened our mouth, never said a word.

So then some of them started coming back and saying, "Well, that's not fair; the Hallecks and the rest of them who've participated in this thing are leaving and they are going to their convention and you just want to have it so that you'll have Humphrey and one or two of them up there taking all the glory and the people that helped do it . . . Why do you wait? Why don't you go on and do it when they pass it?" So I asked them when they thought they'd get through with it, and they said that they thought they'd get through with it by 3[:00] or 4:00. Now they tell me there's some debate that may go on later tonight. I told them that my plan would be to try to sign it as soon as the bill got to me, that I'd already told them how I felt about it; they knew that, there's no point of waiting until the 4th of July, that I thought that'd just irritate a lot of people . . . unnecessarily. And then I didn't think we ought to wait two or three days. So that's kind of how we got off the hook on the 4th of July by signing when it gets to us. Now, when it gets to us, I don't know, but I think it'll be late today. We tentatively told them that we planned to do it today, before we heard about this, before I knew that you thought it'd be better to go over until next week. Now . . . we could back up on it, but I doubt the wisdom of it after we said that if the bill gets to us . . .

Kennedy: I see, I see and I suppose all the Republicans will be gone next week.

President Johnson: Yes, yes, they're quitting tonight.

Kennedy: Well then, I think we'd better go ahead. . . .

President Johnson: I don't even know whether they'll even come or not; I haven't invited them because we don't know what time. I told them to get Lee White and Larry O'Brien, put them in charge of the signings, and get in touch with your people and see everybody that ought to be invited. We'll try to have it in the East Room around 7:00 if the bill's here. If it's not, we'll have it whenever we get the bill, but we're kind of waiting until 2[:00] or 3:00 to see what time . . . whether the bill . . . it's got an hour on the rule, and they come in at 12. If they make them redirect it two or three times, why it may be late, but if we have it, I'd rather have it tonight than to have it Saturday. And if we have it past Saturday, I think they would think that I held it up two or three days until they got out of town because they've been . . . they've . . . they questioned . . . I asked them to stay next week and act on some of these important bills, and they said that wasn't fair play, that I was being unfair to them, and that they wouldn't pass civil rights unless I let them go. Well, I never did agree to let them go, but they kind of had an agreement among themselves to pass civil rights and then go. Now if I held it over I think they'd say that I was trying to take a little glory away from them on the bipartisan basis, don't you?

Kennedy: I see, well you mean, because they won't be here. Yeah, well, I think that's possible. I do think that's possible.

President Johnson: I think that it's important that we extend them an invitation at a time when they can come, even if they can't come. I don't know, Halleck may go fishing. But one of them told me, I've forgotten who it was, I believe Mansfield called up and said that he was going to be in session tonight. He didn't know whether he could come or not, but I believe that we ought to go ahead in light of the fact that they'll be gone next week.

Kennedy: That's fine, I'd like to have a chance to talk to you about Poland. . . .

Thursday, July 2, 1964, 12:09 P.M.

Roy Wilkins

President Johnson: Ah Roy, I need to have you do a little hard thinking for me.

Roy Wilkins: Yeah.

President Johnson: This bill looks like it will be ready late today; they're trying to filibuster it some in the House and it may not be, but word got out that we might have a big celebration and signing ceremony on July the 4th. That came from some of the people on the Hill. We talked around here about it and nearly everybody concluded that the wise thing to do was to sign the bill as soon as we could and name the conciliation director as soon as we could after it became available. So we've planned tentatively to do that this evening.

Wilkins: Yeah.

President Johnson: A question has been raised now. I've talked to Louie Martin and some of the folks here, and they think we ought to sign it as soon as we can after it's passed.[36] But a question has been raised now that if we sign it that quick, that Saturday throughout the South, it's a big day when everybody's in town shooting firecrackers and it's the 4th of July

---

[36]Louis Martin was a former newspaper reporter with a leading black paper, and an adviser to President Kennedy.

and celebrating and fellows get a few drinks of beer and we could kick off a wave of trouble that would wind up a lot of people getting hurt, and maybe we ought to wait until after the weekend. Now we've already tentatively announced that we're gonna do it tonight, if the bill is available, that is my better judgment. But I thought before I did it that maybe I'd better check with one or two of my friends and let them think about it and see what their judgment was. They know the situation better than I do maybe.

Wilkins: Mr. President, I think the idea, which has already been suggested as signing it as soon as it's available is the correct idea. I think you have the right hunch here. I think a delay would simply mean that you felt that you were . . . ought to delay signing it. You know it would be interpreted that way.

President Johnson: I'll tell you another thing that worries me; the Republicans are leaving for their convention and they're getting out tonight. Congress is not going to be in session in the House tomorrow, and I'm afraid . . . I don't know whether they'll come or not, but it was bipartisan and I think that we ought to have Republican legislators like Kuchel and like Halleck just the same. Dirksen just like we have Humphrey.

Wilkins: That was my second reason, the first one had to do with the problem perhaps of violence, but the second one is that the Republicans do deserve a chance at this. . . .

President Johnson: That's what I think and I think they'd charge me with trying to be cute if I put off signing after it's ready to sign until after they left town.

Wilkins: That's right, that's right and this is the overwhelming political reason. And that's what's being talked about in Washington, and I was there last night, and they said the Republicans wanted a chance at it and that's the reason it's being moved up, and I think it would be regarded as a gracious gesture on your part to sign it promptly so they could take part in the ceremony and go about their convention.

They then briefly discussed who the conciliator would be, before wrapping up.

Wilkins: . . . I thank you for what you did on this bill.

President Johnson: Well, I have great confidence in you and I think we've got a long hard fight ahead, but if we work together, we'll find the answers—

Wilkins: We'll do it—

President Johnson:—because we're right—

Wilkins:—yes, we'll do it—

President Johnson:—because we're right. Good-bye.

Wilkins: Thank you.

Thursday, July 2, 1964, 12:09 P.M.

George Reedy[37]

George Reedy: One quick question. If they ask me about that cabinet meeting, what should I tell them?

President Johnson: I'd tell them that we're going to have a cabinet meeting and that I'm going to go over the civil rights bill with them . . . general provisions, ask if they're . . . all of us in cooperation so that the government can all understand its obligations under the bill and the leadership that we're expected to provide. I'll probably ask them to help us every way they can.

Reedy: Right. Okay sir.

President Johnson: Anything else?

Reedy: No, that's all.

President Johnson: You heard any more about the signing?

Reedy: No sir, I talked to Larry about it, and Larry still seems fairly sanguine about 3:00. He says it might even go earlier.

President Johnson: Does he think it ought to be signed today, or put over the weekend?

Reedy: I didn't ask him sir.

President Johnson: Bobby Kennedy called up and said he thought this might cause a lot of violence in the South, but I don't think we ought to wait.

Reedy: No sir, I think it'd be very bad if you wait; it'd look like you were dawdling around just to get a big ceremony or something like that.

President Johnson: I think it'd look like we were waiting until we get out of town, too.

Reedy: Right, I agree. I think it's . . . I think you should handle this as an important bill, one that you aren't playing games with. You're having an appropriate ceremony but you're having it right away because the world has been waiting, this country's been waiting a hundred years for it, and there is no sense in playing around with it now and making what will look like a big public relations ploy. Actually it will be, of course, but it won't look like it this way.

President Johnson: Any other news?

Reedy: No sir, it's pretty quiet otherwise.

．　　．　　．

---

[37]George Reedy was Johnson's press secretary.

Johnson wanted an elaborate signing ceremony. He had a keen under-standing of the need for pomp and circumstance. The event was planned for the early evening in the East Room of the White House and was attended by cabinet officers and Justice Department officials such as Nicholas Katzenbach and Burke Marshall. A place of prominence was reserved for all of the major supporters from the Congress, and for the most significant civil rights leaders—Martin Luther King, A. Philip Randolph, Roy Wilkins, Clarence Mitchell, Whitney Young, and Rosa Parks. The ceremony was televised, and as Johnson set his pen to the 72 copies he was to sign, he addressed the nation once more.

He placed the bill in the context of the American Revolution. "We believe all men have certain unalienable rights," he declared. "Yet many Americans do not enjoy those rights." He said that for more than 180 years, the promise of the Revolution had gone unfulfilled for millions of Americans. Until this day, he intoned, all citizens had been equal in the eyes of God, but as of today, all citizens would also "be equal in the polling booths, in the classrooms, in the factories, and in hotels, restaurants, movie theaters, and other places that provide service to the public." It was time, he declared, to end the moral injustice of racial discrimination. "My fellow citizens," he concluded, "we have come now to a time of testing. We must not fail. Let us close the springs of racial poison."

Just after the ceremony, the President met privately with civil rights leaders and suggested that now that the law had been changed, demon-strations demanding an end to discrimination were no longer necessary. The climate was relaxed and friendly. The assembled leaders, basking in the glow of victory, assured the President that they would do all they could to coordinate their plans with the Justice Department. For now, civil rights leaders did not see the White House as an adversary. They had found an ally in Lyndon Johnson.

Later that evening, after a few congratulatory phone calls, Johnson had a brief exchange with his aide, Bill Moyers. It had been a hard-won fight, he confessed, and though the moral victory was clear, it would have conse-quences. "I think we just delivered the South to the Republican Party for a long time," Johnson remarked, and that fear was not unjustified. In the fall of 1964, Johnson and his running mate, Hubert Humphrey, lost five Deep South states to challenger Barry Goldwater. And four years later, the Republican Richard Nixon narrowly defeated Hubert Humphrey, partly because of unexpected Republican strength in the South. Johnson had done the right thing, but the political price would be high.

Conclusion

The July 4 weekend came and went, and the South did not rise up against the bill. The threatened chaos proved more imagined than real, and while a portion of the South continued to fight on for the lost cause of segregation, after July 2, 1964, the world of Jim Crow began to come to an end.

But that did not mean an end to the civil rights struggle. A bill had become a law, but millions still ardently opposed integration. The President and Congress had crafted a far-reaching piece of legislation, but it did not fully enfranchise African Americans. And prejudice remained part of the fabric of everyday life, not just in the South but throughout the country.

Lyndon Johnson had little time to celebrate the legislative victory. There were scattered episodes of violence, and segregationists like Alabama's George Wallace promised defiance. The atmosphere in Mississippi remained volatile, and the Mississippi Summer Project, which would focus on black disfranchisement, injected considerable energy into the movement, mainly through an umbrella organization, the Council of Federated Organizations (COFO), which was composed largely of SNCC activists. Violence continued to be a way of life for those struggling for racial justice in the South, a fact demonstrated by the disappearance of the three male activists whose bodies were found in an earthern dam a few miles outside of Philadelphia, Mississippi.

COFO also organized the Mississippi Freedom Democratic Party, which would make the right to vote a national issue at the Democratic convention in August. Claiming to represent hundreds of thousands of black Mississippians who were not allowed to vote, its leaders demanded that it be seated as Mississippi's official delegation at the convention, in place of the all-white delegation sent by the state government. Not sur-

331

prisingly, when the convention began in Atlantic City, the Democratic Party found itself in a sharp, brief crisis.

Johnson was furious. He had wanted the convention to be a perfectly staged beginning to a successful presidential campaign. Instead, the Mississippi activists threatened to turn the convention into an embarrassment for the President and his party. Avoiding the public spotlight on the issue, Johnson delegated Hubert Humphrey to settle the matter, and after several days of backroom maneuvers, an agreement was reached that would allow two of the alternate Mississippi delegates to be seated. Only after some distinguished civil rights leaders had urged compromise, was the impasse broken. In their eyes, Johnson had earned the right to request a deal, and beyond that, he was a far better choice than was Republican Barry Goldwater, who had opposed the Civil Rights Act.

But the issue could be shelved only temporarily. The problem of African American voter registration remained acute, and the Freedom Summer had exposed how bad the situation was. Johnson won the fall election overwhelmingly against Goldwater, and of the 6 million blacks who voted, nearly 95 percent supported LBJ. But the number of blacks who voted in the Deep South represented less than 50 percent of those eligible to do so. Discriminatory laws, which had remained on the books since the nineteenth century, prevented many black Americans from registering, and the voting provisions in the Civil Rights Act of 1964 did little to assist them.

To complicate matters, the compromise reached at the convention opened a fissure between the established leaders of the civil rights movement and the younger, grassroots activists who led SNCC and the Freedom Project. Martin Luther King understood as well as anyone that the fight was not over and that maintaining his position as an effective leader meant he would have to tackle the next crucial issue: voting rights.

Lyndon Johnson was not eager for another civil rights crisis. His relationship with Martin Luther King had soured, and he had failed to oppose the personal vendetta against the civil rights leader carried out by FBI chief J. Edgar Hoover, who continued to direct the Bureau to investigate the most intimate details of King's life, in an effort to discredit him. Believing he had gone to extraordinary lengths to advance the civil rights cause, Johnson wanted to turn his administration's attention to the War on Poverty and the programs of the Great Society. Nevertheless, he did not wish to block voting reform, and in his State of the Union address in January, he endorsed voting rights legislation. The black population had supported the Democratic Party in overwhelming numbers, and the more southern blacks were able to exercise their right to vote, the easier it would be for the Democratic Party to compensate for the potential loss of white southerners who felt LBJ and his party had betrayed them. But while Johnson looked eventually toward a bill on voting rights, it was not at the top of his agenda.

Hoping to force the issue, the Southern Christian Leadership Conference (SCLC) targeted Selma, Alabama, a city that represented in microcosm how black southerners were intimidated and prevented from voting in the Deep South. The small city had nearly 30,000 residents, more than half of them black. Yet blacks accounted for fewer than 400 of the city's registered voters. Just as Birmingham had been chosen because of the likelihood of confrontation with its police commissioner, "Bull" Connor, the SCLC chose Selma partly because of its sheriff, James Clark. Like Connor, Clark, with his ruddy complexion and ample paunch, was a caricature of a southern lawman. He was also easily provoked, and King and the SCLC were intent on exposing the violence that kept Selma's blacks living in fear.

The protests began in February 1965, and at first, Sheriff Clark did not respond violently. He arrested the protestors for illegal assembly, but swiftly and without police brutality. Midmonth, one demonstrator, Jimmy Lee Jackson, was shot and killed, but the tragic episode happened away from the glare of television cameras. While Jackson's death inflamed the situation in Selma, the national repercussions were slight.

On March 7, 1965, things changed. Defying an order issued by Alabama governor George Wallace that banned a scheduled march, 500 protestors approached the Edmund Pettus Bridge, where they were met by nearly 100 police officers, mounted on horses and armed with bullwhips. Refusing to disperse, the protestors, led by Hosea Williams and John Lewis, tried to walk across the bridge. Sheriff Clark ordered his men to charge, and in the resulting melee, police officers whipped and bludgeoned the unarmed marchers without mercy. The horrific scenes, captured by television cameras, were viewed throughout the country, and, as had happened two years before in Birmingham, the reaction was swift and unequivocal.

The White House received a flood of calls and telegrams demanding that the President do something to address the situation. Thousands of clergy assembled in Washington or headed to Selma to offer the protestors their support. King and the SCLC organized a march to Montgomery, Alabama's capital, to drive home the point that this was a problem throughout the state and the region, and was hardly confined to Selma or its brutal sheriff.

The Johnson administration responded on two levels. The President sought to get King, Wallace, and officials in Selma to agree to avoid further violent confrontations. Within days, Johnson made a widely publicized speech denouncing the brutality of the Selma officials and assailing those who had tried to prevent black Americans from exercising "the precious right to vote." A week later, on March 14, the President addressed a joint session of Congress and called for the passage of the Voting Rights Act. Validating the rhetoric of Martin Luther King, Johnson declared, "We shall overcome!" A hundred years had passed since the end of the Civil War, he said, yet black Americans were still "not fully free." Only when all state barriers to voting were removed, and when all tests and crafty devices designed to disfranchise blacks were finally abolished would the promise of the Emancipation Proclamation be realized.

It took less than five months for the bill to make its way through both houses of Congress. Whereas the Civil Rights Act of 1964 had faced an arduous road through the House and Senate, the Voting Rights Act confronted fewer obstacles. Having soundly defeated Goldwater and carried with him numerous congressmen and senators, Johnson had considerable authority in Congress. While he needed the support of Republicans to overcome southern Democrats, that was easy to muster. The results of the fall election had strengthened the coalition that had passed the 1964 legislation, and this time a southern filibuster in the Senate was defeated by a resounding cloture vote in days, rather than months. The only serious debate revolved around the ban on the poll tax and the exercise of federal authority, but the final bill would be unequivocal.

On August 6, 1965, in a ceremony in the Capitol Rotunda, Lyndon Johnson signed the Voting Rights Act into law. From that day on, there would be no more literacy tests, no more poll taxes, and no more legal restrictions on the right to vote. "This is a victory for the freedom of the American Negro," Johnson said in signing the bill. "But it is also a victory for the freedom of the American nation." Because of the act, he concluded, "every family, across the great, entire searching land—will live stronger in liberty, will live more splendid in expectation, and will be prouder to be an American."

The effect of the Voting Rights Act was dramatic. While fewer than 25 percent of Alabama blacks had voted in the 1964 election, nearly 60 percent voted in 1968. In Mississippi, 7 percent had voted in 1964; in 1968, the number was 60 percent. These changes occurred throughout the South, and by the early 1970s, African Americans would be elected to statewide offices and federal positions.

Despite the legislation, the second half of the 1960s was not an era of tranquil race relations in the United Sates. The civil rights struggle moved north, and with varying degrees of success, a new generation of leaders began to confront more insidious and no less entrenched forms of racial discrimination. Although the legal barriers had been removed, the law had not changed the hearts and minds of many in the United States.

But the Civil Rights Act of 1964, along with the Voting Rights Act of 1965, remain significant achievements in the struggle for racial justice. That in their wake the country did not immediately succeed in abolishing discrimination, prejudice, and race hatred is not a mark of legislative impotence or failure. It would, after all, be naive to imagine that the enactment of laws could at once cause such age-old problems to disappear. Legislation, no matter how powerfully written, is no substitute for the more deeply rooted changes that take hold slowly in the minds and hearts of a people—changes that cause individuals to believe genuinely in the principle of human equality. The passage of civil rights legislation in these years marked one step, albeit a significant one, on the path to making America a more just society.

Kennedy, Johnson, and Civil Rights

It is worth reiterating that the tape recordings on which this book is based reveal but one aspect of a lengthy struggle. And by themselves, the tapes can present a somewhat distorted picture of the quest for racial justice, making it seem that presidents were the decisive force, responding to pressures from civil rights activists, trying to contain the chaos in the South, and finally, energetically supporting legislation.

But for a long time, the White House was not the key player; indeed, it came late to the struggle. In fact, presidential activism lasted little more than three years, not terribly long in a campaign that had been waged over many decades. For his part, John Kennedy was more reactive than active on civil rights during most of his short presidency. The events surrounding Ole Miss in 1962 represented a civil rights baptism for the young President, and he emerged with a heightened awareness of the volatility of the struggle and the intractability of the race problem in America. Only after Birmingham in May 1963 did he commit his administration's full resources to legislative action, and Kennedy's decision, in turn, placed his successor in a position to make civil rights a key priority.

Taken alone, the tapes do not accurately represent what occurred in these years. In the world captured by the White House taping system, the President and his aides stand at the very center of everything, but on civil rights, this was surely not the case. Clearly, if generations of black Americans had not devoted their lives to making real the promise of equal rights, the White House and Congress would not have acted as they did in 1964. Nevertheless, if Kennedy and Johnson had not embraced the cause as they did, the legal barriers would not have fallen at that time.

The tapes show that Kennedy and Johnson were central to the black freedom campaign, and suggest how crucial it was for the President to endorse the movement's aims. It is worth remembering that without the backing of the White House, no bill could have survived southern opposition in Congress. Just as the civil rights movement had to overcome the resistance and reluctance of the White House, Kennedy and Johnson had to overcome the inertia and opposition on Capitol Hill. While many in Congress supported civil rights reform, those legislators by themselves could not have defeated the determined group of civil rights opponents in the Senate and House. The dynamics in Congress, especially in the Senate, meant a small group of die-hard opponents could kill meaningful legislation.

Until 1963, those opponents had obstructed any substantive changes in federal law on questions of race and equal rights. While the legislation of 1957 and 1960 set a precedent on which the 1964 bill would build, neither of those earlier efforts addressed the core issues at the heart of the Jim Crow system. They did not make it illegal to keep black Americans from eating at a lunch counter, using a water fountain, or sitting where they pleased on a bus. Those earlier laws did not make it easier for a black person, who was denied a job on the basis of color, to sue for discrimination, nor did they provide the federal government with the power to prevent discrimination in the face of state and local officials who wished to maintain it.

But the 1964 Civil Rights Act accomplished precisely these things, and only when the White House used the power of the presidency to pressure Congress into rewriting earlier legislation did it come to fruition. At times, this meant mediating between civil rights activists and congressional liberals who wanted to go farther. At other moments, Kennedy and Johnson refused the demands of civil rights leaders and insisted that half a loaf was better than none. That raised suspicions that they were interested in their political fortunes rather than in the cause of justice, a perception that made civil rights leaders reluctant to trust either man to do the right thing.

But after May 1963, when Kennedy had joined the civil rights crusade, and later, when Johnson signaled his continuing commitment, civil rights leaders recognized that their suspicions had been unwarranted. There were, to be sure, disagreements about how far and how fast to go, but black leaders realized that at last they had an ally not an adversary in the White House. As A. Philip Randolph told President Kennedy on August 28, 1963, just after the March on Washington: "It's going to take nothing less than a crusade to win approval [in Congress] for these civil rights measures. . . . And if it's going to take a crusade, I think nobody can lead this crusade but you." As one of the movement's elders, Randolph knew what it meant to confront an indifferent, even hostile, White House, and after mid-1963, he believed that in Kennedy and then in Johnson, the movement had found reliable partners.

That did not mean the relationship was easy. During Kennedy's tenure, the White House sometimes viewed civil rights leaders as unreasonable in their demands and ungrateful in their responses, and even after Birmingham had caused a shift in public opinion, the White House remained cautious and inclined to move slowly. That made for some tense encounters, but the relationship was no longer adversarial. Almost without exception, civil rights leaders acknowledged at that time and later that Kennedy and Johnson had taken a bold stand and run political risks to end legal discrimination.

It is tempting to close on a triumphal note, but subsequent events make such a conclusion problematic. The 1960s did not unfold as many had hoped, and by 1965, the coalition that had allowed for the passage of the acts was beginning to unravel. Those civil rights leaders who had lobbied the White House two years before found that they no longer possessed the same authority in the African American community. The movement had begun to pass them by, and the civil rights struggle was riven by competing factions and conflicting philosophies with no clear consensus on either methods or goals. After 1965, no longer would a few leaders from the NAACP, the SCLC, or CORE congregate at the White House to coordinate strategy. As the war in Vietnam generated increasing pressures on the Oval Office, Lyndon Johnson would be compelled to wage other battles, and the relationship between the President and civil rights leaders would feel the strain.

Nevertheless, the years documented on the civil rights tapes were marked by a convergence between what was right and what was possible, between what two Presidents believed to be just and what they worked to achieve. John Kennedy's ringing rhetoric announcing his bill in June 1963 and Lyndon Johnson's promise to honor his predecessor's civil rights legacy were framed in terms of fundamental human rights and freedoms. Their language, in many ways, echoed that of Martin Luther King. Despite the political maneuvering that was necessary to pass the bill, the struggle was less about congressional horse trading than it was about attempting to realize ideals that were often proclaimed but rarely fulfilled.

The tapes reveal two men grappling with the sublime and the mundane in politics. In this brief period, the civil rights struggle helped bring out what many Americans yearn for in their political leaders: a willingness to confront seriously the question of what America represents as a nation; a conviction that the fortunes of one's political future or one's party matter less than the common good; and an understanding that a country founded on exceptional ideals will prosper only if those ideals are honored.

Bibliographic Essay

The presidential tape recordings on which this book is based were obtained from the John F. Kennedy Library in Boston and the Lyndon Baines Johnson Library in Austin, Texas. The Kennedy civil rights tapes from 1962 and 1963 are easily accessible to those who wish to listen to them at the John F. Kennedy Library, and copies of the tapes can also be purchased from the library. Tapes of President Johnson's 1963 and 1964 telephone conversations on civil rights are also readily available at the Lyndon Baines Johnson Library, and copies of the tapes can also be purchased from the library.

In preparing this volume, we have consulted and, where helpful, quoted from the following oral histories obtained at the Kennedy and Johnson libraries. From the John F. Kennedy Library: James Farmer, Nicholas Katzenbach, Martin Luther King, Jr., Burke Marshall, Norbert Schlei, Theodore Sorensen, Lee White, and Roy Wilkins. From the Lyndon Baines Johnson Library: James Eastland, James Farmer, Hubert Humphrey, Nicholas Katzenbach, Burke Marshall, Harry McPherson, Clarence Mitchell, A. Philip Randolph, Roy Wilkins, and Whitney Young.

The secondary literature on Jim Crow and the early years of the civil rights struggle is vast. In preparing this volume, the following studies have been particularly helpful: Leon Litwack, *Trouble in Mind: Black Southerners in the Age of Jim Crow* (New York: Knopf, 1998); James M. McPherson, *The Abolitionist Legacy: From Reconstruction to the NAACP* (Princeton, NJ: Princeton University Press, 1975); August Meier, *Negro Thought in America, 1880–1915* (Ann Arbor: University of Michigan Press, 1988; orig. 1963); Wilson Jeremiah Moses, *The Golden Age of Black Nationalism, 1850–1925* (New York: Oxford University Press, 1978); George M. Fredrickson, *The Black Image in the White Mind: The Debate on Afro-American Character and Destiny, 1817–1914* (New York: Harper and Row,

1971); C. Vann Woodward, *The Strange Career of Jim Crow* (New York: Oxford University Press, 1974; orig. 1955); Edward L. Ayers, *The Promise of the New South: Life After Reconstruction* (New York: Oxford University Press, 1992); Charles Flint Kellogg, *NAACP: A History of the National Association for the Advancement of Colored People, 1909–1920* (Baltimore: Johns Hopkins University Press, 1967).

On Booker T. Washington, the standard work is Louis Harlan's two-volume biography: *Booker T. Washington: The Making of a Black Leader, 1856–1901* (New York: Oxford University Press, 1972) and *Booker T. Washington: The Wizard of Tuskegee, 1901–1915* (New York: Oxford University Press, 1983). On W. E. B. Du Bois, see David Levering Lewis's superb two-volume biography: *W. E. B. Du Bois: Biography of a Race, 1868–1919* (New York: Henry Holt, 1993) and *W. E. B. Du Bois: The Fight for Equality and the American Century, 1919–1963* (New York: Henry Holt, 2000). A solid account is Manning Marable, *W. E. B. Du Bois: Black Radical Democrat* (Boston: Twayne Publishing, 1986). On the literary aspects of Du Bois's work, see Arnold Rampersad, *The Art and Imagination of W. E. B. Du Bois* (Cambridge, MA: Harvard University Press, 1976). See also Adolph L. Reed, Jr., *W. E. B. Du Bois and American Political Thought: Fabianism and the Color Line* (New York: Oxford University Press, 1997). Worth mentioning is Du Bois's classic work of 1903, *The Souls of Black Folk* (available in numerous editions), which remains one of the seminal texts of the African American experience.

On African American life and the freedom struggle during World War I and between the world wars, the following studies have been helpful: Arthur E. Barbeau and Florette Henri, *The Unknown Soldiers: African-American Troops in World War One* (New York: Da Capo, 1996; orig. 1974); Florette Henri, *Black Migration: Movement North, 1900–1920* (Garden City, NY: Doubleday, 1976); B. Joyce Ross, *J. E. Spingarn and the Rise of the NAACP* (New York: Atheneum, 1972); Nathan Huggins, *Harlem Renaissance* (New York: 1971); David Levering Lewis, *When Harlem Was in Vogue* (New York: Oxford University Press, 1979); Harvard Sitkoff, *A New Deal for Blacks: The Emergence of Civil Rights as a National Issue* (New York: Oxford University Press, 1978); John B. Kirby, *Black Americans in the Roosevelt Era: Liberalism and Race* (Knoxville: University of Tennessee Press, 1980); Nancy J. Weiss, *Farewell to the Party of Lincoln: Black Politics in the Age of FDR* (Princeton, NJ: Princeton University Press, 1983).

On African Americans and World War II, and the broader question of African Americans in the U.S. military, see the following: Richard M. Dalfiume, *Desegregation of the U.S. Armed Forces: Fighting on Two Fronts, 1939–1953* (Columbia: University of Missouri Press, 1969); Daniel Kryder, *Divided Arsenal: Race and the American State During World War Two* (New York: Cambridge University Press, 2000); Bernard C. Nalty, *Strength for the Fight: A History of Black Americans in the Military* (New York: Free Press, 1986); Sherie Mershon and Steven Schlossman, *Foxholes and Color Lines: Desegregating the U.S. Armed Forces* (Baltimore: Johns Hopkins University Press, 1998). Also worth noting is Barbara Diane Savage, *Broadcasting Freedom: Radio, War, and the Politics of Race, 1938–1948* (Chapel Hill: University of North Carolina Press, 1999).

On the post-1945 era, we have relied on a number of studies and have listed those that have been especially helpful: Mark V. Tushnet, *Making Civil Rights Law: Thurgood Marshall and the Supreme Court, 1936–1961* (New York: Oxford University Press, 1994); Tushnet, *The NAACP's Legal Strategy Against Segregated Education* (Chapel Hill: University of North Carolina Press, 1987); Richard Kluger, *Simple Justice: The History of Brown v. Board of Education and Black America's Struggle for Equality* (New York: Vintage, 1975); Jack Greenberg, *Crusaders in the Courts: How a Dedicated Band of Lawyers Fought for the Civil Rights Revolution* (New York: Basic, 1994); Morton J. Horwitz, *The Warren Court and the Pursuit of Justice* (New York: Hill and Wang, 1998); James T. Patterson, *Brown v. Board of Education: A Civil Rights Milestone and Its Troubled Legacy* (New York: Oxford University Press, 2001); Harvard Sitkoff, *The Struggle for Black Equality, 1954–1992* (New York: Hill and Wang, 1993; orig. 1981); Clayborne Carson, *In Struggle: SNCC and the Black Awakening of the 1960s* (Cambridge, MA: Harvard University Press, 1995); Steven Lawson, *Running for Freedom: Civil Rights and Black Politics in America Since 1941* (New York: McGraw-Hill, 1991); Robert Wiesbrot, *Freedom Bound: A History of America's Civil Rights Movement* (New York: Norton, 1990).

On the influence of Martin Luther King, see Taylor Branch's two masterly volumes: *Parting the Waters: America in the King Years, 1954–1963* (New York: Simon and Schuster, 1988) and *Pillar of Fire: America in the King Years, 1963–1965* (New York: Simon and Schuster, 1998). On King, we have profited from David J. Garrow's superlative study, *Bearing the Cross: Martin Luther King, Jr., and the Southern Christian Leadership Conference* (New York: Vintage, 1988; orig. 1986), and Adam Fairclough's excellent account, *To Redeem the Soul of America: The Southern Christian Leadership Conference and Martin Luther King, Jr.* (Athens: University of Georgia Press, 1987). Note, too, Fairclough's sweeping history of the movement, *Better Day Coming: Blacks and Equality, 1890–2000* (New York: Viking, 2001). For an excellent collection of King's writings, edited and compiled by Clayborne Carson, see *The Autobiography of Martin Luther King, Jr.* (New York: Warner, 1998).

The literature on the Kennedys is enormous. The best study on the Kennedy administration and civil rights is Carl M. Brauer, *John F. Kennedy and the Second Reconstruction* (New York: Columbia University Press, 1977). Works by those in the administration include two by Arthur Schlesinger, *A Thousand Days* (Boston: Houghton Mifflin, 1965) and *Robert Kennedy and His Times* (New York: Houghton Mifflin, 1978). See also Harris Wofford, *Of Kennedys and Kings: Making Sense of the Sixties* (Pittsburgh, PA: University of Pittsburgh Press, 1980); Theodore C. Sorensen, *Kennedy* (New York: Harper and Row, 1965); and Edward Guthman, *We Band of Brothers* (New York: Harper and Row, 1971). For an interesting collection, see Kenneth W. Thompson, ed., *The Kennedy Presidency: Seventeen Intimate Perspectives of John F. Kennedy* (Lanham, MD: University Press of America, 1985). Two of the better sources on the early attitudes of John and Robert Kennedy are Evan Thomas, *Robert Kennedy: His Life* (New York: Simon and Schuster, 2000), and Richard Reeves, *President Kennedy: Profile of Power* (New York: Simon and Schuster, 1993). On the 1960 campaign, see Theodore White, *The Making of the President 1960* (New York: Atheneum, 1961). For critical assessments of Kennedy, see Gary Wills, *The Kennedy Imprisonment: A Meditation on Power* (Boston: Little Brown, 1981); Nigel Hamilton, *JFK: Reckless Youth* (New York: Random House, 1992); and Seymour Hersh, *The Dark Side of Camelot* (New York: Little Brown, 1999). See also Herbert Parmet, *JFK: The Presidency of John F. Kennedy* (New York: Penguin, 1984), and Mark Stern, *Calculating Visions: Kennedy, Johnson, and Civil Rights* (New Brunswick, NJ: Rutgers University Press, 1992).

On Johnson, see Robert Dallek's two-volume biography, *Lone Star Rising: Lyndon Johnson and His Times, 1908–1960* (New York: Oxford University Press, 1991) and *Flawed Giant: Lyndon Johnson and His Times, 1961–1973* (New York: Oxford University Press, 1998). Also note the first three volumes of Robert Caro's projected four-volume study, *The Years of Lyndon Johnson: The Path to Power* (New York: Knopf, 1982), *Means of Ascent* (New York: Knopf, 1990), and *Master of the Senate* (New York: Knopf, 2002). On Johnson's presidency, see Irving Bernstein, *Guns or Butter: The Presidency of Lyndon Johnson* (New York: Oxford University Press, 1996).

Several studies on the history of civil rights legislation in this period have been invaluable in preparing this book. These include Robert D. Loevy, *To End All Segregation: The Politics and the Passage of the Civil Rights Act of 1964* (Lanham, MD: University Press of America, 1990); Robert D. Loevy, ed., *The Civil Rights Act of 1964: The Passage of the Law that Ended Racial Segregation* (Albany: State University of New York Press, 1997); and Charles and Barbara Whalen, *The Longest Debate: A Legislative History of the 1964 Civil Rights Act* (New York: Mentor, 1986). Especially compelling is Robert Mann, *The Walls of Jericho: Lyndon Johnson, Hubert Humphrey, Richard Russell, and the Struggle for Civil Rights* (New York: Harcourt Brace, 1996). See also Hugh Davis Graham's superb study, *The Civil Rights Era: Origins and Development of National Policy* (New York: Oxford University Press, 1990), and John Walton Cotman, *Birmingham, JFK, and the Civil Rights Act of 1963: Implications for Elite Theory* (New York: Lang, 1989).

On key events in the African American freedom campaign during the 1960s, the following books have been especially helpful. On the sit-ins, see William H. Chafe, *Civilities and Civil Rights: Greensboro, North Carolina, and the Black Struggle for Freedom* (New York: Oxford University Press, 1980). On developments in Birmingham, see Glenn T. Eskew, *But for Birmingham: The Local and National Movements in the Civil Rights Struggle* (Chapel Hill: University of North Carolina Press, 1997), and Andrew M. Manis, *A Fire You Can't Put Out: The Civil Rights Life of Birmingham's Reverend Fred Shuttlesworth* (Tuscaloosa: University of Alabama Press, 1999). On the crisis at the University of Mississippi, see William Doyle's excellent account, *An American Insurrection: The Battle of Oxford Mississippi, 1962* (New York: Doubleday, 2001). See also Walter Lord's *The Past That Would Not Die* (New York: Harper and Row, 1965). Also note James Meredith's account, *Three Years in Mississippi* (Bloomington: Indiana University Press, 1966). On the integration of the University of Alabama, see E. Culpepper Clark, *The Schoolhouse Door: Segregation's Last Stand at the University of Alabama* (New York: Oxford University Press, 1993). On the civil rights struggle in the South at the local level, two of the best recent studies are John Dittmer, *Local People: The Struggle for Civil Rights in Mississippi* (Chicago: University of Illinois Press, 1994), and Charles M. Payne, *I've Got the Light of Freedom: The Organizing Tradition and the Mississippi Freedom Struggle* (Berkeley: University of California Press, 1995).

Participants in the African American freedom struggle have penned a rich literature on their efforts. Some of the more compelling accounts include Ralph David Abernathy, *And the Walls Came Tumbling Down* (New York: Harper and Row, 1989); James Farmer, *Lay Bare the Heart: An Autobiography of the Civil Rights Movement* (New York: Plume, 1985); John Lewis, *Walking With the Wind: A Memoir of the Movement* (New York: Simon and Schuster, 1998); Roy Wilkins, *Standing Fast: The Autobiography of Roy Wilkins* (New York: Viking, 1982); and Andrew Young, *An Easy Burden: The Civil Rights Movement and the Transformation of America* (New York: HarperCollins, 1996). From an earlier period, see Walter White, *A Man Called White: The Autobiography of Walter White* (Athens: University of Georgia Press, 1995; orig. 1948).

Key Players

Albert, Carl, U.S. Representative, Democrat from Oklahoma, 1947–1977; House Majority Leader, 1961–1970.

Arends, Leslie, U.S. Representatitve, Republican from Illinois, 1935–1974.

Barnett, Ross R., Democratic Governor of Mississippi, 1960-1964.

Bolling, Richard, U.S. Representative, Democrat from Missouri, 1949–1983.

Boutwell, Albert, Mayor of Birmingham, Alabama, 1963–1967.

Byrd, Robert, U.S. Senator, Democrat from West Virginia, 1959–present.

Celler, Emanuel, U.S. Representative, Democrat from New York, 1923–1973; chairman, Committee on the Judiciary, 1949–1952, 1955–1972.

Connor, Eugene "Bull," Public Safety Commissioner, Birmingham, Alabama, 1957–1963.

Cox, Archibald, Solicitor General of the United States, 1961–1965.

Dirksen, Everett, U.S. Senator, Republican from Illinois, 1951–1969; Senate Minority Leader, 1959–1969.

Farmer, James, Founder of Congress of Racial Equality (CORE); CORE National Director, 1961–1966.

Fulbright, J. William, U.S. Senator, Democrat from Arkansas, 1945–1974; chairman, Committee on Foreign Relations, 1959–1974.

Graham, Katherine, Publisher of the *Washington Post,* 1969–1979.

Halleck, Charles, U.S. Representative, Republican from Indiana, 1935–1969; House Minority Leader, 1959–1964.

Humphrey, Hubert, U.S. Senator, Democrat from Minnesota, 1949–1964, 1971–1978; Democratic Whip, 1961–1964.

Katzenbach, Nicholas deB., Deputy Attorney General of the United States, 1962–1966.

Kennedy, Robert F., Attorney General of the United States, 1961–1964.

King, Martin Luther, Jr., Civil rights leader, Cofounder of the Southern Christian Leadership Conference (SCLC).

Lincoln, Evelyn, Personal secretary to President Kennedy, 1952–1963.

Luce, Clare Booth, Journalist; playwright; U.S. Representative, Republican from Connecticut, 1943–1947.

Macy, John, Chairman of the Civil Service Commission, 1961–1969.

Mansfield, Michael, U.S. Senator, Democrat from Montana, 1953–1977; Senate Majority Leader, 1961–1977.

Marshall, Burke, Assistant Attorney General for Civil Rights, 1961–1965.

McCarthy, Eugene, U.S. Senator, Democrat from Minnesota, 1959–1971.

McClellan, John, U.S. Senator, Democrat from Arkansas, 1943–1977.

McCormack, John, U.S. Representative, Democrat from Massachusetts, 1928–1971; Speaker of the House, 1961–1971.

McCulloch, William, U.S. Representative, Republican from Ohio, 1947–1973.

McNamara, Robert S., Secretary of Defense, 1961–1968.

Meredith, James H., First African American student admitted to the University of Mississippi, 1962–1963.

Mitchell, Clarence, Director, Washington, D.C., bureau of the NAACP, 1950–1978.

Moyers, Bill, White House Press Secretary, 1965–1966.

Mundt, Karl, U.S. Senator, Republican from North Dakota, 1948–1973.

O'Brien, Lawrence F., Special Assistant to the President for Congressional Affairs, 1961–1963.

O'Donnell, Kenneth, Special Assistant to the President, 1961–1963.

Randolph, A. Philip, Founder, President of Brotherhood of Sleeping Car Porters 1925–1968.

Reedy, George, White House Press Secretary, 1964–1965.

Ruether, Walter, President, United Automobile Workers, 1946–1970.

Russell, Richard, U.S. Senator, Democrat from Georgia, 1933–1971.

Salinger, Pierre, White House Press Secretary, 1961–1964.

Sandburg, Carl, Pulitzer Prize–winning poet and biographer.

Shuttlesworth, Fred, Cofounder of the Southern Christian Leadership Conference (SCLC); leader of Alabama Christian Movement for Human Rights (ACMHR).

Smathers, George, U.S. Senator, Democrat from Florida, 1951–1969.

Smith, Howard, U.S. Representative, Democrat from Virginia, 1931–1967; chairman, Committee on Rules, 1955–1966.

Sorenson, Theodore C., Special Assistant to the President, 1961–1964

Valenti, Jack, Special Assistant to the President, 1963–1966.

Vance, Cyrus R., U. S. Secretary of the Army, 1962–1963.

Wallace, George, Democratic Governor of Alabama, 1963–1967

Watkins, Tom, Mississippi lawyer and Barnett aide, who served as an intermediary in the 1962 University of Mississippi crisis.

White, Lee, Associate Counsel to the President, Special Counsel, Adviser on civil rights issues, 1962–1966.

Whittington, Gerri, Secretary to President Johnson.

Wilkins, Roy, Executive Director of the National Association for the Advancement of Colored People (NAACP), 1955–1977.

Williams, G. Mennan, Assistant Secretary of State for African Affairs, 1961–1966.

Young, Whitney, Executive Director of the National Urban League, 1961–1971.

Summary of Civil Rights Act of 1964

An Act

"To enforce the constitutional right to vote, to confer jurisdiction upon the district courts of the United States to provide injunctive relief against discrimination in public accommodations, to authorize the Attorney General to institute suits to protect constitutional rights in public facilities and public education, to extend the Commission on Civil Rights, to prevent discrimination in federally assisted programs, to establish a Commission on Equal Employment Opportunity, and for other purposes."

Title I—Voting Rights

Establishes standards designed to prevent discrimination in determining eligibility to vote. These include the requirement that every standard, practice, and procedure applied to one individual be applied to every other in the same district; that no person can be denied the right to vote because of paperwork errors that are immaterial to voter eligibility; that if literacy tests are to be used, they must be administered to every voter and must be conducted wholly in writing; that any person not judged incompetent who has completed the sixth grade in an English-language school shall merit the rebuttal presumption of being sufficiently literate and intelligent to vote in any federal election; and that the Attorney General can request a finding in court if a pattern or practice of discrimination seems evident and that, at the request of the Attorney General or the defendant, determination will be made in federal court by a three-judge panel.

Title II—Public Accommodation

Bars discrimination based on race, color, religion, or national origin in any public accommodation and establishes remedies in federal court for such cases. Public accommodations include restaurants, lunch counters, hotels, movie theaters, sports arenas, and places that contain such an establishment (e.g., lunch counter in a department store) or are contained within such an establishment (e.g., gift shop in a hotel). These accommodations are included under this law if they affect interstate commerce (hotel guests or movies shipped from out of state) or if the discrimination or segregation is based on state law or regulation. Further the law states that individuals must not be harassed, intimidated, threatened, or coerced with the purpose of interfering with these rights and privileges.

Gives the Attorney General the power to step in on an individual suit if the case is deemed of general public importance. Procedures are established for allowing localities an opportunity to settle the dispute before it is taken to federal court, for determining when a civil suit can be filed if a criminal action is pending, and for bringing the case before a three-judge panel in federal court.

Title III—Desegregation of Public Facilities

Authorizes the Attorney General to pursue legal proceedings in federal court on the basis of any written complaint of an individual deprived of due process of law or access to a public facility owned, operated, or managed by or for a state if the Attorney General determines that the individual either can't afford to pursue action or that such action would jeopardize the personal safety, employment, or economic standing of the person, the person's family, or the person's property. The civil action will be entered in the name of the United States, and the Attorney General may add defendants as necessary to grant effective relief.

Title IV—Desegregation of Public Education

Calls for active pursuit of desegregation of public schools, with desegregation defined as the assignment of students to public schools and within such schools without regard to their race, color, religion, or national origin but not defined as the assignment of students to schools to overcome racial imbalance. Requires a study by the Commissioner of Education concerning the lack of equal educational opportunities for individuals because of race, color, religion, or national origin. Authorizes provision by the Commissioner of Education of technical support, training, and monetary grants to help teachers and administrators effect desegregation and cope with difficulties that may arise.

Allows the Attorney General to seek action in federal court on the basis of a written complaint from an individual if that individual would be unable to afford appropriate legal action, if that individual's safety might be jeopardized as a result of such action, and if the Attorney General certifies that the action would serve generally to advance the cause of school desegregation. Title IV explicitly does not prevent classification or assignment based on factors other than race, color, religion, or national origin.

Title V—Commission on Civil Rights

Sets procedures for the Commission on Civil Rights for hearings, subpeonas, and public access to proceedings and gives the commission directives including to investigate allegations of certain citizens' being denied the right to vote on the basis of color, race, religion, or national origin; to study legal developments constituting denial of equal protection; to appraise the laws and policies of the federal government with respect to denials of equal protection; and to serve as a national clearinghouse for information about discrimination in voting, education, housing, employment, the use of public facilities, and transportation or in the administration of justice. Denies the commission the right to investigate private clubs, fraternities, sororities, or religious organizations.

Title VI—Nondiscrimination in Federally Assisted Programs

Prohibits exclusion on the basis of race, color, or national origin of any individual from programs or activities receiving federal financial assistance. Authorizes each federal department or agency that extends such financial assistance to establish rules and regulations to achieve this provision and establishes rules for enforcement by termination of financial assistance or by any other means authorized by law, provided that the appropriate person or persons have been notified of noncompliance and given the opportunity to voluntarily remedy the failure. Provides the right of the affected party to judicial review when funds are terminated. Excluded is the right of any department or agency to act with regard to the employment practice of any employer, employment agency, or labor organization except where a primary objective of the federal assistance is to provide employment.

Title VII—Equal Employment Opportunity

Declares unlawful for an employer, employment agency, labor organization, or training or apprentice program to discriminate on the basis of race, color, religion, sex, or national origin in hiring, discharging, and terms and conditions of employment or to limit, segregate, or classify employees on the basis of these characteristics in any way that would adversely impact the opportunities or employment status of individuals. Excepted from this provision are cases where religion, sex, or national origin is a bona fide occupational qualification and cases where educational institutions hire employees of a particular religion if the school is substantially owned or managed by a particular religion or if the curriculum is directed toward the propagation of a particular religion. Also bars discrimination against anyone who speaks out, complains, or takes action against an employment practice made illegal in this title. Prohibits advertisements for job openings that suggest preference or classification according to these categories.

Establishes the Equal Employment Opportunity Commission (EEOC) to investigate charges of noncompliance and negotiate for compliance; such investigations and negotiations not to be made public. The EEOC is required to work with state and local agencies, allowing states time to remedy noncompliance before stepping in.

Gives the Attorney General the right to pursue action in federal court under reasonable belief in a pattern of discrimination.

Calls for a special study by the Department of Labor to determine the extent of age discrimination and the impacts (if any) on individuals and the economy.

Title VIII—Registration and Voting Statistics

Directs the Secretary of Commerce to undertake a survey of registration and voting statistics in districts recommended by the Civil Rights Commission; to establish a count of persons of voting age by race, color, and national origin; and to determine the extent to which such persons are registered to vote.

Title IX—Intervention and Procedure after Removal in Civil Rights Cases

Defines the right of appeal and gives the Attorney General the right to intercede in any case in which an individual seeks relief from denial of equal protection of the laws under the Fourteenth Amendment if the case is deemed to be in the public interest.

Title X—Establishment of Community Relations Service

Establishes within the Department of Commerce a Community Relations Service with the task of assisting communities and persons in the resolution of disputes and difficulties arising from discriminatory practices which impair the constitutional or legal rights of persons or which affect interstate commerce. Activities of the service to be conducted in cooperation with local or state agencies. The service will provide an annual report to Congress.

Title XI—Miscellaneous

Defines criminal contempt and prescribes proceedings, bars double jeopardy, places some limitations on the powers of the federal government to impact state law, authorizes appropriation of necessary funds, and declares that if one part is deemed unconstitional, the rest shall nonetheless stand.

Acknowledgments

Without question, *Kennedy, Johnson, and the Quest for Justice* is the product of a collaborative effort. Over many months, each of us drafted and redrafted various sections of the narrative and edited the transcripts; with the process complete, neither of us can tell where the work of one ends and the other begins. But this book was a collaborative enterprise in an even more meaningful sense: It could not have been written without the intensive efforts of the scholars at the Miller Center of Public Affairs at the University of Virginia. Though we participated in the countless hours of work that went into the preparation of the transcripts, we were only two of many. For the Kennedy material, Paul Pitman, Kent Germany, Erin Mahan, and Maria Farkas were instrumental in making the unintelligible intelligible and the incoherent coherent. For the Johnson material, Robert David Johnson, Max Holland, and David Shreve toiled to create accurate transcripts and the results are a testament to their skill. At the Johnson Library in Austin, Texas, we benefited from the research assistance of Don Zinman. With great care, Sarah Stewart read through the transcripts and the narrative to check for inconsistencies and infelicities, and also created a summary of the Civil Rights Act and a glossary of the major figures of the period. We wish to thank Frank Gavin and Tarek Masoud, scholars formerly at the Miller Center, who provided keen insights on the history and politics of presidential decision making. And Pat Dunn and Lorraine Settimo of the Miller Center did a superb job of making sure that the complicated process of coordinating the various parts of the whole enterprise went smoothly.

The Presidential Recordings Project is the brainchild of Ernest May and Philip Zelikow, and we hope this volume has done justice to their vision. We thank them for their incisive comments and for their continued support. Timothy Naftali, the director of the project at the Miller Center, has been both an organizational genius and an insightful scholar. He carefully read and critiqued the manuscript, and we have benefited immensely from his help.

Taylor Branch, William Doyle, David Garrow, Robert Loevy, Robert Mann, and Allen Matusow read all or part of the manuscript, and if we have not followed all of their advice, we have certainly profited from their considerable input. They made us take a second (and a third) look at our assumptions, and steered us clear of pitfalls that we might not have recognized. We are grateful that they took time away from their own work to share their thoughts with us.

At W. W. Norton, Drake McFeeley has been patient, supportive, and enthusiastic, and we have deeply appreciated his calm confidence in this volume. Eve Lazovitz has had to deal with numerous last-minute changes, and we are grateful that she has kept both her composure and her sense of humor throughout a lengthy production process that might have driven many to distraction.

Finally, we offer a word to our respective families. For Zachary, Nicole Alger has listened to countless hours of talk about what must have been less than scintillating details. She provided exactly the type of passionate support that we all hope for but rarely expect and even more rarely find. For Jonathan, his wife, Jane, and his children, James and Isobel, have provided the emotional support (and essential distractions) that are necessary for anyone engaged in the often solitary process of research and writing. For James and Isobel, who wondered when the book would be done, yes, it is finished. In short, we have had an abundance of help from a team of scholars, each of whom is already distinguished or soon will be, from a patient set of editors, and from two families that supported us every step of the way.

Index

357